Those religious are killed by the letter who do not wish to follow the spirit of Sacred Scripture, but only wish to know what the words are and how to interpret them to others.

Francis of Assisi, *Seventh Admonition*

Models for Interpretation of Scripture

• •

John Goldingay

WILLIAM B. EERDMANS PUBLISHING COMPANY
GRAND RAPIDS, MICHIGAN

THE PATERNOSTER PRESS
CARLISLE

© 1995 Wm. B. Eerdmans Publishing Co.
255 Jefferson Ave. S.E., Grand Rapids, Michigan 49503

Published jointly 1995 in the United States by
Wm. B. Eerdmans Publishing Co.
and in the U.K. by
The Paternoster Press
P.O. Box 300, Carlisle, Cumbria CA3 0QS

Printed in the United States of America

00 99   7 6 5 4 3 2

Library of Congress Cataloging-in-Publication Data

Goldingay, John.
Models for interpretation of scripture / John Goldingay.
        p.   cm.
Includes bibliographical references and indexes.
ISBN 0-8028-0145-5 (pbk. : alk. paper)
1. Bible — Hermeneutics. 2. Bible — Criticism, interpretation, etc.
I. Title.
BS476.G65 1995
220.6'01 — dc20   95-4957
                                                        CIP

British Library Cataloguing in Publication Data

Goldingay, John
Models for Interpretation of Scripture
I. Title
220.6

ISBN 0-85364-643-0

To the students and staff of the Evangelical Theological House of Studies (ETHOS) in the University of Natal at Pietermaritzburg, with whom discussion of some of these issues was a revolutionary experience, and for whom interpretation of scripture is not only an examination subject but a matter of life and death.

Contents

PART III
SCRIPTURE AS INSPIRED WORD:
INTERPRETING PROPHECY

PART IV
SCRIPTURE AS EXPERIENCED REVELATION:
INTERPRETING APOCALYPSE, TESTIMONY,
AND THEOLOGICAL STATEMENT

• 1 •

Introduction:
Scripture's Varied Forms

My starting point for considering the interpretation of scripture is suggested by the opening of the Letter to the Hebrews, which observes that "God spoke to our ancestors in *many and various ways* by the prophets." Scripture has a variety of ways of speaking, and the process of interpretation requires a variety of hermeneutical approaches, corresponding to this variety in types of texts.[1] Discussion of how we are to interpret scripture (and how we are to preach on the basis of scripture) has often implicitly assumed that there will be a single approach to the task, but that assumption takes no account of the diversity of the ways in which scripture itself communicates. Scripture utilizes many forms of speech: historical narrative, instructions about behavior, oracles of warning or promise, prayers and praises, manuals of theological teaching, accounts of dreams and visions, . . . Our interpretation and our exposition of scripture need to allow for its diverse forms, and to reflect them.

In a book called *Models for Scripture* I have attempted to consider how we are to think of scripture doctrinally in the light of these diverse forms that the scriptures take. The four "models" that I work with there emerge from scripture itself and are witnessing tradition (a way of looking at scripture's narrative), authoritative canon (a model that applies most directly to scripture's commands in the Torah and elsewhere), inspired word (a term especially at home in connection with prophecy), and experienced

---

1. See the discussion in Ebeling's *Word and Faith* 314-18; cf. Thiselton, *New Horizons in Hermeneutics* 32-34, 557-58.

revelation (covering material such as psalms, apocalypses, and wisdom books and letters). These different types of material also suggest a parallel set of complementary approaches to the task of interpreting the First and Second Testaments.[2]

Approaches to the Interpretation of Scripture

In one sense, understanding is a quite straightforward task, one that people are successfully fulfilling every day as they read newspapers or novels or weather forecasts, watch plays or cartoons or commercials, and listen to confidences or sermons or jokes. At the same time it is a task that periodically catches us out — when we cannot see the point of the novel or the play, or mishear the confidence and hurt the one who shared it. When we are seeking to understand something cross-culturally, the weight of that task of understanding increases, whether one moves within different ethnic or cultural groups in one's own country or between different world cultures. Further, beneath the recurrent experience of failure in understanding or awareness of difficulty in understanding lies something of a mystery: What is this thing called understanding anyway? What makes it possible, what encourages it, what hinders it, and what prevents it?

Understanding scripture is a particular instance of the general task of understanding. "The hermeneutical problem" is intrinsic to Christian faith because of the nature of that faith's origins.[3] Jesus Christ first came to be understood by means of interpretation of the existent Jewish scriptures, and this process involved interpretation of these scriptures in the light of him. Questions regarding the relationship between the Hebrew scriptures and the Christ event are thus a feature of Christian faith from the beginning, and inevitably so if Christian faith wishes to be seen as the fulfillment of a longstanding purpose and promise rather than as an irrational interruption. Jesus' significance is itself interpreted in the church's proclamation, and the church is invited to live hermeneutically by deciphering its own experience in the light of the story of Jesus. The church's proclamation of Jesus is

2. I prefer these terms to the conventional "Old Testament" and "New Testament," which tend to downgrade the Hebrew scriptures: See the Introduction to *Models for Scripture*.

3. See Ricoeur, *The Conflict of Interpretations* 382-88 for what follows. Barton's criticisms of Ricoeur (*People of the Book?* 6-7) warn against an overstatement of this point, but do not undermine its fundamental truth.

interpreted in the writings that came to make up the Second Testament. His significance for us is then ascertained only through an interpretation of these scriptures that enables the written word to become again the living word.

Thus "text interpretation is and must be a basic Christian activity"; while "we believe in the God of Jesus Christ, not in the Bible," the possibility of giving the latter impression stems from the fact that the textual witnesses are quite indispensable if we are to have access to the event and person of Jesus Christ.[4] Acknowledgment of the Bible as canon likewise necessarily leads to the question how scripture is revered concretely. Obedience has to be a matter of acts, not words (1 John 3:18). Faith in scripture is not a mere formal matter: It rests on paying attention to words in their diversity. "For such a true faith in scripture to be meaningful, the interpretation of Scripture is of the essence. . . . Not in separation from, but rather in connection with, the understanding of Holy Scripture does it become evident whether its authority is really honored."[5] This is not so where interpretation is characterized by arbitrariness or subjectivism and scripture's authority is not concretely accepted.

Like understanding in general, understanding scripture is in one sense a quite straightforward enterprise, one that ordinary people accomplish (courtesy of the labor of translators) as effortlessly as they understand newspapers, television, or each other. It, too, like all understanding, periodically catches them out, partly because of the cultural differences that go beyond the linguistic gulf that separates most modern readers from the Bible: These readers make little sense of the ritual instructions in Leviticus or the visionary material in Revelation. They are unsure — or too sure — what we are supposed to learn from healing stories in the Gospels or Acts. Or they read Genesis 1–3 as more historical, or more parabolic, than it may inherently be. Understanding scripture, also like all understanding, raises questions of baffling depth: What do we mean by understanding scripture, anyway? What makes it possible, what encourages it, what hinders it, what prevents it? How can we hear what these human authors wanted to communicate in God's name to their hearers? How can we hear what God wants to say to us through scripture? How far or on what basis can we perceive significances in scripture that go beyond the awareness of its authors, as the Second Testament writers seem to do in their appropriation of the First?

---

4. Jeanrond, *Text and Interpretation* 122, 150.
5. Berkouwer, *Holy Scripture* 105-6.

With scripture, too, occasions when we have difficulty in understanding a text or when an interpretation that is compelling to us is quite unconvincing to someone else remind us of the element of mystery about the task of interpretation and raise a further question. Who knows whether we miss whole aspects of the meaning of particular texts, or fundamentally misconstrue them, even when we feel no uncertainty about their meaning or do not find our understanding of them contradicted by someone else? Texts, after all, cannot answer back ("No, I didn't mean that") as people can. It is an advantage to feel that we have grounds for being confident of the meaning of scripture; we can then obey and preach that meaning with confidence. It is difficult at the same time to be open to being coaxed toward some other understanding of scripture. Openness to new understanding presupposes the willingness to yield old convictions.

The task of understanding can be considered in the abstract, but discussion of it can then become rather rarified, and I propose to forgo discussing the task in its "neat" or theoretical form. Understanding is a multiplex skill or art: understanding *Hamlet,* understanding a football game, understanding an atlas, understanding my spouse. . . . Ultimately a different approach is required for each form of the task. The varying objects of understanding with which scripture presents us similarly require varying approaches. Further, it happens that many of the insights that have emerged from the study of interpretation at the rarified, abstract level over recent decades come into sharper focus and are of more obvious application when applied to specific kinds of material. To be comprehensive would involve examining every scriptural genre one by one — ultimately examining every scriptural text; but that would be to sacrifice ourselves to the concrete as fatally as we might otherwise sacrifice ourselves to the abstract. The four broad genres that provide us with headings for considering how we *think* about scripture in its diversity of form also provide us with headings for considering how we *interpret* scripture in its diversity of form.

In the chapters that follow we will thus examine the task of understanding scripture as it arises in four main blocks of material: in narrative, in material that gives instructions, in prophecy, and in experiential and revelatory material. These include examples of three directions of speech that appear in scripture: God addressing people, especially in prophecy and instruction material; people addressing God, especially in experiential material such as the Psalms; and people addressing each other, especially in narrative. They correspond to four fundamental forms that communicative statements can take: Descriptive statements make factual assertions;

prescriptive statements attempt to lay obligations on others; in commissive statements I commit myself to some act; expressive statements put into words my convictions, feelings, or attitudes.[6] These four forms exemplify speech used for varying purposes: to reassure, the most common function of narrative; to confront, in prophecy and instruction; and to reflect and respond, in experiential-revelatory material.

These four genres take as their point of departure four modes of utterance within scripture: law, prophecy, wisdom, and gospel.[7] They invite varying forms of response: To the witnessing tradition, storytelling and worship are the responses; to the authoritative canon, they are delight and submission; to the inspired word, they are repentance and hope; to the experienced revelation, they are awe and theologizing. These four genres also illustrate the differing points at which meaning may be located in relation to texts: within them, in the intrinsic form and interrelationships of the various elements in the text itself — especially in narrative; beneath them, in the experiences, feelings, and convictions that the text concretely symbolizes and expresses — most specifically in experiential-revelatory material; behind them, in the aims and intentions of the text's author or in the life setting of its tradition — most specifically (paradoxically) in prophecy; or in front of them, in the possible mode of being in the world that the text sets before us — most specifically in instruction material.

The four blocks of material can be related to varying focuses that inter-preters may take for their work: the world out there, the universe as the text sees it, objective truth as the text conceives it — so perhaps in narrative and in reflective and revelatory material; or the needs of the audience to which it was addressed and the effect it had on them — so in prophetic and instruction material; or the personal feelings and experience of the author, which the work expresses — especially in experiential material; or the inner dynamic of the work itself as a world of its own — so in narrative. These four approaches can be related to the feminist version of this typology: Interpreters may focus on the forgotten history that may lie beneath the surface of the biblical text, on the liberating strand within scripture that constitutes the canon within the canon, or on the countercultural impulses within the text that we can identify

6. See Brümmer, *Theological and Philosophical Inquiry* 15-25, developing the work of Austin in *How to Do Things with Words*. Strictly Brümmer is analyzing the particular kind of statements that Austin calls illocutions, and for the first category (descriptive/fac-tual) Brümmer uses Austin's term "constative." Searle (*Expression and Meaning* 1-29) prefers the term "assertive"; he also adds a further category, that of declarations.

7. Cf. Reed, "A Poetics of the Bible" 161-65.

with the aid of our own experience.[8] These four approaches may also enable us to distinguish between seeing texts as windows onto another world, as mirrors reflecting back insight on the interpreter's world, or as portraits with a world of their own.[9] They may illustrate the varying strands to the meaning of the Greek verb *hermeneuein*, "to proclaim," "to explain," and "to translate."[10] And they may make it easier to do justice to both a concern for attaining interpretations (interpretation as a creative act; cf. Luke 24) and a concern for testing interpretations (interpretation as a critical act concerned to avoid misinterpretation; cf. 2 Pet 3:16).

The four genres can be related to different ways of seeing the two Testaments in relation to each other, as salvation history or typology, with the First Testament playing Act 1 to the Second Testament's Act 2; as teaching on a way of life in which the First Testament may more often make allowance for human stubbornness while the Second more often insists on the ultimate standards of God's reign; as promise and fulfillment in which the Second Testament declares that what the First looked forward to has now arrived; and as a statement of a faith with its unity and diversity in which what was before concealed is now revealed. These diverse approaches to that relationship can already be illustrated from the opening pages of the Second Testament, which suggest an understanding of a link with the First in terms of history or story or of a witnessing tradition (Matt 1:1-17), in terms of prophecy and fulfillment or of an inspired word (1:18–2:23; cf. 4:12-17), in terms of theological images and concepts or an experienced revelation (3:1-17; cf 5:1-16), and fourthly in terms of a way of life or an authoritative canon (4:1-11; cf. 5:17-48).

Different genres bring to the surface different questions about interpretation; no one philosophy of interpretation opens up all secrets, just as no one model for a doctrine of scripture brings out all facets of scripture's doctrinal significance. It is unwise to treat all texts as fundamentally expressive of an understanding of human existence.[11] It is unwise to treat all texts as primarily didactic and designed to "teach" something, an assumption for which James Barr faults fundamentalists.[12] It is unwise to treat all

---

8. See Tolbert, *The Bible and Feminist Hermeneutics* 122-23.

9. So, e.g., Abrams, *The Mirror and the Lamp* 3-29; cf. Karris, "Windows and Mirrors"; Poythress, "Analysing a Biblical Text"; Lapointe, *Les trois dimensions de l'herméneutique*; Alonso Schökel, *The Inspired Word* 134-50.

10. Palmer, *Hermeneutics* 12-32.

11. Against Bultmann; see, e.g., the essays in *NT and Mythology*.

12. *Fundamentalism* 76.

texts as either story or poem.[13] The new hermeneutic is more appropriate to some parts of scripture than to others.[14] In preference to open or hidden monisms, biblical study, like literary criticism, needs to cultivate an eclectic "open methodology."[15] This need not mean an unprincipled and casual eclecticism that makes method simply a matter of taste (Eagleton notes how fortunate it is that distaste for method has not yet infiltrated medicine or aeronautical engineering),[16] but a critical pluralism.[17] Method must correspond to text. It is in this sense that there may be a special "sacred hermeneutics" just as there may be a special legal hermeneutics. Texts must be interpreted as what they are.[18]

Such a methodology will indeed then discover that genres overlap in their inner nature, so that questions about interpretation also overlap. An experiential text such as a prayer is implicitly an instruction text telling people how to pray. A narrative text is a fruit of reflection. What a narrative tells a story about, an instruction text expresses as an ethic, a prophecy turns into warning and promise, and experiential-revelatory material makes matter for reflection and prayer. So the distinctions we make in analyzing approaches to interpretation in the pages that follow are made in order to let the issues emerge as sharply as possible; the distinctions can then be allowed to blur in order for the insights to be applied across any artificial divides. The situation throughout is thus similar to the one that obtains in considering approaches to a doctrine of scripture.

Approaches to Preaching

The object of preaching is to do something to people: to engender or to deepen the response of faith, questioning, hope, anger, love, reflection, repentance, obedience, and worship. In order to do that, preaching is also involved in dispensing information, otherwise those attitudes and actions

13. Against Clines, "Story and Poem."

14. Thiselton, *The Two Horizons* 353-54.

15. Valdés and Miller, *Interpretation of Narrative* 10; cf. Mark, "Relativism and Community" 163.

16. *Literary Theory* 198; characteristically he also notes how the abjuring of method can function ideologically.

17. So W. C. Booth. See his *Critical Understanding*, with Tracy's comments in *Analogical Imagination* 112-13, 141.

18. Hirsch, *Validity in Interpretation* 112-13.

would not be a *response*. There is thus an overlap between preaching and teaching. In preaching, however, we are not *merely* dispensing information, and if people have forgotten the content of the sermon by Tuesday, or even by Sunday bedtime, this does not in itself mean that the sermon failed in its object. We are seeking to give people an opportunity to respond to God.

The Bible is entirely at home in the pulpit because its words were spoken and written to do something to people along the same lines. "It is the preaching book because it is the preaching book."[19] Biblical statute, wisdom, prophecy, and epistle overtly urge people toward more confident faith or questioning and more specific commitment and away from disobedience or false trust. Biblical narrative, poetry, and psalmody have similar aims. They offer not merely historical information or aesthetic experience or cultic record but implicit invitation. One reason why works of various kinds were collected and eventually became "scriptures" was so that they might continue to effect something in the lives of people.

In taking the Bible into the pulpit we are thus not doing something alien to its nature. It belongs there. It is perhaps more at home there than in the university study. In the pulpit it can be given the response of mind, heart, and will that it seeks. We open it before a congregation so that the God who long ago acted on people by means of these words may do so again by the same means. The application of the scriptures to the life of the people of God is entirely natural given the origin of the scriptures as words addressed to the people of God. Our aim is to free these words to address that people of God once more.

Arguably any true biblical interpretation must eventually take the form of preaching, and vice versa, because "the Bible itself is preaching."[20]

It is possible and helpful to distinguish between various aspects of interpreting a text: understanding its original meaning, setting it in the context of the rest of scripture, applying its message to our own day, responding to its promise or challenge, and communicating it to a congregation. Yet these distinguishable facets of the interpretive task are often not sufficiently cooperative or predictable to occur in such a logical order, as stages of a linear process. Responding to a passage on the basis of intuitively grasping that it is in some way God's special word to me now may lead to perceiving how it does actually apply, and being charged with communi-

---

19. Forsyth, *Positive Preaching and the Modern Mind* 6.

20. Packer, "Preaching as Biblical Interpretation," in *Inerrancy and Common Sense* (ed. Nicole and Michaels) 189.

cating its significance today may lead to perceiving its original meaning, as well as the reverse in each case.

Attending to the written word is even harder than attending to the spoken word. We easily cut off our partner in midsentence; the text provides the preacher's subject, but the preacher provides the predicate, which decides the nature of the statement made. Alternatively we may rely on having listened to this text on an earlier occasion instead of listening anew in order to see if we are now in a position to hear it more fully or freshly and thus to preach a new sermon rather than repreach yesterday's. Or again, we may assume we know what the text "says" — indeed, we may have chosen this text because we "knew" what it said — and therefore that we have no need to listen to it. The preacher's calling is that of a vicarious listening. We are set aside and invited to spend time listening on behalf of other people. Our task is to do that and then to come before our congregation, not as prophets who speak the word of God, but as those who have heard the prophets and apostles and are therefore in a position to share with them the results of such listening.[21]

I would not want to argue that all preaching must be text-centered — though ninety-five percent of my own is. There is a place for topical preaching, though it may become a sin when indulged in too often. There is a place for preaching that begins from a text but goes on to reflection based on other sources of Christian wisdom and insight. There may even be a place for preaching from Katherine Whitehorn.[22] Yet our study of scripture as a witnessing tradition, an authoritative canon, an inspired word, and an experienced revelation will suggest reasons for finding scripture itself the preacher's supreme source of insight. Preaching on specific texts is our way of exposing ourselves and our congregation to those resources. I have found over the years that the texts I expound have grown longer, so that a "text" more often means a chapter than a verse; the longer the text, the more likely the sermon is to be full of *its* insight, whereas the shorter the text, the more of *me* there needs to be in it.

If preaching involves taking up a task that the scriptures themselves are concerned with, it is natural to examine the ways the scriptures themselves go about the task to see how those ways are instructive for us. This leads us to consider another aspect of the diversity that characterizes all

21. W. W. Johnson, "Ethics of Preaching" 425.

22. So Nineham, *Explorations in Theology* 1:106. Whitehorn is a columnist in a British Sunday newspaper; in scriptural terms, she belongs among the wisdom writers!

aspects of scripture. Preachers often settle into one particular approach to preaching, perhaps one valued in their own Christian tradition. In scripture itself different kinds of texts communicate in different ways, and they point toward diversity in the way we expound scripture.

There is a classic form of expository preaching that works by seeking to explain systematically and explicitly what the central message of a text is and how its various parts contribute to this message. It remains a means of opening up the significance of scripture in a powerful way, and it is vastly preferable to the three-point "thoughts that have occurred to me and that I am prepared to attribute to the Spirit and inflict on you," which can be the fare of the pulpit. But this sort of expository preaching is mainly appropriate for the texts in the Bible that are themselves directly expository or conceptual such as the prophets, the Sermon on the Mount, and the Epistles. It is less appropriate for the history/story material in scripture. A common homiletic approach to the latter has been to summarize the story itself at the beginning of the sermon and then ask, "Well, what do we learn from this?" — at which point the sermon falls flat on its face as the preacher abandons the text's story form and turns it back into the kind of direct teaching that those other parts of scripture offer.

Such expository preaching may also be less appropriate for texts such as the Psalms or other first-person passages. The Psalms, at least, offer not teaching about prayer or stories about prayer but models of prayer. When we read them, we are accepting an invitation to listen in on the psalmists praying, to overhear what was going on between them and God. We are being invited to see if we can make their prayer our own and to test our prayer by theirs. We are not being invited to learn something about prayer but to pray. Such a distinctive method of communicating within scripture points toward a distinctive method of communicating scripture. What could be involved in expounding the Psalms is to pray them oneself in order to draw the congregation into praying them — to preach by praying.

Francis Young likens the preacher to someone offering a performance of a work of art. "A classic repertoire . . . encompasses a variety of genres: symphonies, concertos, tone poems, opera, comedy, tragedy, satire. . . ." These require different styles of performance. Similarly "each genre within the Bible will have its proper mode of performance. Narrative, poetry, prophecy, law, wisdom, hymns, prayers, visions — all these require different approaches"[23] and are not to be assimilated to each other.

23. Young, *The Art of Performance* 26, 27.

Different kinds of texts suggest different, complementary approaches to the interpretation and exposition of scripture as well as to a doctrine of scripture. My aim in the following chapters is to work out these approaches in the light of the view that scripture is a witnessing tradition, an authoritative canon, an inspired word, and an experienced revelation, and is each of these more intrinsically at some points than at others.

PART I

SCRIPTURE AS WITNESSING TRADITION: INTERPRETING NARRATIVE

Witness in the Form of Story:
Beginning from the Text

To view scriptural narrative as a witnessing tradition suggests on the one hand that this narrative is intrinsically concerned with factual events. Witnesses testify to what has actually happened. Tradition (in classic passages such as Luke 1:1-4 or 1 Cor 11 and 15) is the passing on of accounts of real events. On the other hand, witnesses report on things from their individual angles; tradition reflects the personal characteristics of those who pass it on and those whose situation it is designed to address. Biblical narrative is not merely annal or chronicle but story, manifesting an interest in plot and character and written from a point of view. The approaches appropriate to interpreting other narrative literature are thus appropriate to interpreting scripture. The factual basis of narratives such as those of the exodus or the resurrection is important to the validity of their theological messages. But our *understanding* of that message will be gained by the same approaches as we would use in relation to fictional stories such as the parables or to largely fictional narratives (as I take them to be) such as Ruth, Job, Esther, and Jonah.[1]

History and Story

Textbooks such as John Bright's *A History of Israel* have long been popular with people who study the Bible. There a number of reasons for this. The

---

1. Cf. Lundin, *The Responsibility of Hermeneutics* 60. On the model of the witnessing tradition, see further my *Models for Scripture* Part I.

actual history of Israel is to be expected to be theologically illuminating both in itself and as the background to the Christ event and is thus worth studying; further, Bright's work has a relatively high estimate of the First Testament's historical value and is thus a more reassuring example of the genre than some others. But another reason for its popularity is the assumption that in recounting Israel's history it could be presumed to be giving the reader an understanding of the meaning of the First Testament itself.

This assumption takes no account of the fact that the truth of the biblical story is more than its historical facticity. The task of understanding the meaning of that story cannot be reduced to the task of establishing the historical facts that underlie it. Indeed, the understanding of the *story* is not much furthered by books called *A History of Israel*. The scriptural narrative exists in order to offer a patterned portrayal of events, to express a vision. This central aspect of its importance is ignored when interpreters are preoccupied with discovering *what* historical events it refers to (the open, critical approach to the task) or with proving *that* it refers to historical events (the apologetic, conservative approach to the task) — or with disproving that it has any significant reference to historical events (the correlative skeptical approach to the task). Any of these concerns are distractions from the task of interpreting the narrative itself. We may question whether Karl Barth was right to proscribe the attempt to get behind the biblical witness to actual historical facts.[2] There is a place for that. But Barth is right that hearing the witness of scripture is a matter of just this — listening to its actual witness, to the story that it tells, as it tells it.[3]

Concern with the factuality of Genesis 1 offers an instructive instance of the way in which, if we are preoccupied with investigating the historical events to which a narrative refers, our attention easily becomes distracted from the narrative's meaning. Various aspects of the chapter's message or vision become clear when one considers it in its contexts in the literary work to which it belongs (Genesis–Kings; Genesis–Exodus; Genesis 1–11; Genesis 1–8; Genesis 1–3). Other aspects become clear through consideration of its own internal dynamic, for example, its structured form with recurrent features (God speaking, God seeing, God calling) and its double climax in the creation of humanity and God resting. Much of the depth and the excitement of this opening chapter of the Bible has been missed,

2. See, e.g., *Church Dogmatics* III/1, 76-83; IV/1, 335-36.
3. Cf. Gunton, *Enlightenment and Alienation* 121.

however, when the focus in interpretation has been placed on the relationship between its picture and the possible scientific and historical facts about world origins.

Similarly such a focus may be more of a hindrance than a help in interpreting the Gospels. Matthew and Luke offer markedly different accounts of Jesus' birth, the beginning of his ministry, and his resurrection appearances. If the interpretive task concentrates on looking behind these differences or harmonizing them, it ceases to follow the story Matthew or Luke told and to open itself to the world they portrayed.

There is a way in which investigating the events that lie behind a narrative can help us understand the narrative itself. Examining the differences between the events themselves and the narrative's portrayal of them (what is included, omitted, emphasized, or reordered) will help us perceive aspects of the interpretation that the narrative gives them. The difference between the significance of the reign of King Omri when judged by ordinary historical criteria and the insignificance attached to it in the story in Kings provides a convenient example. Comparing a later version of a story with an earlier one can also further the task of interpretation in this way, as the story of Jesus' stilling of the storm as it appears in Mark and in Matthew illustrates.[4] Different views of the prehistory of the text may generate different understandings of its eventual final form.[5] Source criticism, tradition criticism, and redaction criticism can thus contribute to the interpretation of the actual text we have, whether or not their practitioners' own concern lies in this direction or rather in tracing the prehistory of the text or the theology of the individual editors. But it requires some self-discipline to ensure that these methods make this contribution; they have a habit of becoming ends in themselves.

Literary approaches to biblical narrative give concentrated attention to the story in which its witnessing tradition is mediated. Such approaches to interpretation are by no means confined to narrative, but in their application to scripture they have flourished and been especially creative here.

In *The Mirror and the Lamp* M. H. Abrams devised a helpful diagrammatic grid for understanding developments in literary criticism as they then stood. He categorized approaches to interpretation according to where their

---

4. Cf. Josipovici, *The Book of God* 6; for the stilling of the storm, see G. Bornkamm in *Tradition and Interpretation in Matthew* 52-57.

5. Boorer, "The Importance of a Diachronic Approach" (he instances understandings of the theme of hope in Genesis to Kings).

focus lay: in the origins of the text (its date, sources, authorship, and purpose), in the external realities to which the text refers (such as historical and theological matters), in the text itself (for instance, in the structure and language of a story, its plot, characters, and points of view), or in the readers of the text (the nature of the audience presupposed by the text, the way it communicates with them, and the way readers go about making sense of it). Abrams's grid still provides a convenient starting point for a consideration of literary approaches to scripture.[6]

Biblical interpretation has commonly concerned itself with the first two of Abrams's four focuses. Traditional critical interpretation has been centrally interested in establishing the historical background of the narratives, the historical process whereby they came into being, and the historical realities to which they refer. In the precritical period interpreters would have taken for granted that there was no distinction between the story told by a biblical narrative and the events that actually took place in biblical times, or between the figure traditionally associated with a particular book and its actual author. During the critical age it is these distinctions that have been taken for granted, and the major concern in interpretation of the stories has been to establish and defend views of their historical background and reference.

The views that have been held on these matters have varied, and fashions have changed regarding the degree to which we can, for instance, derive historical information from the Pentateuch or recover the historical Jesus. Social context, personality, and personal faith-convictions influence whether scholars take more conservative or more skeptical views on such matters. Yet scholars who take quite different positions on these historical questions share the same understanding of what is involved in interpreting the material. All are concerned with the stories' historical background and historical reference; all overtly agree that the historical method enables one to investigate these matters. They disagree on the results of the investigation but agree on the nature of the questions to be investigated and — formally — on the methods for approaching these questions.

The prophetic books and the Epistles tend to draw attention to aspects of their historical background, and they imply that knowing something of this background will help us to interpret them. The same has been widely assumed to be the case with the narrative books, and scholarship has spent

6. A comparable, apparently independent diagram with an explicit concern for biblical hermeneutics appears in Croatto, *Biblical Hermeneutics* 11.

considerable effort in seeking to place the biblical narratives historically. The value of this can again be illustrated from Genesis 1, since several of its features seem to gain their significance from their exilic context, and an awareness of that context helps one to identify those features. The delay in making reference to sun, moon, and stars until the week of creation is half over, and the failure to name sun and moon even then, are responses to the temptation to overestimate their significance in the Babylonian context. The portrait of God doing a week's work and then observing the sabbath responds to the converse temptation to underestimate the sabbath's significance in that context. General features of Israelite or first-century life are often an important part of the taken-for-granted background to biblical narratives. Nevertheless the value of efforts to establish the narratives' precise historical context has been overrated. It is not usually the case that we are able to place them geographically and historically with certainty and precision. This results from an aspect of their inherent nature: While prophets and Epistles work by revealing their background, intention, and message, narratives work by being more reserved about such matters.

In awareness of such facts, a substantial critique of the historical approach to interpretation has now accumulated.

First, the fact that the practitioners of this approach cannot reach agreed results reflects not merely the fact that some are using the wrong methods or starting from mistaken assumptions, but also the fact that all of them are asking questions whose answers the text by definition conceals. Admittedly this may make these questions paradoxically attractive to a profession that thrives on asking questions that are not very readily answered. Much study of the Song of Hannah in the story of Samuel's birth, for instance, has focused on locating it in a specific sociohistorical setting rather than interpreting it in its literary context in 1 Samuel. There is broad agreement that its origin is later than the events the story is relating, but little agreement about the particular historical context from which it did originally emerge.[7] South African interpreters of the Cain and Abel story have sought to consider it in the light of sociocritical insight, but their study suffers from radical diversity in conclusions even among people committed to the black struggle.[8]

---

7. Cf. Eslinger's comments in *Kingship of God in Crisis* 102.

8. Contrast the work of Wittenberg ("King Solomon and the Theologians": the story emerges from critique of Jerusalem state theology) and Mosala (*Biblical Hermeneutics and Black Theology in South Africa* 33-37: the story was designed to support the ruling classes who were appropriating land from peasants). Cf. G. West, "Reading 'the

Second, and conversely, because the historical approach's interest centers on a topic on which the text does not overtly focus, it misses the text's specific burden and thus misfocuses the interpretive task. It cannot directly help exegesis. We have noted that establishing the historical events that lie behind the story does not in itself establish the story's meaning. The many biblical commentaries that concentrate on the historical background, reference, and implications of their texts and on the process of development whereby the traditions reached their final form are sidetracked by these concerns from the actual task of exegeting the text. The point has been put with special trenchancy by Robert Polzin in a review of works on 1 Samuel. He notes the effort put into establishing its correct text, which is then ignored out of a desire to excavate behind it to its hypothetical earlier forms, so that the object of study is the pre-text rather than the text.[9]

Third, the historical approach is capable of casting doubts on the truth of the text it studies, by questioning its historical value, but it is not capable of vindicating the truth of the text. Its historical results are always tentative, and by their nature thay cannot establish the religious heart of the stories' truth-claim. They cannot establish what is now sometimes called the viability of the world that the texts portray to their audience.

Fourth, again to extend the previous point, the historical approach inevitably thus fails to realize the text's own aim. The form of objectivity it seeks is not only unattainable but also not worth attaining.[10] To whatever degree a biblical text seeks to convey historical information, it seeks to do so not for the sake of that information but in order to bring a religious message. A piece of historical exegesis will generally acknowledge that it is handling a text with a religious message and will summarize that message, but it will not feel obliged to go beyond such a summary of this message's surface structure. This fourth difficulty of the historical approach is compounded by the fact that for many people the stories being studied are not merely religious texts but parts of their scriptures. To put this point in less confessional terms, the historical approach ignores the actual text, which "has helped shape Western civilization and the Judeo-Christian culture at its core."[11] Indeed it may make that achievement rather a mystery.

Text' and Reading 'Behind-the-Text'," in *The Bible in Three Dimensions* (ed. Clines and others) 299-320; also West's *Biblical Hermeneutics of Liberation* 45-62.

9. See "1 Samuel"; cf. *Samuel and the Deuteronomist* 1-17.
10. Cf. Phillips, *Poststructural Criticism and the Bible* 12-13, 37.
11. Polzin, *Samuel and the Deuteronomist* 3.

It is in part the sense of impasse that historical method has reached that makes literary approaches to the text worthy of investigation.

Focusing on the Story's Own Form and Structure

This sense of impasse draws us initially to the "formalist" approaches of what was once the "new criticism." These approaches focus on the story itself, on the precise nature of a text's structure and language, on narrative plot and characterization as these unfold in the work as a whole, and on matters such as the development of themes within a story, its patterns, motifs, images, and actual words, its use of anticipation, flashback, questions, and irony, and the points of view from which it is told.[12] Thus Luke's Gospel might be studied in order to discover not what sources underlie it, nor what these contribute to the attempt to trace what Jesus historically said and did, nor what the work teaches on themes such as the nature of God, the person of Christ, the church, the nature of salvation, and questions of ethics, nor what message the work brought to the particular audience for whom it was written, but the plot of Luke's work as a whole: R. C. Tannehill, for instance, sees it as "a tragic story" about Israel and its Messiah.[13] Formalist criticism seeks to understand works as wholes, even long works such as Gospels or Genesis–Kings, and to see the place of individual sections within such wholes — the way people normally read books!

In the study of Daniel, vast scholarly effort has been expended on establishing the background and historical value of the stories, without its producing a consensus on the matter. A formalist approach looks at the stories themselves, perceiving that chapter 1, for instance, has a chiastic shape. It begins and ends with the story's broad context in imperial history, Nebuchadnezzar at the beginning, Cyrus at the end (vv. 1-2, 21). Inside this pair of brackets appears the theme of the education of certain Judean youths, who in due course prove more able than anyone else at the Babylonian court (vv. 3-7, 17-20). At the center of the chapter is the account of Daniel's insistence on avoiding defilement and his taking on a test in order

---

12. See, e.g., Berlin, *Poetics and Interpretation of Biblical Narrative;* Bar-Efrat, *Narrative Art in the Bible;* Rhoads and Michie, *Mark as Story.* For the background in the application of these approaches in secular poetics see, e.g., Rimmon-Kenan, *Narrative Fiction.*

13. "Israel in Luke-Acts: A Tragic Story." Cf. Moore, *Literary Criticism and the Gospels* 5.

to do so (vv. 8-16). These three elements in the structure of the chapter indicate the story's plot tension and resolution. What will happen when Israel is defeated by Babylon, when its young men are enrolled for a Babylonian education, when they are subjected to the defilement of life at the Babylonian court? By human courage and divine aid they avoid defilement, triumph in learning, and outlast their conquerors. Details of the text's language give clues to such points. Certain words play significant roles in the chapter: One verb meaning "give" or "make" appears three times, in vv. 2, 9, and 17, once for each of the three issues raised by the plot, each time with God as subject — the only times God acts in the story. Another verb meaning "come" or "take" appears four times in vv. 1-3; it plays a key role in the portrayal of Nebuchadnezzar's aggression. And a verb meaning "determine" appears in consecutive verses (vv. 7, 8) at the point where Daniel takes his stand in relation to the requirements of his Babylonian overlords.[14]

The interpretation of a story thus emerges from the story itself rather than from attempts to trace the process whereby it came into being or the historical truth of the events that it refers to. One should not exaggerate the point: We have noted that some knowledge of the events themselves and of a writer's sources may illuminate what the writer has done with the events and the sources. Nor is this to imply that the story is a self-contained world of its own so that we neither need nor should consider anything from outside it in order to understand it. The very fact that it is written in Hebrew or Greek is a reflection of its belonging within a linguistic tradition shared by author and audience, and its modern audience has to enter that broad linguistic tradition (at least vicariously, via the work of translators) if they are to hear the story. Beyond that, there will be matters of social and historical background presupposed by the story that need to be made explicit if the story is to be heard.

The form of the story will also suggest part of the story's meaning. Here an audience has to discover the conventions of the authors' society within which they were working and be wary of imposing alien literary categories on ancient Middle Eastern religious texts[15] — though in principle that is no more of a problem with literary approaches than with

---

14. The verbs are *nātan*, *bô'/hēbî'*, and *śîm*. See Goldingay, *Daniel* 6-12.

15. The issue is raised by Exum (ed.), *Tragedy and Comedy in the Bible*, since (as some contributors note) these categories do not seem to correspond to the biblical material; though if it is a matter of a narrative's tragic *vision* or *dimension* there is not such a problem (cf. Humphreys, *The Tragic Vision*, and Exum's own *Tragedy and Biblical Narrative*).

historical or theological approaches.[16] The notion that a story is its own world does not mean that it can be reckoned to contain within itself everything that is necessary to its interpretation. "Texts are framed in an environment of convention" regarding matters such as genre, a convention specific to a culture.[17] Perhaps all literary texts presuppose earlier texts, as the study of "intertextuality" presupposes.[18] Certainly biblical texts commonly presuppose earlier biblical texts, so that (for instance) the opening references in the story of Ruth to the days when the judges ruled and to the country of Moab presuppose not merely historical and geographical realities but ways these are portrayed in the Torah and the Former Prophets and an awareness of these on the part of an audience. Considering the writings that formed the literary and religious horizon of a story's world thus makes a contribution to enabling us to hear it.[19]

Formalism's stress on rigor of attention to the actual text forms an important complement to talk of intuition and openness in reading stories. Interpreting a story requires a demanding combination of sensitivity, openness, enthusiasm, imagination, and the rigor and slog of hard work that develops ideas and tests them.[20] We do not wish to be reading an alien insight into the text — or more likely a marginal idea into the center of it. I believe, for instance, that *the* theme that runs through Genesis is that of God's blessing — originally given, deservedly compromised, graciously promised, variously imperiled, partially experienced. This understanding is suggested by verbal clues in the text itself, but it must be tested by considering how the book's various episodes relate to this theme.[21] Interpretation is not arbitrary, with imagination imagining its own meanings into the text. It "cannot be based merely on an imaginative impression of the story but must be undertaken through minute critical attention to the biblical writer's articulations of narrative form"; we require not just imagination but also precision.[22] "Imagination and the distrust of imagination go together."[23]

16. Miscall argues that a deconstructionist approach (see pp. 27-30 below) helps one to avoid reading the Bible as a modern Western text: see *The Workings of OT Narrative* 143.

17. Kugel, "On the Bible and Literary Criticism" 229.

18. Cf., e.g., Culler, *The Pursuit of Signs* 103-4, 107.

19. Cf. Josipovici, *The Book of God* 6.

20. Cf. Haller, "On the Interpretative Task."

21. I have sought to do this in "The Patriarchs in Scripture and History."

22. Alter, *The Art of Biblical Narrative* 12, 21.

23. Fisch, *Poetry with a Purpose* 5.

The central principle for interpretation of scripture pressed by Benjamin Jowett in his paper in *Essays and Reviews* was *"Interpret the Scripture like any other book."*[24] Read the text itself. That is the concern of formalist interpretation.

Looking for the Structures under the Surface of the Story

Formalist study aims to understand the specific nature of stories as texts and the unique structure of each story as one aspect of that study. Structural*ist* study of stories is a distinguishable literary, philosophical, and anthropological approach. It, too, is interested in the "narrative *surface* structure" of stories, but it involves looking beneath the immediate surface of stories for their *deeper* underlying structure. The presupposition of such study is that because of consistencies about the way human thinking works, patterns recur in stories. These include patterns of action and of interrelationship between different participants.

Any individual story may typify varying underlying structural patterns, and a knowledge of these recurrent patterns may enable one to perceive aspects of the way a given story works or of the way it has its effect on its hearers by utilizing structures of thinking that both storyteller and hearer may be unaware of. Daniel Patte compares these patterns to the loom and the set of colored threads that someone uses to weave a blanket. The blanket's surface design may be unique, but loom and threads have opened up possibilities and set constraints common to a multiplicity of blankets and weavers. They thus explain a number of the design's features. Structuralist insights similarly help to identify some of the constraints that contribute to the shape of biblical thinking and storytelling. They also enable us to perceive points at which a particular story breaks the bounds of these constraints. In both ways they enable us to see more clearly the nature of and the reasons for the impact a story has on an audience.[25]

Any single structuralist scheme is likely to illumine only some aspects of a story. Structuralism is a "heuristic device"[26] that works in a manner

24. "On the Interpretation of Scripture" 458; his emphasis. See Barr, "Jowett and the 'Original Meaning of Scripture.'"

25. See Patte, *What Is Structural Exegesis?* 21-22. Study of the "art" of biblical poetry (see Alter, *The Art of Biblical Poetry*) serves a parallel function for poetry.

26. Milne, *Vladimir Propp* 264.

parallel to that of form criticism. It enables us to identify features and interrelationships in a narrative, when these features and interrelationships correspond to elements within the scheme, and it also draws our attention to features that do not fit the scheme. David Clines offers an analysis of Esther, for instance, in terms of A. J. Greimas's "actantial" scheme, which identifies six interrelated roles that can be expected to appear in any story.[27] This analysis reveals that in Esther there is no "sender," the person who seeks to communicate the "object" (here deliverance) to the "receiver" (here the Jewish people) in a story. This is the structuralist way of expressing a theologically crucial and distinctive feature of the Esther story, the (apparent) absence of God from the story. Furthermore, the position of the king in the story is ambiguous: He takes both the role of "opponent" and that of "helper." This corresponds to an ambiguity in the book's stance toward the Persian government.

Such observations can be paralleled in the study of other texts. While there is no doubt about the functions fulfilled by some of the characters in the stories in Daniel, there is considerable uncertainty or ambiguity about the functions fulfilled by the king. In the terms of Vladimir Propp's earlier analysis of roles in stories, the king can be both opponent, on one hand, and recognizer, rewarder, and punisher on the other.[28] That puts us on the track of a key feature of the stories (not one that Proppian analysis is capable of handling, but one it is capable of drawing attention to, by default), namely, that the position of the king of Babylon and the relationship between divine and human kingship are key issues in the stories.[29] Again, in Genesis 32, the subject of a famous structuralist study by Roland Barthes, God is both sender and adversary, so that the story begins in the manner of a folktale but then throws the hearer by this strange development.[30]

While structuralist schemes can thus function heuristically, stories can have features that fail to correspond with any one scheme, and the interpreter must resist the temptation to rewrite stories so that they do correspond with the scheme.[31] It is also both the strength and the limitation of structuralism

27. "Reading Esther from Left to Right," in *The Bible in Three Dimensions* (ed. Clines and others) 36-37.

28. See Milne, *Vladimir Propp* 259.

29. Nolan Fewell, *Circle of Sovereignty* (first ed., 1988) 10.

30. See Barthes, *Structural Analysis and Biblical Exegesis* 21-33. On this study cf., e.g., Barton, *Reading the OT* 116-19.

31. Milne's understanding of Daniel 1–2 provides a warning example (*Vladimir Propp* 206-22).

that it focuses on common underlying patterns in stories. From a structuralist perspective, we tell several versions of a story in order to get the underlying pattern home in several different ways. "The order both behind and embedded in the stories is the message."[32] The "redundancy" of repetition aims to ensure that this message gets home; the distinctive features of a particular story are merely "noise" or interference — to use the terminology of communications theory — that the repetition helps us to ignore.[33] The regrettable implication is that the concrete form of a particular story is not a subject of great interest. "It is rather like killing a person in order to examine more conveniently the circulation of the blood."[34]

A second form of structuralism that has been applied to biblical studies is concerned with interpreting features within stories as elements from natural or cultural systems or codes. These codes express themselves in connection with matters such as food, clothing, geography, place, and spatial movement on the local scale, time and temporal sequence, and society in its structures of authority and hierarchies of relationship, as well as in matters within the realm of ideas.[35] The codes are formulated by means of binary oppositions, and beneath the surface polarities are polarities at the level of attitudes and ideas regarding matters of life and death, heaven and earth, and the significance of history. Esther illustrates the alimentary code (feasting and fasting are recurrent events), the code of clothing (normal and deformed clothing, ordinary and festal clothing, the clothing of the powerless and the powerful), and the topographical code (especially the disjunction between outside and inside), and all provide means by which the story handles one of its key themes, the nature and the location of power.[36]

It may seem that structuralism "has contributed very little to understanding the Bible."[37] Its own concern is more with explaining how texts

32. Spivey, "Structuralism and Biblical Studies" 136.

33. Jacobson, "The Structuralists and the Bible" 150. Both Spivey and Jacobson refer to Leach's *Genesis as Myth,* the first application of C. Lévi-Strauss's structuralism to scripture. J. C. Anderson takes up this aspect of information theory in "Double and Triple Stories, the Implied Reader, and Redundancy in Matthew," in *Reader Response Approaches to Biblical and Secular Texts* (ed. Detweiler) 71-89.

34. Eagleton, *Literary Theory* 109.

35. See, e.g., Jobling, *The Sense of Biblical Narrative,* for the application of the structuralist method of Lévi-Strauss (and of Greimas) to the Hebrew Bible.

36. Clines, "Reading Esther from Left to Right," in *The Bible in Three Dimensions* (ed. Clines and others) 37-40.

37. R. Morgan, *Biblical Interpretation* 219; cf. A. C. Thiselton's comments in "On Models and Methods," in *The Bible in Three Dimensions* (ed. Clines and others) 341.

suggest meaning than with generating new interpretations of texts. But the examples quoted above indicate the usefulness of this achievement. Historically structuralism's chief significance may be that it has provided biblical study with a way of breaking the monogamous hold of historical approaches on biblical study. But it may also be that the novelty of its approach and the initial abstruseness of its techniques and procedures mean that its potential has not yet been exploited.

Deconstructing the Structures in the Story

It is often (perhaps always) the case that behind an interpretive method lies a philosophy; this is true of historical criticism and of structuralism, and of formalism when it takes the view that the text is a world of its own with no relationship to a world outside it. Failure to recognize this may make us fail to do justice to the significance of the interpretive method in question or to take account of the far-reaching way in which it may clash with the presuppositions of the gospel. Thus Gunn comments that "reading biblical narrative in terms of its final form is a more radical proposition than perhaps is realized by those who most enthusiastically have embraced the programme (and mocked its historical-critical predecessor)."[38]

This is also true of deconstruction as a philosophy (or an anti-philosophy). The father of deconstruction, Jacques Derrida, observed that as part of its program "the motif of homogeneity, the theological motif *par excellence*, is decidedly the one to be destroyed."[39] In this sense deconstruction cannot be domesticated.[40] And it is in part such considerations that explain the strong feeling expressed in the conscious abjuring of approaches such as deconstructionism in *The Literary Guide to the Bible*[41] — and in the embracing of them in *The Book and the Text*[42] (though it is noteworthy that a number of contributors appear in both books or could have appeared in both).

---

38. "New Directions in the Study of Biblical Hebrew Narrative" 71.

39. *Positions* 63-64; cf. Culler, *On Deconstruction* 135, and 85-225 generally; also Steiner, *Real Presences*, e.g., 133-34, 214-32. Thiselton thus asks whether deconstruction is a worldview masquerading as an approach to interpretation (see *New Horizons in Hermeneutics* 92).

40. J. P. Leavey, "Four Protocols," in *Derrida and Biblical Studies* (ed. Detweiler) 48-49.

41. Ed. Alter and Kermode; see page 4.

42. Ed. Schwartz; see page 1.

Nevertheless, consciously or unconsciously, biblical interpretation characteristically works in dialogue with the intellectual currents of the day. It was so at Alexandria, then during the Reformation, and then in the development of the historical-critical method; nor is there anything distinctively twentieth-century about biblical interpretation being decades if not centuries behind these intellectual currents, often embracing one method just as secular thinking abandons it.[43] Culler comments that "the comprehensiveness of literature makes it possible for any extraordinary or compelling theory to be drawn into literary theory,"[44] and biblical interpretation will hardly be satisfied to make less of a claim.

In any case, to keep up a conversation with the thinking of the day seems a good principle. These intellectual currents are unlikely to be totally wrong, even if they have been distorted, not least through their lack of relationship with the gospel. The ease with which we ourselves domesticate or otherwise distort the gospel makes such intellectual currents positive handmaids, by virtue of their facing issues that we may avoid. Thus the simplicity of the parables, as we may see it, becomes the necessarily extravagant paradoxicality of their portrait of the one imageless God by means of multiple and polyvalent images, a portrait that reflects the ultimate unknowability of God and the necessity that we retrieve a "negative theology."[45]

This is a particularly appropriate perspective with which to approach the application of deconstructive criticism to scripture. As cultural relativism self-destructs because it must see itself as culture-relative,[46] so historicism self-destructs because it must see itself as a relative historical truth, text-as-world-of-its-own self-destructs because it is only a theory in a world of its own, and deconstruction defeats itself because it deconstructs.[47] Treated as more limited aids to interpretation, all may be fruitful.

Writing is a creative activity: It brings a world into existence, creating order where otherwise there is only miscellaneous data. Texts bring a vision of order to data, and interpretation (itself, like writing, a creative activity) brings order to texts. By their nature, then, texts and their interpretations

43. Keegan, *Interpreting the Bible* 14-22.

44. *On Deconstruction* 11.

45. Crossan, *Cliffs of Fall* 58; cf. Moore, *Literary Criticism and the Gospels* 140.

46. Trigg, *Reason and Commitment,* e.g., 2-3; cf. Barton, "Reflections on Cultural Relativism" 103-4.

47. Cf. Grant, *Reading the NT* 6; also Moore, *Literary Criticism and the Gospels* 145-46.

may beguile us into thinking that things are simpler than they are.[48] In the light of this, deconstructive criticism "reaches beyond structuralism in an exploration of how these elements [of binary opposition] render the text *unstable*"; it assumes that "any reading which produces a text with complete thematic unity (which every reading inevitably does) is a misreading."[49] After all, the assumption that a text is internally consistent is just that — a presupposition, "no less arguable and contentious than any other."[50] Deconstruction's concern is not to be destructive; again, Derrida himself has said that "when I say deconstruct a thing, I do not say we are against it, or that in any situation I will fight it, be on the other side."[51] Deconstruction does seek to dismember oversimple constructions, to "identify grafts in the texts it analyses" — not to introduce an alien principle into the text, but to analyze the self-deconstruction that is present in the text itself.[52] It wants to face ambiguity — not the ambiguity that results from insufficient evidence or material, but that which may issue from *too much* evidence.[53]

Deconstruction thus looks beneath the surface of the construction that the text may put on matters, or the construction interpreters put on the text, to the more complex questions and uncertainties that may lie beneath the text and that the text may be concealing. It "permits me to read [the Bible] on its own terms without having to force it into modes of meaning and interpretation that gloss over, harmonize, or remove its repetitions, contradictions, details, gaps, etc."[54] It remystifies the text that interpretation seeks to demystify and rationalize.[55] As Terry Eagleton puts it, "the aim of 'deconstructive criticism' is to confront *ideology* with *textuality*."[56] It is to

48. Cf. Lundin in *The Responsibility of Hermeneutics* 34-40, summarizing Derrida.

49. Nolan Fewell, *Circle of Sovereignty* (first ed.) 15-16 (emphasis original); "Feminist Reading of the Hebrew Bible" 82.

50. Eagleton, *Literary Theory* 81; on deconstruction, see further, e.g., 132-34; also, e.g., 142 on the historical background post-1968: "unable to break the structures of state power, post-structuralism found it possible instead to subvert the structures of language."

51. Speaking (with reference to the Enlightenment) in London in 1985, as quoted by E. Graham and H. Walton, "A Walk on the Wild Side," *ModT* 33 (1991) 1.

52. Culler, *On Deconstruction* 135, summarizing Jacques Derrida; Culler, *The Pursuit of Signs* 15-16, summarizing Paul de Man and J. Hillis Miller, American literary deconstructionists.

53. Miscall, *I Samuel* ix.

54. Miscall, *I Samuel* xxiv.

55. Greenstein, "Deconstruction and Biblical Narrative" (with a particular focus on the story of the death of Aaron's sons in Leviticus 10).

56. "Text, Ideology, Realism," in *Literature and Society* (ed. Said) 149 (emphasis original).

allow the complexity of the text to break the silence imposed on it by our constructions.

The tension between patriarchal and egalitarian stances within scripture, for instance, may be seen as illustrating a process of deconstruction beginning within the biblical text itself, one that feminist interpretation may help along.[57] In the Book of Job, Job's eventual submission to God and God's restoring of Job may seem to silence the Job of chapters 3–31 in such a way that the book's final incoherence witnesses to the fact that no way of speaking of God and suffering will do.[58] Male interpretation has seen Judges as focusing on national, political, and religious history, but it has imposed this coherence on a book that "is also about lineage, fatherhood, and the lives of young girls . . . virginity, mothers, and violence . . . sex, obedience, and death . . . power and its dissymmetrical distribution . . . ," especially between women and men.[59]

In Daniel, Nolan Fewell pays particular attention to the opposition of divine and human sovereignty as fundamental to the tension of the narratives. The stories assert the priority of divine sovereignty over human sovereignty, but it is characteristic of the secondary element in a binary opposition constantly to undermine the primary element. So

> Daniel 1–6 makes point after point about God's sovereignty over human beings, but God's sovereignty is undercut by the way in which human sovereignty keeps pushing to the fore: God's power and presence is constantly being screened through human characters' points of view; God's identity is expressed in terms of human identity; God's wisdom is translated by a human mediator and so forth.[60]

Any interpreter could have noted the concern with the relationship between divine and human sovereignty in the stories; deconstructive criticism may enable the interpreter to analyze more sharply tensions and undercurrents that are present within the text and that contribute to the subtlety of its handling of reality, but that the interpreter may be inclined to simplify out.

---

57. K. M. Craig and M. A. Kristjansson, "Women Reading as Men/Women Reading as Women," in *Poststructural Criticism and the Bible* (ed. Phillips) 120-21.

58. So Tilley, "God and the Silencing of Job"; cf. Clines, "Deconstructing the Book of Job," in *The Bible as Rhetoric* (ed. Warner) 65-80 = Clines, *What Does Eve Do to Help?* 106-23. Tilley, however, actually speaks in terms of reader-response theory rather than deconstruction.

59. Bal, *Death and Dissymmetry* 16-17.

60. *Circle of Sovereignty* (first ed.) 16.

The Story and Its External Referents

A story creates a world before people's eyes and ears and invites them to recognize that they do or can live in that world. It is in part this concern that literature has in common with scripture that makes methods of interpretation appropriate to the former also fruitful with regard to the latter. But J. D. Crossan asks "Is story telling us about a world out there objectively present before and apart from any story concerning it, or does story create world so that we live as human beings in, and only in, layers upon layers of interwoven story?" He believes that the latter is the case. God is unknowable and "we can only live in story."[61]

One reason for disquiet at the idea of treating the Bible as literature is the conviction that it was brought into existence not merely through an act of artistic creation or a desire to entertain but to convey information to people.[62] But this risks a false antithesis. The biblical authors are capable of the richness of great literature yet are also aware that they are in opposition to mere literary creativity; indeed, the antithesis between literary and referential is questionable even in literature itself.[63] To put it another way, stories are windows or portraits as well as mirrors. "The literary venture is never dissociated from value and belief and is never, consequently, far from religion."[64] If formalist, structuralist, and deconstructionist critics say they are not concerned with "objective truth" or truth in the world outside the text but only with truth in the terms of the text's own world, they may only mean that their particular interpretational stratagems work, in fact, by focusing on the meanings of texts as opposed to their reference — what they refer to. But both the friends and the enemies of these approaches are mistaken when they infer that this focus is incompatible with a concern that "there is reality out there" to which the text refers.

The tellers of biblical stories are creative artists. Their stories do not claim to be God-given, as prophetic oracles do. They are works of creative human imagination. Treating them as a witnessing tradition, however, implies the conviction that these particular stories do reflect God's story. Their

61. *The Dark Interval* 9, 40-41; cf. Kermode, *The Sense of an Ending* 36-40.

62. E.g., Barton, "Reading the Bible as Literature"; cf. Reed, "A Poetics of the Bible."

63. See, e.g., Fisch, *Poetry with a Purpose* (the title is significant) 2. Cf. T. R. Wright, *Theology and Literature* 20-40; Green, *Scriptural Authority and Narrative Interpretation* 79-96; Walhout in *Responsibility of Hermeneutics*; Eagleton, *Literary Theory*, e.g., 17-31; contrast Barr, *The Bible in the Modern World* 55.

64. Kort, *Story, Text, and Scripture* 3.

world may have been imagined, but that does not in itself mean that it is merely imaginary. As witness, their stories have reference, not merely sense.[65] While that may come about in part because "the sense of the text is not behind the text, but in front of it" as it "points towards a possible world,"[66] if the stories lacked any historical reference they would arguably also lack sense; they would self-deconstruct. To seek to understand biblical stories in their own right leaves quite open the possibility that they need to have, and do have, some historical reference in order to "work" as stories.

If a story is to do something to us, give us something to live by, its reference to the real world outside itself matters in a way that it does not to a structuralist interpretation, for which "the referent of a text is not something out there in the real world, but the text itself."[67] It is not mere chance that most biblical narratives have historical concerns as well as literary features. They are not novels or short stories, even though they share the literary and rhetorical form of novels or short stories. Thus Sternberg describes Hebrew narratives as combining ideology, historiography, and aesthetics — they aim to inculcate a worldview and to relate history, but they use the conventions of art to do so.[68] They are more than history, not less than history. That makes both historical and literary approaches to interpretation appropriate to them. The literary approaches themselves suggest no answer to the question of their own relationship with historical study, and it is only by systematically bracketing the question of that relationship that they can concentrate on the matter that is their particular concern, the actual meanings of texts. That they focus on this does not mean that the texts do not refer to realities outside themselves; the study of that reference is simply not the particular aim of those approaches.

65. Cf. Ricoeur, "Response" 79; *Time and Narrative* 2:77-82; cf. D. S. Greenwood, "Poststructuralism and Biblical Studies"; Lentricchia, *After the New Criticism;* Lischer, "The Limits of Story."

66. Ricoeur, *Interpretation Theory* 87.

67. Nolan Fewell, *Circle of Sovereignty* (first ed.) 15.

68. *Poetics of Biblical Narrative* 1-57. Cf. T. R. Wright, *Theology and Literature* 41-42; also Barr, *Scope and Authority of the Bible* vi, on scripture as story yet as still having a concern with history.

Authors and Audiences

As much as other texts can, stories can also be described as "speech-acts." Speech-act theory asks what an author was seeking to *do* in a given text.[69] It assumes that authors are not merely aiming to convey some propositional content, but that their works have "illocutionary force," that they are designed to effect something.[70] This approach might be expected to attract some biblical interpreters (though also to alienate others) because it is more obviously compatible with historical concerns than the other approaches that we are considering in this chapter and the next.[71] Just as (and because) the historical reference of narratives remains important, so does the historical background against which stories need to be read.

Speech-act theory takes us back to authors and their intentions, the first focus in Abrams's grid. The parables, for instance, were designed to effect something in the context of the mission of Jesus and the church. M. A. Tolbert, D. O. Via, and B. B. Scott can offer valuable Freudian, Jungian, and structuralist interpretations of the parable of the prodigal son, each of which may uncover aspects of the story's underlying patterns, and thus illumine timeless aspects of how and why the story works.[72] But to treat such features as *central* to interpretation of the parable involves ignoring the specific features that first gave the story its importance in its context in the mission of Jesus and the church. It was preserved in connection with that which it did in that context. Lifted from that context, how far it can still work becomes questionable.[73] Polzin thus exaggerates in describing the whole effort to read biblical narrative historically (in terms of the historical context of its final form, and of the nature of its relationship to earlier material) as unbiblical on the grounds that the text tells us to read it not that way but as a present confession.[74]

---

69. See, e.g., H. C. White (ed.), *Speech Act Theory and Biblical Criticism,* esp. Lanser, "(Feminist) Criticism in the Garden" (67-84) on Gen 2–3; also Thiselton and Walhout in *The Responsibility of Hermeneutics.*

70. Cf. Eagleton, *Literary Theory* 118.

71. Cf. Porter, "Why Hasn't Reader-Response Criticism Caught On in NT Studies?" 283.

72. *Polyvalent Narration* (ed. Crossan) 1-73. See also Tolbert, *Perspectives on the Parables.* Cf. the existentialist interpretation of parables, positively assessed by Thiselton (*Two Horizons* 6-7) as enabling us to perceive features which *are* there.

73. Lischer, "The Limits of Story" 27. Wink (*Transforming Bible Study* 164 in both editions) dismisses psychological readings as allegory — though he half-recognizes that he risks this in his own approach (see p. 11 in the second ed.).

74. Polzin, *Moses and the Deuteronomist* 7-8, 12.

Ascertaining the original meaning of a story has traditionally been equated with ascertaining its authors' intention when they wrote it[75] — in the sense of what they themselves meant by the words they used.[76] Abrams's grid reminds us that authors' intentions are extrinsic to their stories — and are elusive. We might hope to discover such intentions in narrative works by assigning dates of composition to them, so as to discover their purposes in their historical contexts. But we noted at the beginning of this chapter that this task generally produces conclusions that are so hypothetical as to be unsafe foundations for further construction (in the case of the Gospels and Acts) or that seem to illuminate only a few aspects of the material (in the case of Genesis or 1 Samuel, the final form of which seems to come from the exile, but much of whose content does not obviously connect directly with that context). Thus biblical interpretation often seems to spend vast amounts of effort discussing or establishing when a given story was written and then runs out of steam before going on to interpret it.[77]

It is the work itself that has to provide our information on its meaning, purpose, and intention. In Luke, John, and Acts, the authors insert themselves into their story at the beginning or end to state their intentions, and they thereby remind us that narratives do have authors who intend to communicate and to effect something by their work. At the same time these interesting exceptions to the rule prove the rule because they still involve information on the intention and meaning of a story coming from within the text itself.

Further, talk in terms of the authors' intention may sound as if it limits the meaning of the story to what the authors were consciously seeking to achieve. In practice authors may well have been unconscious of some of the implications inherent in what they said. Sacred texts are usually anonymous, and this is linked to the fact that they have their meanings by virtue of what they say rather than because of who says it. There may be more depth of meaning the less we know of the author.[78] Such possibilities are not limited to sacred writings. It might be argued that the equality of slave and free, of black and white, of immigrant and native, and even of woman and man was implicit in the American Declaration of Independence's asser-

75. So Hirsch: See *Validity in Interpretation* and *Aims of Interpretation*. For the debate on intentionalism, see Newton-de Molina (ed.), *On Literary Intention*.

76. Cf. Juhl, *Interpretation* 14.

77. Moore, *Literary Criticism and the Gospels* 9, noting the parallel between this assessment and Wellek and Warren's in *Theory of Literature* 139.

78. So Croatto, *Biblical Hermeneutics* 19.

tion of the equality of "all men," even if long periods lapsed before these implications were perceived and even though they were remote from the intention of the Declaration's authors. Indeed, Hirsch observes that the crucial problem in interpretation is discerning which implications belong to a text and which do not.[79] But these implications are still part of the intrinsic meanings of works, that which their audience may discover; and when an audience does so, what they are doing is discovering part of the meaning that the authors gave to the work, even if unconsciously: It is not the audience that gives the work its meaning.

That the day of a historical approach to texts is not over is also suggested by the fact that the results of literary approaches to stories turn out to be little more assured or objective than those of historical approaches. Indeed, historical approaches can still offer some safeguard against subjectivist understandings of stories, whether by "historical approach" we mean "what its author meant by it, or what it would have meant to an ideal audience of its day, or what accounts for its every detail without violating the historical norms of the genre."[80] The idea that the meaning of a text is there in the text where it was put by its authors remains worth holding onto.

The implication is that we ought not to be thinking of a simple abandonment of the second focus in Abrams's grid, the concern with the historical and theological realities to which stories refer. There is no one method of study appropriate to all texts and no one method that will give an audience access to all features of any single text. There is insight to be gained from study with all the focuses included in the grid. One discovers by trial and error which method proves illuminating with regard to particular texts. David Clines's study of Esther, for instance, shows how formalism, structuralism, feminism, materialism, and deconstruction can all contribute to "an integrated but polychromatic reading" of the book.[81] The eclectic methodology for which we have argued in chapter 1 is proved valuable by its fruits.

79. *Validity in Interpretation* 62.

80. Culler, *Pursuit of Signs* 48; Culler does not himself agree with such statements of the goal of interpretation.

81. "Reading Esther from Left to Right," in *The Bible in Three Dimensions* (ed. Clines and others) 51.

• 3 •

Beginning from the Audience

In chapter 2 we have considered the move from concentration on a story's possible historical background and referents to concentration on the text itself. But it would be naive to leap from the unsatisfying arms of historical method into the embrace of text-centered approaches as if we have at last found interpretation's long-sought dream bride. The era in literary criticism that sought to understand poems and novels on the basis of their background in history and in their authors' experience was indeed followed by an emphasis on the autonomy of the literary work, but that has in turn been supplemented by further critical approaches, in particular ones that focus on the readers or audience who receive and respond to works, the fourth of the foci identified by Abrams's grid.[1] Theologically, Anthony Thiselton argues, such approaches begin from the fact that the gift of the scriptures is, indeed, a gift, which as such — like the gift of the land to Joshua — is only actualized when it is appropriated.[2]

The Audience Implied by the Story

Stories themselves presuppose certain sorts of hearers and sometimes indicate what sort of audience can hear them aright. Reader-oriented approaches to interpretation ask questions about the nature of the readers

1. A number of the issues raised here express in another form the debate over issues such as preunderstanding, to be considered in Part IV below. Thus Eagleton moves seamlessly between reception theory and consideration of romanticist hermeneutics (see *Literary Theory* 74-77). See Moore, *Literary Criticism and the Gospels* 76-77, 84-88.
2. See *New Horizons in Hermeneutics* 63-64.

presupposed by a story and about the effect a story is designed to have on them. It is appropriate to think at least as much in terms of audiences and hearers as of readers. In the ancient world, as far as we can tell, the normal way to attend to scripture would be hearing it read, not reading it silently; few people had access to a personal copy of a biblical scroll in order to read it for themselves. For Jews, even private reading of the Torah was a spoken act. If scriptural authors had in mind a means of the dissemination of their work, then, it would have been the reading of it to a congregation or group. This has implications for interpretation of their work. "In the beginning was the word," Martin Buber was fond of pointing out — the spoken word. The reading of a story is indeed a *speech*-act.[3]

The human authors of a story are all-important to its existence, but the form of a story enables them to hide; its audience is invited to collude with them in acting as if the story came into existence of itself and is its own authority. In the same way, the audience of a story is usually not directly addressed by the story, as they are in some other forms of speech, but the audience is thereby the more compellingly manipulated. Although formally absent from the story, the audience is substantially omnipresent insofar as stories are created not just for their own sake but in order to do something to some people. A story has "implied readers"[4] — people who are in a position to make the proper response to it. A story is told in such a way as to work for an audience — for example, by means of the order in which it relates events (commonly not the chronological order) and the rate at which it releases information. It tantalizes, teases, challenges, upsets, makes the audience think, forces it to come inside the story and involve itself with it if it is to understand.[5]

In Luke-Acts and John, the implied audience of the narrative sometimes becomes visible as the narrative addresses that audience directly, just as the narrators themselves also occasionally become visible and speak about their purpose. But the narratives indirectly offer further clues regarding the audience for which they are written, the audience that will be able to "make sense" of them. The language of all four Gospels, for instance, identifies their audience as Greek-speaking and thus probably urban com-

3. See, e.g., Talmon, "Martin Buber's Ways of Interpreting the Bible" 202-3. Graham's *Beyond the Written Word* is a systematic study of the importance of the orality of scripture.

4. Iser, *The Implied Reader* and *The Act of Reading;* see also W. C. Booth, *The Rhetoric of Fiction.*

5. Keegan, *Interpreting the Bible* 84-85.

munities, people living in the theological space between Jesus' resurrection and his final appearing.

In the case of Matthew, J. D. Kingsbury collects references that suggest that the audience is a firmly established and well-to-do Christian community living after the fall of Jerusalem, one with a substantial Jewish element, though (to judge from the Gospel's Gentile bias) also with a Gentile element. They stand outside the orbit of official Judaism but in close proximity to both Jews and Gentiles and under pressure from both. They are also under pressure from within, from miracle-working false prophets and from people who wish to impose a more hierarchical leadership pattern.[6] They thus differ quite markedly from the audience presupposed by Luke, with its well-known stress on the poor. Such differences in slant hint at and reflect differences in audience. There is material here for consideration as interpreters seek to take account of Jesus' "bias toward the poor" and to discover what attitude he would take to the not-so-poor.

Given that we are not the originally envisaged audience of any biblical story, we are invited to an act of imagination that takes us inside the concerns of that audience. That we cannot precisely locate those hearers geographically or chronologically need not matter because it is the concerns that the stories themselves express that we seek to share. We are invited to listen to them as people for whom the stories were told, to listen to them from the inside. We have noted in chapter 2 that interpretation involves not the exercise of untrammeled imagination but close attention to the particularities of *this* text, but also that it is not merely an analytic and intellectual affair but one that involves being willing to be drawn into stories. Thus with regard to interpretation of the biblical stories "a man without an imagination is more of an invalid than one who lacks a leg."[7]

We cannot live our real lives inside these stories. We have to live our lives in our own contexts, confronted by their questions, needs, and pressures. If the stories are to do to us what they were designed to do to their original hearers, a further act of imagination is needed, one that sets some of our questions, needs, and pressures alongside those that the stories directly address, and we need to do so in a way that is open to seeing how they address our questions, needs, and pressures, so that we may respond to the stories by telling our story in a way that links it to the biblical stories.

---

6. *Matthew as Story* 120-33; cf. Culpepper, *Anatomy of the Fourth Gospel* 204-27, on the "implied reader" of John.

7. Barth, *Church Dogmatics* III/1, 91.

Conceptually these two acts of imagination can be clearly distinguished, but in their operation they are likely to interpenetrate each other. Grasping the biblical stories' significance may enable us to see how to tell our story; bringing the latter to the biblical stories may also fill out our grasp of their own significance. Interpretation involves the whole person — feelings, attitudes, and wills as well as minds; it also involves *us*, not merely people 2500 or 1900 years ago.

Specifically, there are religious and person-involving aspects to biblical stories, and in themselves formalist methods are no more designed to handle these aspects than are historical approaches. Both didactic and historical approaches tend to overwhelm concern for the text itself, and a literary approach therefore stands apart from didactic approaches with their theological or ethical concerns as much as it does from historical approaches. Nevertheless, a holistic study of the text ultimately cannot stop at the literary approach, which still allows interpreters to distance themselves from the text. To avoid imposing our own questions on the text is not yet to let it press its questions on us, only to overhear it talking to itself. Interpreting biblical narratives involves more than merely understanding a text as an object over against me, of which I seek to gain a rational, objective grasp. The stories were written to do something to people, and our approach to interpretation needs to be able to handle — or to be handled by — this aspect of them. It involves the possibility that what the story had the power to make happen to its audience will happen to us.

The Role of Ambiguity and Openness in Stories

One of the ways in which stories do things to an audience is by leaving questions and ambiguities for their audience to answer or to resolve. We have to recognize and accept the presence of such ambiguity in texts rather than working on the assumption that if only we had all the right information everything would be clear. Sometimes authors do not make themselves clear. This may happen either by accident or on purpose; whichever is the case, ambiguity is then a fact to be acknowledged and made the most of. It can be creatively provocative. Beyond this kind of deliberate or accidental ambiguity, no story can tell us everything that happens in the course of the events it relates, or everything about its characters. "There is something more to the reception of the meaning of a literary work than simply its decoding by means of universally held deep structures. What is in need of decoding by the reader is not entirely determined. . . . The structure itself involves potentialities. Gaps that occur in the text are deliberate and essential." As a result, the same story can be actualized in a variety of ways by different readers.[8]

Traditional biblical interpretation has difficulty tolerating ambiguity and openness; it assumes that the author aimed at clarity and precision, and it brings all the resources of historical and linguistic scholarship to bear on elucidating the text's clear meaning. It is likely to assume that apparent ambiguity in texts is there because we do not share the conventions and assumptions that the text's author and first audience shared. Formalist interpretation also seeks by means of its close study of the objective data provided by a biblical text to discover its inherent meaning and to provide a check on our intuitions as to that meaning. But there are aspects of the intrinsic meaning of biblical stories for which such data seem to be missing.

But an audience-oriented approach to interpretation presupposes that ambiguity is inherent in a story and asks what its opennesses do to an audience, or what it does with them, aware that precisely in its ambiguity at such points the story can challenge an audience regarding its own attitudes. This comes about through the need for us to "fill in the blanks" in the story.[9] We do not do that once and for all; the openness of the story means we have to keep coming back to it, "brooding over gaps in the information provided."[10] In this sense the meaning of a story is something that its audience provides; "readers make sense."[11]

There are irresolvable ambiguities in the portraits of biblical characters such as Moses, Saul, or David that prohibit simple understandings of their stories. Is David raised up by God to be Israel's king, or does he emerge as an epic hero? Is he the man who does the right thing and the man with God's blessing, or is he the man with an eye to the main chance and who always manages to fall on his feet? What are we to make of the two accounts of his introduction to Saul?[12] When Moses strikes out at the sight of an

---

8. Keegan, *Interpreting the Bible* 80, 103-4, summarizing W. Iser, "Interaction between Text and Reader," in *The Reader in the Text* (ed. Suleiman and Crosman) 111; cf. Iser, *The Act of Reading*.

9. So, e.g., Miscall, *The Workings of OT Narrative*.

10. Alter, *The Art of Biblical Narrative* 12.

11. McKnight's repeated aphorism in *The Bible and the Reader*, e.g., 133.

12. See Alter, *The Art of Biblical Narrative* 147-53; cf. 141-47 on the two accounts of creation, where superficially contradictory material is again juxtaposed — in each case fairly self-consciously on the author's part, as Alter sees it (see 154).

Egyptian beating an Israelite (Exod 2:11-15), is he using the wrong method to reach the right end, or is he manifesting the qualities of spirit worthy of one who is to be the means for Yahweh to smite Pharaoh? There are hints in the passage pointing both ways, so that it brings out rather than resolves the ambiguities in the act of violence.[13]

Alter suggests that the "indeterminacy of meaning" characteristic of much biblical narrative, with its "complex moral and psychological realism," reflects an implicit theology. "God's purposes are always entrammeled in history, dependent on the acts of individual men and women for their continuing realization. To scrutinize biblical personages as fictional characters is to see them more sharply in the multi-faceted, contradictory aspects of their human individuality, which is the biblical God's chosen medium for His experiment with Israel and history."[14] This is linked to the disinclination of biblical narrative to pronounce on people's inner thoughts: Leaving such gaps unfilled leaves room for the "conjectures of grace" and "the mystery of God-with-us."[15]

Pannenberg makes a parallel point when he urges the historian to focus on the particularities of history and not to rush into speculating about God's providence, because it is through human activity that God works in the world — indirectly, though as its Lord.[16] Allusiveness regarding the character of human actors both honors them and highlights the importance of the divine director of the story. It offers an indirect witness to the God who is the story's ultimate subject. It invites an act of faith in God, not in God's human agents, on whom the narrative is content to be unclear. The example of Job's submission and restoration, referred to above in chapter 2, implies that allusiveness and ambiguity in portraying biblical characters does not stop short of the character of God.[17] That means that the stories offer true witness to the complexity and mystery of God's character; it also highlights the fact that "a coherent reading of the biblical narratives" is as much an act of faith as a ground for faith.[18]

13. So Childs, *Exodus* 46; cf. Mendenhall, *The Tenth Generation* 20-21.

14. *The Art of Biblical Narrative* 12; cf. 22, 33, 114-30 for a treatment of David along these lines.

15. Buttrick, *Homiletic* 334.

16. "Redemptive Events and History," in *Basic Questions in Theology* 1:79.

17. Thiselton sees the Book of Job itself, and Ecclesiastes, as requiring their readers' involvement in working their way toward a conclusion, rather than offering an already packaged answer (see *New Horizons in Hermeneutics* 65).

18. Cf. R. F. Thiemann, "Radiance and Obscurity in Biblical Narrative," in *Scriptural Authority and Narrative Interpretation* (ed. Green) 28-31 (quotation from 30); cf. T. R. Wright, *Theology and Literature* 62-66.

What We Bring to Stories

If understanding stories inevitably involves *us* as whole people, it involves our hearing them with the advantages and disadvantages of our background, experience, and commitments. Colluding with custom, I began by treating the historical and formalist approaches as if they were objective and positivist rather than hermeneutical in their own nature. But this is not so.

Formalist interpretive methods that claim to be objective and analytical can be very fruitful in enabling a modern audience to be drawn into the text itself and addressed by it. But they do not always have this fruit; they can seem to be a matter of dry word-counting. In having these two capacities, they parallel other methods of exegesis and illustrate how exegetical method and hermeneutics may not be as separate in practice as we may assume they are in theory. This phenomenon is not confined to the application of formalism to biblical material. Literary criticism itself is both a would-be objective, scientific affair and an enterprise that hopes to discover and unveil truth about the world and about what it means to be human. Even formalist reading of stories will be influenced in what it looks for, or limited in what it perceives, by the historical and social position of its practitioners. Paying close attention to the text does not in itself solve the question how stories in their foreignness are grasped by people and grasp them.[19]

Many stories are rich in theme and defy simple analysis in terms of their "intention" or "message"; different audiences (or the same audience at different times) perceive different aspects of this richness. These differences do not indicate that only one or another theme belongs to the story; they reflect the differences among the audiences and the different ways in which the story of their own life resonates with that of the story they are listening to, at the point their own story has at a given moment reached. It is sometimes asked whether there is any point in the continuing production of new works of interpretation.[20] One aspect of the answer is that interpretations in their variety give testimony to the richness of texts as they are read out of different contexts.

Liberation and feminist hermeneutics illustrate the way in which audiences with particular backgrounds are able to perceive, articulate, and

---

19. Poland, *Literary Criticism and Biblical Hermeneutics;* cf. M. Gerhart, "The Restoration of Biblical Narrative," in *Narrative Research on the Hebrew Bible* (ed. Amihai, et al.) 3-24. Moore makes the same point regarding reader-response approaches to the Gospels ("Doing Gospel Criticism" 89-91).

20. Cf. Culler, *The Pursuit of Signs* ix.

respond to aspects of texts that audiences with other backgrounds may miss and be missed by, even though they also illustrate how the same audiences (like all audiences) are also by virtue of their background liable to mishear the text in other respects. Both can be seen as instances of reader-response approaches to scripture, ones that use their particular initial horizons or preunderstandings as their ways into the text's concerns, and both make it clear that what we are able to see reflects not merely our intellectual preunderstanding but our practical precommitment. Interpretation is shaped by the way we live. This has been so for slaveholders, and with racism, sexism, homophobia, and capitalism (which has discounted the Hebrew Bible's proscription on usury).[21] It has also been so with their antonyms.[22]

Approaches to interpretation presuppose and support value systems and systems of power. For the most part they do so unconsciously, but they do so none the less for that. Sociocritical hermeneutics requires an awareness of the ideological factors that shape academic work. In Daniel some prominence is given to institutional academia. Its question is: Can Judean exiles work within the parameters of academia? One's teaching position will have an influence on how one interprets Daniel's handling of this question. In some institutions a scholar could not discuss Daniel on the assumption that it has a second-century date, let alone offer a deconstructionist understanding of what it says about divine sovereignty or divine revelation, without imperiling his or her post. In other institutions (or at least in learned societies) a scholar could hardly discuss Daniel on the assumption that it has a sixth-century date. The pressures of certain seminaries may drive an interpreter toward commitment or in a conservative direction, and the pressures of certain universities may drive the interpreter toward objectivism or in the direction of novelty. Personality factors and how much we believe or do not believe also do one or the other; politics is not everything.

In practice some of the most interesting or suggestive or illuminating or life-changing exercises in narrative interpretation integrate one of the more text-centered approaches with one of the more self-consciously committed approaches. Liberationist or feminist approaches may be combined with deconstructive criticism.[23] Materialist understandings may combine a

---

21. Cannon, in *Interpretation for Liberation* 18. Quietistic pietism's typologizing of the exodus story with its political implications provides another example.

22. See Swartley, *Slavery, Sabbath, War, and Women.*

23. D. Jobling, "Writing the Wrongs of the World: The Deconstruction of the Biblical Text in the Context of Liberation Theologies," in *Poststructural Criticism* (ed. Phillips) 81, 93-94.

structuralist approach to understanding the actual text with Marxist insights into the relationship between literature (and our interpretation of it) on the one hand and social contexts on the other. There is no necessary implication that the aesthetic and the social-functional aspects of the text are reducible to one another.[24] Russian formalism and Marxism might seem a natural pairing (Propp was actually a student at the time of the 1917 revolution), though the Russian formalists of the 1920s were too interested in literary study for its own sake for the liking of Marxist critics; this fact lies behind the neglect of Propp's work until after the Second World War.[25]

Alongside liberationist interpretation, feminist interpretation also illustrates the way in which illuminating or life-transforming exercises in narrative interpretation may combine a self-consciously committed approach with one of the more text-centered literary methods. This is so with Phyllis Trible's formalist work on some agreeable texts in the opening chapters of Genesis, Ruth, and the Song of Songs and some more terrifying ones later in Genesis, Judges, and 2 Samuel, with Mieke Bal's deconstructionist work, and with Elizabeth Schüssler Fiorenza's historical-critical study.[26]

The admission that one is using historical-critical methods with a "bias" may seem scandalous, but it is becoming clear that historical-critical history always functions ideologically in the nature of the concerns and presuppositions that determine what counts as history.[27] Since historical-critical exegesis is the ruling method in professional biblical study, one purpose of its exercise is now to legitimate the members of the scholarly guild in their position of power.[28] Thus Schüssler Fiorenza issues a feminist challenge to the "objectivist-factual" pretension of traditional critical scholarship and its failure to acknowledge the (e.g., male) "interests" it serves, and urges that recognition of bias and enthusiasm about looking at questions in the light of a different set of biases will lead to new historical discoveries.[29]

Of course, no prior commitment is immune from leading to misreadings or incomplete readings. Feminist interpreters have found Trible too

24. See Füssel, "Materialist Readings of the Bible" 23.

25. See Milne, *Vladimir Propp* 19-32.

26. See Trible, *God and the Rhetoric of Sexuality* and *Texts of Terror;* Bal, e.g., *Lethal Love* and *Death and Dissymmetry;* Schüssler Fiorenza, *In Memory of Her* and *Bread Not Stone;* also Yarbro Collins (ed.), *Feminist Perspectives on Biblical Scholarship;* Tolbert (ed.), *The Bible and Feminist Hermeneutics.*

27. See Brueggemann, *Abiding Astonishment* 37-46.

28. Füssel, "Materialist Readings of the Bible" 15.

29. *Bread Not Stone* 141-47. Cf. Bal, *Death and Dissymmetry.*

unequivocal in her reading of Genesis 2–3, Song of Songs, and Ruth.[30] David Clines regards the whole enterprise of a feminist reading of a passage such as the Genesis creation story anachronistic if it pretends to be exegesis. He sees it rather as an (in principle) entirely appropriate readerly approach to the text, which is as such no more anachronistic than nineteenth-century concern to relate Genesis 1–11 to scientific study or to Middle Eastern creation and flood stories.[31] Those who pretend to be objective and critical and then find their own (Enlightenment or existentialist or feminist) concerns in the texts they study need to take a dose of self-suspicion.[32]

Every audience comes to a story with different prior commitments. Our hearing of it is never exclusively objective. Both historical and formalist study are undertaken by interpreters who belong in particular contexts and do their work out of particular commitments. That is ground for (self-)suspicion and a longing to test my reading of stories by readings from other commitments.

What We Read into Stories

There is another sense in which the objectivity of formalist interpretation may be questioned. It might seem that analyses of the structure of texts were objective and easy to agree on, but this does not seem to be so. The theory was that formalist approaches should enable us to discover something of the stories' own burden. By taking their own structural, rhetorical, and linguistic features as the key to identifying their central concerns, we should be able to concentrate attention on questions raised by the chapters themselves rather than ones extrinsic to them.

The conviction that there is some objectivity about these matters is subverted by the fact that reports of chiasms, for instance, have a habit of appearing more objective than they may seem when one checks them by the text.[33] Even the process of "positing various structures" in works may thus be seen as part of "the activity of the reader" in interpretation.[34] Chiasms apart,

30. See Nolan Fewell, "Feminist Reading of the Hebrew Bible" 80-82, following Landy, *Paradoxes of Paradise;* E. Fuchs, "Who Is Hiding the Truth?" in *Feminist Perspectives on Biblical Scholarship* (ed. Yarbro Collins) 137-44; Lanser, "(Feminist) Criticism in the Garden" 79.
31. See Clines, *What Does Eve Do to Help?* 25-48; Rogerson, *Genesis 1–11* 11-17.
32. Lundin in *The Responsibility of Hermeneutics* 23.
33. Cf. Kugel, "On the Bible and Literary Criticism" 224-25.
34. Culler, summarizing Stanley Fish, in *The Pursuit of Signs* 121.

different scholars often give different accounts of the structure of a story. While some stories give objective markers regarding their structure, many do not. The structure of a story may thus be difficult to identify, and interpreters may differ in how they understand it, as is the case with the Gospels and with Genesis.[35] This may mean that no one analysis is exclusively "right" and that different aspects of the story's meaning emerge from various analyses of its structure. Perhaps structure lies in the eye of the beholder — it is something that we as readers of a narrative find helpful. Even the analytic aspect to interpretation cannot claim to be wholly objective.

There is a real distinction between the literary-critical approaches of formalism that focus on the text itself and approaches that focus more on the process of reading and the contribution of the reader; but it is readers who undertake formalist readings. Like fact and interpretation (of which they are actually a version) formalism and questions about readers can be distinguished but not ultimately kept apart. Structuralism, indeed, is often described as a theory of reading rather than a theory about writing.[36] To emphasize this interweaving is not to collapse Abrams's categories; perhaps it makes them more important. That we read with the advantages and disadvantages of our background and commitments is reason for doing so reflectively and self-critically rather than unthinkingly if we want to have a chance of seeing what is actually there in the text. "No close reading of a work is ever close enough" in that it involves trying to make sense of it, and thus "inevitably, we ignore, leave out, suppress" elements from it in the light of our background and prejudices.[37] There is always more to discover.

Is It Audiences That Make Sense of Stories?

When we move away from objective-looking matters such as structures to inquire more broadly about the meanings of works, the question whether stories have objective meaning becomes yet more difficult. Does Jonah tell a story to bring home the love of God for all peoples, to dramatize how not to be a prophet, or to invite Israel itself to return to Yahweh? According

35. The articles on Genesis in *Narrative Research on the Hebrew Bible* (ed. Amihai and others) 31-50 offer two accounts, both of which differ from mine referred to on p. 23 above.

36. So, e.g., Barton, *Reading the OT* 126.

37. Nolan Fewell, "Feminist Reading of the Hebrew Bible" 79, 80; the first quotation paraphrases P. de Man, "Introduction," *Studies in Romanticism* 18 (1979) 498.

to the Genesis creation story, do men and women have equal authority and responsibility, or are men given authority over women? Are Ruth, Naomi, and Boaz all selfless, enlightened, and honorable people, or are they self-centered and ambiguous like the rest of us? If it is of the very nature of narrative works such as the Gospels to have many meanings and to be open to many understandings,[38] do such questions have answers, or does everything depend on the hearers of the stories? Do texts have determinate meaning at all? The observation that "readers make sense"[39] can be understood more radically than we have allowed so far: The meaning of a story is always provided by its audience. A text is only a matter of marks on a piece of paper. Despite exegetes' continuing attempts to state the objective meanings of texts, "criticism is an ineluctably creative activity. Prior to the interpretive act, there is nothing definitive in the text to be discovered."[40]

There are a number of difficulties with this view. When we speak of "making sense" of a statement, we usually mean "discovering the sense that must somehow be there," not creating sense in something that lacks it. We presume that the statement was an attempt at communication, and we wish to receive the communication. Like many writers, the biblical authors wrote in order to be heard and understood and on the assumption that they could be — and without the aid of critics or interpreters.[41] This coheres with the observation by Abrams himself that in general authors surely write to say something of determinate meaning, that readers read (or audiences listen) reckoning to discover what that meaning is, and then share their understanding of it with other people in the expectation that they can be understood and can carry conviction.[42] Susan Suleiman begins her standard introduction to audience-oriented criticism by discussing the literary text as a form of communication between author and reader.[43] And without the assumption that texts have determinate meaning, interpretation as a cognitive activity becomes logically impossible.[44]

38. See, e.g., Kermode, *The Genesis of Secrecy* 145.

39. McKnight, e.g., *The Bible and the Reader* 133. Cf. Gunn, "New Directions in the Study of Biblical Hebrew Narrative" 68-69.

40. Moore, *Literary Criticism and the Gospels* 121.

41. Keegan, *Interpreting the Bible* 10. Cf. Thiselton, *New Horizons in Hermeneutics* 72.

42. "The Deconstructive Angel" 426.

43. *The Reader in the Text* 7. Cf. Rimmon-Kenan's opening remarks in *Narrative Fiction* 2 on narration as a communication process.

44. Lentricchia, *After the New Criticism* 190, quoted by Davis, "The Theological Career of Historical Criticism" 281-82.

While a writer such as Nolan Fewell says that "textual meaning is undecideable," she also speaks of narrative as a form of discourse, "designed to communicate certain knowledge to its audience,"[45] and thus implies that stories do have determinate meaning. When she describes her understanding of the stories in Daniel as "one long exercise in filling in gaps" she could be implying that there is no distinction between one way of filling in the gaps and another and that the gaps are so extensive that interpretation has no fixed points. But she also speaks of the possibility (nay certainty) of her reading being a misreading, which implies that there is a difference between right and wrong ways of filling in the gaps; and she sees interpretation as analogous to putting together a puzzle, which does not seem to imply that interpreters construct whatever picture they like.[46]

The view that narratives have different meanings in different contexts or for different audiences offers openness and scope to interpreters, but it also threatens arbitrariness and relativism. R. F. Thiemann suggests that it both reflects and shares the strengths and the dangers of cultural and moral pluralism in society.[47] An emphasis on objective meaning can conversely be an ideological concern designed to support the status quo and can be self-deceived regarding its own subjectivity.[48] But to abandon it may be to submit oneself to something just as ideological.

Stanley Fish, a key theorist of this approach to interpretation, suggested that right interpretation is interpretation that accords with the conventions of a particular interpretive community. He sees this as the safeguard of objectivity in interpretation.[49] But such a way of attempting to handle this question only serves to underline the problem. An interpretive community may be a safeguard against individual oddity, but otherwise it merely replaces individual subjectivism with communal subjectivism or relativism.[50] Or perhaps it institutionalizes an already existing communal subjectivism, since readers inevitably read out of the corporate context in which they are embedded, not as independent individual selves.[51] A. N. Whitehead

---

45. *Circle of Sovereignty* (first ed.) 16, 17-18.

46. See *ibid.*, 17-18.

47. "Radiance and Obscurity in Biblical Narrative," in *Scriptural Authority and Narrative Interpretation* (ed. Green) 22-24.

48. K. M. Craig and M. A. Kristjansson, "Women Reading as Men/Women Reading as Women," in *Poststructural Criticism and the Bible* (ed. Phillips) 121-22.

49. *Is There a Text in This Class?* 14.

50. Jeanrond, *Text and Interpretation* 113.

51. Keegan, *Interpreting the Bible* 88, following the work of W. B. Michaels.

famously observed that "in the real world, it is more important that a proposition be interesting than that it be true." But he added that "the importance of truth is, that it adds to interest."[52]

T. F. Berg remarks that it is difficult for Christians to move to a post-structuralist reading of the Second Testament: "Adherence to a transcendental signified keeps them in the structuralist camp."[53] In general, as we have hinted already, it may be reckoned that "arguments over method are fundamentally differences in assumptions or beliefs."[54] It is for this reason that Christians have taken a long time to come to terms with historical-critical method. Ironically, when that venture may be largely over, another replaces it. "As the challenge was once to come to terms with the modernist Bible, so now the challenge is to come to terms with its postmodern successor."[55] As with the older challenge, we now have to live through a period in which we do not yet entirely know how to come to terms with the new challenge — but in the light of the earlier experience we may live through that period reckoning that we will eventually do so.

Hirsch argues that it is worth betting on the reality of determinate meaning because — as with Pascal's wager — if it is indeed real, we have gained, whereas if it is not, we have lost nothing. Further, Boone adds, like Pascal's, the wager is at least open to verification at the End.[56] If our discussion takes place within the context of the view that God is there, the odds in the wager may seem stacked Pascal's way. As we may believe that it is more likely that God would have ensured that an adequate witness to the Christ event would have survived than that it would have been allowed to disappear, so we may believe that the texts' witness to that event has meaning of its own rather than having meaning only when we provide it.

Theological and philosophical as well as personal factors thus enter into the judgment whether determinate meaning is possible or important. It is perhaps for this reason that the acrimony and contentiousness of

52. Quoted from *Process and Reality* (corrected ed., New York: Free Press, 1978) 259 by T. J. Altizer, "Demythologizing as the Self-Embodiment of Speech," in *Orientation by Disorientation* (ed. Spencer) 157. Thiselton's *New Horizons in Hermeneutics* 515-55 offers an extensive critique of Fish.

53. See "Reading in/to Mark," in *Reader Perspectives on the NT* (ed. McKnight) 192.

54. Greenstein, "Theory and Argument in Biblical Criticism" 90; cf. Polzin, "1 Samuel" 305.

55. Moore, *Literary Criticism and the Gospels* 129-30.

56. Hirsch, "The Politics of Theories of Interpretation" 243-44; Boone, *The Bible Tells Them So* 67-68; cf. Steiner, *Real Presences* 214-16.

literary-critical debate sometimes appears also in biblical studies.[57] In my view, all three factors direct us to an attempt to hold onto a both-and rather than submit to an either-or. Audiences contribute to the identification of meaning, but their contributions are subject to the meaning of the text, not creative of it. Awareness that all facts are interpreted facts need not make us conclude that there are no such things as facts; there is an equivalent truth here about the factuality of textual meaning.

Textual criticism proceeds as if it were possible to reach a 100% correct version of the text. This is only theoretically possible — indeed, perhaps not even theoretically possible. Yet as an aim it fulfills an important function. In a parallel way we will never attain a 100% correct understanding of a text, or of anything else. For instance, if meaning is context-dependent we can neither in theory nor in practice attain the total mastery of the total context in which a text came into being that is necessary if we are to understand its meaning.[58] Yet the impossibility of total understanding does not negate the worth of attempting whatever degree of understanding will turn out to be possible. The attempt is likely to be more successful if we behave as if total understanding is possible. If you aim at the moon, you may hit the lamppost. The notion of determinate meaning has functional efficacy.[59]

Why Is There Diversity in the Way People Understand Texts?

Works on biblical interpretation have often given the impression that the central question in hermeneutics is how we decide between conflicting interpretations of texts — how we avoid misinterpretation.[60] The more dominant recent view is that this misconceives the central concern of hermeneutics, which is rather how interpretation can happen at all, how our eyes and ears can be opened to what texts have to say. Nevertheless it

57. See Culler, *On Deconstruction* 17. Cf., e.g., Nolan Fewell and Gunn, "Is Coxon a Scold?"; also the acrimony and belligerence of attacks on fundamentalism, notably those of James Barr in, e.g., *Fundamentalism*.

58. F. W. Burnett, "Postmodern Biblical Exegesis," in *Poststructural Criticism and the Bible* (ed. Phillips) 62; cf. Culler, *On Deconstruction* 110-34.

59. Against A. K. M. Adam, "The Sign of Jonah," in *Poststructural Criticism and the Bible* (ed. Phillips) 179.

60. Cf. Hirsch, *Validity in Interpretation*.

may be argued that "the diversity of readings is *the* fact to be explained by any literary theory."[61] If we resist the idea that there is no such thing as determinate meaning, what explanation for this diversity do we offer?

The question might first be countered by another. If meaning is indeterminate, why is there so much overlap between interpretations? Our concentration on differences and disagreements in interpretation may mask the degree of commonality. Why does no one take up the theoretical possibility of understanding as adverbs all words that have henceforth been taken as verbs? Formally the answer may be that the interpretive community has a tacit agreement on grammar, but that agreement surely includes a presupposition that this understanding of grammar corresponds to something inherent in the text that establishes objective constraints within which anything that is to count as interpretation takes place. It is difficult to know whether Genesis begins with "In the beginning God created . . ." or "In the beginning *when* God created . . . ," but there is no doubt that it excludes "In the beginning the world came into being by accident or by the activity of Marduk." The ways in which a text can be understood are finite in number, and some understandings of them can be said to be wrong.

Traditionally interpretation has sought to safeguard the importance of objectivity in interpretation by seeing its goal as ascertaining the original meaning of the text or its meaning in the context in which it was written. One may affirm this principle but still recognize that different people can come to different legitimate interpretations of a story. There are in fact a variety of explanations of diversity in readings, some already hinted at in this chapter; different explanations will apply to different texts.

First, all texts have some degree of openness; if every point in them were to be made explicit, the story would never be finished. Our assumption in writing and reading, in speaking and hearing, is that enough is said to make communication possible, but the inevitable allusiveness of writing and reading means that more than one understanding of aspects of them can coexist.

Second, there are texts that achieve part of their effect by leaving an extra degree of ambiguity and openness. That the stories of Saul and David attract widely varying interpretations[62] is an indication that they are texts of this kind, but not that all texts are.

61. F. W. Burnett, "Postmodern Biblical Exegesis," in *Poststructural Criticism and the Bible* (ed. Phillips) 59.

62. Cf. D. M. Gunn's comments in "Reading Right," in *The Bible in Three Dimensions* (ed. Clines, et al.) 62-63, on his own understanding of Saul and on that of Sternberg in *The Poetics of Biblical Narrative*.

Third, many stories are rich and complex. We do not have to argue about whether the stories in Daniel are really about the significance of imperial kingship as opposed to the possibility of being a successful but faithful Jewish politician — really about the kings or the Jewish sages — because both can be true. The reason why different people may offer varying legitimate interpretations of some stories is that a story's meaning may have a number of facets.[63] Its meaning is an objective matter, something there in the text, but it may nevertheless be quite complex. Part of the greatness of some stories is a richness that cannot be encapsulated in a simple formula ("this story is about x"). It is in this sense that the question of the right interpretation of a text is as inappropriate to the Bible as it is to Shakespeare: The question to ask about interpreting *Hamlet* is how we can feed on such a rich work.[64]

This is not to imply that there is no such thing as a wrong understanding of a work such as *Hamlet,* only that concern with that possibility misses the point. Missing right understandings is a more threatening danger than arriving at wrong ones. Reading the parable of the workers in the vineyard from the perspective of the oppressed uncovers a message about human solidarity to add to the parable's message about the grace of God.[65] Polyvalence involves a story having many facets; it does not mean questions about meaning are inherently arbitrary or even that such analytic models "provide meaning *to* the text rather than discovering meaning *in* the text."[66] One can grant that there are very many aspects to a story's meaning but still assume that there are limits to what can be read out of a story, and it may be that interpreters can agree on meanings that do not belong to a story — not so much because author or audience could or would not have envisaged them but because they are not a natural understanding of this actual story.

Indeed, one aspect of the problem in this discussion is the actual notion of the meaning of a story. The meaning of a story cannot really be abstracted from the story itself, as if a summary of the principles it illustrates could adequately represent the story itself. In the case of Hamlet or Ruth or a parable, the story *is* the meaning or the message. An author only discovers

63. Hirsch, *Validity in Interpretation* 128.

64. Josipovici, *The Book of God* 5.

65. L. Schottroff, "Human Solidarity and the Goodness of God," in *God of the Lowly* (ed. Schottroff and Stegemann) 129-47.

66. Against S. Wittig, "A Theory of Multiple Meanings," in *Polyvalent Narrative* (ed. Crossan) 90.

what to say by saying it, and an audience only understands it by hearing it.[67] What a story says in a detailed and concrete way by means of a portrayal of events, characters, and conversations achieves something for both parties that an abstract of a story cannot. Even though a story does not convey new information, it may still convey new knowledge.[68]

Fourth, a text may have one intrinsic meaning (even a complex and rich one) but many significances or applications, or one sense but many references. Many diversities of interpretation are differences over the way a story applies to different people or in different contexts rather than differences about its inherent meaning.[69] It is this that makes the story something of inexhaustible significance, something that needs to be grasped by every age in its own terms, which may be different from those of its authors.[70] Statements of the text's significance may be mutually incompatible in a way that statements of the text's actual meaning may not.[71] Statements of a text's reference may also be mutually incompatible in a way that statements of its meaning may not.[72]

When an account of an event is put into writing as a narrative, there is a sense in which this definitively determines the event's meaning. Yet paradoxically when the narrative comes into being as an independent object, it is simultaneously opened up to a multiplicity of new readings.[73] When a person speaks, what he or she means by his or her words largely dominates the way those words are heard; words in written form can more easily be heard independently of their author's purpose and meaning. "Writing is central to the hermeneutical phenomenon, insofar as its detachment both from the writer or author and from a specifically addressed recipient or reader has given it a life of its own."[74] The specific weakness of writing is that no one can come to the aid of the written word if it falls victim to misunderstanding, intentional or unintentional.[75]

---

67. Moore, *Literary Criticism and the Gospels* 64-65.

68. Bambrough, *Reason, Truth and God* 119-25; cf. Ford, *Barth and God's Story* 48.

69. So Hirsch, e.g., *Validity in Interpretation* 8, 140.

70. So Gadamer, e.g., *Truth and Method* 265-66, 280.

71. Hirsch, *Validity in Interpretation* 227-30.

72. Cf. W. J. Houston, " 'Today, in Your Very Hearing,' " in *The Glory of Christ* (ed. Hurst and Wright) 37-41, following Caird, *The Language and Imagery of the Bible* 40.

73. Croatto, *Biblical Hermeneutics* 16-20, 41, following Ricoeur, e.g., *Interpretation Theory* 25-44, 75-76. Croatto thus speaks of the meanings of the text once it is independent of its author. But it seems to me wiser to speak of one meaning and multiple significances (so Hirsch, *Validity in Interpretation*).

74. Gadamer, *Truth and Method* 353.

75. So Plato, e.g., *Phaedrus* 275; cf. Gadamer, *Truth and Method* 354. But the orality

Ironic readings of biblical stories illustrate this difficulty. L. R. Klein's interpretation of Judges, for instance, sees it as a systematically ironic book.[76] On what basis can we evaluate that understanding? We cannot ask the authors whether they intended the book ironically. We can only ask ourselves whether that understanding corresponds best to the nature of the book that we have or whether an ironic understanding of the book, starting from our inability to take seriously a more straightforward understanding of it, is the only way that we can "make sense" of it. Unconsciously we may be finding *significance* in the story rather than the story's *meaning*. Similar questions arise from David Gunn's ironic reading of the "innocuous 'only'" in the statement that Solomon was faithful, "only he sacrificed and offered incense at the high places" (1 Kgs 3:3; cf. the "only" in 15:5; 2 Kgs 14:4; 15:4) and from Gunn's identification of irony in the portrayal of David in 2 Samuel 21–24.[77] Irony is "the mother of confusions"; it is especially tempting to designate as ironic something that implies beliefs that seem absurd to us.[78] Similar possibilities and questions arise from the application to biblical narrative of the theory of the "unreliable narrator," the narrator whose rendering of the story or interpretation of events the audience is actually invited to question rather than to trust.[79]

Howard Marshall began the symposium *New Testament Interpretation* with a consideration of John 4 and noted that the story has been seen as an instance of Jesus' pastoral dealings with people that provides an example for his followers,[80] but this is hardly at the center of the passage's intrinsic meaning. It might be a secondary aspect of the story's meaning, part of its richness as a story; it might be an implication of the story, given the Gospel's conviction that Jesus' disciples are sent by the Father as he was (John 20:21); it might be not part of the story's meaning but an aspect of its significance for hearers involved in pastoral ministry, justified by the general Second Testament assumption that Jesus is a model for ministry. Which is correct

---

behind the superficially written form of (some parts of) scripture has been emphasized by writers such as Kelber (*The Oral and the Written Gospel*).

76. *The Triumph of Irony in the Book of Judges.*

77. "New Directions in the Study of Biblical Hebrew Narrative" 70-72.

78. W. C. Booth, *A Rhetoric of Irony* ix, 81-82.

79. See W. C. Booth, *The Rhetoric of Fiction* 158-59, 294-309; cf. Rimmon-Kenan, *Narrative Fiction* 100-103. Moore (*Literary Criticism and the Gospels* 33) sees the application of this theory to scripture as anachronistic, though whether it is should surely not be determined a priori.

80. *NT Interpretation* 14.

makes little difference, as is often the case with arguments about right and wrong interpretations, though there is a point of more importance in the reminder that whichever is right the story centrally concerns how Jesus revealed himself rather than what disciples should be.

One might draw a parallel with Bible studies in grassroots communities such as those collected by Cardenal in *The Gospel in Solentiname*.[81] His book begins, for instance, with a transcript of a discussion of John 1:1 that understands the identification of Christ as the Word as signifying that God expresses himself through Christ to denounce oppression. That is hardly an example of "liberating exegesis," which is the title of a book on the Bible study in grassroots communities by Christopher Rowland and Mark Corner, but it is indeed an example of liberating exposition. It discerns not the meaning of the text, but its significance for these audiences. The discussion in *The Gospel in Solentiname* of throwing pearls to pigs further illustrates the application of the text to a context rather than insight into the inherent meaning of the text out of a context. The difference remains worth preserving.

That fifty preachers might produce a dozen different sermon angles from the same text[82] is not necessarily cause for concern. The opposite phenomenon might be more worrying.

81. For what follows see 1-2 and 238-39.
82. Buttrick, *Homiletic* 242-43.

• 4 •

Scripture as Witness: Some Implications for Interpretation

What are the implications for interpretation of viewing the scriptural story as a witnessing tradition? As a whole the witnessing tradition is the story of God's work in the world. As witness it points us to the grace of God active on our behalf more than to our obligations to God. Seeing it as one whole, a macro-story that embraces many individual stories, points us to the presuppositions of typological interpretation of biblical stories and offers pointers regarding the logic of liberationist interpretation.

As Witness Scripture Points Us to God's Deeds
More Than to Our Obligations

The nature of the Bible as a witnessing tradition points to a fundamental aspect of its practical significance for its hearers, of the aim of its stories. They focus on God's activity, on God's grace, on God's achievement of an aim or aims, rather than on human activity, humanity's reaching out to God, or humanity's activity in the cause of God.

When Jesus commissioned his disciples he declared that he was sending them as the Father had sent him (John 20:21). It is likely that one motive for telling stories about Jesus was to provide a model for people who had come to share his calling: As he lived and worked, so should they. Similarly, the believing communities preserved stories about Abraham or Moses, Joshua or Ruth, Josiah or Daniel, Nehemiah or Esther, Stephen or Paul, partly to offer examples for other believers called to live by faith, to exercise leadership, to withstand the pressures of life in a foreign land, and to witness boldly before Jews and Gentiles. It is this function of stories that is taken up by a passage such as Hebrews 11. In the First Testament it is perhaps more prominent in Chronicles than it is in the Samuel-Kings account of the same period. Stories illustrate the commitments that the faith entails.

Focusing the interpretation of biblical narrative on its capacity to provide examples of how believers should or should not behave is thus a quite biblical procedure. Yet books on preaching often protest at such a "moralizing" approach,[1] and the protest is substantially justified. This way of using stories is very common in the church, especially with children and in "all-age" or "intergenerational" services; in scripture it is much less so. There are theological and spiritual reasons for that. It is a use of scripture that focuses on God's word to people as a challenge to them to perform certain acts or to manifest certain characteristics, and this is the fundamental limitation of this way of using scripture. The focus of the gospel story lies on what God has done for us. The Second Testament is thus strikingly reticent in its use of the First to provide examples for our behavior.[2]

When we take stories as examples of what we should do or be, we risk turning the faith into something we do rather than something God has done. Further, it is striking that biblical stories that center on human initiative, bravery, faith, and fortitude commonly concern rather out-of-the-ordinary characters such as foreign heroines, Israelite kings, young princes, imperial officials, and exiled queens. People such as these will not commonly be direct examples for anyone else to follow, and their stories appear in scripture at least in part because in their out-of-the-ordinariness they became part of *God's* story. Thus when Wesley Kort identifies four elements in biblical narrative, he sees all four as means whereby God's person, power, wisdom, and grace are revealed: in plot (in a book such as Exodus), in characterization (in a book such as Judges), in atmosphere (in a book such as Jonah, with its apparent negativeness but its actual inclusiveness), and in tone or point of view (in a book such as Mark, with its authoritive stance).[3]

Perhaps one reason why preachers are inclined to use stories as examples for human behavior to a greater extent than scripture itself does is

1. So, e.g., Keck, *The Bible in the Pulpit* 100. See also Greidanus, *Sola Scriptura* and *The Modern Preacher and the Ancient Text.*
2. Barton, *Oracles of God* 161-66.
3. *Story, Text, and Scripture* 24-49.

that as preachers we may feel that we only fulfill an aim and actually achieve something in our preaching if we tell our congregations what to do — they can then go and do it. Perhaps scripture gives this concern less prominence because it recognizes that when believers do not act or live as they should, it is commonly not because of ignorance, in such a way that being given the right example will show us something we do not know. We need to be affected at a different level in order for our attitudes and behavior to change. Merely being given the correct positive or negative example may not help a great deal. "If we are to have changed obedience, we must have transformed imagination."[4] Indeed, scriptural history implies that God's story advances despite the deeds of the people of God (let alone those of outsiders) as often as through them. Here, too, it is not a question of "examples to be avoided"; the story is too realistic to think that such examples will in fact be avoided. Rather it portrays for us a world in which human sin and tragedy are real, but God's grace and providence are bigger, and it invites us to flee from moralizing to grace.

Thus scripture uses stories to illustrate the experiences that the faith may involve at least as commonly as it uses stories to illustrate the commitments that the faith entails. The stories are about God and the ways of God with the people of God; they show us how God characteristically relates to people like us. They encourage and challenge us not by giving us a clearer picture of what we should or should not be but by giving us a clearer picture of who God is. The stories in Genesis, for instance, focus more on the way God deals with Abraham and Sarah than on the way Abraham and Sarah relate to God. Their emphasis is on God's purpose, God's promise, God's initiative, God's blessing, and God's covenant undertaking. They offer mirrors for identity more than models for morality.[5] The First Testament relates *God's* story. It is the person and activity of Yahweh that are its narratives' supreme interest and that come into clearest focus there.

Sometimes Genesis expresses implicit or explicit approval of human attitudes and actions (e.g., 15:6; 22:16), but this is relatively rare. We noted in chapters 2 and 3 that it is commonly difficult to tell whether people are doing the "right" or the "wrong" thing or acting from right or wrong motives, as is reflected in the long-standing difference of interpretation of passages such as the Hagar story in Genesis 16. If Genesis were presenting Abraham and Sarah primarily as examples for us, rights and wrongs would

4. Brueggemann, *Interpretation and Obedience* 2, following Paul Ricoeur.
5. J. A. Sanders, *From Sacred Story to Sacred Text* 71.

surely have to be made clear. If the stories mainly function to show how *God* fulfills a purpose for the world, despite as much as through human actions and circumstances, clarity about human motivation is less important. It is thus natural that Isaiah 51 appeals to the story of Abraham and Sarah as an example of what God can do, not as an example of what human faith can achieve.

It is likely that similar considerations lay behind the telling and preserving of stories about Jesus. The primary burden of these stories is not to set him forward as an example of what we are called to go out and do. One hint of this is that the stories do not seem to be told so as to demonstrate that Jesus always loved his enemies or was always a model of humility; when the Second Testament does look to Jesus for an example it is his incarnation and cross to which it appeals.[6] More fundamentally the stories show us what Jesus can be and do for us. They render Christ, recreating him before our inward eyes and ears. In appropriating these stories we do not see ourselves as taking Jesus' position but as taking the position of disciples (or opponents) for whom or despite whom Jesus can achieve his purpose.

To take stories as illustrations of the experiences that the faith regularly involves comes closer to their intrinsic nature, but it leaves certain problems unresolved. Not all stories embody characteristic experiences of faith. In particular, what is the purpose of miracle stories? If God marvelously delivered Israel at the Red Sea, rescued Daniel from the lions, brought the widow's son at Nain back to life, and resurrected Jesus himself from death, we cannot infer that God with any frequency acts in that way for later believers. Martyrdom may be an infrequent occurrence, but it is much more common than miraculous rescue. The prominence of such miracle stories in the Bible, raising the question what message the preacher is to draw from them, brings to the surface particularly clearly an issue that arises with many stories. They do not indicate what God may do with us, any more than what God expects of us.

A factual story can come to have a symbolic significance for later hearers. Jesus delivered his disciples from a literal storm on the lake; he also delivers his church from metaphorical storms that assail it. Like appealing to biblical stories as examples to follow, interpreting factual stories symbolically is thus a biblical practice. But like the former it may be utilized more frequently by contemporary preachers than by biblical preachers, and

6. Harvey, *Strenuous Commands* 179-89.

it risks compromising a key feature of biblical preaching that is encapsulated in the description of scriptural narrative as a witnessing tradition.

Stories that do not indicate what God may literally do with us, any more than what God expects of us, bring out a key characteristic of the biblical story as a whole: They bring to life the events on which the faith is based. The story of what God has done in Israel and what the God of Israel has done in Christ, as well as recounting the characteristic pattern of events that Christian faith can look to see repeated, also recounts the once-for-all events that are the foundation and object of the faith — its aetiologies and not merely its paradigms.[7] This faith is a piece of good news with implications for the present and for the future, but it is news about events that are essentially past; they have happened once for all.

The statements in Luke-Acts and John regarding the purpose that those Gospels were designed to fulfill (Luke 1:1-4; John 20:30-31; Acts 1:1-5) point to this significance in the story they tell. In the opening chapters of Mark, the chief significance of Jesus' miracles stories seems to be historical: They indicate that Jesus has won a victory over forces of evil that inaugurates the reign of God in this world and this age.[8] In 1 Corinthians 15, Paul assumes that the story of Jesus' resurrection is important, not because it models the kind of experience of new life Christians may have in this life (though this point is made elsewhere), but because that was the once-for-all event in the past that guarantees our own rising from the dead at the End.

Stories in the First Testament, too, were written to bring to life the once-for-all past events on which faith for the present and the future have to be based. The Abraham story reminded the people of Israel that they possessed their land only as God's gift, in fulfillment of God's promise. The exodus story reminded them that they had been only a herd of demoralized slaves in a foreign country and would still be that but for the exercise of Yahweh's power on their behalf. The Books of Kings showed how Israel had ignored Yahweh's expectations over centuries, and they thus explained why Israel had ended up in exile. The fundamental function of biblical stories in general is to bring to life the events on which the faith is based. They are events that will not be repeated in our experience, but they are events that remain of crucial importance for us. The Bible's nature as a witnessing tradition suggests

7. R. Smend, "Tradition and History," in *Tradition and Theology in the OT* (ed. Knight) 56-60 — though Smend implies that aetiologies are generally fictional, which is not my assumption here.

8. I am indebted to my colleague Colin Hart's dissertation on *The Use of Miracle Narratives in Mark* for comments on the Gospels here and in Part IV.

that its primary concern is to relate what God did for us once for all, not what God does every day, still less what we are supposed to do for God.

Individual biblical stories are not limited to fulfilling only one of the three aims just described; their depth may derive partly from their fulfilling several functions at once. Yet in any story one function will usually be more important than others. The dominant point in Ruth may be the way God's providence takes two women through bereavement and exile into new life ("experiences that the faith may involve"), though it also makes these events part of the introduction to the story of David ("events on which the faith is based") and probably implies that Ruth is a model of caring for a widow in need, Boaz of caring for a girl in need, and Naomi of how to get God and people to act. Disagreements about the present relevance of some stories (e.g., the use of Exodus in liberation theology or the use in charismatic renewal circles of stories from the Gospels and Acts about healing or raising the dead) are sometimes disagreements about whether these stories relate solely "events on which the faith is based" or also offer paradigms of how God may act now or of how we should act now.

Witness to One Story:
Implications in Terms of Typology

The nature of the Bible as a witnessing tradition suggests that the various individual stories it tells need to be understood as part of one macro-story. Episodes within one long narrative have to be interpreted in the light of the narrative as a whole: accounts of creation in the light of accounts of deliverance and vice versa, accounts of cross in the light of accounts of resurrection and vice versa. Luke's story of Jesus has to be read in the context of Luke's story of the spread of the gospel from Jerusalem to Rome, and vice versa. That much would be true of any narrative. But something further emerges from the awareness that one story runs through the Bible as a whole. Different witnesses tell us of the exodus from Egypt and the occupation of Canaan, of the triumphs under David and Solomon, of the exile and the restoration, of the oppression by the Seleucids and again by the Romans, of the Christ event and the beginning of the work of the Spirit in the church. Their witness is set in the context of an account of the unwitnessed Beginning of this history at creation and its not yet witnessed End in the new Jerusalem. The story accumulates throughout biblical times.

It is a story of a series of liberating exoduses: Abraham's exodus from

Egypt, which foreshadows Israel's greater exodus from bondage to Pharaoh, the exiles' exodus from Babylon, the exodus Jesus accomplishes in Jerusalem, and the liberation to which the children of God still look forward. It is a story of covenants ever being remade: perhaps with humanity at creation (though the word does not appear there and covenants perhaps presuppose sin in the world), certainly with Noah to promise the survival of humanity, with Abraham to initiate the blessing of humanity, with Israel to draw its people into a response to Yahweh's acts on their behalf, with David to guarantee the persistence of his line, with Israel returning after the disaster of exile, with Israel reconstituted as the family of Jesus, with Israel at the End when they are finally saved. It is a story of a share in God's rest ever being offered: at creation, in the entering of the promised land, in life in the land, in that ceasing from labors that Christ makes possible (see Hebrews 3–4).

Each individual biblical story belongs in the setting of the story as a whole, stretching from Beginning to End, with the Christ event at the center. The Second Testament story has to be read in the light of the story related in the First and vice versa. The two Testaments are like the two acts of one play.[9] People cannot expect to understand Act II if they miss Act I, nor Act I if they leave at the intermission; neither act can be understood independently of the other.

The events related in the two Testaments form one story. While this is arguably the only way to read the Second Testament, despite Marcion's attempt to understand it as a wholly new story, it is not the only way to interpret the history of Israel. A non-Christian Jew will read it very differently. Whether people read Israel's history in this way will depend on what they make of Jesus. If they believe that he is the Christ, then they will believe that he is the climax of Israel's history. If they do not, they will not. Admittedly, whether they think Jesus is the Christ may depend on whether they reckon it plausible to read Israel's history that way; a dialectic is involved here. But once they do read Israel's history in that way, it makes a difference to their understanding of all the events that comprise that history. The significance of Abraham's leaving Ur, the Israelites' exodus from Egypt, David's capture of Jerusalem, and succeeding events through the history of Israel emerges with fuller clarity when they are seen in the light of each other and of the Christ event, which is their climax — just as the Christ event is seen with full clarity only in the light of those other events.

If the Bible witnesses to one connected series of events, it is natural to

---

9. Bright, *The Authority of the OT* 202-3.

look for links in the inner structure of these events. Presupposing such links is one starting point of typology as a way of interrelating events within the biblical story.

Typology has three fundamental features. First, it presupposes that there is an essential similarity between certain significant events or significant acts or significant people. The similarity reflects their interlinking through their belonging to a liberating purpose of Yahweh, the God of Israel who is also the God and Father of our Lord Jesus Christ. Thus the Israelites' original exodus from Egypt, their later release from exile in Babylon, and the potential release of Israel and the world from other forms of bondage through Christ are events of a deeply similar kind. The sacrificial acts of the Jerusalem temple have a parallel significance to Christ's act when he lets himself be killed; both are means by which human beings are put right with God. There is also a parallel between Christ and the priests of the temple in that both offer sacrifices, and a further parallel between Christ and the Davidic kings in that both have a son-father relationship with God and a special role in relation to God's rule over the world.

The second feature of Christian typology derives from its starting point in faith in Christ. The conviction that Christ is *the* ultimate means through which the purpose of God is fulfilled in the world naturally carries with it the conviction that the later events or acts or people referred to above are in key respects more far-reaching or significant than the earlier ones. The Israelites' exodus from Egypt gave them release from material bondage only, and their exodus from Babylon, though in some ways more impressive (according to the promise in Isa 52:12), is in that respect no different. Through Christ, however, people gain their release from the inner bondage of sin that underlies other bondages. The father-son relationship between the Father and Jesus and the significance of Jesus for the implementation of God's rule in the world utterly overshadows those features as they appear in the story of the Davidic kings. What the sacrificial death of animals in the temple could achieve pales into insignificance alongside what Christ's death achieves, and what the priests of that temple could do pales into insignificance alongside what Christ as *the* high priest could do. This point is elaborated in Hebrews (chapters 9–10), the great repository of typological exposition in scripture, which makes this second feature of typology explicit by referring to the first set of realities as *foreshadowings* of the second set. There is a provisionality about the first; it is the second that really counts.

The third feature of typology is that the events, acts, and people with which it concerns itself have a literal reference when they first appear but come to have an increasingly metaphorical significance as they reappear. The exodus from Egypt is a literal departure from a foreign country and a literal emergence from slavery, whereas the act of redemption or liberation brought about by Christ is metaphorical. Christ's death is not literally a sacrifice and he is not literally a priest; he does not belong to the tribe of Levi. Nor is he literally a king, even though as a descendant of David he is better qualified for that position. Exodus, kingship, priesthood, and sacrifice have become symbols with which the first Christians could come to an understanding of the realities that have grasped them — Christ and what he achieved.

As we have noted, Hebrews is *the* repository of typological thinking in the Second Testament, but modern interpreters continue sometimes to use typology as a means of making links (or of identifying links) between the two Testaments. Its possible fruitfulness and possible difficulty can be illustrated from Barth. His exposition of the doctrine of election in *Church Dogmatics* II/2 includes an extensive study of what he sees as the First Testament's witness to Christ in the form of anticipatory announcement of him as simultaneously *the* elect one and *the* rejected one.[10] This anticipatory announcement appears in the stories of people in Genesis such as Abel and Cain, Isaac and Ishmael, Jacob and Esau, and Rachel and Leah, where in each case the one who is blessed is also condemned and the one who is condemned is also blessed. It appears in the ritual laws regarding the two birds and the two goats in Leviticus 14 and 16, where identical birds and goats receive contrasting but overlapping destinies. It appears again most systematically in the opposing but overlapping figures of Saul and David, and also in the strange story of the man of God from Judah and the old prophet of Bethel in 1 Kings 13. Barth also offers an extensive typological interpretation of the Second Testament figure of Judas.

Three features of Barth's interpretation deserve note. First, he recognizes that there are no exegetical grounds for making a link between these various phenomena and the person of Christ (or of Paul in the case of Judas), but he also suggests that if we do not make that link, the phenomena are simply enigmatic: We do not know what sense to make of them. This latter point seems to me an exaggeration.

Second, Barth's typological approach does enable him to perceive theologically significant aspects of the stories he is studying, aspects that other interpreters commonly miss. His typological approach is heuristically ef-

10. See *Church Dogmatics* II/2, 354-411. Barth does not himself use the expression "typology," but this seems to be the approach he is using.

fective — though this may be more because he is an instinctively insightful reader of scripture than because the typological approach itself is inherently illuminating.

Third, however, that same typological approach makes him read alien significances into other aspects of the material. Of the examples from the First Testament, this seems particularly clear with Leviticus 14 and 16.[11] Indeed, typology has a built-in danger of turning real people or events that had significance of their own into mere representative symbols or puppets in a cosmic drama. Thus Judas is "a planned figure in a planned role."[12] There are grounds for this statement in the Second Testament, but it imperils the human reality that scripture very clearly attributes to Judas.

Reading of significances into scripture is also a danger posed by the more pietistic typology that (for instance) sees the blue, purple, and red coloring of the tabernacle hangings as pointing to Christ's heavenliness, kingship, and death. Such conceits may be harmless, though they run the risk of foregoing the actual message of the First Testament for the sake of statements about the Christ event that we can in any case make on the basis of the Second Testament. Thus the nature of the various sacrifices that were offered in Israelite worship is illuminating with regard to biblical worship, spirituality, and obedience, but such insights tend to be lost when they are approached with an all-pervasive concentration on sin and atonement.

Typological interpretation of the exodus carries with it even greater risks. The exodus is a key event in Israel's story; it is in the light of this event that Israel looks to the past and envisions the future as another release from bondage. The exodus is important to the first Christians as they look for stories that will help them understand the significance of Jesus and as they themselves also look to the future. But there is a danger that such Christian appropriation of stories such as the exodus, especially by means of the symbolic interpretation involved in typology, skews the inherent meaning of these stories. It turns something essentially (though not exclusively) this-worldly and material into something that belongs centrally (though not exclusively) to the religious realm.

The conviction that Christ comes as the climax to the First Testament's story implies that this story plays a part in the interpretation of the Christ event. As the exodus is to be understood in the light of the coming of Christ,

---

11. Cf. also Klopfenstein's critique of Barth's third example in his "1 Könige 13."

12. *Church Dogmatics* II/2, 460. For a critique of Barth's interpretation of Judas see Ford, *Barth and God's Story* 91-93.

so the coming of Christ is to be understood in the light of the exodus —
with the latter not merely a symbol but an event. But the typological
approach to the exodus story facilitates only the first move; it interprets
realities in the First Testament in the light of the Christ event but constricts
the extent to which those realities can interpret the Christ event. The move
is from the Second Testament to the First and not the reverse. To put the
point sharply, typology is a means of castrating the First Testament.

Witness to One Story:
Implications for Liberation Hermeneutics

From the beginning, liberation theology, too, made much of the exodus story.
That is its "privileged text."[13] Its approach to the exodus story was quite
different from the typological approach characteristic of traditional Christian
appropriation of the story. It claimed the exodus story on behalf of people in
the world today who live in an experience of physical bondage analogous to
that of the Israelites in Egypt and encouraged them to hope and act for a future
in the light of the story of Yahweh's release of the Israelites from their bondage.

The awareness that individual biblical stories are part of the biblical
story as a whole is also suggestive for a critical appreciation of this central
feature of liberation theology and its hermeneutics. Two issues come up
for discussion, both aspects of the question whether the exodus story can
be appropriated in isolation from its context in the story of Israel.

First, whose story can be looked at in the light of the story of Israel?
Liberation theology assumes that the exodus story provides a paradigm for
the way God may be expected to deal with oppressed peoples today. Is this
assumption justified? Like white colonists arriving in North America, many
of the white settlers who trekked into black Africa saw themselves as a
contemporary embodiment of that ancient people of God to which God
promised the land of Israel, and they saw tribes such as the Zulus as the
contemporary equivalent to the Canaanites, as those whom they were free,
indeed commissioned, to dispossess.[14] Is the white claim disputable? Does
either group have grounds for claiming the support of scripture?

---

13. Kirk, *Liberation Theology* 95; cf. Assmann, *Practical Theology of Liberation* 35.

14. See, e.g., West, *Biblical Hermeneutics of Liberation* 35; R. A. Warrior, "A Native
American Perspective: Canaanites, Cowboys, and Indians," in *Voices from the Margin*
(ed. Sugirtharajah) 287-95 (see 289).

One reason Exodus suggests for Yahweh's acting on behalf of Israel in Egypt is Israel's position as the people of Yahweh; rescuing Israel from that bondage is an act of faithfulness to the covenant people (cf. Exod 3:7, 10; 7:4). If that is the basis for the exodus, this may cut away the ground from application of the exodus story to any nation today, for no modern nation is God's people as Israel was. The story could only be applied to the church as the people of God.

In Israel's later history Yahweh often fought against Israel, when right demanded it, and this points to a second reason for Yahweh's taking Israel's side at the time of the exodus. Egypt is the oppressor and Yahweh is responding to the cry of the oppressed. Yahweh's attacks on the Egyptians are "mighty acts of judgment" (6:7; 7:4, NEB): "Judgment" is the work of the judges in the Book of Judges, whose task is to act decisively in history in the cause of what is right. The act of God at the exodus was an act of justice whereby the oppressed were released and the oppressors punished.

There were no doubt other oppressed peoples in the ancient world, perhaps even other oppressed foreigners in Egypt who groaned under their bondage and cried to heaven for deliverance, but Yahweh is recorded only to have responded to the Israelites, because of the covenant with their ancestors (2:24; 6:5). Yet that same covenant links Israel with the rest of the world, including oppressed peoples today, in that God's purpose for Israel was that they should be a paradigm for the lives and experience of all nations. Abraham was promised extraordinary blessing, "so that all the families of the earth will pray to be blessed as you are blessed" (Gen 12:3 NEB). The promise draws attention to the magnitude of Abraham's blessing, but it also implies that such blessing is also God's purpose for other peoples. This suggests that it is quite justifiable to understand the exodus story — and other aspects of the story of Israel — as a paradigm of how God might deal with any oppressed people, a story in whose light they might come to understand their own story.[15] Conversely there are no grounds for seeing white settlers in Africa as in a position theologically or morally to displace the black inhabitants of southern Africa, and good grounds for the reverse now, whether or not then.

The second question raised by liberation theology's appeal to the exodus story concerns that story's setting in the rest of Israel's story as the

15. So Miranda, *Marx and the Bible* 90-91. Cf. Cone, *A Black Theology of Liberation* 21, arguing that it is the Christ event that universalizes the concern for oppressed *Israel* expressed in the exodus story. Contrast Stott, *Christian Mission in the Modern World* 95-97.

First Testament tells it. The exodus was of key importance to Israel, but it was not God's last deed. It stands as a programmatic event, the beginning of a project to be brought to fulfillment; it therefore puts the later events of Israel's history into a context and illuminates them. Conversely, later events also help to bring out more fully the significance of earlier ones, as J. S. Croatto notes in connection with the exodus.[16] Thus the subsequent history of Israel brings out and refines the meaning of the exodus. There is a version of the hermeneutical circle to be observed here: The exodus both explains and is explained by later events.

The most significant point on the path traced by the idea of the exodus within the First Testament is the exile and the ministry of Isaiah of Babylon, which gives considerable prominence to the exodus motif and to other aspects of the Book of Exodus. In the exile, the other great pole of Israel's history with Yahweh, the story of God's people, once liberated from bondage, covenanted to Yahweh, and enjoying freedom in the land of promise, reaches its nadir with the covenant destroyed, the land lost, and the bondage reentered. Isaiah 40–55 addresses a people demoralized by this experience.

In doing so, it offers what almost amounts to a systematic midrash on Exodus, so methodically does it take up its themes. To a people once again under foreign oppression it promises liberation from bondage and restoration to the land of promise, a new exodus achieved by the violent action of the warrior Yahweh fighting on Israel's behalf and using the Persian Cyrus as an agent, as Israelite kings and foreign emperors had been used before the exile. Isaiah 40–55 as a whole, however, also unfolds a very different method by which Yahweh's purpose is achieved in the world, one that involves the renewal of Israel's downcast spirit and moral intransigence at the cost of the personal suffering of those who minister to Israel. One climax of the chapters is reached as the deepest account of the paying of this price by an unidentified agent of Yahweh is prefaced by the declaration that in his affliction "Yahweh's arm is revealed" (53:1). Yahweh's arm had rescued Israel from Egypt and dispossessed the Canaanites (Exod 6:6; 15:16); it is ready to crush the Babylonians in turn (Isa 40:10; 48:14; 51:9; 52:10). But here is a quite different manifestation of the power of Yahweh, made perfect in weakness in the act of restoring relationships with humanity.

In Isaiah 40–55 Yahweh is still concerned for freedom from oppression and the achievement of justice in this world through the events and agents

16. *Exodus* 12-16.

of history and the processes of war that are integral to that freedom and justice. But it has also become clear that what Yahweh achieved through such processes, though real, was limited and transient. With the exile the people of Yahweh ceases to be a politically independent or militarily active entity. The one through whom Yahweh operates on the political scene is the Gentile Cyrus, not an Israelite figure such as Zerubbabel. A military victor can bring the Jews back to Jerusalem, but their history has exposed the depth of their inner need. It will take a suffering servant to bring them back to God.

The drift of the Second Testament takes further the line developed in Isaiah 40–55. Arising out of a context when the Jews are once again unjustly oppressed, the Second Testament makes little reaffirmation of God's commitment to political liberation, and instead uses the motifs of exodus, redemption, and liberation not in their original political significance but as a means of picturing liberation from sin. Redemption from sin is the central idea, because humanity's moral weakness and willfulness is its deepest problem, without which its political and social problems cannot be adequately confronted.

The hermeneutical significance of setting exodus and exile or exodus and Christ event alongside each other has been understood in two ways. We have noted that traditional Christian theology has read the exodus in the light of the Christ event and has spiritualized it.[17] Liberation theology stresses the opposite implication, that the nature of the Israelites' deliverance from Egypt should continue to form the focus of a biblical understanding of liberation.

So do we follow Exodus or the Second Testament? It is surely not a matter of a choice of that kind. The interpretive relationship between the two must be seen as dialectical; when different events are juxtaposed for the purposes of interpretation, they throw light on each other. Insofar as people who experienced the Christ event appealed to the earlier event related in Exodus, they draw us to take seriously the nature of what God was doing then, in both its political and its spiritual aspects, which justifies the contemporary claim that God is concerned for political and social liberation. The God and Father of our Lord Jesus Christ is one who has shown a concern for the release of the oppressed from bondage; the nature of the Christ event does not change that.

On the other hand, the conviction that the exile and the Christ event

17. As Gutiérrez protests in *A Theology of Liberation* 166-67.

form part of the same story as the exodus draws us to see the exodus in the context of those later events. Understanding the story related in the First Testament in the light of the Christ event highlights for us that concern with the spiritual liberation of the spiritually oppressed that is present in the exodus story itself and that becomes more pressing as the story of Israel unfolds. Any concern with political and social liberation that does not recognize spiritual liberation as the more fundamental human problem has failed to take account of the development of the story of Israel after the exodus via the exile to Christ's coming and his work of atonement.

The biblical story has to be understood as a whole, and each episode has to be understood in its place in the whole. The Second Testament's story about a spiritual exodus, a liberation from sin, is not to be read apart from the context of the story in the First that demonstrates God's concern with the political and the material. The story in Exodus of the achievement of a people's political release by the act of the just and faithful God is not to be read out of the context of the way their story continues, demonstrating that they have a need that is more far-reaching than their physical bondage. The exodus story on its own cannot be taken as a paradigm for today; but neither is it to be silenced by approaches such as typology.

J. L. Segundo asks rhetorically whether Israel should be expected to act differently if they find themselves in the same situation now as they were on the eve of the exodus, notwithstanding the development in the biblical story toward a greater concentration on issues that are less overtly political.[18] It is regrettable, however, if we have to take for granted that people can never learn from history and are condemned to repeating its mistakes, being able to hear the message of the exile and of the cross only when they have personally experienced the disappointment of exodus/resurrection hope. After its initial focus on the exodus some liberation theology did in fact come to look at its people's experience in the light of the exile. In turn the prospect of a transition to democratic government in South Africa, for instance, has led people to turn to the story of the early Second Temple period (e.g., Ezra-Nehemiah) with its account of the restoration of a degree of freedom yet also a realism about living both in this age and in a new age.[19]

18. *Liberation of Theology* 115.
19. P. Lee, "A Land No Longer Desolate?"; cf. Boff and Boff, *Introducing Liberation Theology* 35.

• 5 •

How Stories Preach

Stories are a key means by which scripture communicates and therefore a key resource for the preacher. How do these stories work as a way of preaching? How do they suggest we go about preaching on them?

We have noted in chapter 1 that classical expository preaching has essentially one form, taking an analytic and discursive approach to all kinds of texts and thus not utilizing a variety of methods of communicating in the way that the Bible itself does. Some years ago I took a course on communicating on television. We had to do a five-minute presentation of one of the parables, and I adopted an abbreviated version of the usual approach I would use for the exposition of a story, summarizing the story at the beginning of the talk, asking "Well, what do we learn from this?" — and then telling the audience. The tutors on the course pointed out that this was *not* how the biblical stories themselves work. Further, they pointed out, when the sermon makes the transition from retelling the story to analyzing its lessons, the sermon's dynamic collapses. I think I recognized the point, but did not quite know what to do about it.

As I was wondering how to develop an approach to preaching that would deal better with story texts, I came across a book called *Communicating the Word of God* by John Wijngaards that looks helpfully at appropriate ways of preaching on many different kinds of scriptural material. It was the chapter on history/story that especially interested me. I was due to preach on Abraham soon after, and decided to try a method Wijngaards suggests, retelling part of the story fairly straight, then reflecting on that part (perhaps talking about a modern experience that might be equivalent), then telling more of the story, then reflecting again, then telling more of the story once again. . . .

As I preached the sermon, I quaked at the knees, feeling I was taking people back to an old-fashioned children's Sunday School. Yet I do not remember ever receiving more appreciative feedback on a sermon. I proved to myself that there is a power about stories that reaches adults as profoundly as it reaches children. Like children, they will collude with us if we tell the story in a way that invites them to forget that they know it (avoiding the use of phrases such as "As we know . . ."), so as to allow themselves to be drawn into its wonder once again. A. T. and R. P. C. Hanson criticize a preacher who, despite not taking the view that the story of Jesus and Nicodemus actually happened, in preaching on that story retold it in the way one would if it had actually happened.[1] Even an undeniably fictional story such as a parable needs to be preached in such a way that it works once more as a story; all the more so, then, the realistic stories in the Gospels. Many of these we may not be able to locate with certainty on the continuum between fact and fiction; but that may make no difference to the way they are preached.

The Hansons' remark does raise an issue that church life needs to handle. James Smart tells a story about the introduction of a new Christian education curriculum. For the first time historical and literary questions were to be covered and questions about matters such as the factuality of Genesis 1–3 were to be raised. The new literature was met by a storm of protest.

> In one village three men, prominent in the local church, were standing in the street reviewing the situation with some concern when a retired minister, who had been their pastor many years before, joined them. They told him what they were discussing and received from him the assurance that there was nothing really new or disturbing in the approach of the curriculum to the Bible. "We had it all in seminary fifty years ago," he said, to which the immediate retort of one of the men was, "Then why in hell didn't you tell us about it?"[2]

The pulpit is rarely the place to do so, because the pulpit is designed for another purpose and because it does not allow the kind of discussion that the issues need (though when I preach on material such as Genesis 1–3 or Jonah where the issues are already in people's awareness I generally tell people my view on the story's historicity; this usually brings apprecia-

1. *The Bible without Illusions* 5-6.
2. *The Strange Silence of the Bible in the Church* 69. On how to handle such questions in a church context, see Franklin, *How the Critics Can Help.*

tion from members of the congregation who are glad to be given a way into thinking about the question, but sometimes induces concern in the resident minister for one reason or another!). Elsewhere in the church's program there need to be occasions when people can think about these questions as part of their Christian maturing. It is pardonable that the minister in seminary fifty years ago found the questions difficult to handle. It is easier now for us to see how to hold together (for instance) a confidence in the witnessing tradition's trustworthiness with an openness to its being imaginative rather than positivist history. As ordinary Christians help theologians keep in touch with God's speaking to us through scripture, so theologically literate Christians owe it to their brothers and sisters in Christ to facilitate their thinking through of these issues.

So how do stories preach?

How Biblical Stories Preach

The Gospels illustrate four ways of going about relating a story so as to enable it to be effective. One is by simply telling it. Interpretive comments by the narrator are rare; events speak for themselves. Many narratives in the Hebrew Bible work on this basis; but Mark's Gospel is the most powerful driving straight narrative in scripture. In this breathless accumulating chain of stories, John Drury notes a "lack of relaxation or indulgence"; "every incident is a summons to recognize the mystery of Jesus and to follow him."[3] In this sense the story is quite straightforward in its message and way of working. At the same time readers who try to give themselves to individual stories in Mark find that they are puzzlingly opaque in their straightforwardness. They rarely tell us what to learn from them beyond what they contribute to the thrust of the Gospel as a whole. Drury comments that this work, in which Mark first "took the momentous step of presenting the (Pauline) gospel of the cross entirely as history," has the "primeval power" of something done "powerfully and roughly for the first time," compared with the "more elegant and digestible" work of subsequent masters such as Matthew and Luke.[4] The latter do much more of the work for their readers. There is a theology implicit in Mark's story of Jesus, but it is less overt than the theologies of the other Gospels.

3. *Tradition and Design in Luke's Gospel* 32.
4. *Tradition and Design in Luke's Gospel* 6.

The reminder this issues to the preacher is the power of the bare story. The philosophy of story presupposes that a story can communicate and convey a world without the storytellers necessarily making explicit what principles or lessons they want people to draw from it. Mark's Gospel points us toward a style of preaching that is simple, the mere retelling of a story, but that may be extremely powerful. The openness of the bare story means that neither the Evangelist nor the preacher can control what the listeners hear or receive and how they respond. The preacher realizes this and feels a responsibility to make explicit and underline what that point is. But by doing so we may destroy the dynamic of the story itself, which gets home in power precisely by working more subliminally.

Matthew's Gospel illustrates a second way of telling stories, by building an application of the story into the way one tells it. We noted how Matthew contemporizes Mark in order to draw his readers into his story (see pages 17 and 38 above). This is the way he makes his story work as "preaching," as the bringing home of a message from God intended to change the faith and life of the hearers. A story such as that of the storm on the lake becomes a story about what can happen when you "follow" Jesus (the technical term for Christian discipleship). Matthew's version of the story is distinctive first for the addition of two of Jesus' sayings about such "following" (8:19-22). After that Matthew tells us that the disciples themselves "follow" Jesus into the boat (Mark says they "took him along"). So getting into the boat is an act of following Jesus, the storm is the kind of experience that sometimes comes to Christian disciples, "save, Lord" is the way they pray in crises, and "of little faith" is his assessment of his followers (8:23-26).

In subtle ways, then, Matthew brings home the story's application to the life of the church by the way he retells the details of the story. Similarly the preacher's occasional sentences expressing what Jesus "said" (that is, what he would have said) to people like us make it possible both to keep the story form, with its potential for reaching mind, heart, and will, and also to make clear how the story applies to us, without appending another sermonette on the end of the story, which would risk destroying its impact.

There is another implication of the difference between the approaches of Matthew and Mark. In the terms we have used in chapter 4, Mark is mainly concerned with "events on which the faith is based," with the Jesus of Galilee and Jerusalem to whom its readers have committed or should commit themselves. Matthew is more concerned with "experiences that the faith may involve" and "the commitment that the faith entails" — with the Christ event's continuing concrete implications for discipleship.

The point should not be exaggerated; Mark's healing stories likely presuppose that the living Christ will continue to exercise his Lordship over the forces of evil in the church's life as he did in the context of his earthly ministry. Conversely, that Matthew begins with a list of names establishing Jesus' Jewish and Davidic ancestry indicates that Matthew is interested in the once-for-all historical Christ event. But a concern with the church's life is nearer the surface in Matthew than it is in Mark.

In the First Testament, Kings is more like Mark: As we have noted, it is an account of how the exile came about, "an act of praise at the justice of the judgment of God,"[5] not an attempt to draw detailed lessons from the distant past for the present. Genesis and Chronicles are more like Matthew, retelling the story not only out of a concern that people come to the right act of faith in regard to the events of the past, but also so that they may see the story's implications for ongoing life in the present. Genesis is concerned to suggest what sabbath, abstaining from blood, and circumcision signify for people taken into exile, while Chronicles emphasizes what David's arrangements for the temple and the defeats and triumphs of preexilic history signify for people after the exile.

John's method of contemporizing the story of Jesus is less subtle than Matthew's. He offers examples of something like the procedure that subsequent preachers have often used (but is rarer in scripture itself), whereby the point of the story is driven home by direct teaching material attached to the story to bring out its theological and ethical implications. Even here, however, the teaching can be presented as the words of Jesus himself rather than as those of the Evangelist (one might compare sermons within the First Testament such as the one in Joshua 1) so that the framework of the story form is kept.

A fourth form of biblical storytelling is seen in Luke, which continues the Gospel story into the life of the church. Luke's Gospel "becomes a sort of Old Testament to which the Book of Acts is the New Testament."[6] Our story is thus linked to the biblical story. This process had a long history in Israel, most clearly in the way that Ezra and Nehemiah continued the story told in Kings and Chronicles. It also probably underlies the accumulation of the history in Genesis to Kings as a whole, which was repeatedly brought up to date by having new episodes linked onto it, as well as by being itself

---

5. My rendering of *Gerichtsdoxologie*, which von Rad uses in this connection. The translation in von Rad's *OT Theology* (2:343) is "doxology of judgment."

6. J. M. Robinson, "The Gospels as Narrative," in McConnell (ed.), *The Bible and the Narrative Tradition* 109.

retold in updated ways. The eventual result of this process that contributed to the development of the scriptures as a whole is the macro-story that stretches from Beginning to End, with Christ at its center.

Because it looks forward to the End as well as back to the Beginning, the biblical macro-story thereby actually embraces our story. It is possible to present a sermon by setting a biblical story and a modern story side by side. But whether we do precisely that in the pulpit, Luke's work offers a suggestive clue to a way we may go about preparing the sermon (or studying scripture for ourselves). We are seeking to set an appropriate aspect of our story alongside the biblical story. We are linking our story to God's story.[7] Perhaps the untidiness, even incompleteness, of Luke-Acts (and of Kings and Ezra-Nehemiah) constitutes an invitation to do this — as if to say "We have added our story to what came before; now we leave it open to you to add yours."[8]

How Stories Engage Their Readers

Stories engage their readers. How do they do that, and how do we enable them to do that in the retelling? The following observations may not be universal, but they may serve as broad generalizations.

First, each story has a beginning, a middle, and an end; that is, stories are structured. Each story has a plot of some kind. We are presented with a problem that is to be solved; quite likely there are difficulties to be overcome on the way or consequences when the main events are over. In Gospel stories some point in them may lead to a significant remark by Jesus, and it is for the sake of the remark as much as for any other reason that the story is told. Interpreting a story involves discovering how it works; it may then be natural for the sermon's structure to follow that of the biblical story. The sermon may not have a structure in the sense of four points beginning with R or three with P, but it will still (for the congregation's sake) be a structured entity rather than a ramble, in the more subtle way that a story is.

Second, each story offers a concrete portrayal of a series of events against a particular historical, geographical, social, and cultural background. There is movement from one area to another, political and religious heroes and villains pass before the audience's eyes, and pressure points of

7. Cf. Frei, *The Eclipse of Biblical Narrative* 3.
8. I owe this point to Peta Sherlock.

economic or family or social life are alluded to or emphasized. For the story to grasp its modern hearers, the significance of these allusions has to come home to them. It is possible to convey this information in a hamfisted way; there is no need to incorporate *all* the learning that may be gleaned from valuable works such as de Vaux's *Ancient Israel* or Jeremias's *Jerusalem in the Time of Jesus,* and one should spare the congregation "When I was in Israel . . ." (as rigorously as "The Greek word means . . ."!) — invaluable though a visit to the scene itself is to understanding and preaching on biblical stories. The skilled storyteller can bring to life the concreteness and thus the reality of a story by more subtle, low-key explanations of the meaning of this detail or that, in the course of the imaginative reconstruction of a significant scene.

A third feature of biblical stories is that they invite their hearers to identify their life and circumstances with those that they presuppose. In this way a story makes clear in the telling that it is about the hearer as well as about the subject. Features that mark biblical stories as unhistorical often originate with this characteristic. We have noted it in a Gospel story such as the stilling of the storm, which makes Jesus and his disciples use the language of the life of the church. In the First Testament, Chronicles pictures priest and people of old behaving the way they would in the Chronicler's day. The preacher, in retelling the story, similarly encourages the congregation to see the story as about people like them in situations like theirs — not by telling them that this is so, but by using the kind of language that makes it so.

In order to do this, as well as portraying the scene, the setting, and the action the preacher may look at the events through the eyes of each of the characters in the story. One needs to be wary of psychologizing characters, imposing on the story modern interest in and modern forms of expression of the inner workings of people's minds. And one needs also to be wary of biographizing, since biblical stories do not share our interest in how characters develop over time. Yet we can ask what the event concerned would mean for the kind of person involved and how these characters would relate to each other, noting especially what we can learn from the words, feelings, and actions that are actually attributed to them.

For a fourth feature of many stories is their focus on individual people with whom the hearers are invited to identify. Luke 7, for instance, offers its hearers a series of brief sketches involving a galaxy of players: Jesus, centurion, slave, elders, friends, crowd (vv. 1-10); Jesus, disciples, crowd, widow, mourners, youth (vv. 11-17); John, his disciples, Jesus, crowd, recipients of Jesus' ministry, Pharisees, lawyers (vv. 18-35); Pharisee, sinful woman, Jesus, guests (vv. 36-50). The stories engage their hearers by offering them various characters with whom to identify. Different hearers then grasp different facets of the stories' significance, so that group meditation on a story naturally leads different people to focus on and identify with different characters in a way that can then be illuminating for the whole group. Different facets also come home to individual hearers at different times in their lives; there is no once-for-all hearing of a story. Our task as preachers is to open up as much as possible of the resources that lie in these various character portrayals, all of which can open up for people aspects of the gospel. Our task is to help people to get into the story, identifying with characters and situations as if hearing it for the first time, so that they can in doing so respond to the gospel in the way that they must.

Luke and John imply that their Gospels, at least, were not written with already committed insiders primarily in mind. A key purpose of the tradition preserved in scripture is to witness to people outside the church. The demand the witnessing tradition makes is that we free it to do its work in the world; we must not confine it to preaching to the converted. The method of communication demanded by its inherent nature and purpose is one that will enable it to speak to the world. Its own combination of faithfulness in witnessing to the key gospel events with dynamic flexibility so that new audiences may have the opportunity to see the significance of these events for themselves is the model for our witnessing to these events and the canon by which we will be judged.

Interpreting the Parables

Among the stories in scripture, for a number of reasons the interpretation of Jesus' parables deserves particular attention. One reason is that they have been the subject of much productive modern study with challenging but helpful implications for the pulpit.

One stream of that recent study is represented by books on the parables by C. H. Dodd, J. Jeremias, and A. M. Hunter, whose concern has been to locate the origin and significance of parables in the life of Jesus.[9] It has tended to stress that they were designed to make one point, often a different

---

9. See Dodd, *The Parables of the Kingdom;* Jeremias, *The Parables of Jesus;* Hunter, *Interpreting the Parables.*

point from the one on which modern preachers focus. Thus the meaning of the Parable of the Talents (Matthew 25) does not lie in the varying numbers of talents that the different servants are given, nor should these talents be confused with "talents" in the sense the word has for us. The question the parable asks is "What would you do with a bag of gold?" (cf. NEB); the Pharisees were like people entrusted with a bag of gold (God's revelation), who looked after it instead of "investing" it.

This parable, and others, thus have their original context in the life of Jesus with the crises that his coming brought to people. That is a different context from the one presupposed by the interpretations given to the parables by the Evangelists, who were also concerned for the parables' significance in the life of the church. This tradition of understanding the parables can seem to imply that we simply throw away the Evangelists' additions to and interpretations of the parables. But our attitude to the additions and interpretations should surely rather be that the Evangelists are modeling what we ourselves have to do, taking the kind of thing Jesus was saying and applying it to the situations of their day in the context of the church, living as they did (like us) after the resurrection.

A second fruitful modern approach to the parables is the stream associated with the "new hermeneutic" in Germany and with literary-critical study in the United States and represented by works of writers such as E. Fuchs, E. Linnemann, D. O. Via, J. D. Crossan, and R. W. Funk.[10] The key aspect of the parables from which the new hermeneutic begins is the way in which they concern the ordinary, everyday world of their hearers.[11] Sometimes they do so by telling a straightforward story about everyday life that they imply embodies what the rule of God is like, without quite making it clear how the parable illustrates the nature of God's rule. Thus people's response to the Parable of the Sower (Mark 4) is puzzlement: It is a clear enough story, but what is its point? Stories like that make people think and help open their eyes to the gospel, if they are willing to open them; but they do so indirectly and let people off the hook if they want to avoid seeing the point.[12]

10. See, e.g., Robinson and Cobb (ed.), *The New Hermeneutic;* Linnemann, *Parables of Jesus;* Via, *The Parables;* Crossan, *In Parables;* Funk, *Language, Hermeneutic, and Word of God.*

11. On this see also Bailey, *Poet and Peasant* and *Through Peasant Eyes,* two studies of the parables in Luke against their everyday Middle Eastern background.

12. Cf. Funk, *Language, Hermeneutic, and Word of God* 133-36; he is actually taking up an observation by Dodd in *The Parables of the Kingdom* 16-18.

Jesus' parables thus communicate in a different and less direct way from that which is characteristic of the Gospels as a whole or of more direct forms of preaching. "The *Gattung* gospel tends to make *explicit* what is only *implicit* in the parable — and thus violates the intention of what may be the dominant mode of discourse in which Jesus taught. . . . The mystery of the kingdom held in solution in the parables precisely as mystery, tends to be profaned, made public, by the *Gattung* gospel."[13] The parables share in the mysterious revelatory but unauthoritarian persuasive power of other fiction. "To save sinners, God seizes them by the imagination"; preachers place themselves at the service of this saving act by the engagement of their own imagination.[14]

If understanding a factual story depends on allowing ourselves to be drawn into it, this is the more true of a fictional story such as a parable. The new hermeneutic has shown special interest in the kind of parable in which Jesus begins in people's realistic, everyday world, the world of home and family, of work and worship, of sowing and harvest, of shepherding and laboring, of weddings and funerals, of Pharisees, tax farmers, priests, Levites, and Samaritans. He thus draws his hearers into his stories, because they manifestly relate to their world. They are at home in these stories, nodding in understanding as they unfold.

Near the end Jesus' stories turn surrealist; they eject out of that world and somersault into a topsy-turvy one in which the tax farmer finds God's favor, some people get a day's pay for an hour's work, the people we would expect to help a victim do not, and the last person we would expect to do so does. The parables make a backdoor assault on the familiar worlds in which people live with God, with a lightning speed that the evasive heart of the listener is hard put to match. "Myth establishes world. Apologue defends world. Action investigates world. Satire attacks world. Parable subverts world."[15] The parables portray a realistic but strange world — a threatening but better world, one transformed by God's grace. They create a world before people's eyes and ears, a familiar world into which people cannot help but be drawn, but then challenge them as to whether they will

---

13. Funk, "The Parables" 295.

14. Green, *Imagining God* 149.

15. Crossan, *The Dark Interval* 59. Cf. H. White's grid of "modes of emplotment" and "modes of ideological implication" that links romance and anarchism, tragedy and radicalism, comedy and conservatism, and satire and liberalism (*Metahistory* 29; also "Interpretation in History" 307); and B. Harrison, "Parable and Transcendence," in *Ways of Reading the Bible* (ed. Wadsworth) 190-212.

live according to the logic of merit that is inherent in this familiar world or go with God into a world that lives according to the illogic of grace. They create a new world, the price being the destruction of the old one. They are understood only by those who are drawn into them and go through this world-destroying, world-creating process. In telling parables, a language-event takes place.[16] The hearers do not interpret the parables, the parables interpret the hearers.

It is not the case that all the parables suggest the revolution of grace. They can be mysterious or shocking: God is like an absentee landlord, a silly old fool, a judge who fears neither God nor human beings, a hard man who reaps where he has not sown, a person in bed who does not want to be disturbed by having to get up to help a friend. The parables burst apart our picture of God in worrying ways, but ways that make God correspond better to reality and experience.[17] This tougher side of the parables reflects their link to their predecessors, for this somersaulting from the familiar to the unfamiliar, into a different world, is not new in the parables. It can be seen in a prophet such as Amos. His book begins with a series of declarations of God's judgment upon Israel's traditional enemies, and one can imagine the enthusiasm with which Israel hears these oracles. But the Israel whose assent has been won suddenly finds that it is cheering its own judgment as Amos turns to speak of Israel in the same terms in which he has spoken of others (Amos 1–2). The prophet invites people to worship, to come to the sanctuary with their tithes and sacrifices, speaking like a priest exhorting people to worship ("Come into his presence singing hallelujah"); but when they hear more clearly, the hearers perceive the wicked irony in his invitation (4:5). Later the prophet takes up the form of a funeral dirge (5:1-2): You ask who has died, and you realize it is your own death he is singing about. He has entered the people's world, then turned it upside-down in a way that reveals that mysteriously and worryingly God's world, while one with Israel's, differs radically from it.

The nature of what was going on when Jesus told parables enables us to perceive where the central problem in preaching on them lies. Jesus moved from people's familiar, everyday world to an unfamiliar, revolutionary world. But where people were once at home, now there is obscu-

---

16. Fuchs, *Studies of the Historical Jesus* 141; cf. Thiselton in *The Responsibility of Hermeneutics* 108-9.

17. R. White, "MacKinnon and the Parables," taking up MacKinnon, *The Problem of Metaphysics*, e.g., 137-38.

rity for us. We wonder why the bridesmaids were having to wait for the bridegroom at night; the arrangements for the wedding seem very strange (unlike our entirely rational way). Precisely because Jesus started from the everyday life of his culture, what was formerly familiar is now quite obscure. We are no longer instinctively aware of the resonances of words such as "Pharisee" and "Samaritan" in the vocabulary of a first-century Jew.

Conversely, what was previously surprising and objectionable is now familiar and natural. We know the tax farmer will go home justified, so we identify with him; we know the Samaritan will help the mugged man, and we are happy to identify with him. It is difficult for us to take account of the way in which words such as Pharisee and Samaritan have turned 180 degrees around in their meaning since Jesus' day. "Pharisee" then meant someone who was especially committed to a life of faith and obedience, and the word carried no overtone of hypocrisy; the change in the term's meaning causes us inevitably to miss the scandal of Jesus' claim that God preferred the tax farmer's prayer to the Pharisee's. The Samaritans were the apostate people from the north, far from being (as they are now for us) the people we can be sure will listen to us when no one else will. We inevitably miss the impossibility in Jesus' juxtaposition of the words "good" and "Samaritan."[18] At best, the parables are now obscure; at worst, when they seem clear they make a point contrary to the one Jesus wanted to make.

We have noted already that a common way to preach on the parables, as on other stories in scripture, is first to summarize the story, then to offer straightforward direct teaching on the topic the parable covers, of the kind that appears in the Sermon on the Mount or the Epistles. The fatal weakness of this approach is that it fails to do what Jesus was doing when he himself spoke his parables.

It is possible to talk people through the parables, explaining who Pharisees, publicans, and Samaritans were and other matters in such a way that people are then able to hear the parable again, able this time to get inside it. We are inviting them on a fantasy journey or acting like the critic who explains a poem for people in order to enable them to go back to the poem and read it better. David Clines once suggested that the place for the

18. Crossan, "Parable and Example in the Teaching of Jesus" 295; *In Parables* 64; cf. Thiselton, "Understanding God's Word Today" 107.

text in a sermon is at the end, and this is the kind of sermon in which this is appropriate. Of course, he pointed out, we do not normally end our sermons with texts, because what we want to leave people with is not scripture, but our words![19]

Alternatively, the preacher may be able to tell an updated version of a parable. Anthony Thiselton relates:

> A former student of mine . . . attempted to engage with the horizons of his Protestant congregation in Liverpool by re-telling the parable [of the Good Samaritan] in terms of an Orangeman who passed by on the other side, and a Roman Catholic priest who ministered to the man in need. John D. Crossan . . . envisages telling a Roman Catholic Irish audience how a member of the IRA passed by the man, as did a Catholic nun, whilst a Protestant terrorist stopped and helped him.[20]

In the area of Britain where I live, I can imagine how the parable might have been adapted in the context of the miners' strike in the 1970s. More recently I heard a Jewish believer in Israel imply that the Good Samaritan might be a Palestinian. The preacher knows when he or she has retold the parable faithfully: It leads to a lynching.

Admittedly such adaptations can themselves become fatally predictable, even in their concern with grace. "To certain listeners long conditioned by legal demands, a story of surprising grace might be given. To others beginning to include a rescue by grace in their calculations of the Kingdom, might come a story of straight justice." F. B. Craddock appends to this observation a story that illustrates how modern hearers might be scandalized by the parabolic declaration of justice that denies their expectations as Jesus' parables did. He recalls students adapting the Parable of the Two Sons so that the father refuses to have the boy back and the elder brother appeals for him.[21] In general, Craddock suggests, the problem is that people already know — they have too much information; they can be reached by putting them into the position of overhearing rather than directly hearing, so as to avoid fruitlessly and exhaustingly confronting them.[22] In our

---

19. "Notes for an OT Hermeneutic" 10.
20. "Understanding God's Word Today" 107-8; cf. Crossan, *The Dark Interval* 106.
21. *Overhearing the Gospel* 104-40.
22. Thiselton, "Understanding God's Word Today" 109, following Fuchs, *Studies of the Historical Jesus* 129, 155.

preaching they overhear rather than hear Jesus telling parables, and they may have their defenses down.

There is one further feature of the parables that makes interpretation of them deserve special consideration. There is something characteristic and distinctive of the parables in the ministry of Jesus. He made a point of communicating by this means. Indeed, parables are not merely a dynamic way of communicating but a witness to the love of Jesus for those he addresses. The picture part of the parable constructs a "world" into which the hearers may enter. In the picture part Jesus does not simply, in the first place, make the hearer adjust to Jesus' viewpoint; instead Jesus himself enters the everyday world of the hearer. Hence he speaks about farming, housekeeping, trading, children's games, and looking for lost objects, not merely to give sermon illustrations or to make his teaching more vivid, but quite literally to enter the world of the hearer. "The parables embody in microcosm the principle of the incarnation. Jesus comes and stands where the hearer already stands."[23]

Indeed, even when a parable somersaults into a fantastic world, it is "a fantastic that remains a fantastic of the everyday, without the supernatural, as it appears in fairy tales or in myths."[24] Here, too, the parables of Jesus correspond to the person and life of Jesus. They "manifest this incarnational principle — this serious treatment of the everyday — by combining the realistic with the extra-ordinary and improbable."[25] Jesus did that not merely in his words but in his life. He is "God's Parable" (the title of a book by F. H. Borsch). Grace is the most prominent theme of the parables, grace is a fundamental feature of the way they communicate (because they do not force anything on us but leave us room to maneuver), and grace is what the parabler himself is.[26]

The Parable of the Broadcaster

Radical updating becomes the telling of a new parable. The story that follows is a sermon preached by Trevor Williams, now leader of the Corymeela Community in Belfast, when he was a student in my sermon class. Like Jesus'

---

23. Craddock, *Overhearing the Gospel* 88-89.
24. Ricoeur, "The 'Kingdom' in the Parables of Jesus" 167.
25. Via, *The Parables* 105.
26. Peta Sherlock (in a private communication).

original version, it starts in people's everyday world — so much so that it is only as the preacher hits us over the head with his sledgehammer that we realize that we are the victim of a specific parable of Jesus.

Patrick Murphy works at Rolls Royce in Derby as a fitter. The moment he gets up and goes down to the kitchen on goes the radio. He has turned on a constant flow of chat and music, news, weather forecasting, religion (thought-for-the-day style), and happy disc jockey. As the radio is blaring away Paddy is reading the back of the cornflakes package and skimming over the newspaper.

Having swallowed his flakes and toast he climbs into his car and turns on the radio, just to keep a check on the time, but he gets a lot more than that: more chat and more music, as well as a "What's on Today" spot. Meanwhile he is driving his car, and there is an almost constant traffic jam. He cannot let his concentration wander from his driving for a moment. But he is looking at road signs and traffic lights, all telling him what to do: "Turn Right," "No Left Turn," "STOP!" So it goes on and on. Over the day as a whole, Paddy is likely to see hundreds of advertisements, watch about four hours television, and also try to fit in some talk with his wife and children.

All day long he is exposed to a constant flow of information. He is told to change his brand of toothpaste, drink more Guinness, redecorate his house, and have a holiday in Majorca. If a god were told to do so many things at the same time he would probably have a nervous breakdown from sheer confusion.

How then does Paddy survive? He has a cut-off switch: He only hears what he wants to hear. The sole reason he has the radio on at breakfast is to hear the time. The rest of the chatter and music might as well be wallpaper. He takes it for granted without noticing.

Despite Paddy's cut-off switch, occasionally something gets through. He noticed the car bomb in Dublin. His mother always shopped in that street. She would usually have been there at this time. He was worried and tried to telephone her, just in case. But the lines were jammed with hundreds of people trying to phone Dublin. On another occasion he heard an appeal for refugee children from Vietnam and sent a donation to help support an orphanage. He got a reply to thank him for his generous donation. The idea came to him: Why didn't they offer to adopt one of those orphans? He thought about it for a couple of days, but then somehow never got around to it. He doesn't exactly know why, but he remembers thinking that saying you would like to adopt and actually having another baby in the house are two very different things. Another baby would change their life as a family quite a lot. Things were just about getting comfortable now that Jamie and Trisha had both started school. So Paddy didn't bother telling his wife about his idea. Maybe it wasn't such a good one after all. A seed-thought choked; too many things would have to change.

My name is Patrick Murphy and so is yours. None of us listen to most of what we hear. And if we do listen, we won't allow it to change us very much. We can't afford to. So how much that God wants to say to us never gets through?

If you have ears to hear, then hear.

PART II

SCRIPTURE AS AUTHORITATIVE CANON: INTERPRETING TORAH

• 6 •

Scripture as a Collection of Norms for Behavior

The model of the authoritative canon suggests that scripture provides norms for behavior. It especially fits material in scripture such as the instructions on behavior in the Torah: Indeed, "Torah" might be seen as the biblical equivalent to "authoritative canon."

Now humanity's need East of Eden to enable it to live the right life is not primarily more commands or more advice but more strength, and that depends on a transformed imagination. "We are not changed by new rules. The deep places in our lives . . . are not ultimately reached by instruction . . . only by stories, by images, metaphors, and phrases that line out the world differently" and evoke transformed listening. The role of preaching in relation to obedience is not so much to offer concrete moral admonition, at least not without also ensuring that the sermon is more fundamentally the place where the church's imagination is fed with dreams and hopes and visions.[1] It is the place where revolutionary attitudes can be portrayed and crazily extreme instances of familiar attitudes be represented.

In transforming imagination, scripture creatively affects behavior in a number of ways.[2] Its story of Israel and of Jesus shapes our understanding of ourselves within the purpose of God at work in the world. The Prophets emphasize ethical values and principles such as holiness, justice, and love,

1. Brueggemann, *Finally Comes the Poet* 109-10 and the chapter as a whole, following Ricoeur, e.g., *Essays on Biblical Interpretation* 117; cf. the comments in chapter 4, pp. 56-61 above.

2. See my *Approaches to OT Interpretation* 38-43 and *Models for Scripture* chapters 7 and 8.

which they see as implicit in the Torah. Theologians such as Paul develop a whole perspective on life lived in the light of cross and resurrection. Ethicists have pointed out that all these and more shape the persons we are and thus have a decisive influence on the life we live and the decisions we take. This shaping takes place not merely through individual academic study but in the ecclesial and liturgical context of corporate exposure to scripture enacted and narrated.[3]

The presence of many detailed commands in scripture nevertheless suggests that when these points have been granted and as long as the primacy of the gospel is safeguarded, standards for behavior can be granted their important but derivative place. Calvin attempts this balance in a way that Luther does not, though he also thereby makes possible the Puritan degeneration into moralism as Luther would not. If we had to choose between witnessing tradition and authoritative canon, it would be better to choose the former. But it is not complete on its own. "Story does not provide the resources for implementing ethical growth or socio-political change" even though it provides the inspiration for it.[4] And "the goal of biblical interpretation is not only understanding but also ultimately a new, different praxis."[5]

That underlines the questions raised for us by the many direct imperatives that appear throughout the scriptures. How do they exercise their particular authority? "Love God" and "love your neighbor," for instance, are principles for the whole of human life. What that twofold love looks like in practice is illustrated by many individual commands in scripture, which provide us with canons by which to measure our attempts at love. Our study of these individual commands involves confronting at least two major issues: the meaning and the transferability of the individual sayings and how they are interrelated. It involves discerning how to handle the diversity of standards in these commands and in scriptural attitudes to lifestyle more generally.

3. Guroian, "Bible and Ethics"; cf. more generally Fowl and Jones, *Reading in Communion;* Birch and Rasmussen, *Bible and Ethics in the Christian Life* 125-41.

4. Lischer, "The Limits of Story" 35. Cf. Eagleton, *Literary Theory* 207.

5. Schüssler Fiorenza, *Bread Not Stone* 136; she notes that this conviction is characteristic of liberation theology as opposed to hermeneutical theology.

The Meaning and Applicability of Scriptural Commands

Many biblical injunctions such as the love command are of clear meaning and often of clear application to our lives. At many other points it is more complicated to see how scripture as authoritative canon effects its shaping of us and therefore more complicated to see what meaning attaches to the notion of scripture's authority. Barr thus declares that "the locus of the authority question has shifted. The critical question is no longer 'What was said back then?' but 'What should we say now?' "[6] The biblical message is addressed to the accidental particularities of the human situation at specific moments. Even if we can establish that particular actions were incumbent on people in Israel in 500 BC or in Corinth in AD 50, that may not help us because we live in different times. Conversely, biblical commands do not cover areas in which we need to make decisions in our different world. Not the authority question but "the hermeneutical question is *the* question";[7] or rather, the one collapses into the other, so that "the concentration on the hermeneutic question corresponds to Reformation theology's adoption of the *Sola Scriptura*."[8]

One appropriate response to this statement of the problem is to call its bluff. First, scripture does, in fact, address a wide range of contemporary questions about the nature of society, the family, property, land, mobility, the role of the state, and structures of government. Unfortunately it is mostly the First Testament that addresses these issues, and it is not read much in the church. Study of this biblical material in story and statute with the aid of critical tools and models from the social sciences has hardly begun, so we cannot yet claim that it lacks underlying principles or middle axioms or that it does not present paradigms that could illuminate our own policy making in these areas.[9]

Other questions are raised when life in the modern world requires consideration of issues that are not directly handled in scripture. Yet among the most impressive exercises in biblical interpretation of recent years is Dale Aukerman's attempt at a "biblical perspective on nuclear war," *Darkening Valley*, only one instance of scriptural interpretation that proves

6. "The OT and the New Crisis of Biblical Authority" 36.
7. Buttrick, *Homiletic* 241.
8. Ebeling, *Word and Faith* 10.
9. But see, e.g., C. J. H. Wright, "Ethics and the OT"; *Living as the People of God; God's People in God's Land*; Schluter and Clements, *Reactivating the Extended Family;* Schluter, *Family Roots or Family Mobility.*

the Bible's capacity to speak authoritatively to the most unbiblical of issues.[10]

Nevertheless the Bible is rooted in another set of cultures, and working out the significance of its commands is not always straightforward. One complex of questions raised by the direct commands in scripture is their specificity or particularity. Most are not universal absolutes but enactments made to fit concrete situations. Yet they are hardly random enactments but concrete expressions of principles. They are thus of use to us in their concreteness, because they show principles applied in concrete ways; but in interpreting them we need to move behind the concrete command to the principles that underlie it, not so as to stop there but so as to turn these principles back into concrete commands applicable to our own situations. Building walls around the roof of a pitched-roof house would be a literalistic obedience to Deut 22:8; providing speed bumps to slow the traffic in the street in front of the house might be a more faithful embodiment of the principle expressed in the Deuteronomic command.[11] It must be admitted, however, that the principles underlying biblical commands may often be difficult to discern. "You are not to boil a kid in its mother's milk" is an injunction famously important enough to be repeated three times in the Torah, but its rationale is also famously difficult to be sure of.

Implementing such an injunction is in one sense complicated, in that it is difficult to know whether we are living by its spirit, but in another sense straightforward and uncontroversial, since it is evident what its letter asks for. This is not the case with the requirement that people guilty of adultery, among other acts, must be put to death (Lev 20:10). There are many references to adultery in scripture, but no record of this punishment being exacted (even John 8 in the end only proves the rule). This has raised the exegetical question whether we misunderstand such a command when we read it as designed for literal implementation. Perhaps such injunctions are not instructions to be obeyed but teaching about behavioral priorities. Some of Jesus' more extravagant expectations may parallel them in this respect.

Of pressing practical significance is the material in scripture relating to homosexuality. If passages such as Rom 1:24-27 indeed condemn any homosexual practice, the only interpretive question raised by them is whether we feel committed to live by them.[12] The more these texts are studied,

10. Compare also Bauckham, *The Bible and Politics.*
11. See further my *Approaches to OT Interpretation* 51-55.
12. On both questions, see especially Hays, "Relations Natural and Unnatural" and his references.

however, the more complex become the questions regarding what is being condemned and why and what its contemporary implications might be. Sometimes, at least, Paul may be referring to pederasty or casual homosexual relationships, and such a critique might be irrelevant to committed adult homosexual relationships. Sometimes, at least, his interest may lie in arguing on the basis of moral views that his readers would themselves have held rather than being concerned with the theoretical question whether these practices are wrong. Accepting for the sake of argument the view that homosexual practices are wrong, he utilizes that view as part of his theological argument that moral wrongdoing issues ultimately from the world's turning its back on God.[13] He is seeking not to determine what is the need that the gospel answers but to commend the gospel by relating it to the felt need that it answers.

As regards the contemporary implications of what Paul says, sometimes, at least, his views may presuppose attitudes in his culture that are no longer shared in ours. In 1 Cor 11:14 he asks whether "nature" itself does not teach that long hair is degrading for a man and gives pride to a woman. He has reason to think that people in first-century Corinth will answer "Yes," but in other cultures such as those of contemporary North Atlantic countries the answer would be "No." When Paul refers to nature, then, he refers to nature as conceived in a particular culture. The question arises whether the human relations of Rom 1:26-27 are only "natural" and "unnatural" in his context.[14] In other contexts homosexual relations may seem quite natural.

Such uncertainties suggest that a biblical consideration of an issue such as homosexuality has to proceed on the basis of biblical-theological considerations rather than merely biblical-exegetical considerations. Jowett once invited his readers to "consider, for example, the extraordinary and unreasonable importance attached to single words, sometimes of doubtful meaning, in reference to any of the following subjects: — 1, Divorce; 2, Marriage with a Wife's Sister; 3, Inspiration; 4, the Personality of the Holy Spirit; 5, Infant Baptism; 6, Episcopacy; 7, Divine Right of Kings; 8, Original Sin."[15] Single texts tend not quite to prove a point, and this may perhaps cohere with and be a parable of the fact that laying down the law about behavior is not the most central preoccupation of scripture. Its central concern is witnessing to the gospel.

---

13. Cf. Lindars, *The Use of Scripture* 13, quoting Cranfield, *Romans* 1:127.
14. "Nature/natural/unnatural" involves the word *physis* each time.
15. "On the Interpretation of Scripture" 434; see further 434-38.

The Diverse Perspectives and Levels
of Scriptural Commands

The authoritative canons given to Israel in the centuries before Christ and to Christians in Corinth in AD 50 were quite different, both because different accidental particularities attached to these differing moments and also because of differences in the priorities God apparently brought to different situations. Even people who are committed to the strictest understanding of scriptural authority and inerrancy necessarily assume that not all scriptural commands are directly normative for us; for a command to be inerrant does not imply that it is permanently binding as a command. There are biblical injunctions proscribing eating meat containing blood (Gen 9:4), performing any work on the seventh day of the week (Exod 20:9-10), and swearing of any oaths (Matt 5:34) and an injunction requiring that the church elders be summoned to pray when a person is ill (Jas 5:14). Groups within the church may observe one or another of these, but such groups are the exception rather than the rule. The Bible is more explicit in banning lending money at interest than it is in disapproving of same-sex lovemaking, but the former injunction can be ignored with impunity in a way that the latter cannot. Jowett thus adds to the texts of scripture that are subject to "unfair appropriation" others that are subject to "undue neglect" such as its blessing on poverty and its warning about wealth, its command to wash one another's feet, and its prohibition of oaths.[16]

In practice more controversy attaches to the varying attitude to one topic that different parts of scripture sometimes show. Some Epistles urge congregations to accept the subordination of slaves to masters and of wives to husbands. 1 Pet 2:18–3:6 sets before slaves the example of Christ's willing submission to harsh treatment, and before wives that of Sarah's acceptance that Abraham is her "master."[17] 1 Timothy 2 specifically envisages a situation where the slave owners are Christian, and it requires their slaves to serve them particularly well.

Such instructions contrast with the vision of humanity set forth in the creation stories in Genesis 1–2, where human beings as such are seen as created in God's image. It is in humanity in its diversity, and specifically the diversity of male and female, that this image of God is realized. The

16. Jowett, "On the Interpretation of Scripture" 434; see further 438-42.

17. There are illuminating discussions of passages such as these in *Perspectives on Feminist Hermeneutics* (ed. Gerber Koontz and Swartley).

notion of rule and hierarchy is essential to being human, but it is a rule that humanity as such exercises over the rest of creation, not a rule exercised by some human beings over others (see Gen 1:26-28; 2:15-25). The latter form of rule emerges as a consequence of human disobedience (3:16) rather than being explicitly part of creation itself.[18] In parallel with Genesis, Paul notes that both slave and free, and both male and female, become children of God on the same basis, that of faith in Jesus (Gal 3:28). It is worth beginning from examples where the problem lies in the Second Testament's sometimes seeming to have lower standards than the First since Christian apologetic often uses the former as a criterion for evaluating the latter: The traffic has to be both ways. Where Christians find the First Testament's moral assumptions questionable, it is worth noting that often Jews also do so, as for instance with the story of Elisha, the children, and the bears in 2 Kings 2.[19]

The Second Testament's teaching on the state's authority (e.g., Romans 13)[20] and on the institutional authority of the church's ministers — though the actual word "authority" is not used in the latter connection — also stands in some tension with parts of scripture such as the vision of humanity set forth in Genesis 1–2. The former contrasts, too, with the negative attitude to authorities taken elsewhere in the Second Testament (e.g., Revelation 13), while the latter, authority in the church, contrasts with Jeremiah's vision of a covenant that involves the programming of the Torah into people's minds so that they will not need to give each other instructions (Jer 31:31-34). The emphasis on racial privilege in much of the First Testament may likewise sit in tension with Genesis 1–2, and the converse anti-Judaism of much of the Second Testament sits in tension with its attitude elsewhere to Israel as the people of God: De-anti-Judaizing the Second Testament has been reckoned a more pressing question than demythologizing it.[21]

Variety in attitude appears within individual biblical books. Genesis itself provides examples. If its opening chapters imply an egalitarian vision of human relations, its later chapters record and apparently condone conduct and attitudes that presuppose hierarchies of gender, class, and race.

18. 1 Tim 2:13-14 bases the submission of women on their being created first and sinning first, but Genesis 2–3 itself does not make this point.

19. See N. M. Sarna, "The Authority and Interpretation of Scripture in Jewish Tradition," in *Understanding Scripture* (ed. Thoma and Wyschogrod) 14-15.

20. Cf. Munro, "Romans 13:1-7: Apartheid's Last Biblical Refuge."

21. Van Buren, *A Theology of the Jewish-Christian Reality* 1:135.

Deuteronomy affirms both the unnaturalness of debt and slavery within Israel and their inevitability. It contains regulations affected by sexism and patriarchy, yet also emphasizes the rights and responsibilities of women as well as men.

Pointers from Jesus' Handling of the Torah

Why is there this diversity within scripture, and in the light of it how can all the authoritative canons in scripture have normative authority? The phenomenon of varying levels of demand appears in the First Testament itself. Jesus has to handle it, and he provides us with approaches to our question.

In Mark 10 Jesus is asked what attitude he takes to divorce. He asks his questioners what the Torah says, and they quote the acceptance of divorce presupposed by the regulation regarding divorce certificates in Deuteronomy 24. He counters this with a reference to the passages in Genesis 1–2 noted above, which he takes to imply that marriage is by its very nature lifelong; the Mosaic regulation was given "because of your stubbornness." He does not seek to introduce a new standard for marriage that subverts what is stated in the Torah. He points his hearers to another aspect of the Torah's teaching that they have not considered and then suggests a way of interrelating its diverse perspectives. There is a difference between the ideal divine standards implied by the creation stories and a lower standard required in other parts of the Torah. The latter presuppose the fact of human sin, which — for instance — means that marriages do break down. In God's mercy humanity is not simply left to cope with the consequences of that but is given commands that start realistically where people are as sinners and help bring some structure and order to their sinful and ruined lives.[22] There are indications of this understanding in the Torah itself: Deuteronomy emphasizes that its commands are given to sinners, people characterized by stubbornness.

The Christ event brings a challenge to let the Torah's creation ideals be taken seriously. In analyzing the tensions between what was intended "from the beginning" and what was written "because of your hardness of heart,"

---

22. I assume (with Matthew 19!) that Jesus does see Deuteronomy 24 as a concession, though it may *also* be a judgment; von Campenhausen (*The Formation of the Christian Bible* 8-9) thinks that it is *only* a judgment.

Jesus points out how easily people settle for the latter and have to face the challenge of the former. The challenge to his hearers and readers comes from him, but it also comes from the scriptures on which he builds.

He comments earlier, in Mark 7, that the failure of his audience with regard to the scriptures lies not in taking their authority too seriously but in not taking it seriously enough. Human traditions by means of which the scriptures are interpreted should be abandoned where they obscure the scriptures themselves. Here he is involved in scriptural controversy over a religious or ceremonial matter. He has been asked why his disciples do not observe Jewish rituals for ceremonial cleansing. The question leads him to reject ritual practices that have arisen as means of applying scripture to the detail of everyday life and belong to Israel's distinctive tradition, but that threaten to obscure the scriptures themselves. Indeed, it leads him to reject all ceremonials for ritual cleansing, including those in scripture, on the basis of the principle that the real source of human defilement is not food, which enters the body from outside, but the evil thoughts and actions that issue from inside the person. In saying that, Mark comments, "Jesus declared all foods clean."

Jesus is concerned with the observing of "the command of God" expressed in "what Moses said" about attitudes to parents. He presupposes that the Torah is a normative guide to the kind of behavior God expects. Yet in the same breath, by declaring all foods clean, he subverts considerable parts of the same Torah, annulling many of its commands. The conviction that all foods are clean and that evil originates within people is implicit in the Torah (see Genesis 1–4; also Jer 17:9), but subsequent parts of the Torah make normative distinctions among foods, norms that are then put in question through the coming of Christ. Perhaps Jesus actually meant "defilement issues *more* from what comes out of a person than from what goes in."[23] That the church took time to clarify its mind on the question of food regulations (see, e.g., Acts 15) suggests at least that it did not immediately make the inference that Mark makes in verse 19. Either way Jesus is again setting one scriptural principle against another and suggesting priorities among them.

Something similar takes place in another discussion of a ceremonial or religious matter, in Mark 2:23-28. The Pharisees understand the sabbath command to exclude plucking of heads of grain; it is a "work." Jesus first

23. Cf. R. P. Booth, *Jesus and the Laws of Purity;* cf. Stanton, *The Gospels and Jesus* 244.

counters that with another passage from scripture that concerns food, an incident from the life of David that involved a contravention of the Torah. The principle underlying David's action, Jesus implies, was the priority of human need over ritual obligation. In a parallel way "the sabbath was made for human beings," not vice versa. All the more is the Son of Man Lord of the sabbath. The parallel passage in Matthew 12 adds an allusion to Hos 6:6 with its principle that mercy matters more than sacrifice; this is not the only passage where Matthew indicates that a commitment to love and mercy is a fundamental scriptural norm that as such provides a principle for discerning the relative significance of other commitments required by scripture.[24]

In each of these passages in Mark 2, 7, and 10 Jesus is affirming the priority of one passage from the Torah or the Prophets[25] over another. He is doing so in the light of his own coming, but he seems to see himself as undertaking scriptural interpretation, not as introducing quite novel elements into Jewish faith.[26] The passages that are regarded as of subordinate significance do not lose their scriptural status;[27] Jesus is not in that sense our authority for a critical hermeneutic of scripture.[28] Levitical regulations continue to function as normative scripture, forming a key theological resource for the early church as it seeks to articulate the significance of Jesus' death and the nature of the church's salvation in Christ; Hebrews takes this up systematically. Without this material, the theological work of the Second Testament would at points look very thin.

Yet their authority *as commands* is over. The logic of Jesus' remarks is that these regulations were *always* subordinate to material in scripture concerned with moral matters. Theologically, the place of the ceremonial commands was to safeguard the identity and distinctiveness of Israel through the period before Christ so that Israel could be God's means of reaching the world. When the gospel is to be preached to all peoples such

24. Dunn, *The Living Word* 53.

25. The story of David alluded to in Mark 2:25-26 belongs to the "Former *Prophets.*"

26. Though Hengel suggests that in a saying such as Matt 8:22 Jesus' authoritative summons is assumed to override the honoring of parents (*The Charismatic Leader and His Followers* 8-15; cf. E. P. Sanders, *Jesus and Judaism* 252-55). Hengel notes parallels with Jeremiah 16 and Ezekiel 24, so that it may again be a matter of exercising discernment within the scriptural tradition. Mark 3:31-35 raises similar questions: See Moltmann, *The Way of Jesus Christ* 143-44.

27. As Dunn implies; see *The Living Word* 113-15.

28. Against Schüssler Fiorenza, *Bread Not Stone* 13; cf. Käsemann, *NT Questions of Today* 271.

commands are abandoned for the sake of that same purpose (see Acts 10).[29] At the same time, they were an Israelite version of rites that appear among other Middle Eastern religions and among traditional peoples elsewhere. In adapting such rites, the Torah starts where people are in their cultural context as well as where they are as sinners. We might note that even rites of sacrifice and the idea of building a temple first appear in scripture as human ideas accepted by God, with overt misgivings in the latter case, rather than as originally divine intentions (Gen 4:3-4; 2 Samuel 7). Perhaps regulations regarding cleanness and uncleanness have a similar status, as not ultimately good ideas but as helpful to people in certain cultures and capable of being harnessed to embody real truth.

The Authority of Jesus and the Authority of the Torah

So what is the relation between Christ's own moral teaching and that of the Torah? The Sermon on the Mount declares that Jesus comes not to annul the Torah and the Prophets but to fulfill them (Matt 5:17; cf. John 10:35). One might expect the "fulfilling" to have a similar meaning with regard to both the Torah and the Prophets, and one suggested understanding that goes back to Irenaeus[30] infers that the reference to the Torah is to passages within it that could be interpreted eschatologically (e.g., Gen 49:9-10; Num 24:17; Deut 18:15-19). But the Gospels do not otherwise refer to such passages (though Num 24:17 presumably underlies Matt 2:2) and Matthew's many quotations from the Torah relate rather to its teaching on behavior.

We might consider what fulfilling the Torah and the Prophets might mean by looking at what Jesus actually did with the Torah and the Prophets. He *confirmed* them, declaring that God had indeed made these promises and warnings and had given these commands. He *embodied* them, putting into practice the concerns regarding commitment to God that underlie the Torah and making actual what the prophecies picture. He *broadened* and *extended* them, making clear that justice begins with the Torah but then goes beyond its demands in order to realize the full depth of God's expectations of humanity and that God's purpose of salvation begins with the Prophets but goes beyond what they envisage when it achieves its further-

29. Cf. Dunn's discussion in *Jesus, Paul, and the Law.*
30. *Against Heresies* 4.34.2; he compares Rom 3:21.

most aim. He *interpreted* them, as we have seen, indicating inherent priorities within them and thus identifying their own highest principles. Aspects of that or the whole of that may be involved in the fulfillment of which Jesus spoke. His teaching indicates that his affirmation of the smallest letter and the smallest part of a letter of the Torah (Matt 5:18) does not mean that he is committed at every point to observing the Torah or supporting observance of it; nor was that the way he was understood, or Paul would not have been able to get Peter and James to sanction his mission.[31]

The juxtaposition in Matthew 5 of "not an iota or a dot will pass from the Torah until all has been accomplished" with "You have heard that it was said . . . but I am saying to you . . ." may not be as paradoxical or as singular as it first seems. In line with the characteristics of gospel material elsewhere, Matthew 5:21-48 approaches the Torah with a Yes and a No. It affirms and extends the Torah's ban on murder and adultery, but thereby revokes its acceptance of divorce. Further, it attaches the same seriousness and thus the same penalty to the apparently lesser deeds and even the mere attitudes that lie behind the acts of murder or adultery as apply to the acts themselves. The Torah's insistence on only true oaths and equivalent vengeance is taken further: Now there are to be no oaths and no vengeance at all. The requirement regarding oaths and vengeance is extended by being abrogated. The Torah's exhortation regarding love of one's neighbor is extended explicitly to include one's enemies: The First Testament of course includes no exhortation to hate one's enemies (so that any actual exhortation of this kind to which Jesus is referring must be a postscriptural maxim), and it contains some pointers in the opposite direction — the "neighbor" envisaged in the love command may be one's enemy — but it does not quite say "love your enemies." So Jesus affirms and develops one strand of its attitudes as he puts a query by another. Even in such passages Jesus may be extending rather than opposing the Torah, in that "it is not against the law to be stricter than the law requires"; here as in Mark Jesus is not setting his own authority against the Torah, for "what Jesus presents as his own view is interpretation, not a new law."[32] If Jesus is a liberal,[33] then so are other Jewish interpreters of his day, including some who would have seen themselves as conservative.

31. E. P. Sanders, *Jesus and Judaism* 261; but Sanders doubts whether any of 5:17-48, or Mark 7:15, comes from Jesus.

32. E. P. Sanders, *Jesus and Judaism* 260; *Jewish Law from Jesus to the Mishnah* 93; cf. conservative writers such as G. L. Archer, "The Witness of the Bible to Its Own Inerrancy," in *The Foundation of Biblical Authority* (ed. Boice) 94.

33. Dunn, *The Living Word* 54.

An opposite view of the relationship between the Torah and the Sermon on the Mount emphasizes the gap between the two rather than minimizing it. Under the influence of the evolutionary thinking that pervades Western culture, the relationship between the morality and theology of the First Testament and of the Second has commonly been understood in developmental terms. The ethics of the former are thus seen as understandably primitive compared with the latter; the fully mature form of Jesus' teaching could only emerge when Israel had passed through less advanced stages of thinking. The ethics of the Torah can then be affirmed as a necessary stage in this development but treated as superseded because they belong to an outgrown stage in that development.

Such approaches to the morality and theology of the First Testament have a long history. Paul, indeed, speaks of the Torah as given to look after people in their minority, before Christ came (Gal 3:23-25), though here the Torah fulfills a restraining or controlling function rather than an educational function, and he does not query its standards so much as its theological role. Chrysostom can speak in terms of the need for humanity to have developed beyond the stage the Jews had reached before the fullness of Second Testament truth could appropriately be revealed,[34] and the developmental approach appears in a baptized form as the theory of progressive revelation. Such approaches are now inextricably interwoven with evolutionary thinking, and they persist despite widespread recognition of the fact that the model of evolutionary development is quite misleading when applied to the Bible or to other areas of the humanities.

Three alternative models are more illuminating. The one suggested by Mark 10 is that of ideal and condescension. It is sometimes the case that the commands of the First Testament start where people are as sinners and in their cultural context while the Second Testament asserts the ultimate will of God, though we have noted that the ideal sometimes comes in the First and the condescension in the Second, so this is not strictly a model for understanding the relationship of the Testaments as such. Indeed, the element of condescension reappears in the Gospels' own handling of divorce. In Matthew's version of Jesus' controversy with the Pharisees, Jesus' ban on divorce is qualified by an exception in the case of "fornication."[35] It has been argued that Matthew is making explicit something that Jesus and Mark took for granted, or alternatively that he is putting onto Jesus'

34. E.g., *Homilies on Genesis* 2.7-9, on Gen 1:1.
35. *Porneia;* the meaning of the term is a matter of debate.

lips what Jesus would surely have said if he had been confronted by the pastoral needs of the church. On either theory Jesus as Matthew presents him is condescending to the realities of human sin, failure, and suffering. Jesus accepts that divorce sometimes happens and sets an example for his followers in the way they handle real life within the people of God still living East of Eden. The presence of the phenomenon of "early catholicism" within the Second Testament[36] is another facet of this realism.

A second model is that of foundation and superstructure: The external commands of the Decalogue provide the necessary basis for more demanding requirements that can be built on them.

A third model is that of boundaries and what fills them. The negative commands of the Decalogue mark the limits of acceptable behavior; beyond these, one operates in unequivocally foreign territory. The commands are our boundary markers; when they are established, we can begin to "possess the land" by filling in the positive content of behavioral style and attitude that are appropriate to this country.

Either model enables us to see the complementary nature of the Decalogue's commands when they are negative or external and those of the Sermon on the Mount when they are positive or interior — and to perceive the continuing significance of the former in relation to the latter. The building always needs the lower courses of bricks as well as the superstructure; the land needs frontiers as well as policies for internal development. In John Jesus is not interested in internal attitudes *rather than* external actions, but in both: It is he who tells someone not to commit adultery again (John 8:11).

In handling individual aspects of the Torah Jesus raises questions about the whole, though he does not make these questions explicit. Paul takes up the systematic question, declaring the end of circumcision, sabbath, and food regulations. He had once found all the treasures of wisdom and knowledge in the Torah, but now he discovers that these reside actually in Christ (Col 2:3). All that the Torah could give him seems mere rubbish once Christ has taken hold of him (Phil 3:4-11).

Paul's attitude to the law has been described as "the most intricate doctrinal issue in his theology."[37] To understand it we need to distinguish between obedience to the Torah as essential to salvation or membership in

---

36. Käsemann, "The Canon of the NT and the Unity of the Church" 100-3.

37. Schoeps, *Paul* 168; cf. Cranfield, "St Paul and the Law" 44. Westerholm's *Israel's Law and the Church's Faith* surveys recent discussion.

Israel, obedience to the Torah as an expression of Christian discipleship, and utilization of the Torah as a theological resource. For each there is some distinction between Paul's attitude to the moral and the ritual side to the Torah, though the distinction is not formalized, as it later was.

Paul takes for granted what the Torah has to say in the moral sphere and believes that the gospel establishes rather than subverts that (e.g., Rom 13:8-10). Yet he refuses to let the Torah as such retain the religious significance it once had (e.g., Gal 5:3). It cannot bring anyone salvation; indeed, it was never intended to, because the example of Abraham shows that salvation comes from faith in God's promise. Christians do fulfill the moral concerns of the Torah, but not because they are actually aiming to do that. While Paul occasionally notes warrant in the Torah for action he commends (e.g., 1 Cor 9:8-9[!]; 14:34[!]; Eph 6:1-3 [if Pauline!]), he does not generally base his moral teaching on this foundation but on the nature of the gospel, the guidance of the Spirit, and the practice of the churches. As regards what the Torah has to say in the ritual sphere, he takes for granted its theological value (e.g., Rom 3:25) but refuses equally radically to let it still be normative for behavior (e.g., Gal 2:11-14; 4:10; 5:2-3). He is nevertheless willing for Jewish believers themselves to continue to maintain distinctive Jewish practices as long as by wanting to impose them on others they do not imply that they believe them to be essential to salvation.

7

Handling the Variety
of Levels in Scripture

As a collection of authoritative canons scripture is intended to shape the life of the believing community and the life of the world. To describe scripture itself as a canon or rule is to imply that it is the standard by which we measure how straight other things are. "It is written" determines a question and decides an issue. I do not apply a rule to scripture; it *is* the rule. The notion of canon thus links with the hermeneutical, consensual approaches to interpretation adopted by Barth, Gadamer, Stuhlmacher, or Childs. "Scriptural exegesis rests on the assumption that the message that Scripture has to give us, even its apparently most debatable and least assimilable parts, is in all circumstances truer and more important than the best and the most necessary things that we ourselves have said or can say."[1] It presupposes a fundamental trust in the tradition on the basis of its having been granted a status rather like that of the classic, the work that has filtered out bad influences so that subsequent generations can *reasonably* submit their finite judgment to it; the two Testaments are a repository of the communities' most valuable traditions, those that have demonstrated their truthfulness over time. It adopts the working hypothesis that the Bible results from the best theological "science" or critical reflection to come out of the biblical period and thus respects its content as a whole rather than reckoning that we will wish to do the evaluative work for ourselves on the basis of the beliefs of the age in which we live and the views of the believing community in our age.[2]

---

1. Barth, *Church Dogmatics* I/2, 719.
2. Brett, e.g., *Biblical Criticism in Crisis?* 95-98, 132-34, 143-50. See, e.g., Gadamer,

How do we relate this stance to an awareness of the variety of levels in scripture noted in chapter 6?

The Canon within the Canon

In noting variety in the levels of demand in scripture we have been considering some of the phenomena that have generated discussion of a "canon within the canon." This discussion has been the subject of a vigorous but confusing debate.[3]

The inner canon may be identified with a particular book or section of material such as Exodus or Romans or Jesus' parables, or with the "New" Testament over against the "Old," or with the books that were the earliest to gain uncontroversial recognition in the canonical process, or with a key theme such as liberation or the reign of God or justification, or with an underlying dynamic such as a commitment to equality and compassion, or with an external referent such as Jesus himself, or with the earliest apostolic witness, or with the gospel itself. This inner canon may function as the real locus of normative authority, or as the locus of deepest insight, or as the aspect of the canon that is directly binding, or as the center and focus of the formal canon and thus the key to its interpretation, or as the part or aspect of the formal canon that is especially important to a particular community. In a number of these connections the idea of a canon within the canon may thus be a valid and helpful one.

Sometimes a clue from outside the canon may enable us to perceive something of importance in the canon itself, or to perceive relative priorities in the canon. It may thus help us to interpret and to allow the canon as a whole to be canonical. The study of Romans in the context of awareness of individual guilt in the late Middle Ages and the study of Exodus in the context of Latin American oppression are standard examples.[4] The relativity of such judgments is illustrated by contrasts one can make with Luther's dismissal of Esther and James in favor of Romans. Since the Holocaust,

---

Truth and Method 266-68; Stuhlmacher, *Historical Criticism and Theological Interpretation of Scripture* 83-91.

3. See further my *Theological Diversity and the Authority of the OT* 122-27.

4. In his introduction to Romans Calvin says, "if we have gained a true understanding of this Epistle, we have an open door to all the most profound treasures of Scripture" (*The Epistles of Paul the Apostle to the Romans and to the Thessalonians* 5).

Esther has moved for Jews from the periphery to the center of the canon.[5]
James provides a particularly helpful way into the Second Testament in a
Buddhist context in Thailand,[6] while in the Church of the Lord (Aladura),
a Nigerian independent church, James is the book most commonly
preached on — and in the First Testament Ecclesiastes holds this position.[7]
It is characteristic of literary and musical canons for works to move from
the center to the margins and back again.[8]

Everyone has a "working canon,"[9] but to call scripture itself the canon
is to imply that scripture as a whole is our norm. A canon within the canon
or a clue from outside the canon is not the means by which we decide what
material in the canon itself really is normative. "One ought not to make
the canon within the canon into the canon."[10] The Reformation principle
"the whole of scripture" stands alongside that of "scripture alone." If we
are to make distinctions within scripture, then, these distinctions are not
between normative and nonnormative material. Further, insofar as we measure what is said by what is meant[11] or conclude that some material has
higher status than other material, we do so on the basis of criteria from
within scripture.[12]

The Place of a Hermeneutic of Suspicion

What room does this leave for approaches to interpretation that are suspicious, critical, and evaluative rather than merely empathetic, dialogical,
canonical, consensual, or hermeneutical?[13] Jesus' attitude to the Mosaic
divorce provision implies an awareness that the canon itself is affected by

5. Fackenheim, *The Jewish Bible after the Holocaust* 62.

6. Koyama, *Waterbuffalo Theology* 161-69.

7. Mbiti, *Bible and Theology in African Christianity* 35, 38, following H. W. Turner,
Profile through Preaching (London: Edinburgh, 1965). Mbiti also notes that African
churches preach more on miracles than do Western churches, which are "numbed by a
scientific explanation of the world" (43).

8. Young, *The Art of Performance* 31-32.

9. Tracy, *The Analogical Imagination* 254.

10. Lönning, "*Kanon im Kanon*" 271.

11. Bultmann, "The Problem of a Theological Exegesis of the NT" 241-42.

12. Childs, *OT Theology in a Canonical Context* 11-12; cf. Brett, *Biblical Criticism
in Crisis?* 98.

13. Schüssler Fiorenza, *Bread Not Stone* 39, 97, 108, 133-41. Cf. J. T. Sanders's
approach to normativity in *Ethics in the NT*.

human sin, and in principle this points us to a form of critical interpretation. We need both a hermeneutic of trust and a hermeneutic of suspicion, both "willingness to suspect" and "willingness to listen";[14] retrieval itself may depend on suspicion.[15]

In declaring the need for critical interpretation Habermas describes Gadamer as too conservative in his trust of tradition and insists on the need to take a suspicious stance with regard to the inevitable ideological biases of the individuals and communities who shaped texts as they are. Gadamer does not ask questions about the social constraints that limit people's horizons.[16] Marx, Nietzsche, and Freud, the three "masters of suspicion," have taught us to question whether any statement can be treated at its face value.[17] "There is no innocent interpretation, no innocent interpreter, no innocent text."[18]

In Habermas's words, "language is also a medium of domination and social power. It serves to legitimate relationships of organized force," without being overt in doing so, and is therefore also inherently "ideological."[19] Literature is a product of social praxis and reflects the clash of classes and ideologies. It is a form of ideological praxis that takes sides in the struggle between the rival ideologies at work in societal formation. Recognizing that this is so, interpretation should seek to do justice to the material features of the production of texts.[20] Even the love command may turn out to be "ideological" insofar as it "redounds to the advantage and maintenance of the status quo."[21] Everything is affected by ideology; how can we exempt scripture from that judgment?[22] Critical thinking thus seeks to expose what has been suppressed even there.

Alongside these considerations has to be set the difficulty that neither can we ourselves and our critical thinking be exempted from the judgment that everything is affected by ideology.

Even Marxism, for instance, is a historical phenomenon, a reaction to

14. Ricoeur, *Freud and Philosophy* 27; cf. Thiselton's discussion of Ricoeur in *New Horizons in Hermeneutics* 344-78.

15. West, *Biblical Hermeneutics of Liberation* 29.

16. Bleicher, *Contemporary Hermeneutics* 155-56.

17. So Ricoeur; see his *Freud and Philosophy*, e.g., 33.

18. Tracy, *Plurality and Ambiguity* 79.

19. *On the Logic of the Social Sciences* 172; cf. J. B. Thompson, *Critical Hermeneutics* 82.

20. Füssel, "Materialist Readings of the Bible" 19-20.

21. Segundo, *A Theology for Artisans of a New Humanity* 5:125.

22. Brett, *Biblical Criticism in Crisis?* 95-96, 150-52.

particular circumstances, "dependent upon a social a priori" and "open to error."[23] Marxian insight can expose hidden biases in theology or interpretation, but Marxism itself is not an absolute. Its effectiveness in subverting certain ideologies in certain circumstances does not make it incapable of functioning ideologically in other circumstances or at other points.[24] Is liberation theology, then, able to be self-critical or does it inevitably subvert that possibility by an unequivocal affirmation of Marxian theory and the priority of praxis? A parallel question arises with regard to feminist interpretation, for even feminist theology needs self-criticism if it is to avoid self-deception and ideology.[25] For women as for men "so-called immediate consciousness is first of all 'false consciousness.' "[26] Again, Gadamer sees positivistic historicism as naive in failing to allow for its own historicality and in refusing to allow tradition to be the other voice that questions us and reveals our prejudices to us.[27] Thus Anthony Thiselton's repeated question to liberationist and feminist interpretation is whether they embody a sociocritical principle — that is, whether they are capable of generating insight that offers their communities correction, transformation, and enlargement of horizons — or can only function sociopragmatically — that is, systematically filtering out from the text any signal that does anything other than affirm the perspectives and aspirations of their communities and reflect back their existing horizon.[28]

The argument that everything is affected by ideology turns out to resemble the argument that everything is culture-relative — of which, indeed, it is a variant. I cannot be excluded from its judgment, and I need to recognize the inevitability of my ideological bias and seek to identify its particular nature. That which comes to us from the past with the status of "tradition" — material in which other peoples and generations have recognized particular insight — may as such have the capacity to uncover to us our own prejudices, if we are open to that happening;[29] but if we insist on formulating our own critical faith and in the light of that then determine

---

23. From Cone's discussion of the sociology of knowledge, *God of the Oppressed* 44.

24. Kirk, *Liberation Theology* 191-92.

25. Stroup, "Between Echo and Narcissus" 27, 31-32.

26. Ricoeur, *The Conflict of Interpretations* 18; cf. 101, 148-49.

27. See Gadamer, *Truth and Method* 265-73; cf. Brett, *Biblical Criticism in Crisis?* 137-43.

28. See *New Horizons in Hermeneutics* 410-70.

29. Gadamer, *Truth and Method* 245-49.

what actually counts as God's word and what does not, "we circumvent the best that contact with the Scripture yields to us: the hearing, amazement and discovery of that about which we knew nothing."[30]

Scripture has a givenness that enables it to stand over against me and my "story," and it is partly on these grounds that A. Dumas advocates "metatextual" existence, a life lived in dialogue with the biblical texts, rather than the metaphysical existence that dogmatic theology tends to encourage or a metahistorical existence such as that of Marxism.[31] Metatextual existence involves "trying to listen to a God who is other than our aspirations or our energies," and it avoids the risk of putting one's fancies in place of what one might hear. It introduces more, not less, realism into one's politics than an absolutizing of Marxism, because at key points the Bible's insights are more profound.[32] Similarly, G. Fackre argues, while women's experience is of key significance for the correction of distorted reading of the text, "human experience as such — including men's as well as women's . . . is in thrall to our self-serving agendas and cannot as such disclose ultimate truth." It is for that reason that both men and women turn to the scriptural story of God's engagement with human experience, in the conviction that the critical turning points of that engagement lie in the story of Israel and in the Christ event, so that we let these stories shape our thinking, our experience, and our decisions about behavior.[33]

Stanley Fish sees literature as having both a rhetorical aim and a dialectical aim: The former confirms and supports readers and the latter seeks to transform and convert.[34] The Bible as a whole is a dialectical book. It offers both legitimation and confrontation. It reassures hearers of God's involvement with them and provides them with a context of meaning for their experience, and it also challenges them about their commitment to God's purposes. Usually the same texts will contain both elements, as is illustrated by a consideration of Exodus, Isaiah 40–55, the teaching of Jesus, or the Revelation to John. God consistently confronts and encourages both oppressors and oppressed, often by opposite features of the same texts. As a result, any text may offer both true and false comfort to different readers.

30. Bornkamm, *Early Christian Experience* 4.

31. *Political Theology and the Life of the Church* 47-51, 54-55.

32. Dumas, *Political Theology and the Life of the Church* 130; cf. the critiques of Marxism in Kirk's *Liberation Theology* and Miguez Bonino's *Revolutionary Theology Comes of Age.*

33. *Authority* 111-12.

34. *Self-Consuming Artifacts* 1-2.

The psalms of praise, for instance, as texts expressing Israelite convictions over against those of an imperial world, may form a counterrecital, not least in relation to modernity. But as establishment texts they may marginalize and oppress elements within Israel who do not share their experience of God's goodness — elements who find their voice in the protest and questioning in other psalms.[35]

When we find scripture speaking in terms that we find objectionable, that is where we are tempted to locate its ideological element. Actually the challenge we need to hear may lie there if we are to move on from our present limited perspectives. A wise interest in the Bible allows itself to be both encouraged and confronted by the Bible's total message, both by the points to which we feel drawn because they speak to our circumstances and questions and also by other passages that bring other challenges and encouragements. Passages that seem to undermine the commitment we have already made will be those we hear especially attentively in the hope of opening ourselves to constructive criticism. They will not be passages that we seek to subvert by declaring them historically or ideologically conditioned and irrelevant.

Oppressive Christianity in South Africa has long used scripture as the means of its oppression. When "the oppressed take up the tools of the oppressors"[36] and use scripture to feed their own identity and to encourage them to work for their liberation, that is a step in a positive direction, but it does not in a full sense take oppressed or oppressor to that goal. It must be added, however, that such use of scripture by different communities in a context such as South Africa merely to affirm their own positions may only provide a spectacular example of the way scripture is quite normally used in North Atlantic countries simply to affirm and undergird positions. A test whether this is so is to ask when was the last time one changed one's mind (or better, one's behavior) because of something one read in scripture. In general, we all use scripture to confirm rather than to confront, merely to "replicate ourselves."[37] The advantages of immediate contextual fusion with the text are complemented by the corresponding disadvantage that it encourages a premature fusion that assumes that the text is saying what we think or what we think we need. This disadvantage draws attention to the need of a distancing from the text that can make it possible for us to hear

35. See Goldingay, "The Dynamic Cycle of Praise and Prayer in the Psalms"; cf. Brueggemann's comments, *Abiding Astonishment* 47-53.

36. Thiselton, *New Horizons in Hermeneutics* 450.

37. N. Holland, "Transactive Criticism," *Criticism* 18 (1976) 334-52 (see 342).

it in its own right and to be open to ways in which it confronts as well as confirms.[38]

Therefore liberation theology has to ponder the fact that political liberation was not central to Jesus' teaching and activity, in a context when this would have been possible and natural,[39] and that the rest of the Second Testament concentrates more on how Christians can hold on under pressure than on how they can make a revolution. Theology has a habit of swinging from overemphasis on one insight, treating one half-truth as the whole truth, to some opposite overemphasis or half-truth: from other-worldliness to politicization, from passivity to revolution, from rejection of the world to assimilation. Attentiveness to the diversity of scriptural paradigms may aid us in holding the tension between these various poles.[40]

In the Book of Micah as we have it there are traditions expressing a commitment to justice, solidarity, struggle, and vigilance, but they are set in the context of other material that stresses stability, grace, restoration, creation, peace, compassion, and salvation; the former encourage people toward liberation, the latter encourage them to be tolerant of things as they are and to accept their subordinate place in society.[41] Indeed, we can discern interwoven in the First Testament as a whole both a revolutionary Mosaic covenant tradition and a Davidic tradition oriented to the status quo.[42] Even in the Second Temple period the two stances continue. They appear in the Book of Daniel: The stories portray a world in which alien Judeans work with the government rather than against it; their implicit sociology is consensual rather than conflictual. But the stance of the Danielic visions is different: Here believers have to be prepared to stand up to political authorities in a way more reminiscent of the stance taken in Exodus or Amos. Within the Second Testament F. Belo analyzes a parallel tension between a system based on human equality and one that supports sacral and royal power.[43]

Despite their focus on politics, the stories in Daniel have not attracted

---

38. Cf. Thiselton, *New Horizons in Hermeneutics* 530-31, from which I derive the quotation from Holland.

39. Cf. Segundo, *Liberation of Theology* 110-12; Dumas, *Political Theology and the Life of the Church* 42.

40. Cf. Dumas, *Political Theology and the Life of the Church* 13.

41. Mosala, *Biblical Hermeneutics and Black Theology in South Africa* 101-53.

42. See Brueggemann, "Trajectories in OT literature and the Sociology of Ancient Israel"; *idem*, "A Shape for OT Theology."

43. See *A Materialist Reading of the Gospel of Mark*. Cf. earlier Cone, *God of the Oppressed* 81-82.

materialist or liberationist interpreters. Their political stance makes them uncongenial in Latin America: In a seminar on Daniel I was once taken to task by a Latin American participant for colluding with Daniel's own bourgeois political stance. This person approached Daniel with a suspicious hermeneutic rather than a consensual hermeneutic. It is indeed the case that differences within the First Testament, let alone between it and the Second, drive us toward a comparative and critical evaluation of the worlds it sets before us, an evaluation that is facilitated in this case by the framework of Mosaic and Davidic trajectories. The idea of scripture as canon suggests that we should allow it to set the criteria for evaluation by means of such a framework, rather than importing criteria from elsewhere, and it suggests that even our evaluative work should enable us to hear the text as a whole, not to dismiss aspects of it.[44] Latin America may provide interpreters with a better contemporary context for hearing Exodus than the North Atlantic countries do, as its message may address that context with particular appropriateness. But the political context of Europe and North America, with the possibilities and temptations of political involvement on the part of believers there, may provide a good contemporary reading context for Daniel, one in which the message of its stories can be heard with particular profit.[45] The reverse might also be considered, that those stories represent the possibility that Latin America has to be open to and Exodus the possibility that the North Atlantic countries have to face.

The exception that proves the rule regarding Daniel is W. H. Joubert's dissertation on "Power and Responsibility in the Book of Daniel," accepted by the University of South Africa in 1979. It is not strictly or overtly a liberationist study, but the emergence of a thesis on this subject from that context generates a certain frisson. Alongside it may be put the contrasting South African readings of Genesis 4 by Alan Boesak and Itumeleng Mosala. Boesak takes a literary approach, working with the story itself in a way likely to be more compelling in a context such as that of the African Independent Churches. Mosala takes a sociocritical approach, looking beneath the text's surface for the material conditions that generated it and the ideology it serves.[46] The difference between Boesak and Mosala overlaps with C. Boff's

44. I have discussed this issue in *Theological Diversity and the Authority of the OT* 97-133.

45. Cf. my "The Stories in Daniel: A Narrative Politics" 99.

46. See G. West, "Reading 'the Text' and Reading 'behind the Text,'" in *The Bible in Three Dimensions* (ed. Clines, et al.) 299-320, referring to A. Boesak, *Black and Reformed* (Johannesburg: Skotaville, 1984) 148-57, and Mosala, *Biblical Hermeneutics and Black Theology in South Africa*. Cf. West, *Biblical Hermeneutics of Liberation* 42-62.

typology of liberation hermeneutics, which distinguishes a method that looks for straightforward parallels between the biblical story and contemporary history from a method that sees scripture as resulting from a creative reinterpretation of events in relation to its context and looks for a parallel creative reinterpretation of the text in relation to our context.[47]

Another issue is raised by G. H. Wittenberg's alternative sociocritical-liberationist understanding of the Cain and Abel story, which comes to different conclusions from Mosala's.[48] There is inevitably a degree of speculation in liberationist and feminist historical-critical work, as there is in all historical-critical work insofar as it involves looking "behind the text." It is thus easy for the results to be not merely influenced but effectively determined by the starting point. The results then have "pragmatic" value, but it is surely in the interest of those whose cause they are designed to support that they should also have *critical* value. Thus Thiselton critiques Elizabeth Schüssler Fiorenza's feminist historical reconstruction on the grounds that "the selectivity of a small segment of gender-related explanatory hypotheses for historical or textual data erodes claims to offer a genuinely critical rather than pragmatic-orientated enquiry, in which social interest . . . forecloses certain possibilities before they are examined."[49]

Liberation theology in effect canonizes conflict models of social organization and social change with the emphasis on revolution found in such models, rather than consensual models with their valuing of order, as Mosala indicates.[50] People in power have an interest in affirming the latter, the powerless an interest in affirming the former. Scripture contains pointers toward both. It does not assume that the struggle against the bourgeois state is the ultimate question. Thus Gerd Theissen, for instance, looks at early Palestinian Christianity in the light of "a sociological theory of conflict: religious renewal movements develop out of social tensions and attempt to give new impulses for their resolution," while "a sociological theory of integration" is a more appropriate perspective from which to consider the more positive welcome given to the Jesus movement in the Hellenistic world, reflected in the Epistles.[51]

A parallel point could be made in terms of class. Mosala is inclined to

47. See the excerpt from his *Theology and Praxis* (ET Maryknoll, NY: Orbis, 1987) included in *Voices from the Margin* (ed. Sugirtharajah) 9-35.

48. "King Solomon and the Theologians." Cf. the comments in chapter 2 above, pp. 19-20.

49. *New Horizons in Hermeneutics* 447-48.

50. *Biblical Hermeneutics and Black Theology in South Africa* 61-65.

51. Theissen, *Sociology of Early Palestinian Christianity* 114.

view scripture as a whole as a ruling class document from which the top ideological layer needs to be peeled away; in effect in this way he decanonizes the Davidic tradition, as Brueggemann does not.[52] Croatto, too, sees the Bible as by and large put together and structured by a comfortable middle class and ruling class.[53] Analysis of the Book of Proverbs supports the connection with a middle class. It represents a variety of attitudes to wealth and poverty, including views characteristic of ordinary people and of the more well-to-do, though not a radical dissatisfaction with a status quo that tolerates the existence of destitution.[54]

Yet Croatto also observes that the Torah closes with promises unfulfilled and thus reflects the viewpoint of the oppressed.[55] Earlier versions of the story surely went on to relate the people's occupation of the land, and this suggests that even if reinterpretation can obscure the perspective of the oppressed, it can also introduce that perspective. It can render the text more middle class or less so. The Bible is indeed good news for the poor and bad news for the rich, but not exclusively so in relation to either group. While the canonical form of the text can be calculated to reinforce the status quo,[56] it does not always do so. Scripture as a whole has features that affirm and challenge both rich and poor; it is not identified with any one class. The communities that produced the two Testaments included people who identified with the ruling class, the middle class, and the underclass.[57]

Compromises in the Canon

Scripture combines radicalism and realism, vision and practicality. "Any exercise of freedom demands an act of imagination by which certain constraints in reality are transcended." But

> the flight of imagination that is used to transcend limitation, and hence to change and exercise freedom, must be temporary. Having transcended

52. See Brueggemann, "Trajectories" 180; Mosala, *Biblical Hermeneutics and Black Theology in South Africa*, especially 119-21.

53. *Biblical Hermeneutics* 51.

54. Whybray, *Poverty and Wealth in the Book of Proverbs;* cf. *idem,* "Poverty, Wealth, and Point of View in Proverbs."

55. *Biblical Hermeneutics* 62.

56. Gottwald, "Social Matrix and Canonical Shape" 319.

57. See, e.g., R. H. Smith, "Were the Early Christians Middle-Class?"

reality it must then return to it, and submit the dream to the test of actual experience and action. Only in that way can limited creatures explore their opportunities for freedom, limited but real. Never to dream is the path of passive accommodation, but to refuse to turn from dream to reality is equally ineffectual

— and enslaving.[58] We can see how this works out in several connections.

It may be designed to serve Christian mission. In Belo's analysis, just noted, Jesus stands solely for a system based on human equality, but the Second Testament tradition quickly modifies his radicalism. Theissen suggests that the radical Jesus movement failed whereas in the wider Hellenistic world "Jews and Gentiles, Greeks and barbarians, slaves and freemen, men and women, come to form a new unity in Christ" by means of "a more moderate patriarchalism of love" within a community that is more mixed in class, more urban, more integrated into the political structures, and more capable of addressing the world.[59] Such willingness to compromise may aim to avoid giving a wrong impression of Christianity's subversiveness to the non-Christian world, or perhaps more specifically to dissociate the church from the rebelliousness expressed in the Jewish revolts, as well as to protect the church from excesses of enthusiasm within.[60] A parallel in Israel's history might be its narrowing attitudes to sexuality and diet and its suppression of "female power" as the price of the crucial victory of Yahwism over Baalism.[61] The safeguarding of one important principle is allowed to lead to compromise in regard to another.

The objective may be to set the dynamic of the gospel behind the morally enlightened thinking of the day. While Christian preaching may reshape traditional or conventional moral teaching in the light of the Christian experience of God, it also works on the assumption that people's more fundamental problem is not ignorance regarding morality but unwillingness or incapacity to live by what they know.[62] The commands of the First

58. Shaw, *The Cost of Authority* 12-13.

59. *Sociology of Early Palestinian Christianity* 115. Even if Stegemann's critique of Theissen is correct (see his "Vagabond Radicalism in Early Christianity?" in *God of the Lowly* 164-67) the presence of both these strands within the Second Testament is significant.

60. See, e.g., Munro, *Authority in Paul and Peter.*

61. Ogletree, *The Use of the Bible in Christian Ethics* 61. Barr (*Beyond Fundamentalism* 91-95) illustrates this by a comparison of specific statutes in Exodus 21 and in the laws of the Babylonian king Hammurabi.

62. Cf. Malherbe, "Exhortation in First Thessalonians"; cf. more generally Perkins, "NT Ethics" 321-22; and the comments at the beginning of chapter 6 above.

Testament already constituted an Israelite version of the characteristic norms of the ancient Middle East, sometimes informed by particular Israelite concerns such as protection of the vulnerable or features of Israelite faith such as a hope for the future.[63] The Second Testament has a similar relationship with its context. Thus the difference between ethics inside scripture and ethics outside scripture is less than one might have expected, and indeed sometimes the latter are more demanding than the former; what scripture more often offers is a new motivation and energy for fulfilling expectations that all the world knows about, as it encourages people to allow (for example) an Aristotelian ethic to influence the life of the church.[64]

In the Second Testament as well as the First mission and pastoral strategy may thus involve starting where people are as sinners and in their cultural context.[65] The presence of this element of condescension in biblical injunctions and their background in the fact of creation as well as the fact of redemption point to the possibility of applying God's standards to our own real world. They show how God "compromised" in relating to a sinful humanity and a sinful church rather than insisting on a standard it would never reach or abandoning it because it failed to reach that standard. It thus offers us a paradigm for our own application of God's ultimate standards to the situations of sinful humanity that we encounter.

This suggests one aspect of the answer to the question whether commands that are given within the covenant apply outside the covenant people. In principle they can be more generally applicable because they were given to ordinary human beings, even though they were human beings in a special relationship with God. The commands thus reflect the manner of humanity's creation, not merely that of its redemption; their background lies in the nature of human beings as human beings and in their relationship with their creator. For that reason, too, they can be applied outside the people of God as well as inside. Similar considerations suggest that it is not only justifiable to apply the concern for fairness in society that appears in the prophets to an ordinary nation of today, but also quite justifiable to apply to that nation promises about the blessing that can come when a people returns to the ways of God (2 Chr 7:14); indeed the book of Jonah pictures a prophet himself doing this in his own age.

63. Ogletree, *The Use of the Bible in Christian Ethics* 55-57, 69-71.
64. See Schüssler Fiorenza, *Bread Not Stone* 65-92.
65. See further my *Theological Diversity and the Authority of the OT* 153-66.

E. D. Cook has analyzed seven Christian moves in handling passages such as 1 Corinthians 11 and 14 and 1 Timothy 2:

The text does not mean what it appears to say;
it means what it says, but it is wrong;
it means what it says, but it all depends on the context;
it means what it says, but it may mean something different to me;
it means what it says, and it must be obeyed literally;
it means what it says, but what is crucial is the basis it rests on;
it means what it says, but that needs to be put alongside all the other
   things the Bible says on the subject.

Cook sees the last three possibilities as those that actually involve taking scripture seriously. On this basis he suggests that we ask of each passage what theological and moral principles are at stake, what other scriptures need to be considered in setting the particular text in the context of the whole counsel of God, and how can we take seriously what is said by acting on it.[66]

In the light of the diversity of attitudes in scripture it is not surprising that scripture has been used on both sides of debates concerning slavery and concerning the role of women in church and society. W. Swartley has analyzed how this took place in the nineteenth century, while E. Schüssler Fiorenza notes how in the patristic period advocates of women's leadership in the church pointed to Mary Magdalene, Salome, Martha, the women prophets in Israel, the women in Romans 16, and the principle stated in Galatians 3:28 while their opponents pointed to the absence of women from the groups Jesus commissioned and from the Last Supper and passages such as Genesis 2–3, 1 Corinthians 14, the household codes, and 1 Timothy 2.[67] It is tempting for Christians to claim that the gospel has been a force for liberation in the world, but K. Stendahl declares that "slavery in the western world would have been overcome considerably more quickly, had not slavery been part of the landscape in the Holy Book,"[68] while feminist critique sees the whole Bible as androcentric and patriarchal, written largely

---

66. *Are Women People Too?* 16-19.

67. See Swartley, *Slavery, Sabbath, War, and Women;* Schüssler Fiorenza, *In Memory of Her* 53-54; also the comparison of positions in the 1970s in Johnston's "The Role of Women in the Church and Home."

68. "Ancient Scripture in the Modern World," in *Scripture in the Jewish and Christian Traditions* (ed. Greenspahn) 205.

by and about men, marginalizing women, and assuming, accepting, and sometimes advocating the authority and power of men over women.[69]

While scripture countenances and has been used to encourage slave-holding and sexism, it also expresses another vision that has worked in the opposite direction. The dynamic of this process may be considered in the light of the study of legal hermeneutics. Ronald Dworkin has devised a typology of legal hermeneutics that distinguishes between legal judgments that proceed strictly by literal application of precedent, those that take no substantive note of precedent and are based on a vision of a just society, and those that take precedent into account but set its contribution in the context of present convictions regarding a just society. Linell Cady has analyzed feminist biblical hermeneutics by the same grid, though without making it clear how the second and third really differ.[70]

Sandra Schneiders has taken the matter further.[71] She compares the relationship of the United States to the Declaration of Independence with the church's relationship to scripture. Both involve a sense of indebtedness combined with embarrassment. The Declaration of Independence declared that "all men are equal." What its authors meant was that white men west of the Atlantic were equal to white men east of the Atlantic. They did not affirm the equality of white and black, master and slave, immigrant and native American, nor of males and females or adults and children. Yet the society that developed from that Declaration has come to affirm those other equalities, not least under the stimulus of the Declaration. Those other equalities can now be seen to be implicit in the Declaration of Independence — not in the form of its words but in the vision it expressed and let loose. The text's vision subverts its own statements. The texts that in practice encouraged oppressive structures also contributed to the process whereby oppression came to be recognized.[72]

In a parallel way (indeed a linked way) scripture, which assumes sexism, slaveholding, and racism and was used to encourage such practices also expressed and let loose a vision that was capable of issuing in commitment

---

69. See, e.g., Hampson's writings for a powerful statement of feminism's challenge to Christianity ("The Challenge of Feminism to Christianity," in *Theology and Feminism*).

70. "Hermeneutics and Tradition," following R. A. Dworkin, "'Natural' Law Revisited," *University of Florida Law Review* 34 (1982). Tolbert's overlapping analysis (in *The Bible and Feminist Hermeneutics* 122-24) in part answers the last-mentioned point.

71. See her "Feminist Ideology Criticism."

72. Tolbert, *The Bible and Feminist Hermeneutics* 120.

to oppose sexism, slaveholding, and racism. Its text creates a new world.[73] We must not claim that it does so exclusively or invariably or directly or unequivocally, but there is a substantial link between scripture itself and the contemporary vision in whose light scripture is being evaluated. Perhaps the vision could not have been generated without scripture or without the gospel, and perhaps (because of *men*'s hardness of hearts!) scripture or the gospel could have generated it in no other way.

As we look back on the nineteenth century debate on slavery, it is easy for us to see which side perceived the essential implications of scripture. It may be that the same will be true in a decade or two over the parallel debate on the position of women. Might it also be true with regard to aspects of sexual morality? This takes us back to the question of attitudes to homosexuality, which we noted in chapter 6. What theological considerations underlie the biblical material on this subject?

The biblical disapproval of homosexual behavior derives in part from the concern for ritual cleanness, which was abandoned through the coming of Jesus. If the Second Testament continues to reject homosexuality, this might then parallel its approval of slavery: The inherent implications of its theological position have not yet been drawn. Something parallel might be said regarding adultery. One reason for the disapproval of adultery in many cultures is the assumption that a husband owns his wife; adultery is an infringement of his property. Is it the case, then, that biblical disapproval of homosexual behavior and adultery stems chiefly or exclusively from the collocation of "dirt, greed, and sex"?[74]

It may be that one reason for the biblical and modern disapproval of homosexuality is a sense among heterosexuals that there is something distasteful or unclean about homosexuality, and that one reason for the equivalent disapproval of adultery is the assumption that a wife is her husband's property. But there are other theological and ethical reasons for this disapproval that imply that an abandonment of the cleanliness and property perspectives does not mean the approval of homosexuality and adultery. The sexual relationship is designed to embody complementarity and diversity within humanity — the complementarity and diversity that make it possible for men and women together to represent the image of God. It is designed to embody a faithfulness that triumphs over every

73. Ricoeur, "The Hermeneutical Function of Distanciation," in *Hermeneutics and the Human Sciences* 140-42; cf. Schneiders, "Feminist Ideology Criticism" 7.

74. See Countryman, *Dirt, Greed, and Sex.*

obstacle, again representing the nature of God to the world. Neither committed homosexual love nor the abandonment of committed heterosexual love seems able to image the nature of God in the way that humanity was designed to do, and it is this falling short of the human vocation that makes them wrong, whatever the interpretation of the enigmatic biblical texts. It is now customary to apply the principle of condescension to acceptance of divorce and remarriage within the Christian community, and it may follow that it can also be applied to acceptance of committed homosexual love — though acceptance of some acts of adultery may follow close behind!

8

Interpretation as a Feature
of the Canonical Process

The scriptures as we know them are the subject of our interpretive work, but they are also the fruit of interpretive work within the believing communities that passed them on. Once certain stories, imperatives, prophecies, and other material come to be of normative significance for the people of God beyond their original context, such material is not only preserved for new situations but also reinterpreted so as to speak to these new situations. In due course it is collected as whole works, designed to function canonically in the ongoing life of this people on a long-term basis, and this process also involves the reinterpretation of the material. Such works in turn come to form parts of greater wholes, collections with a message of their own. The whole canonical process is an interpretive process.

Canonical Reapplication

The reshaping and development of normative traditions is the focus of "canonical criticism," though that phrase is used in several connections. One aspect of this process is the adaptation of material so that it speaks relevantly to a new context as it spoke relevantly before. The development of the books of the Bible toward the form in which we know them can be studied as a traditio-historical, literary, and redactional process, analogous to the process whereby other literatures developed. But its fuller significance is not appreciated until we have perceived its interpretive and canonical concern.

The process can be seen in the Torah. Its first body of divine commands comes in Exodus 20–24, where it is said that they were put into writing, and to put authoritative commands into writing might seem to make them unalterable. In practice they were open to change as times changed. Deuteronomy portrays God giving in Moab a further set of commands to cover the circumstances of the settlement in Canaan, the monarchy with its temple, the exile, and the returned Judean community. In these commands the Sinaitic commands are reinterpreted and reapplied so that they speak as authoritatively and canonically in the context of life in the Land as they did before. Deuteronomy is an adapted and expanded form of Exodus 20–24, and the Decalogue itself appears in a different form in Deuteronomy 6. A comparison of the Torah and the narrative books, for instance, suggests that the material in Deuteronomy developed over the centuries in response to differing situations as Israel experienced them; portraying the new commands as all given by Moses on the edge of the land is a parabolic way of affirming that they were indeed a reinterpretation of Moses' own teaching. But even if Deuteronomy actually represents Moses' words in the Plains of Moab, they are still a reinterpretation of God's words at Sinai designed to enable them to speak afresh in a new context.

Deuteronomy requires rigorous attentiveness to Yahweh's commands, but it expresses its own faithfulness by articulating those commands in quite new ways, in an exercise of obedient socially aware and concerned imagination.[1] Deuteronomy affirms the immutability of the word of God, which must be obeyed, but it witnesses to a changing word that is not the same as that in previous parts of the Torah — and that is in turn interpreted with further flexibility in Joshua (for example, when Rahab is exempted from the requirement that all Canaanites be killed). It speaks against "an immutable orthodoxy that would petrify the living word of God. . . . The word of the LORD is not static or unchangeable."[2] Even God's authoritarian dogmatism does not have the last word. There is both an absoluteness and a flexibility about God's commands: They can be reinterpreted in the light of new situations. God's promises also have a built-in flexibility and are open to reinterpretation. Joshua 21:41-43 speaks of the kind of fulfillment one might have expected; Joshua 13:1 gives another impression. In general this process of reinterpretation, rethinking, reworking, and reappropriation

---

1. Brueggemann, "Imagination as a Mode of Fidelity."
2. Polzin, Moses and the Deuteronomist 67, 82. See 80, 126-28 for the parallel point about God's promises, which follows.

can be described in terms of the phenomenon of intertextuality or "transposition," whereby a text from one "signifying system" is articulated anew when it passes to another such system.[3]

When prophets repreach the significance of Israel's ancestral traditions, when teachers declare the contemporary significance of old teaching, and when storytellers retell familiar stories, they do so with an innovatory freedom that implies that they have as much authority as the material they take up. In the dialogue between present and past "the present norms the past — judges it, provokes and validates its reformulation — as often as the past norms the present."[4] Yet the development of the tradition is "authorized" by the tradition itself: The tradition both establishes a given that sets circumscribing limits for what can follow it and stimulates creativity and exploration by the potentialities it opens up, leaves open, and necessitates.[5] The tradition exercises its authority by sharing its authority, in the manner in which God does.

On the traditional conservative view the whole pentateuchal story from Genesis to Deuteronomy, as well as the imperatives in the different codes, were written by Moses — though the narrative itself is of anonymous authorship. On the traditional critical view the narrative came into being through the reworking of a series of earlier narratives from several periods. Critical views are currently in some ferment, but there is no doubting that some process of retelling the pentateuchal story went on in Israel, in which (for instance) Genesis 2–3 told the creation story in one context, perhaps that of the monarchy, while Genesis 1 retold it to bring out its significance for people in exile. Chronicles' subsequent retelling of the Samuel-Kings story of the preexilic community further illustrates this process. The story was retold each time not merely for storyteller's and people's delight but to enable it to address and challenge people in a new context.

Within the Book of Isaiah are phrases that have been added to an earlier form of the text to explain a possible obscurity or reapply a passage to a later situation.[6] These notes are often bracketed, emended, or removed by

---

3. Kristeva, *Revolution in Poetic Language* 59-60; cf. Thiselton, *New Horizons in Hermeneutics* 80-81. On intertextuality, see further chapter 10 below, pp. 157-59.

4. D. Brown, "Struggle till Daybreak: On the Nature of Authority in Theology," *Journal of Religion* 65 (1985) 15-32, here 23, referring to the essays in *Tradition and Theology in the OT* (ed. Knight).

5. J. Z. Smith, *Re-Imagining Religion* 52. Cf. Brown, "Struggle till Daybreak" 26.

6. See, e.g., R. E. Clements, *Isaiah 1–39* on passages such as 5:17; 6:13; 7:8, 17, 20; 8:7; 29:10.

modern translations. They reflect a process whereby Israelite theologians clarified within the text of the prophecy its meaning and challenge for a subsequent generation. A number of longer passages in Isaiah 1–39 may reflect more systematic reflection in later contexts than Isaiah's such as the decline and fall of the Assyrian Empire in the seventh century (for example, 10:16-19) and Judah's experience of exile in the sixth with its hope of a full restoration (for example, 30:18, 19-26; 31:6, 7). One significance of Isaiah 40–55 is that it offers an account of the implications for people fifty years in exile of Isaiah's vision of the holy one of Israel and of Jeremiah's experience of being a prophet. Isaiah 56–66 in turn reworks material from chapters 1–39 and 40–55 (not that these sections of the book were in their final form at the time) in a way that involves something nearer actual quotation of and midrash on earlier passages, working out their implications for people living back in Palestine at the beginning of the Second Temple period. Prophecy is thus enabled to speak authoritatively and specifically to a later context. This likely also happens in the deuteronomists' repreaching of the message of Jeremiah that is preserved in the stories and sermons in the Book of Jeremiah and in their less substantial work in other prophetic books.

Daniel is a further repository of the repreaching of earlier traditions, traditions that in many cases are already actual scripture for the author of Daniel. Jeremiah's prophecy that the exile would last seventy years, which is reinterpreted in one way in Zechariah (see 1:12; 7:5; also Hag 1:2; 2:6) and in another way in 2 Chronicles (see 36:21), is reapplied in yet another way in Daniel 9. Jeremiah's unidentified foe coming from the north to overwhelm Judah (e.g., 1:13-15), reinterpreted as a figure belonging to events of the "latter years" in Ezekiel 38–39, becomes a historical figure again in Daniel 11, where the "Gog" pattern is applied to concrete second-century events.[7]

The text of scripture thus manifests the results of Israel's reflection on material that had spoken authoritatively to it. Traditional critical interpreters of scripture are inclined to discard material that does not go back to the text's original speakers or authors, while traditional conservative interpreters are inclined to seek to establish that the entire text as we know it goes back to these figures. Both imply that authenticity and authority lie only in material that goes back to the original speakers or authors; material that is secondary is thereby spurious. Study of the canonical process offers

7. Grech, "Interprophetic Re-Interpretation" 257; see further Goldingay, *Daniel.*

a different perspective on this question. Material that was added to the text over time is just as authentic and authoritative as the first layer of material. It is designed to enable that first layer to continue to exercise canonical authority.[8]

The hermeneutics of canon has its starting point in the instinct to confront the people of God. It is concerned with identity and lifestyle, with who we are and what we do,[9] but it works by declaring that we are not who we are tempted to think we are and that we should act otherwise than we are inclined. This confrontation does not necessarily constitute bad news; scripture may be telling us that the news is better than we dare hope (so, for example, much of Isaiah 40–55). It can thus confront even when it is comforting.

Using canonical texts to answer new questions about identity and lifestyle can formally respect the meaning of those texts but substantially deny it. In Jeremiah's day other prophets spoke in line with traditions in Exodus, Deuteronomy, the Psalms, and Isaiah, but they did not speak the word of Yahweh. The true prophet is one who knows what time it is and is "able to distinguish whether a historical hour stands under the wrath or the love of God."[10] What was true in one context is false in another. The Qumran community applied scripture's words of judgment to outsiders and its words of promise to itself. Jesus reestablished the confrontational stance of scripture and paid the penalty. The Christian community was then open to repeating the Qumran community's move: Words of judgment on Israel became comfort to that community. This continues when (for instance) we identify the false prophets or the Pharisees of the Gospels with groups other than ourselves so as to confirm us in our self-righteousness, or when we identify ourselves with heroes such as Jeremiah or Jesus rather than with their opponents.[11]

Conversely communities that are committed to keeping faithful to the thrust of the original may alter its actual text. One might expect that a canonical text would be unalterable, but there is much evidence that this is not so. J was expanded by P, Exodus 20–24 was reworked in Deuteronomy,

8. J. A. Sanders, *Canon and Community* 38-39.

9. J. A. Sanders, *From Sacred Story to Sacred Text* 17.

10. E. Osswald, *Falsche Prophetie im Alten Testament* (Tübingen: Mohr, 1962) 22, as quoted in Crenshaw, *Prophetic Conflict* 20; cf. Sanders, *From Sacred Story to Sacred Text* 93.

11. See J. A. Sanders, "The Ethic of Election"; "From Isaiah 61 to Luke 4"; *From Sacred Story to Sacred Text* 70-72.

the oracles of the prophets were reinterpreted by the deuteronomists, and Samuel-Kings was rewritten in Chronicles. The text of Jeremiah was abbreviated by the Septuagint translators (or expanded for the Hebrew version that we have), the Qumran Psalter expands on the 150 Psalms, and the Second Testament writers alter the scriptural text as they expound it. At least some of this material was canonical when it was reworked, which indicates that within the biblical period writers do not seem to have inferred that when a work became canonical it became unalterable, or conversely that flexibility over the details of the text imperils its authority. Thus the fact that the Qumran community produced another Torah-like work, the Temple Scroll, that Matthew rewrote Mark, and that Tatian produced a harmony of the Four Gospels does not in itself indicate that the Torah or Mark or the Four Gospels lacked normative authority, or even that they were not strictly canonical — though other considerations may suggest that.

Concern with establishing one correct text of scripture began with the Masoretes and continued with the invention of the printing press. It is now undermined at the popular level by the existence of a multiplicity of translations and at the scholarly level by our awareness of the existence of a multiplicity of varying manuscripts, and this may take us into an atmosphere more like that of the biblical period itself. Further, the production of targums or interpretive translations coexisted with the Masoretic concern for preserving the true text in detail, and in the modern world related conservative circles have produced and appreciated both the *Living Bible* and the *Dramatised Bible,* rewritten versions of the scriptures, and the *New International Version* and the *New American Standard Version,* fairly literal translations with very conservative policies regarding emendation of the text. The evidence thus suggests that conservative and flexible attitudes coexist. Jewish interpretation of scripture insisted on literal interpretation in connection with halakah (questions of behavior) but allowed other methods of interpretation in connection with haggadah (edifying storytelling). We cannot press a theory that a scriptural text is handled conservatively when it is used as an authoritative canon but flexibly when it is used noncontroversially; this does not fit the way Israel's earlier collections of Torah were open to development. Nevertheless, conservative and flexible attitudes coexist, perhaps in part because they fulfill different functions.

If many scriptural writers saw themselves as taking part in the exposition of an already existing normative tradition, that may in large part explain why they produced considerable material in the name of some significant figure such as Moses, David, Solomon, Isaiah, Daniel, Paul, or Peter, a process also evidenced by material outside scripture written in the names of these and other figures such as Enoch, Baruch, Ezra, Philip, and Thomas. The object of such a practice is not to deceive readers into giving works an authority that they would not grant them if they were aware of their origin. It is, rather, to invite readers to receive them as expositions of what these key figures would speak into the present context. Like other exercises in reinterpretation, these works reaffirm in a new context the truths that their eponymous heroes themselves declared in their contexts and that anticipates that of the later readers, or they declare the truths those heroes would affirm if they had lived in the later readers' different context, or they make explicit an interpretation of their heroes' message that now needs clarifying in the light of later conflict or debate.[12]

Forms of Books

We have been studying the development of the books in the First Testament as a hermeneutical process analogous to the process that takes place when we take an ancient word from God and seek to see how it applies today. That development can also be seen as a canonical process in a narrower sense.[13] It was designed to fulfill a function that was not merely interpretive for one new context but regulative for the ongoing life of the people of God. "The heart of the canonical process lay in transmitting and ordering the authoritative tradition in a form that was compatible to function as scripture for a generation that had not participated in the original events of revelation."[14]

As the material developed, individual stories became part of a Story, social conventions became Torah, occasional oracles became part of prophetic scriptures, sayings became part of Wisdom, and prayers and praises became part of a Psalter. Understanding these sections of scripture requires that we take account of their being designed to be canonical writings. The hermeneutical process we have just been considering is clearly historical, and those who have studied it take a consciously historical approach to that

---

12. See Meade, *Pseudonymity and Canon*.

13. So Childs, from whom most of the examples that follow come; see especially his *Introduction to the OT as Scripture*.

14. Childs, *Introduction to the OT as Scripture* 60.

form of canonical criticism. The further stage we are now considering of course also has a historical setting but it is more reticent about that setting in the course of seeking transhistorical significance, and its exponents refuse to see it as another historical-critical approach.[15]

On the traditional critical view, the Torah in its final form, for instance, abbreviates and conflates Israel's earlier accounts of its story. By implication none of these accounts of Israel's origins is now fully normative on its own; the version designed to function canonically is the Torah as we have it.

Isaiah lived in the eighth century BC. The prophecies in Isaiah 40–55 presuppose a setting two centuries later and need to be considered against that background. Yet they are set in the context of the Book of Isaiah as a whole. By implication the prophecies in Isaiah 1–39 and those in Isaiah 40–55, along with the subsequent ones in Isaiah 56–66, which presuppose a later period again, should not be read in isolation from each other; they are not normative on their own. The message of judgment, the message of comfort, and the message to the day of small things have to be brought into relation with each other. One hermeneutical clue to the Book of Isaiah is provided by its drawing attention to a concern with Judah and Jerusalem in a particular historical context in Isaiah 1:1 and by the historical rooted-ness evident in much of the book's material. Another is provided by the way attention is drawn to a concern with Judah and Jerusalem in days to come in 2:1 and by the relative scarcity of concrete historical references in many of the collections of material in the book (none in chs. 24–27 and 56–66). These clues invite the book's hearers to affirm that it was not to be limited in its application to one set of contexts, and indeed has a perspective that embraces the End.

On a smaller scale, the last oracle in Amos, which offers a promise of restoration, sets the book as a whole in a new context, one that declares that punishment, though it turned out to be inevitable, is not God's last word, while allusions to Judah here and elsewhere in prophecy from the northern kingdom invite Judah to read God's words to northern Israel as also having significance for Judeans.[16]

In the Book of Daniel, the visions in chapters 7–12 confirm and eluci-date the vision in chapter 2 in the light of the second-century crisis. But the visionaries conceal themselves because they seek to be merely expositors

15. So J. A. Sanders, e.g., *Canon and Community* xvi, 18, with his reference to Childs, "The Canonical Shape of the Prophetic Literature" 54.
16. Croatto, *Biblical Hermeneutics* 55-56.

of earlier material, and their vision accounts make no explicit reference to their second-century context. They themselves invite us to treat their visions typologically and to refer them beyond their context to further oppressors such as Rome and our own oppressors rather than discarding them as failed prophecy.

Ecclesiastes is characterized by a grim weariness over the possibility of finding meaning in "life under the sun," encapsulated by the gloomy aphorism that brackets the sayings and reflections collected in the book: "Emptiness, emptiness, everything is empty" (1:2; 12:8). Outside this bracket, however, there appear further comments on the book's significance that instruct us on how to read it. It comes from one who can be described as a churchman[17] and as son of David and king in Jerusalem (1:1) — in other words, as one who bears the mantle of Solomon, the patron of true wisdom in Israel. The book does mediate true wisdom. This is explicit in the closing comments (12:9-10), which also affirm that the uncomfortable tone of Ecclesiastes' wisdom does come from the one divine Shepherd (12:11). On the other hand, it goes on, enough is enough with material of this kind (12:12); all these questions do need to be set in the context of the true certainties of the faith (12:13). The heading and postscript provide indicators regarding how to read the book as normative scripture.

The main content of narrative and wisdom books issues from the collective reflection of the Israelite community, which has made these books what they are. We cannot usually trace the moments of that reflection. We may be sure that Genesis 1 comes from the exile, and we may be able to hear it in that context, but we can have much less conviction about the origin of Genesis 2. What Genesis itself offers us is the fruit of Israel's reflection on its origins over the centuries, in a form that now largely conceals the contexts in which Israel did that reflecting and told its stories. The canonical process is "largely inaccessible to historical reconstruction";[18] the effect is to avoid circumscribing people's hearing by means of too much reference to historical particulars. The canonical form of the text is that testimony to God that Israel actually wished to live by and bequeath. The canon consists not in a set of concepts or a set of historical events, as the biblical theology movement implied, but in a set of documents. The object of interpretation is those texts, not earlier forms of them or intentions held

17. The Hebrew title *qōhelet* is related to *qāhāl*, the word for a religious assembly; hence the Greek equivalent *ekklēsiastēs*.

18. Childs, *Introduction to the OT as Scripture* 67.

by their authors in hypothetical contexts. It is not necessarily the case that "the sharper the historical focus, the better the interpretation";[19] the amount of historical detail that might be reckoned relevant to understanding a text is literally infinite (a hermeneutical equivalent to the point made in John 21:25), and increase in historical detail simply does not necessarily mean better understanding.

What we have said about the development of material that in due course found a place in the First Testament is also true of Second Testament material. Its development, too, was a historical process, but writers who worked in history were seeking to achieve something that had a significance not confined to the historical.

We have noted the way the gospel narrative in general and the parables in particular developed to enable stories located in the past context of Jesus' ministry to function canonically in the ongoing life of the church. The kind of change that the canonical process could bring to early Christian letters was of a different kind. Some had their texts modified in order to tone down their specificity — for example, by removal of the specific address (Rom 1:7, 15; Eph 1:1) or by broadening of the address in some other way (1 Cor 1:2).[20] Thus it may not be surprising that intensive efforts to identify the historical context to which Romans is addressed have not proved as fruitful for the letter's interpretation as one might have expected; these studies work against the intention and nature of the work itself. Letters such as 2 Corinthians and Philippians may have come into existence through a process of compilation and redaction; if so, this was part of a canonical process. "The need to preserve the letters as items of correspondence addressed to a particular situation disappears. What is of interest is no longer the fact that Paul wanted to say something to earlier readers, nor what he wanted to say to them in particular, but his letters are now interpreted as an apostolic legacy to the whole Church."[21] This desire may lead to conflation of traditions or materials and may explain unevennesses — which thus need no other, perhaps more forced, explanation.[22]

In the precritical period there was a tendency to treat Paul's letters as timeless doctrinal and ethical expositions; this has been succeeded by a tendency to see them as merely time-conditioned situational statements.

---

19. Childs, "A Response," in Birch, et al., reviews of Childs's *Introduction to the OT as Scripture* 205; cf. Brett, *Biblical Criticism in Crisis?* 100-3.

20. Dahl, "The Particularity of the Pauline Epistles" 266-70.

21. Marxsen, *Introduction to the NT* 67; cf. Childs, *The NT as Canon* 336-37.

22. Brett, *Biblical Criticism in Crisis?* 46.

But they are, rather, documents that looked at contexts in the light of the gospel and were shaped so as to make normative theological statements that would speak to, but also beyond, their particular contexts, and they were preserved in collection(s) that enabled them to fulfill an ongoing normative function.[23]

Deutero-Pauline letters (if there be such) take the process further, extending the Pauline witness in new directions. They are not a way of foisting alien views on Paul in order to give them a spurious authority. They interpret Paul for the circumstances of their time in the life of the church, "since only in this way can the word of the apostle be directive, instructive, and supportive for the new situation."[24] They "indicate how Paul is to be appreciated and understood by the Church,"[25] how to keep living in Pauline faith and hope when (for instance) the appearing of Christ no longer seems to be right around the corner (for example, Ephesians), where there may be some danger of the Pauline stress on faith leading to mere beliefism (see James), or when the church is assailed by novel idiosyncratic views or questionable extensions of Paul's own teaching (see the Pastorals). By their nature these letters conceal their historical contexts, and the effort to derive from them historical information about Paul himself or about their contexts works against their own nature.[26]

A World Council of Churches discussion document once asked: "Does authority attach only to the finished form of the Bible, or does it attach also and equally to sources used by redactors, to earlier forms of the tradition where such can be discovered, to glosses and alterations and to redactional activity?"[27] Scholars who have studied the development of the biblical tradition have sometimes done so in the conviction that every stage in this development is potentially as significant theologically as was the first creative statement of some theme,[28] though one misses criteria beyond our preferences for deciding what is theologically significant material.[29] Childs's

---

23. See, e.g., Childs, *The NT as Canon* 281, 310.

24. Brox, *Die Pastoralbriefe* 68. Cf. Childs, *The NT as Canon* 385; the model of "extending" Paul is Childs's.

25. Muddiman, *The Bible* 80. The Pastorals may be combating the extension of Paul represented by the *Acts of Paul and Thecla*: see MacDonald, *The Legend and the Apostle.*

26. Childs, *The NT as Canon* 385-87.

27. See Barr, et al., "The Authority of the Bible" 145.

28. See Knight in Knight, ed., *Tradition and Theology in the OT* 5; cf. Anderson, "Tradition and Scripture."

29. Brett, *Biblical Criticism in Crisis?* 94-97.

approach presupposes that tracing the development of Israelite and early Christian tradition is a historically significant task, but also that the eventual form of the text as we have it is the one that the believing community has judged to be theologically significant. The older traditions that the community affirmed survive within the text as it exists; those it rejected do not. Likewise by drawing attention to authors and historical contexts or by not doing so the text affirms the significance of the authors' intentions and the importance of reading the text against a specific context, or does not do so. It is for reasons such as these that the particular "freezing" of the biblical tradition represented by the canon is appropriately distinguished from earlier and later stages.[30]

Complexes of Books

In the scriptures themselves the individual books do not appear in isolation but within complexes with varying degrees of interlinking.[31] The Torah and the Prophets, which provide the synagogue with its weekly scriptural lessons, portray the story of Israel from its beginning (indeed from creation) to its apparent end in the exile and the future that hangs over Israel as threat or promise. Von Rad's organization of his *Old Testament Theology* in terms of "the theology of Israel's historical traditions" and "the theology of Israel's prophetic traditions" corresponds broadly to these two, the Torah and the Prophets.

The narrative from Genesis to Kings has magnificent highpoints in the time of Moses and Joshua and that of David and Solomon, but it has an ultimately tragic shape. There are hints that the story remains open to the future — the promise to David still stands and Jehoiachin is released in the

30. See Best, "Scripture, Tradition, and the Canon of the NT" 259-67. Similarly Dunn, while wanting to affirm the significance of various "levels of canonical authority," sees the level of final composition as "the clearest norm both for exegesis and for faith" (*The Living Word* 172).

31. The Hebrew Bible (as used in the synagogue) and the First Testament (as used in Protestant churches) include the same books, but differently arranged. The Hebrew Bible includes the Torah (the Pentateuch), the Former Prophets (Joshua to Kings, without Ruth), the Latter Prophets (Isaiah to Malachi, without Lamentations and Daniel), and the Writings (the remainder). The First Testament includes the narratives from Genesis to Kings (incorporating Ruth) and from Chronicles to Esther, the poetic books (Job, Psalms, Proverbs, Song of Songs, and Ecclesiastes), and the Prophets (Isaiah to Malachi, incorporating Lamentations and Daniel).

work's last frame — and this aspect of the Torah is taken up in some of the Qumran documents and in the Second Testament, which sees the Torah, like the Prophets, as prophecy (Matt 11:13).[32] But in Genesis to Kings the note of hope is muted and the story is a tragedy. It takes us as far as Israel's history can, but that is to its "miscarriage."[33] The prophetic books are different in final cast. The predominantly threatening ministry of individual prophets such as Amos or Isaiah is in due course set in the context of promises of restoration on the other side of disaster. The corpus as a whole has the form of comedy rather than tragedy. The Prophets begin with forebodings of disaster but promise blessing and hope. They recognize that Israel's hope must lie in a new act of God, and they promise this new act.

This understanding presupposes that the books form complexes that include respectively the books from Genesis to Kings and those from Isaiah to Malachi. The distinction between Torah and Prophets associates Joshua to Kings with Isaiah to Malachi. The former provide background for the latter. But this understanding obscures the dynamic of a story that runs continuously from Genesis to Kings. Joshua to Kings has been called "prophetic history," but such a description is likely a rationalization for a division introduced because the importance of Torah in the Second Temple period meant that Deuteronomy was the last book that really mattered. The modern understanding of Joshua to Kings as a deuteronomistic history suggests another form of link with the Prophets, since the prophetic books reached their final form through a deuteronomistic editorial process. The Christian order, which places the Prophets last in the canon, perhaps reflects their extra importance within Christianity.

In the Pentateuch command material is more prominent in the later strata, the deuteronomic and priestly strata, than in the earlier Yahwistic and Elohistic strata (even though P, too, has a story framework). Torah is a quite general word for "teaching" and is capable of referring to a narrative such as that which holds the Pentateuch together. But as time goes on the notion of Torah comes to suggest instruction more than story, and it becomes less clear how far obedience to commands is a response to what God has done and a condition regarding what God may do in the future.[34] The separation of Genesis to Deuteronomy from the books that complete

32. Clements, *OT Theology* 17-18, 149-54.

33. Bultmann, "Prophecy and Fulfillment," ET in *Essays on OT Interpretation* (ed. Westermann) 72.

34. See, e.g., Clements's discussion of Torah, *OT Theology* 104-30.

its story with the occupation of Palestine and the succeeding events also reflects this increasing concentration after the exile on Torah as commands.[35]

The relationship between Torah and Prophets can also be portrayed as one between order and freedom.[36] The former establishes the norms that are vital to identity, and the latter prevents order from becoming institutionalized and fossilized. The Hebrew scriptures as a whole thus canonize diversity and creative tension, letter and spirit. They seek to keep alive both founding events and charismatic impulse without leading either to bureaucratization or sectarianism. The Prophets actually end with an exhortation to observe the Torah of Moses and with a promise of the coming of a final prophetic figure, a new Elijah, to prepare people for the day of Yahweh (Mal 4:4-6), and thus themselves hold together Torah and Prophecy.

Compared with the Torah and the Prophets or Genesis–Kings and Isaiah–Malachi, the third division of the Hebrew Bible has less coherence, and it may be that all that holds it together is that its books are not used in the weekly lectionary of Judaism.[37] By their very nature the Psalms and Lamentations are, in a more explicit sense than other books, "Israel's response" to Yahweh.[38] Job, Ecclesiastes, Daniel, Ezra-Nehemiah, and Chronicles are all attempts to find ways of living through a time when the old faith of Israel may seem to have gone dead. The Writings as a whole are books produced "between the times" and designed for people living between the times.[39] If Genesis to Kings is tragedy and the Prophets comedy, the Writings occupy the interval. They are attempts to keep faith alive when tragedy was all that could be said by way of story, and when the hope expressed in prophecy did not seem to be coming true.

The wisdom books in general are particularly closely linked with non-Israelite works, and they and the other books among the Writings have closer relationships with their postbiblical equivalents: Psalms and Lamentations with other psalmody; Proverbs, Job, and Ecclesiastes with the Wisdom of Solomon and Ecclesiasticus; Esther with Judith; Ezra-Nehemiah

---

35. J. A. Sanders, *Torah and Canon* 53.
36. See Blenkinsopp, *Prophecy and Canon.*
37. Barton, *Oracles of God* 35-95.
38. Von Rad, *OT Theology* 1:355; cf. Jacob, "Principe canonique" 106.
39. Cf. Wolff, *The OT: A Guide to its Writings.* He treats the books under the headings "Past" (Torah/story), "Future" (Prophets), and "Present" (the other books); he includes Chronicles and Ezra-Nehemiah under the first heading.

and Chronicles with 1 Esdras; Daniel with 1 Enoch and other apocalypses. The Writings stand "between text and community" (to adopt D. F. Morgan's title for his book on the interpretation of the Writings): They reflect a hermeneutical dialogue between the accepted canonical text of the Torah and the Prophets and the Second Temple community seeking to live its everyday life with God. They are in more than one sense on the boundary of the Hebrew Bible — though the boundary is an interesting place to be, as Paul Tillich for one has pointed out.[40] They are farther from the dynamic center of the Hebrew Bible and thus provide a plausible way into it for many people. They sit cheek-by-jowl with what lies beyond the boundary — for the distinction between one side of a boundary and the other is characteristically not very marked. It is not surprising if there is some uncertainty regarding which documents belong on which side of the boundary. Morton Smith sees these Second Temple documents as responses to the impingement on Israel of the Gentile world.[41]

The Mishnah and the Tosephta — collections of rabbinical opinions and judgments from the two centuries following AD 70 — make observations regarding the use of the Writings that reflect an awareness of such features.[42] If the Writings are by definition books not read in the course of the regular synagogue lectionary, it will be even clearer that "common writings" may not be read (Tosephta Shabbat 13:1). Observations regarding the use or origin of the Writings suggest awareness that they had more in common with works outside scripture, including an entertaining and secular quality, than did the Torah and the Prophets. The Song of Songs was read at banquets by some Jews (Tosephta Sanhedrin 12:10). Some Jews though Ecclesiastes was intended to embody Solomon's own wisdom (Tosephta Yadaim 2:14). A number of the Writings provided diverting and lively reading to keep the High Priest awake throughout the night before the Day of Atonement (e.g., Mishnah Yoma 1:6-7).

One should not draw too sharply the distinction between the ethos of the Torah, the Prophets, and the Writings. Links between books such as the Pentateuch and Joshua, Deuteronomy and Proverbs, Jonah and Ruth alone forbid that. But there is a set of family resemblances within the three divisions of the canon.

Rabbinic Judaism came to believe that the Torah, as direction for

---

40. See *On the Boundary: An Autobiographical Sketch.*
41. E.g., *Palestinian Parties and Politics That Shaped the OT* 122-23.
42. Beckwith, *The OT Canon* 146-49.

behavior, was the key section of the canon. To judge from their manuscript collection the Qumran community valued the Latter Prophets and Psalms more than the Torah. To judge similarly from quotations in the Second Testament the early Christians, as well as agreeing with that assessment, also reaffirmed the importance of the Torah as story over that of the Torah as direction for behavior. It is commonly thought that the division of the Hebrew scriptures into Torah, Prophets, and Writings corresponds both to the order in which they came to be scripture and to an ordering of their relative authority, but there is little evidence for either of these points. As far as authority is concerned, the Torah was all-important while the remaining books seem to have been on a similar level. Indeed, for Philo, the Second Testament writers, and the Mishnah, the Psalter is the book of greatest significance outside the Torah, except for lectionary purposes.[43] There is a case for viewing the actual arrangement of the canon as conveying no negative value judgments; it is the links between the first and last books, Genesis and Chronicles, making them an arc embracing the whole, that have struck Sarna and Josipovici.[44]

It has been suggested that the question of the ordering of the books in the canon may be artificial until several centuries after Christ, since it was only then that the books came to be collected in a book rather than as scrolls, which as such could not have an "order."[45] Yet the notion of ordering of books is known from earlier times in connection with the listing and shelving of works in libraries.[46] The threefold ordering of the canon was coming into being by early Christian times, and it is striking that there came to be a standard Christian order closing with the Prophets and a standard Jewish order closing with the Writings. Westermann thus sees the Christian order as suggesting a God who acts, a God who speaks, and a human response.[47] All three groups of books provide the Second Testament with interpretive frameworks and have such frameworks brought to them. The Torah is a story now brought to a climax (rather than a code for

---

43. Barton, *Oracles of God* 42-43.

44. N. M. Sarna, "The Authority and Interpretation of Scripture in Jewish Tradition," in *Understanding Scripture* (ed. Thoma and Wyschogrod) 12; Josipovici, *The Book of God* 46-47.

45. Barton, *Oracles of God* 82-91.

46. N. M. Sarna, "The Bible: Canon," *Encyclopaedia Judaica* 4:827-28, referring to Baba Bathra 14b in the Babylonian Talmud (reproduced in Leiman, *The Canonization of Hebrew Scriptures* 52).

47. See, e.g., *The OT and Jesus Christ*.

behavior, as it is in Judaism). The Prophets voice expectation now fulfilled. The Wisdom books open up the possibility of interpreting the significance of Jesus in the context of a wider intellectual world.

There are then some subcollections within the Second Testament. It includes four Gospels, one for each corner of the world. It includes twice seven Pauline letters (if we include Hebrews) and seven Catholic letters, while Muratori's canon notes that both Paul and John write to seven churches. Together these writings thus address the whole church.[48]

Each of these four Gospels is entitled "*The* Gospel according to . . . ," with the implication that there is only one Gospel proclaimed by four different Evangelists. Independent presentations, perhaps rival ones (cf. Luke 1:1), are thus brought into interrelationship. In its original form Mark's Gospel ends at 16:8 in such a way as to address Christian readers who would have known of the appearances of the risen Jesus from the church's preaching. In its final canonical form it possesses a further ending (vv. 9-20) that conforms it more to the other Gospels by providing it with an account of those appearances, mostly adapted from the other three Gospels. Its witness is thus not muted — indeed it adds to the original ending's stress on the disciples' unbelief — but Mark's witness is thereby drawn into harmony with the witness of the other Gospels.[49] Among the Pauline letters, those written to churches appear before those written to individuals, and they appear in approximately descending order of size within these two blocks, as do the Catholic letters within their block.

Some significance can also attach to the order of the blocks of books in the Second Testament. Greek manuscripts usually locate the Catholic letters between Acts and the Pauline letters, perhaps partly because the authors to whom they were attributed were associated with Jesus, partly because they were addressed to Christians in general rather than to specific churches or individuals.[50] The order in English Bibles puts first the first acknowledged and least disputed letters; by putting Romans first, it may imply it has special status, providing a key to interpreting the Epistles as a group.

As we noted at the beginning of this chapter, canon and interpretation are thus shown to be in various ways interrelated concepts. The develop-

---

48. See Metzger, *The Canon of the NT* 306-7; cf. Dahl, "The Particularity of the Pauline Epistles."

49. Childs, *The NT as Canon* 94-95, 152-53.

50. Metzger, *The Canon of the NT* 296.

ment of the material in scripture before the books reached their final form was in part designed to reinterpret it in order to enable it to function canonically. The development that turned this material into the written books we know had a similar function. And the same is true of the shaping of the canon(s) as a whole. The canon offers us not merely canonical content but a canonically instructive process.

PART III

SCRIPTURE AS INSPIRED WORD: INTERPRETING PROPHECY

9

The First Testament Prophets
in the Second Testament

When the prophets assert that they speak Yahweh's word, they thereby declare that this word will come true. When the Second Testament writers refer back to such a word as having been given through the involvement of the Holy Spirit, they thereby declare that it was not of significance merely for the day in which it was given, but also for the subsequent life of the people of God and for the time in which they themselves lived. How does such a word of God come to address people like us who live later still?

When we ask how we are to go about interpreting the words of the prophets in such a way as to enable them to address us today, the opening words of their books provide us with a key hermeneutical pointer. These opening words characteristically combine two features. One is some allusion to the book's human and historical origins: We are told who the prophet was, perhaps something of his family background, what historical period he lived in, and what community his words were given to. We are also told that the material we are to read is "the word of Yahweh" or "the vision" that the prophet saw. What we are to read is both the words of human beings and the vision or word or oracle that Yahweh gave. After these opening words, the books combine ongoing allusions to their historical context with repeated reminders that the prophets function as Yahweh's messengers, those who declare "thus Yahweh says." Their words relate to particular contexts, but the presence of these words in scripture reflects the conviction that their significance transcends that historical context and is relevant beyond it in ways that their human authors could not have envisaged. Their human and historical origin demands that we interpret them

in accordance with their meaning as it would be understood by intellectually and spiritually competent contemporary readers such as God was originally seeking to address by means of these human agents. That they are
God's words opens up the possibility that God might have intended more
by these words than human author or original hearer would have realized.
They may have a "fuller sense" than their authors knew, a "surplus of
meaning" beyond what was originally apparent.[1]

In portraying Jesus, the first three Gospels begin with his historical and
human background and then tell a story that indicates from that beginning
that there is more to him than that. John begins from the divine Word and
then goes on to the incarnation. Either move is possible in understanding
Jesus, and either move is possible in understanding scripture. In each case,
either can lead to people never quite reaching the other perspective. The
key question is not which comes first but whether both occur. We will begin
here from the text as God-given, following an equivalent to John's order,
but without implying that this approach uniquely conveys the text's significance. We have to begin somewhere.

Prophecy in Matthew 1–2

The opening pages of the Second Testament already provide examples of the
way in which its use of the First presupposes that there was more in the text
than its human author would have realized. After its opening genealogical
summary of the First Testament's witnessing tradition, this Gospel begins the
story of Jesus' own life with a five-scene account of his first months. As well
as continuing that witnessing tradition, in two senses this account of Jesus'
beginnings takes up the First Testament's declaration of the inspired word of
God. It proclaims that those effective words have come true, and it interprets
them in the same intuitive spirit (or Spirit) as the one that inspired them. The
Gospel takes a stance like the one that is implicit in 2 Peter 1:16-21, where
Peter speaks as an eyewitness of Jesus' majesty, as a person who was there and
who saw, and also as one who places firm trust in the prophetic word and has
the key to interpreting its Spirit-inspired message.[2]

1. See, e.g., Brown, The Sensus Plenior; "The Sensus Plenior in the Last Ten Years";
"The Problems of the 'Sensus Plenior'"; Ricoeur, "The Hermeneutical Function of Distanciation"; Croatto, Biblical Hermeneutics.
2. On issues raised by the passage's translation and its pseudepigraphical nature,
see Bauckham, Jude, 2 Peter.

Each scene in Matthew's account of Jesus' birth gives a key place to a passage from the Prophets that is said now to find its fulfillment. The verb "fulfill" comes in four of the five paragraphs. Three times it states a particular event's purpose: "All this took place to fulfill" (1:22); "this was to fulfill" (2:15); "that what was spoken . . . might be fulfilled" (2:23). Once it states an event's result: "Then was fulfilled" (2:17). In the remaining paragraph an event takes place "because so it is written . . ." (2:5). Twice God's authorship of the prophecy in question is noted: "What the Lord had spoken by the prophet" (1:22; 2:15). Three times the prophet's own activity is referred to: "It is written by the prophet" (2:5); "what was spoken by the prophet[s]" (2:17, 23).

In the first of these vignettes Joseph is reassured that his fiancée's pregnancy results not from her promiscuity but from the Holy Spirit's activity, which will bring about the birth of someone who will save his people. The point is clinched by a reference to something the Lord said by means of Isaiah concerning a girl who would have a child called "God-with-us" (1:18-25; cf. Isa 7:14). In the second, the place where "the king of the Jews" will be born is discovered to be Bethlehem through priests and scribes referring Herod and the eastern sages to a prophecy in Micah concerning the birth there of a ruler over Israel (2:1-12; cf. Mic 5:2). In the third, the account of the departure of Joseph, Mary, and Jesus to Egypt is brought to a climax by a description of it as a fulfillment of what the Lord had spoken by means of Hosea about a son having been called out of Egypt (2:13-15; cf. Hos 11:1). In the fourth, the story of Herod's massacre of baby boys in Bethlehem is brought to a climax by the event being described as a fulfillment of Jeremiah's words describing Rachel mourning for her children (2:16-18; cf. Jer 31:15).

In the fifth, the account of the family's move back from Egypt beyond Judea to Nazareth is clinched by being the event described as a fulfillment of the statement in the Prophets about one who would be called a Nazarene (2:19-23). The reference here is unclear, as there is no passage in the Prophets that makes quite this point, though three passages may underlie it. Isaiah 11:1 describes a coming ruler as a "branch" growing from the "tree" of Jesse, which was "felled" by the Babylonian capture of Jerusalem; the Hebrew word for "branch" has the same consonants as the word for "Nazarene," so to describe Jesus as a Nazarene could be taken as an unwitting recognition of him as this "Branch-man." Isaiah 52:13–53:12 describes a servant of Yahweh who is despised and rejected by people; Nazareth was a city in the despised and alien far north, Galilee of the Gentiles, the land of darkness

(Matt 4:14-16, actually quoting Isa 9:1-2), and Nazareth in particular was a city proverbially unlikely to produce anything good (John 1:46), so a Nazarene aspiring to be taken seriously would be likely to be despised and rejected by people. And Judges 13:5 describes Samson as a Nazirite to God from birth; the story of events surrounding the birth of Jesus' forerunner also reflects the story of the angel's visit to Samson's mother (see Luke 1:15; also 1:31).

In each of these scenes from the opening months of Jesus' life, then, a key place is taken by a reference to scriptural prophecy, with the implication "You will understand Jesus aright only if you see him as the fulfillment of a purpose of God contemplated and announced centuries before." In particular, if it seems surprising that he should be conceived out of wedlock, born in a small town such as Bethlehem rather than in Jerusalem, hurried off to Egypt as a baby, indirectly responsible for the death of scores of other baby boys, and eventually brought up in unfashionable Nazareth, then consider the fact that all these features of his early years are spoken of by the prophets.

The pattern continues in the very next paragraph of the Gospel with the designation of John the baptizer as "the one spoken of by the prophet Isaiah when he said, 'The voice of one calling in the wilderness...'" (3:3; cf. Isa 40:3). It is a common feature of Second Testament reference to the First.

Matthew's Aims and Methods

The utilization of scriptural prophecy in the Second Testament raises a number of questions. One is the critique of this utilization as mere "proof from prophecy" designed to remove the scandal from the story of Jesus and to win cheap debating points over other Jews.[3] In fact, Matthew's use of prophecy hardly has a primarily apologetic concern. It is of a piece with the Gospel's interest in other aspects of the scriptures. It provides the church with an understanding of Jesus by providing it with an understanding of the Scriptures. The Gospel is not concerned to prove something to unwilling hearers or to explain away something to disciples of shallow faith. It simply presupposes that Jesus is to be understood in the light of scriptural prophecy, of which he is the fulfillment, and seeks to work out the implications

3. So Bultmann, "Prophecy and Fulfillment," in *Essays on OT Interpretation* (ed. C. Westermann) 50-55.

of that conviction. The scriptures are functioning as a resource for early Christian reflection on the significance of Jesus.[4] The Second Testament writers gain from the scriptures not merely evidence for what they know already from their faith in Christ, but greater clarity on what faith in Christ means. If there is a claim implicit in Matthew's use of the First Testament it is that Jesus' significance is established by demonstrating not that he fulfills prophecy that is otherwise unfulfilled but that he alone makes sense of prophecy that is otherwise enigmatic.[5]

A second issue raised by Matthew's use of scriptural prophecy is the nature of the meaning that the Evangelist finds in the text. Second Testament interpretation of prophecy as instanced in Matthew 1–2 takes clear account of the origin of prophecy in God's purpose, but often seems to ignore its human and historical significance. In Hebrews this feature is even more marked: All twenty-nine scriptural quotations there ignore the human author and present God or Christ or the Holy Spirit as speaker of the words in question, except in its allusion to Psalm 8 in 2:6-8, where God is the addressee (and the speaker is "someone"!).[6]

There is some variety in the degree to which Matthew's use of the Prophets stands in tension with the prophetic passages' historical meanings. Micah 5 is future-oriented in its original context and Matthew's use of it is arguably quite in accord with its historical meaning. Exegesis of the passage is not in itself capable of affirming that Jesus specifically is the coming ruler of whom it speaks; Matthew's use of the text goes beyond its statements in the light of faith in Jesus, but not in a way alien to the sense of those statements and no more than would be the case with any other attempt to identify a person Micah refers to. In contrast, Matthew's appeal to Hosea 11 takes the text in a quite different sense from the sense it would have had for Hosea and his hearers. The chapter is a portrayal of God's inner wrestling over whether to deal with Israel in mercy or in judgment. It opens by recalling blessings God had given Israel, beginning with their being "called out of Egypt" at the time of the exodus. Hosea 11:1 is not a prophecy at all, in the sense of a statement about future events that as such could be fulfilled. It is a historical statement.

---

4. So Juel, *Messianic Exegesis;* cf. Gundry, *The Use of the OT in St. Matthew's Gospel,* and Westcott's comments in *Hebrews* 481; contrast Lindars's understanding of their use as *NT Apologetic.*

5. So Barton. See his discussion of the Second Testament's use of prophecy in *Oracles of God* 179-92.

6. Westcott, *Hebrews* 469-95.

Between these two extreme examples of Matthew's use of prophecy are others that are future-oriented but that relate to the fairly immediate future of the prophet's day — as is characteristic of scriptural prophecy and may indeed be the case with Micah 5. Rachel's weeping (Jer 31:15) is the lament she will utter as the people of Judah trudge past her tomb on their way to exile. The voice in the wilderness (Isa 40:3) is one that speaks at the end of the exile, commissioning Yahweh's servants to prepare the road for Yahweh's return to Jerusalem. If "he will be called a Nazarene" refers back to Judges 13, then it, too, takes up a statement that originally referred to a specific imminent event, though if it alludes to Isaiah 11 or 52:13–53:12 it more closely resembles the appeal to Micah 5.

The child to be born of a young girl (Isa 7:14) is a more controversial figure, though this promise, too, seems to refer to an event to take place soon. Even if the traditional translation "virgin" (NIV) rather than RSV's "young girl" is right, this need not imply that the girl in question will still be a virgin when she conceives and gives birth. To say that the Prince of Wales will one day rule Great Britain does not indicate that he will rule as prince; it presupposes that he will rule after he has become king. In a parallel way, if Isaiah 7 refers to a virgin, it likely promises that by the time a girl yet unwed has married and had her first child — within a year, perhaps — the crisis Ahaz so fears will be over, and in her rejoicing at God's deliverance of Israel, she will be able to call her child Immanu-el, "God-is-with-us." Here again the prophecy thus refers to an incident soon to take place within the life of the people.

In most if not all these passages, then, Matthew attributes to prophecies meanings they would not have had for their authors. The theological presupposition that underlies his activity is the one stated in 1 Peter 1:10-12, as well as 2 Peter 1:20-21. Even if the minds of prophets are engaged when they speak and they understand the words they utter, they are not to be expected necessarily to know what their prophecies refer to. As their own testimony makes clear, when they speak it is not because they decide to do so. Their experiences and words are truly human and thus historically rooted, but do not have their origin in human initiative or creativity. They are God-given. The Petrine passages imply that the interpretation of such prophetic experiences and words is also out of the control of the prophets themselves; they are not privileged interpreters of their words. Their words came from God, and God is their only privileged interpreter. Although the meaning that emerges from the context in which they are given would generally be taken as their God-given meaning, this generalization does not always hold. Sometimes another meaning is the God-given meaning. The divine initiative and activity that lie behind the human authors can give their words a meaning beyond the one these authors are aware of.

If the interpretation of a prophecy does not derive from a historical approach to it, then where does it come from? I have assumed above that the NIV points us toward the correct translation of a key observation in 2 Peter 1:20: "no prophecy of Scripture came about by the prophet's own interpretation."[7] But the RSV renders the verse "no prophecy of scripture is a matter of one's own interpretation"; whether or not that translation is correct, it expresses a sentiment the author would have accepted. Second Testament writers would not have seen themselves as generating their own interpretations of scripture. Their interpretations were revealed to them by the Holy Spirit (cf. v. 21), who enabled them to look at the scriptures in the light of their knowledge of Jesus (cf. vv. 16-18). The Qumran documents indicate that Christians were not the only Jews who believed that it was the Spirit of God who inspired the interpreters of scripture as well as the prophets themselves. What Christian faith added to this was the conviction that the Spirit who had impelled the prophets to speak was the Spirit of Christ: One might compare passages such as 1 Corinthians 12:3 that link the Spirit and testimony to Christ. In parallel, 1 Peter 1:10-12 refers to the Spirit of Christ within the prophets predicting the sufferings and glory of Christ; the prophets did not know who or what they were speaking of, but they knew they were speaking for the sake of that future generation in whose time Christ would actually come.

The Second Testament writers' belief that the scriptures came into being through the initiative of the Spirit who is the Spirit of Christ backs up their conviction that passages without overt reference to Christ may refer to him covertly. When 2 Timothy 3:15 declares that the "sacred writings" make known "the wisdom that leads to salvation through faith in Christ Jesus," the last phrase is not included just as a matter of convention: "Although what we call the Old Testament scriptures were able to instruct one for salvation, they will not necessarily do so unless interpreted by faith and with Christ as the clue."[8] The Second Testament's interpretation looks arbitrary when assessed on exclusively historical presuppositions, but less so when this other factor is taken into account. The prophets were God's

---

7. On the passage, see again Bauckham, *Jude, 2 Peter.*

8. A. T. Hanson, *Studies in the Pastoral Epistles* 43, following Barrett, *The Pastoral Epistles.* For what follows, see also Hanson's *Jesus Christ in the OT.*

instruments; God spoke by means of their mouths. Christ is and always has been God's means of acting and speaking in the world, so it was he who spoke through them. It will not be surprising if he meant some things that they would not have understood; he can now reveal what he meant through others who know him.

Matthew's utilization of prophecy in the story of Jesus' beginnings also illustrates the assumption that the way in which the inspired word finds its fulfillment can sometimes be allowed retrospectively to affect the form of the text itself. In the quotation from Micah 5 "insignificant Bethlehem" becomes "by no means insignificant Bethlehem," which was indeed the result of Micah's prophecy being fulfilled. The way the scriptural text comes true influences the way it is now read and quoted. Both among Christian Jews and among other groups such as the authors of the Qumran scrolls, textual work characteristically paid close attention to the text itself in the conviction that one is handling the very word of God. The conviction that one now sees God acting in fulfillment of prophecy enables one to make clearer in the actual form of the words the nature of that fulfillment.

Conscious and Unconscious Meanings

It has often been suggested that some of the surprising ventures in interpretation undertaken by a writer such as Matthew can be understood if we become aware of principles of interpretation with which he worked. Of particular importance on this view is the principle of typology, which we have considered already in chapter 4 and which may be reckoned to underlie a passage such as Matthew 2:15.

Theologically we might indeed say that there is a typological relationship between the experience of Israel and that of Jesus, but the way Matthew 1–2 introduces passages from the First Testament that we have surveyed gives no indication that Matthew himself was working with such principles. Such a reading of his work may resemble Matthew's own reading of the First Testament in that it seems to be reading into the text a concern that is not there, in the light of the concerns of the later reader who (in this case) wants to be sure that Matthew's interpretation reflects some rational criteria. R. B. Hays's observations regarding Paul apply also to Matthew. While Philo does expound scripture in accordance with a systematic method, that of allegory, Paul or Matthew

by contrast offers helter-skelter intuitive readings, unpredictable, ungener-
alizable. . . . He adheres neither to any single exegetical procedure, nor
even to a readily specifiable inventory of procedures. Modern biblical
scholars fascinated by the heuristic power of their own conception of
exegesis as a rule-governed science have frequently sought to retroject such
a conception onto Paul [or Matthew] by ascertaining the methods that he
employed. . . . Paul [or Matthew] did not do his work of interpretation
with such analytic categories in mind; the modern concern for methodological control in interpretation is foreign to him.[9]

A passage in John's Gospel enables us to see presuppositions that more
likely resemble Matthew's at work in a different connection. At a meeting
of the Sanhedrin called to discuss what is to be done about Jesus, Caiaphas
declares that "it is expedient for you that one man should die for the people,
and that the whole nation should not perish" (John 11:50). Jesus must be
killed lest he continue to arouse messianic expectations and ultimately cause
a revolt that the Romans will have to crush violently. But John can see a
hidden meaning in Caiaphas's words: "He did not say this on his own
initiative, but being high priest that year prophesied that Jesus would die
for the nation" (11:51). John knew well, no doubt, that at one level Caiaphas
did speak on his own initiative and knew what his words meant. But John
finds his words remarkably significant when understood in a way Caiaphas
did not intend, and he cannot believe that it is mere chance that as Jesus'
death draws near the high priest, of all people, speaks words that express
what this death will mean for Israel. The significant second meaning of
which these words were capable implied that they must have been uttered
by a divine prompting, of which Caiaphas was unaware.

A similar approach to interpretation could have led people to identify
passages in the First Testament as prophecies of Jesus when this was not
their straightforward meaning. Whatever meaning they had historically, at
certain points they offered remarkable anticipations of aspects of the gospel
story. A writer such as Matthew infers that in that special sense, which
2 Peter points to, these sentences were not uttered on mere human initiative
but by a divine prompting. It was this that gave them a meaning that their
human authors and their first hearers could not have perceived and that
would only emerge in the light of the event they referred to. John can see

9. *Echoes of Scripture in the Letters of Paul* 160; he compares Barr, *Old and New in
Interpretation* 143.

a hidden providence of God in a high priest speaking in a certain way; Matthew can see a hidden providence of God in a prophet speaking words that had both a God-given historical meaning and also a God-given meaning that would emerge through the coming of Christ. It is this latter meaning to which 2 Peter 1:21 refers.

This is not the totality or even the norm of Second Testament interpretation of scripture. Matthew and other writers commonly refer to the First Testament in its literal historical meaning, as is illustrated by the genealogy with which Matthew begins — though this, too, is hardly a criterion with which Matthew himself consciously operates. A further consideration of John's approach to Caiaphas's "prophecy" may help to make the point. John does not imply that there is a double meaning in every human statement, even in every statement by a high priest, even in every statement about the future by a high priest, or even in every statement about the future by this particular high priest in this particular year. He rather presupposes that the significance of Jesus as the Christ makes it possible to perceive when *occasionally* the form of words that a person uses is so striking, looked at in the light of Christ, that the question of a second meaning arises.

The passage in John reflects how this process of interpretation works not forward *from* Caiaphas's words *to* Christ, but vice versa. This is also an important aspect of the Second Testament interpretation of the First. It looks back to the scriptures in the light of what it knows about Jesus and on that basis sometimes finds in them statements so appropriate to the circumstances of the Christ event that it infers that this reference must have been present in them from the beginning, by God's will if not in the awareness of their human authors and thus in their historical meaning. It moves back from some aspect of the Christ event to a passage that turns out to illumine it rather than forward from texts in scripture toward what Jesus must be. This is not to imply that the scriptural text merely confirms what people knew already and contributes nothing to their actual understanding of Christ. The kind of text to which people turn and the kind of meaning they perceive there is determined by what they already know of Jesus and by the questions this raises for them, but it is the scriptural text that helps people provide the actual answers to their questions and thus articulate who Jesus is.

As we have noted, in their philosophy and method of interpretation Matthew and 1 and 2 Peter are one with other Jewish interpretation of scripture of their period. The early Christians shared with the Qumran community in particular a special interest in prophecy and a parallel approach to interpretation of prophecy. God's "mysteries" or "secrets" were revealed to the prophets, but their meaning was hidden from them; it was their own "Just Teacher," the Qumran community believed, to whom that meaning or reference was revealed. The conviction expressed in 1 Peter 1:10-12 that the prophets did not know what they were talking about is paralleled in the Commentary on Habakkuk from Qumran,[10] according to which in Habakkuk 2:1-2 "God told Habakkuk to write down the things that would come upon the last generation, but the consummation of the time he did not make known to him," nor the fact that the one who "can read it running" is the "Just Teacher." The Second Testament interpreters of the First Testament differed from their fellow Jews not so much in their methods of interpretation but in their conviction that Jesus is the hermeneutical key to the Hebrew scriptures.

10. Column 7; cf. Vermes, *The Dead Sea Scrolls in English* 239 ([3]286).

The First Testament Prophets
in the Modern World

Can we reproduce the exegesis of the Second Testament? This question comes from R. N. Longenecker[1] and is phrased with deliberate ambiguity. We might be able to explain how the Second Testament's exegesis of the First works and thus reproduce in that sense, but can we thus reproduce it in the sense of imitating it? Can we use the First Testament in the way that Matthew does?

Traditional Figurative Interpretation

The textual method that Matthew shared with other interpreters within Second Temple Judaism can be paralleled to one degree or another in a variety of Christian writings over the past two millennia. A well-known traditional implementation of it is the understanding of Genesis 3:15 as "the first statement of the gospel." The Genesis passage refers to the conflict between the seed of the snake and the seed of the woman; the former will bruise the latter's heel, the latter bruise the former's head. Since Irenaeus[2] the final phrase has been taken to refer to the crushing of Satan through Jesus, the seed of Mary. Historically considered, there is no reference to

---

1. See his article "Can We Reproduce the Exegesis of the NT?"; also his *Biblical Exegesis in the Apostolic Period.*
2. *Against Heresies* 5.21.1. Luther emphasizes a reference to Jesus rather than Mary (*Lectures on Genesis* 1:184, 191); cf. H. Bornkamm, *Luther and the OT* 101.

Satan in the passage; the idea that the snake stands for the Devil appears first in Wisdom 2:24, and only in the light of that passage (and later of Rev 12:9) is the snake interpreted as anything other than one of "the wild creatures that Yahweh God made" (Gen 3:1). Nor does the "seed" of the woman refer to an individual; it denotes her descendants in general. Nor does the phrase refer to a far future final clash between the two seeds; the passage as a whole refers to the continuing consequences of Adam and Eve's disobedience. Indeed, this context shows how the statement does not offer good news at all; it speaks of an ongoing conflict between humanity and the animal world. But in the fullness of time Jesus, *the* seed — of *the* woman? — *did* bruise *the* snake's head, and Christian interpreters have found a reference to this event in Genesis 3:15.

Another well-known test case appears in Psalm 22. Several phrases from this cry of a person abandoned by God and attacked by enemies are quoted in the Second Testament as "fulfilled" in Jesus. In addition to these, v. 16 declares "a company of evildoers encircle me; they have pierced my hands and feet" (RSV). Since Justin Martyr[3] many Christians have found a reference to Jesus' crucifixion here by means of a nonhistorical approach to interpretation like that of the Second Testament. There is no hint that the author of Psalm 22 saw the cry of lament expressed in this psalm as a messianic prophecy or that other Israelites would have understood it so. The suggestion that it refers to Jesus works back from the Christ event to the text and intuits that the crucifixion must have been in the back of God's mind when a cry of this kind was drawn from some afflicted Israelite.

As is the case with the use of Micah 5 in Matthew 2, this use of Psalm 22 may also illustrate the process whereby working back from the Christ event to the text can affect how the form of the text is read. In v. 16 text and translation are problematic. As the marginal note of the RSV indicates, the Hebrew manuscripts read not "a company of evildoers encircle me; they have pierced my hands and feet" but "a company of evildoers encircle me, like a lion [at] my hands and feet" — a minute difference in Hebrew.[4] The RSV's translation follows the Greek, Syriac, and Latin versions of the psalm. As far as we know, the development of this Christian textual tradition originated after the Second Testament; indeed, the reason the Second Testament does not refer to this tempting text from Psalm 22 may be that it did

---

3. *Dialogue with Trypho* 97-106. Cf. Luther's treatment in *WA* 5:633 (see Bornkamm, *Luther and the OT* 97-98).

4. "Like a lion" is *kā'arî*; "they have pierced" presupposes *kā'arû*.

not know the reading represented by the RSV text but only the less striking reading noted in the RSV's margin.

At least the difference between the Hebrew and these early translations is hardly a coincidence. The Christian textual tradition preserves a reading amenable to a christological interpretation of the verse, while the Jewish textual tradition preserves a reading that is less so. Each could be working back from what they believe or decline to believe about Jesus — either that he is the crucified Messiah and that the scriptural text may be expected to hint at this, or that he is not and it is not. At least one of these forms of the text illustrates how the text's preservation can be influenced by the same factors as the interpretation of the text. The movement can be *from* contemporary beliefs *to* the text as well as vice versa.

While the patristic writers were concerned for the literal sense of scripture, they also developed approaches to interpretation that looked beyond the literal or historical for a range of figurative or metaphorical or allegorical senses in scripture. Three are commonly distinguished. The theological sense, that to which the word "allegorical" most commonly refers, is use of the text to elucidate aspects of the faith itself. The moral or "tropological" sense is application of the text to questions about human behavior. The eschatological or "anagogical" sense is application of the text to questions about the invisible realities of heaven. A standard example is that an allusion to Jerusalem that refers literally to the actual city might also be expected to offer illumination with regard to the church (the theological sense), civil society (the moral sense), and the life of heaven (the eschatological sense). This particular ordering of the senses is suggestive: The theological builds on the historical, the moral on the theological, and the eschatological on the moral.[5]

For an interpreter such as Augustine the importance of allegory lay in its capacity to respect and release scripture's power as God's word. Allegorical interpretation did not add to the truths received from scripture; it worked within the framework of the rule of the faith, understood to be a summary of the teaching of scripture. It "was not merely a cognitive exercise, but an emotional one"; it "kindles ardour, arouses the affections, and strengthens the soul."[6] It begins from the conviction that God is there behind the words but greater than mere words.

5. Louth, *Discerning the Mystery* 116.
6. L. Poland, "The Bible and the Rhetorical Sublime," in *The Bible as Rhetoric* (ed. Warner) 37.

Contemporary Figurative Interpretation:
Allegorical, Devotional, Liberationist,
and Preterist-Millennialist

Allegory has long been intellectually unfashionable. Lynn Poland suggests that our difficulty with it is a by-product of romanticism, under whose influence symbol comes to be the key form of figural language and to eclipse allegory; symbol and allegory "cease to be descriptive terms, and become normative judgements."[7] Even the now fashionable reading of biblical texts within a literary rather than a historical framework can domesticate their religious power, their capacity to provoke a sense of the holy. It assumes that the relationship between God and language is essentially continuous rather than discontinuous. It thereby removes mystery from revelation and replaces it not merely with clarity but with banality. Allegory, in contrast, "is a way of entering the 'margin of silence' that surrounds the articulate message of the Scriptures."[8] Scripture is inherently characterized by depth, complexity, and difficulty — not merely the contingent difficulty of the inevitable occasional obscurity of a text from another culture but the onto-logical difficulty that reflects mystery.[9] Its contingent difficulty can be a parable and allegory a recognition of this ontological difficulty. Allegory helps us acknowledge — but not dissolve — the mystery of Christ.

Parallel considerations underlie some of the variety among English translations of the Bible and some of the passion with which preferences for translations are felt. One reason for the continuing popularity in some circles of the King James/Authorized Version and its revisions (and the continuing advocacy of the *Book of Common Prayer*) is that they now have resonances from their long use in Christian theology and devotion com-parable to the resonances of great medieval cathedrals. They, too, now point toward that margin of silence that surrounds scripture's articulate message. It is to similar effect that the Church of England's *Liturgical Psalter,* which is included in *The Alternative Service Book 1980,* preserves some of the archaic phrases of Coverdale's Psalter: God is still "a very present help in trouble" (Ps 46:1). In contrast, translations such as the Good News Bible and the Jerusalem Bible seek "to use language that is natural, clear, simple, and

---

7. Poland, "The Bible and the Rhetorical Sublime" 30-31; see further 29-47 gener-ally. Poland is following P. de Man, *Blindness and Insight* (New York: OUP, 1971) 188.

8. Louth, *Discerning the Mystery* 96.

9. Cf. Steiner, *On Difficulty* 18-47; cf. Louth, *Discerning the Mystery* 110.

unambiguous" (to quote the 1976 preface to the first of these). They thus remove any possibility of preserving mystery, suggestiveness, complexity, or ambiguity that might be present in the text (as Prickett notes, with an interesting study of the "still, small voice" in 1 Kings 19),[10] let alone pointers toward the margin of silence that some resonances of the older translations offer.

Allegory reappears in modern writing on spirituality. The investigation of the wilderness theme in a work such as Kenneth Leech's *True God* illustrates this by bringing together references to geographical wilderness in the First Testament and "the wilderness period" as holding "a key place in Christian spirituality."[11] It reappears in the commendation of silence on the basis of texts such as "Be still and know that I am God" (Ps 46:10, which was actually concerned to silence rebellious nations attacking Jerusalem). It reappears in modern liturgy, as in the thanksgiving prayer in the *Alternative Service Book*'s baptism liturgy with its manifold celebration of the significance of water in scripture, continuing the manner of liturgical use of scripture that goes back to the patristic writers.[12]

There is a more down-to-earth Christian appropriation of scripture of this kind; indeed most contemporary Christian listening to scripture may have some family resemblance to the Second Testament's use of the First and to the allegorical instinct. It begins from one of the key implications of scripture's identity as the inspired word of God, the assumption, that is, that this text speaks beyond its original context. It expects to hear the text address issues that concern our own day. It discovers how the text does so, perhaps by a method parallel to that of allegory, perhaps by a procedure more like free association that parallels the Second Testament's method. For us such approaches to discovering the meaning of scripture are often denigrated, and they have not been given serious theological reflection. But they seem to be too important and effective to be dismissed or ignored. They also reappear in more modern approaches to experiential Bible Study such as those of Walter Wink.[13]

10. *Words and* The Word 4-36.

11. *True God* 33; see further 27-38, 127-61.

12. See Daniélou, *The Bible and the Liturgy*. The "biblicism" of liturgical texts is criticized by T. G. A. Baker in " 'This Is the Word of the Lord' "; cf. his "NT Scholarship and Liturgical Revision," in *What About the NT?* (ed. Hooker and Hickling) 187-97.

13. See *The Bible in Human Transformation* and *Transforming Bible Study;* though Wink (*Transforming Bible Study* 164 [²164]) criticizes the work of Via and Tolbert as allegorizing (see p. 33 above).

At the end of the summer during which I first drafted the material in this chapter, the issues were in my mind as I prepared to preach at the beginning of the new year in the theological college where I teach. I spoke in that sermon about the possibility of letting God's word show its capacity for speaking today and its effectiveness in our lives. I invited people to spend half an hour each day considering the scriptures we read together in chapel and to keep a notebook in which they recorded what God said to them through these scriptures. Having made the suggestion, I then had to put it into practice myself. It happened that the winter that followed was an extraordinarily difficult one for me in my personal life and one during which I myself had to prove what truth there was in the affirmations I had made about scripture at the beginning of the year. Again and again I found that some aspect of one of the daily readings addressed the particular despair or temptation or challenge or darkness that overwhelmed me in different weeks and that it spurred me on or drew me out. In my notebook I collected pages and pages of evidence that scripture had the power and the relevance that I had spoken and written of before the year started. Some of the encouragements I received from scripture could be easily justified by literal exegesis of the text, but others could not. When that dark period in my life passed, so did that particular experience of finding scripture speaking to me directly each day. But in principle there is nothing unusual about such experience; it has been Christians' common experience with scripture when they were not writing essays or books. But we have lacked a place for it in our discussion of biblical interpretation.

One modern way of approaching figurative interpretation considers it in the light of literary study of intertextuality, the way in which all texts depend on each other so that poems, in particular, gain a significant proportion of their insight and power by taking up motifs from earlier poems. T. S Eliot argued that "not only the best, but the most individual parts of [a poet's] work may be those in which the dead poets, his ancestors, assert their immortality most vigorously";[14] he was aware that *The Waste Land* illustrates the point well. It is not merely that writers use their predecessors' works to support or express points that they have independently formulated. Echoes of and allusions to earlier works reflect the way that these works have influenced the actual content of the later work. They have stimulated thought and generated insight that went beyond what their

---

14. *Selected Essays* 14 (American ed., 4); cf. Hays, *Echoes of Scripture in the Letters of Paul* 16.

authors saw or intended but that was not reached without their stimulus and help. There is thus both continuity and discontinuity between the earlier works and the later one, both dependence and independent creativity in the latter. Indeed, George Steiner argues, new art is the best criticism or interpretation of the old.[15]

R. B. Hays sees such a relationship between the First Testament and Paul's writings. When Paul declares in the context of his imprisonment and consequent preaching that "this will turn out for my deliverance" (Phil 1:19) he follows the exact wording of Job 13:16. That suggests a number of resonances in the general context of Job 13 and invites us to see Paul as a Job-like righteous sufferer troubled by his "friends" but looking for a favorable outcome of his afflictions, though also then to see differences between Job and Paul. Hays describes Paul's intertextual use of the First Testament, his allowing scripture to echo allusively and evocatively in his text in such a way as to suggest patterns of meaning wider than his own interpretive claims, as the most interesting feature of his approach to interpretation. The point Paul illustrates is that

> despite all the careful hedges that we plant around texts, meaning has a way of leaping over, like sparks. Texts are not inert; they burn and throw fragments of flame on their rising heat. Often we succeed in containing the energy, but sometimes the sparks escape and kindle new blazes, reprises of the original fire.[16]

Paul does also practice a more explicitly text-based approach that more resembles that of Matthew, which we have considered — though Paul is concerned to use scripture to throw light on what the church is rather than on who Christ is, as a consequence of the fact that he is writing pastoral letters to deal with issues in the life of the church. In Romans 10:5-10, what Paul does is "read the text of Deuteronomy 30 as a *metaphor* for Christian proclamation"; Hays describes Paul's reading of Habakkuk 2 and Hosea 1–2 in similar terms. "What he does is use Christian experience in the church as a hermeneutical paradigm for reading Scripture, from which he is then able to draw material for the guidance of his community." This move is implicitly justified by the fact — on the assumption that it is a fact —

---

15. See *Real Presences* 11-21.

16. *Echoes of Scripture in the Letters of Paul* 21-23, 155, 33. On the links and contrasts between premodern and postmodern interpretation, see Thiselton, *New Horizons in Hermeneutics* 142-78.

that what God has done in Christ in reaching out to the Gentiles is indeed the fulfillment of the purpose announced in Abraham.[17]

The figurative approaches we have been considering also parallel the approach of liberationist interpretation.[18] *Liberating Exegesis* by Christopher Rowland and Mark Corner offers a series of examples of Latin American Christian experience with scripture. The parable about the vineyard workers (Matt 20:1-16), for instance, highlights the vulnerability of the workers when they lose solidarity and turn against each other instead of standing together against their exploiters, and it speaks along these lines to victims of injustice in contemporary British or American society.[19] Such interpretation may ignore the historical significance of the parable for Jesus and his hearers, but it emerges from a direct, positive, and fruitful interaction between Christian experience and the text of scripture. We have noted in chapter 3 that it is a way of seeing scripture's significance for us rather than a method of exegesis; like allegory it is concerned to release scripture's power as God's word.

Another approach, one that is quite different and that has had a place in interpretation of prophecy for over two thousand years, sees prophecies in books such as Ezekiel or Daniel as referring to events of the interpreter's own day or of decades still to come. It appears in modern books such as Hal Lindsey's *The Late Great Planet Earth,* according to which Ezekiel 38:14-16, for instance, "describes" the following attack on modern Israel: "When the Russians invade the Middle East with amphibious and mechanized land forces, they will make a 'blitzkrieg' type of offensive through the area." In the verses that follow, "Ezekiel sounded the fatal collapse of the Red Army." At the opening of chapter 39, "the description of torrents of fire and brimstone raining down upon the Red Army, coupled with the unprecedented shaking of the land of Israel could well be describing the use of tactical nuclear weapons."[20]

These chapters of Ezekiel could not do this if they were an exercise in

17. *Echoes of Scripture in the Letters of Paul* 84, 162, 82, 104; see also, e.g., 117-18 (on Galatians 4), 140 (on 2 Corinthians 3), and 165 (on 1 Corinthians 9).

18. C. Mesters, "How the Bible Is Interpreted in Some Basic Christian Communities in Brazil," in *Conflicting Ways of Interpreting the Bible* (ed. Küng and Moltmann) 42, with his examples; cf. Rowland and Corner, *Liberating Exegesis* 39.

19. Cf. L. Schottroff, "Human Solidarity and the Goodness of God," in *God of the Lowly* (ed. Schottroff and Stegemann) 129-47; cf. Rowland and Corner, *Liberating Exegesis* 19-26.

20. *The Late Great Planet Earth* 157, 160, 161.

communication between God and Israel through a prophet in the time of the exile or soon after, but we have acknowledged that Second Testament writers sometimes ignore this meaning. The question is, then, does reinterpretation in terms of current events in the Middle East carry conviction for us today in the way that the Second Testament writers' reinterpretation did for the early church, with the result that their work came to be recognized as scripture alongside those earlier words?

The Characteristics of Figurative Approaches

A number of features that appear or questions that arise are common to these figurative approaches to interpretation — Jewish, early Christian, traditional allegorical, devotional, intertextual, liberationist, and preterist-millennialist approaches that accidentally or deliberately bypass what the text would have meant to its human author.

First, allegory has often been a means of avoiding the literal sense of a passage when this caused difficulties or raised objections. For Origen, these were often historical difficulties or moral difficulties. C. S. Lewis provides a modern example of the allegorizing of a theological or moral difficulty when he relates the enemies in the Psalms to the wickedness within us that we must oppose; he is reviving an interpretation of Origen's.[21] But the essence of figurative interpretation is not merely to enable us to cope with aspects of a text that we do not like. It is nearer to being a way of enabling us to discover something from a text that would otherwise be mute. Barr sees theological interpretation of scripture as characteristically allegorical in this sense.[22] Allegory may make it possible to handle difficult texts; more fundamentally it makes it possible to hear something that speaks to us from texts that may not otherwise do so.

Second, the correctness of figurative interpretations is difficult to evaluate. On the assumptions of the Second Testament's interpretation of the First — and in the case of Psalm 22:16, the Second Testament's interpretation of this Psalm in particular — it is entirely plausible to take the passage as referring to Jesus, but there is no way of moving from acknowledging this as a possibility to affirming that the interpretation is probable or

21. *Reflections on the Psalms* 136 (Fontana ed., 113-14); cf. Origen, *Against Celsus* 7.22.

22. "The Literal, the Allegorical, and Modern Biblical Scholarship."

compelling. We cannot establish what was in the back of God's mind at a given moment unless God reveals it; any true interpretation of this kind comes as the gift of the Spirit who inspired scripture. Purported instances of such Spirit-given interpretation involve us in difficulties like those that come with other forms of inspired utterance. Such claims are difficult to test, sometimes possible to disprove, always impossible to prove. Acceptance of Matthew as Second Testament scripture may carry with it an acceptance of his intuitions about the interpretation of particular passages in the First; there is no parallel way by which our own intuitions regarding interpretation can carry the same conviction. "Discovering" new meanings in a passage of scripture in the light of other passages of scripture is thus encouraged by the Second Testament and is certainly difficult to prohibit, but it is as difficult to evaluate.

The object and the effect of the christological interpretation of Psalm 22:16 may be to facilitate Christian devotion to Jesus, the one who was treated in the way the psalm describes. If this is its function, then proving that he was the person originally spoken of or speaking in the psalm may be beside the point. I have the impression that the christological interpretation is believed in some way to generate or reinforce faith by means of the wonder that the event of the crucifixion was anticipated in the psalm. If this is so, it is more of a problem that we can hardly prove that this is the correct interpretation of the psalm — prove it, that is, in a way that is convincing outside the context of faith. Further, such appeal to the First Testament falls afoul of Bultmann's criticism of the proof from prophecy (noted in chapter 9): Faith that requires such props may not be true faith.

When interpreters such as those who take a preterist or millennialist approach interpret scripture as prophecy of events of their own day or of coming events, they often emphasize that they are taking the relevant passages of scripture literally and commend this as a reason for accepting their interpretation. In practice, they are only selectively literal, especially in interpreting prophecy: A literal interpretation of the thousand-year reign of Christ but not a literal interpretation of every feature of Revelation. In applying Ezekiel 38:14-16 to a prospective Russian attack on Israel, Lindsey takes the allusion to a mighty army coming from the north literally, but makes no reference to that army being mounted on horses.[23] This approach to prophecy characteristically appeals to a passage's particular close correspondences to some modern situation but makes no comment on other

23. See *The Late Great Planet Earth* 157.

elements of the prophecy or on other aspects of the modern situation that the prophecy does not hint at. Therefore, the links between the text and the modern event tend to look less impressive when examined closely. People who stress literal interpretation of prophecy rarely understand the Song of Songs literally or fail to find Christ in the Psalms.[24] Of course such literal interpreters do not see themselves as literalist interpreters. They allow that the intrinsically figurative must be interpreted figuratively. But their judgment on what is figurative and what is literal seems actually to be arbitrary.

In any case, of course, the mere fact that there is some match between an interpretation of prophecy and the modern events it is said to refer to (or predict) is not enough to make us accept it. The words of false prophets can come true (see Deuteronomy 13). We need to test the interpretation by some other criteria. F. W. Farrar notes how "You have put all things under his feet" (Ps 8:6) was applied to the authority of the pope and "Gather the weeds to be burned" (Matt 13:30) was applied to the methods of the Inquisition.[25] Figurative interpretation can be used to many ends.

A third feature of figurative approaches is significant in this connection. Traditionally they implicitly work within the positive constraint of the rule of the faith, the framework of orthodox doctrine, ethics, and spirituality with Christ at its center that is believed to underlie or to emerge from scripture as a whole. They presuppose the framework of what is stated directly in other passages of scripture, being committed to allowing scripture to be its own interpreter and avoiding the kind of interpretation that Satan adopted in testing Jesus (Matt 4:1-11).

Preterist interpretation is again in difficulty here. In general it seems to fail one implicit test that the Second Testament writers passed in order to be so recognized. Those writers began from the Christ event and interpreted the First Testament in the light of it; their interpretation receives part of its justification from its faithfulness to God's speaking in the Son. Preterist interpretation reinterprets the First Testament in the light of the newspaper and then builds novel teaching on an unacknowledged figurative approach to the text.

We may grant that God could have spoken through the prophets about events that would not take place until the twentieth century AD. The question is whether God would have done so, whether that is the kind of thing

24. Sandeen, *The Roots of Fundamentalism* 109.
25. *History of Interpretation* 297-98; cf. Thiselton, *The Two Horizons* 316.

that the God of the Bible does, and whether God did do so, whether this is the kind of prophecy that appears in the First Testament. To both questions the answer seems to be negative. The God of the Bible is not inclined to reveal dates, as remarks of Jesus make especially clear (see Mark 13:32-37; Acts 1:7). When God makes statements about the future, they are not so much detailed outlines of history to come, a history predetermined to unfold like the schedule of games on a sports calendar that we can tick off one by one as they take place. They are promises, warnings, and challenges designed to call people to decision in the present. The God of the Bible does not generally help along this decision and bolster people's faith by revealing to them exactly what is to come. Any "signs" that Jesus does offer (Luke 21:25) are of a rather general kind; he is more inclined to warn his disciples about their curiosity concerning "signs" and to remind them that they do not know when the time will come (Mark 13:4, 22). They are called to a trusting faith and hope that can face an unknown future confident that they are safe in God's hands. God explicitly denied that Ezekiel's prophecies concerned some far-off day (Ezekiel 12:26-28). They were warnings and promises for those to whom they were given, immediately relevant to their present and demanding a response from them.

God does sometimes grant special revelations to people who cannot believe without them, and we cannot exclude the possibility that the prophets received such revelations. But Jesus declared God's blessing on those who believe without that kind of experience (John 20:29), and this is how God usually deals with people. This suggests that we should assume that the prophets do not contain such revelations unless there is evidence in a particular case that they are there revealing the future in an exceptional way, perhaps because of some specific need that God is condescending to. It is not obvious that this is the case with prophets such as Ezekiel and Daniel.

The rule of the faith thus works against preterist and millennialist interpretation. It presupposes a dubious understanding of God, a dubious understanding of morality, and a dubious sidestepping of Jesus.

In a similar way, the formal parallel between the hermeneutical approach of liberation theologians and that of the Second Testament or the Fathers does not establish the validity of the former.[26] Its validity depends

---

26. Against C. Boff, *Theology and Praxis* (ET Maryknoll, NY: Orbis, 1987), as quoted by Rowland and Corner, *Liberating Exegesis* 61-62. Cf. Croatto, *Biblical Hermeneutics* 3-5.

also on there being some more substantial link between the two. In fact, as Rowland and Corner note, the hermeneutic is different; liberation exegesis has a novel starting point, the "preferential option for the poor." Where devotional or experiential interpretation is individualistic or pietistic or both, liberation interpretation is corporate and this-worldly.[27] The parallels between early Jewish, early Christian, patristic, devotional, millennialist, and liberationist interpretation do not somehow prove the validity of the last, as Rowland and Corner seem to imply; they rather make it important to analyze the differences between the convictions in whose light different groups use similar methods.

Fourth, figurative interpretation is not a way of bringing a predetermined meaning to the text; the content of the interpretation is determined by the text itself.

> Paul finds in Scripture language and images that allow him to give expression to his kerygma. In reactivating these images, he necessarily (and sometimes artfully) twists them in such a way that new significations arise out of the interplay between the old and the new. Gospel interprets Scripture; Scripture interprets gospel.[28]

On the other hand, figurative interpretation does take its angle of approach from outside the text, which does not have an opportunity to correct it. The problem with much figurative interpretation is then not what it discovers in scripture but what it fails to discover. The rule of the faith (as fallibly understood within the church) is both the text's protection and its limitation. Conversely, figurative interpretation may now seem to have less point than it had in Second Testament times. By definition the new meaning we are discovering is already explicit in some other passage. It is on the basis of the fact that the Second Testament tells us that Jesus was crucified that we discover a reference to this in Psalm 22. But since we now have the Second Testament to tell us directly about Christ, we can allow the First Testament to press its own explicit agenda on us rather than risk that giving way to an agenda determined by later considerations.

Louth rightly notes that fear of allegory accompanies commitment to the view that scripture is "the objective truth of God's revelation"; it reads "tradition from the perspective of the letter of the scriptures."[29] But if (as

---

27. See Rowland and Corner, *Liberating Exegesis* 43; cf. 14.
28. Hays, *Echoes of Scripture in the Letters of Paul* 160.
29. *Discerning the Mystery* 98, 96.

he grants later)[30] "the heart of Christianity is the mystery of Christ, and the Scriptures are important as they unfold to us that mystery," then objective historical interpretation of the scriptures is important because Christ is a historical person. The way tradition has interpreted scripture or Christ may well aid me in hearing them aright, but it may sometimes obscure them. Allegorical approaches enable me to perceive aspects of the truth that the church has already seen or that my context already presses on me. Historical approaches may help me see quite new things. In a parallel way liberationist approaches enable us to gain insights from within the preferential option for the poor, but they do not enable us to broaden out from that principle. The universal significance of a parable[31] is compelled to work within certain parameters — apparently different parameters from those with which Jesus was working when he told the parable. If I am to see who is the priest, the Levite, and the good Samaritan in a contemporary society, I need to know who they were then.

Fifth, whether figurative interpretation "works" is a matter of taste. A preacher given the opportunity to preach on the passage about Christians being strangers and pilgrims (1 Pet 2:11) found that the modern translations abandon the rendering "pilgrims," so he declared his intention to ignore them and work from the rendering that he found more suggestive, and he preached an edifying, helpful sermon. Another preacher took as his text the affirmation that God gives "wine to gladden the heart of man, oil to make his face shine, and bread to strengthen man's heart" (Ps 104:15) and took these gifts to denote not strong drink, after-shave lotion, and solid food, but joy in Christ, the anointing of the Holy Spirit, and the bread of life. I would find the second sermon much more difficult to "hear" than the first, but it would also be difficult to give objective reasons for the first being more acceptable than the second. When Psalm 45:1 speaks of a heart overflowing with a goodly word, Theophilus of Antioch takes this to refer to God's giving forth the Word through whom all things were made.[32] I find it difficult to use the text that way, but also difficult to suggest objective reasons for that being more objectionable than devotional appropriations of the Psalms in which I have myself indulged.

Sixth, I must also add that I am acquainted with the specific congregation that is fed by allegorical preaching such as the second sermon just

30. *Discerning the Mystery* 102.
31. Rowland and Corner, *Liberating Exegesis* 32.
32. *To Autolycus* 2.10; cf. Rogerson, *The Study and Use of the Bible* 37.

noted, and that congregation is characterized by Christian joy, the fruit of the Spirit, and a love for the bread of life. The interpretation that wins people to a love for scripture and a trust in scripture often adopts a figurative approach to scripture. It has been said that the nineteenth-century critics had become Christians under the influence of the "old Bible," not the new, and that there is a link between the old religion and the old attitude to the Bible.[33] When people move from a figurative to a historical approach to scripture they can feel that their existential involvement with scripture disappears and can become aware of a need to work against the grain to maintain the living relationship with scripture that won their love for it in the first place.

In one of his hermeneutical reflections Paul described the scriptures as designed to encourage us in steadfastness, harmony, and the glorifying of God (Rom 15:4-6).[34] Augustine likewise once declared that the purpose of scripture was to encourage love for God and for other people and suggested that it did not matter too much if one's detailed interpretation of a particular passage was mistaken if the interpretation still served that end: The interpreter "goes astray in much the same way as a man who by mistake quits the high road, but yet reaches through the fields the same place to which the road leads." He therefore offers as a rule for interpretation that we "turn over carefully in our minds and meditate on what we read until we find an interpretation that tends to establish the reign of love" — an allegorical one if necessary.[35] Liberationist interpretation can have the same spiritual (i.e., material!) strength.[36]

There are advantages and drawbacks to a figurative approach to interpreting the words of God. The advantages encourage us to follow Matthew's interpretive method, while the drawbacks make us ask whether we may seek to understand and acknowledge Matthew's interpretive method without being committed or even licensed to imitate it.

33. See Glover, *Evangelical Nonconformists and Higher Criticism* 223, following S. G. Green, *The "Psalms of David" and Modern Criticism* (London: Religious Tract Society, 1894) 52-54.

34. Cf. Hays, *Echoes of Scripture in the Letters of Paul* 192.

35. *Christian Doctrine* 1.36.41; 3.15.23; 3.10.14; cf. McKnight, *Postmodern Use of the Bible* 33, 39.

36. Fowl and Jones, *Reading in Communion* 85.

11

Interpreting a Historical Word

The characteristics, rationale, advantages, and drawbacks of historical approaches to interpretation offer a mirror image of those of figurative approaches. They begin from the fact that the books of scripture explicitly come from human authors, invite us to approach them historically, and open themselves to the illumination that comes from the use of the methods of biblical criticism.

The Place of Historical Interpretation

The least controversial shibboleth of biblical interpretation for a century has been the conviction that any passage of scripture should be understood against its historical background. It is striking that the scriptural material that most overtly claims a divine origin is also the material that most consistently draws attention to its own historical background and thus to the need to understand it against that background. We sometimes speak of the timelessness of scripture; within scripture itself one of the key implications of the idea of inspiration is that scripture is capable of speaking beyond the context in which it was written. But scripture itself also refuses us the option of understanding the word of God as a timeless word in the sense of one without historical rootedness. It is not a set of timeless propositions that have immediate universal application because they have no inherent connection with any particular context. It requires us to see God's word operating in relation to particular sets of circumstances.[1]

1. See Thiselton, *The Two Horizons* 95-99.

We have noted that a historical approach to interpretation is the one toward which the prophets themselves point; its theological rationale lies in the fact that the God of Israel, who is the God and Father of our Lord Jesus Christ, both acted and spoke in history. The practical advantage of a historical approach to interpretation is that it makes it in principle feasible to discuss a text's meaning in such a way as to come to some conclusion about whether or not we are right. We are asking ourselves what was in the front of God's mind at particular moments in dealing with people in their concrete situation. That lends itself to reasonable discussion, as considering what may have been in the back of God's mind on such occasions does not. Some passages of scripture may have an inspired second meaning, an extra level of significance beyond the historical sense, but that second meaning is difficult for us to identify. All scripture has an inspired first meaning: its meaning as an act of communication between God and Israel in the context of their life together. We can have access to that meaning by the usual methods for interpreting texts. Going by way of the meaning of the scriptures when they were written is thus a more straightforward route to discerning their meaning for us.

The patristic writers developed figurative approaches to interpretation, but the Antiochene exegetes were particularly committed to a historical approach. Thus Diodore of Tarsus declined to find any reference to Christ in Psalm 22, and Theodore of Mopsuestia declined to see one in a passage such as Hosea 11:1.[2] They did not rule out prophetic references to Christ in the First Testament; they simply did not believe that historical interpretation indicated that these were examples. While they did themselves interpret scripture christologically, both the Schoolmen and the Reformers emphasized the literal sense of scripture. William Tyndale declared: "The scripture hath but one sense, which is the literal sense. And that literal sense is the root and ground of all." Packer comments "The literal sense is itself the spiritual sense, coming from God and leading to Him."[3]

Talk of the "word" of God or of God "speaking" has to be seen as analogical language, not literal. By definition "words" are human. "Only human beings use words; and so, when one has entitled divine communica-

---

2. See Rogerson, *The Study and Use of the Bible* 38-39, referring to Diodore, *Commentarii in Psalmos* (Corpus Christianorum, Series Graeca 6; 1980) 142 and Theodore, *Patrologia Graeca* 66:189 (text in Zaharopoulos, *Theodore of Mopsuestia on the Bible* 158).

3. Tyndale, *Works* 1:304; see Packer, *"Fundamentalism" and the Word of God* 103.

tion 'word of God,' one has already indicated that the divine communication is in human words"[4] and needs to be understood as such. If God spoke through human writers who themselves spoke and wrote messages designed to communicate to other human beings of their day, that implies an approach to understanding God's words that seeks to understand the human words of these messengers. Interpreting scripture is like interpreting other books. God's words are words; there is no sacred hermeneutics if that would imply that in scripture God spoke a language different from ordinary human language.[5] Interpreting scripture is like interpreting other collections of books: While all point to the same reality, the words they use come from different speakers, whose vocabulary (for instance, when they use words such as "faith," "salvation," or "grace") has to be understood in its own terms before we seek to set it in the context of other speakers' words about the same realities.

To a degree the need for scripture to be understood against its historical context implies that biblical interpretation is a task for experts in ancient history and culture. A group of ordinary English-speaking people who picked up the Bible as it was written in order to see how it applies to them would not even be able to read the alphabets in which it is set down, let alone understand its words. In order to read it at all they would be dependent on experts who have translated it. To say that they will also benefit from the work of such experts who can tell them more about the background and meaning of the words they have translated is not to add a new principle. The other side to God's speaking and acting in particular historical contexts, and thus to the nature of the gospel itself as involving events in history, is that God's speech and acts have to be understood in their historical particularity. Even God could have it no other way.

The prophetic books also draw our attention to their authors, with their own backgrounds, in such a fashion as to imply that none of them can be fully understood or preached except as the message of this or that particular prophet. One reason for this becomes clear as we go on to read their books. Their persons, lives, and personalities commonly enter into their messages or embody them in some way; the insights the prophets offer, the ways in which they express themselves, and the emphases they bring reflect their individuality. They are directly prompted and addressed

4. Brown, *The Critical Meaning of the Bible* 21.
5. See, e.g., Ebeling's comments on Barth and Bultmann in *Word and Faith* 310-11.

by God and given God's words, but the message they hear and transmit is the message as *they* can hear and transmit it. It is significant that Amos is a Judean prophesying among the northern tribes, that Isaiah's name means "Yahweh is salvation" and embodies his message, that Hosea's marital experience shapes his interpretation of Yahweh's relationship with Israel, that Jeremiah ministers in Jerusalem as a member of a priestly family from one of the northern tribes, and that Ezekiel prophesies as someone who would be a priest if he were not in exile. The prophetic books are not books that came directly from heaven or whose "real" author is God, with human scribes functioning merely as his typists. These books issued from the depths of human personalities and have power to speak now partly because in their humanness they spoke to people then. Their humanness is also significant for the task of interpreting them.

Each of the prophets is a different person, and their differences come out in their prophecies. God does not bypass them or speak despite who they are. He uses them and speaks through who they are. The words of God that they utter are also quite human words — not words that are thereby spoiled and not exactly what God really wanted said, but precisely what God wanted said, yet also what the prophet wanted to say. If we are to understand them aright, then, we take the same approach as we do to any other human words. We hear and obey the words of God by listening to the human words in which God spoke. We ask what these words meant to the prophet and his audience, knowing that this was where God's message lay. When a book such as *The Late Great Planet Earth* applies prophecies to the twentieth century, it ignores their meaning for the prophet and his audience. It takes no note of the pointers that the prophets themselves give regarding the way to discern their meaning: the general pointer with which their books commonly begin and the specific pointers they give as they go along.

It is the nature of narratives not to reveal their author or the intentions that that author had in writing. When we seek to discover the intention of a narrative we have to look between the lines of the narrative itself. Prophecy characteristically reveals rather than conceals its author and its author's intention, and discerning the intention of the author has a more intrinsic role in the task of interpretation than is the case with narrative because author and intention are explicitly present in the text; they cannot be dismissed as irrelevant to the text's interpretation. It is here that an interest in the author's intention in the sense of the meaning the author intended to convey by means of the actual words used seems a clearly justifiable aspect of interpretation.[6] Indeed, it seems perverse if not immoral to ignore what the author intended to say for the sake of other meanings that the text's words might be capable of, unless (perhaps) the author actually invites that — in which case the alternative meanings become part of the author's implied meanings. Following Ricoeur, Croatto argues that a statement's original speaker, recipients, and horizon or context disappear when the statement becomes a written text; questions of the statement's meaning are now discussed independently of these.[7] But the introductions and contents of the prophetic books seem designed to preserve the presence of the original speakers, recipients, and contexts. The implication is that the spiritual meaning of the text is the meaning that the Spirit inspired the human author to convey and that the way to discover the text's spiritual meaning is to investigate the author's meaning by the normal procedures for interpreting texts. "A gracious text gives the meaning over to the readers, but a gracious hermeneutic gives the initiative back to the author."[8]

The Process of Historical Interpretation

There are thus standard insights regarding the nature of exegesis that apply to the interpretation of inspired texts. Interpretation is contextual: Words are taken in the context of sentences, sentences in the context of the work from which they come, works in the context of the author's writings as a whole. One cannot read into an occurrence of a word the many nuances it may have in other contemporary contexts, even in the same author's own writings, still less the nuances it may have in other historical contexts. Nor can one ascertain a word's meaning from its etymology rather than from its usage. In English "goodbye" does not mean "God be with you" and "worship" does not mean acknowledging the worth of something; still less is the latter fact of English etymology a basis for an understanding of what any First or Second Testament writer means by worship. There are no lessons about meaning to be learned from the fact that Paul's word for power, *dynamis*, in due course generated the English word dynamite. The Greek word for a servant in 1 Corinthians 4:1 originally meant an under-

---

6. See Hirsch, *Validity in Interpretation; Aims of Interpretation;* cf. Juhl, *Interpretation;* E. E. Johnson, *Expository Hermeneutics* 23-30.

7. *Biblical Hermeneutics* 16-17; cf. p. 53 in chapter 3 above.

8. So Peta Sherlock in a private communication.

rower, but there is no indication that Paul or his readers would have been conscious of the fact. The Hebrew word *dābār* means both "word" and "event," but in itself this does not indicate that Israelites saw word and event as the same thing or as inextricably linked. The relationship between language and thought is less predictable than that, as is suggested by Hebrew's lack of a word for history and Greek's lack of a word for sex.[9]

The historical context often alluded to by the introductions to the prophetic books can be illumined from sources inside scripture such as Kings, Chronicles, and Ezra-Nehemiah and from sources outside scripture that tell us more about their international context in particular. It has sometimes been maintained that scripture is self-interpreting and that we should not need to look outside it for information to help us interpret it. In principle this seems a mistaken inference: The notion that scripture is self-interpreting is designed not to safeguard scripture from illumination from elsewhere but to safeguard us from interpretations imposed on scripture that are not justified by the text itself. Nevertheless neither scriptural nor extrascriptural sources are as helpful as one might expect to an understanding of the prophets, as we have already noted is the case with the interpretation of biblical narratives (which, for instance, have interests of their own that shape what they include and what they omit in their presentation of events). Extrascriptural sources, for their part, rarely clarify the content of the biblical documents in any direct way, and often an interest in archaeology and the ancient Middle Eastern background of the Bible constitutes a diversion from seeking to interpret the texts themselves — as T. S. Eliot noted to be the case with parallel study of the "background" to the interpretation of English literature.[10] B. S. Childs observes that the debate over Romans illustrates the fallaciousness of the view that "the sharper the historical focus, the better the interpretation."[11]

The same is true with attempts to date material in Isaiah 1–39 to the periods of Josiah, the exile, or the Second Temple: The historical concern seems to beguile scholars away from the task of exegesis. On the other hand, it is strange that Childs believes that reading Isaiah 40–55 against an exilic background works *against* the text's own intention and makes its appropriation more difficult.[12] The text explicitly directs our attention to a

---

9. On such issues see, e.g., Caird, *The Language and Imagery of the Bible* 37-84; A. C. Thiselton, "Semantics and NT Interpretation," in *NT Interpretation* (ed. Marshall) 75-104, from which some of these examples come.

10. *On Poetry and Poets* 112; cf. Jowett, "On the Interpretation of Scripture" 466.

11. *The NT as Canon* 51; cf. Hays, *Echoes of Scripture in the Letters of Paul* 35.

12. See his *Introduction to the OT as Scripture* 324.

specific context after that of Isaiah of Jerusalem, which Isaiah 1–39 does not do, and it requires us to reconsider the first impression created by Isaiah 1:1 concerning its historical context. Countless readers of Isaiah 40–55 have found that this introduces them into a newly living interaction with the text as the deposit of God's truly ministering to people where they were in their exile and hopelessness; indeed, even before the critical era these chapters were read against this historical background because of the indications that they provide concerning their intended audience, even if it was assumed that the oracles had been delivered in an anticipatory manner a century and a half earlier.

The books of the prophets themselves are our major resource for a knowledge of the situations that the prophets address and of the questions they are concerned to answer. So one of the interpreter's first tasks in studying one of the Prophets is to read through the book with this interest in mind: What were the various aspects of the circumstances, beliefs, lives, or needs of the hearers that the prophet had to address? Even when we have understood clearly the words that a person uses, we have not understood what they mean until we know "what the question was (a question in his own mind, and presumed by him to be in yours) to which the thing he has said or written was meant as an answer."[13] Thus Amos gives us many indications of the situation he was addressing, against which he thereby invites us to read his actual oracles.

That it is from the contents of the book itself that we learn most about its historical context provides us with an approach to prophetic books that do not begin by telling us about their authors, context, and background. Joel is the best example. It offers no concrete indications of its date or authorship, beyond the bare name, but its contents make quite clear what *kind* of circumstances it addressed and what aims the prophet had in relation to the needs he perceived. Biblical scholarship has been centrally concerned with tracing the actual historical process whereby Israelite religion developed, and locating each of the prophets chronologically is of key importance for this purpose. Whether we date Joel to the ninth, fifth, or third century, three favored possibilities, affects our understanding of the development of Israel's religion. It makes less difference to the meaning of Joel itself. What matters more in that connection is the kind of context the Book of Joel was addressing, and the nature of this is made clear by the book. The kind of context decided, for instance, the form of continuity and

13. Collingwood, *An Autobiography* 31.

discontinuity the prophet had to manifest in relation to where his audience was, and thus determined whether his ministry was fundamentally one of reassurance or one of confrontation.

The Role and the Nature of Biblical Criticism

Because the scriptures are human writings and because the eternal word of God only manifested itself in historical process, the methods of criticism, and in particular historical-critical interpretation, are appropriate to the scriptures.[14]

With the witnessing tradition the theological significance of historical criticism arises from its concern with establishing what historical events underlie a narrative; we are willing to be critical of traditions concerning the authorship of the Gospels because we want to attain as much well-grounded information as we can on the actual Jesus. Our interest now, however, lies in another, logically prior aspect of that significance, its concern with establishing the original nature and background of documents, which has the potential to put us into closer contact with the meaning of the word of God as it was originally given.

The notion of biblical criticism need not suggest the aim of criticizing the Bible, just as literary criticism does not mean criticizing literature. The object of literary criticism is appreciation of literature, facilitation of an appropriate response to it. In the same way, biblical criticism can take as its object appreciation of the Bible and facilitation of the response of appropriation, faith, humility, obedience, and commitment through the investigation of the Bible's text, origin, sources, and composition. We are critical in the sense of circumspect, not in the sense of judgmental,[15] though we might reckon that if the texts or traditions are worthy of respect, they will emerge from critical judgment triumphant and with added glory.[16]

Criticism has the capacity to help us respond to scripture itself by being critical of received theories regarding the origin, nature, and meaning of the works it studies. Jewish and Christian tradition has believed, for instance, that Moses wrote not only Exodus to Deuteronomy, in which he is

---

14. O'Donovan, *On the Thirty Nine Articles* 58-61.

15. Gunton, *Enlightenment and Alienation* 112.

16. R. M. Fowler, "Who Is 'the Reader' in Reader Response Criticism?" in *Reader Response Approaches to Biblical and Secular Texts* (ed. Detweiler) 9.

central, but also Genesis, in which he is unmentioned. Christian tradition has believed that the disciple Matthew wrote the Gospel that appears first in the Second Testament, that Paul's associate Mark wrote the Gospel that appears second, and that Paul wrote Hebrews. Such beliefs overcome the anonymity of authorship that is common in scripture. Tradition has also assumed that the statements regarding authorship that do appear in the Prophets, the Wisdom Books, and other Epistles are to be taken at their face value. It has developed a set of standard positions regarding the genre to which some works belong, such as the assumption that the Book of Jonah is a piece of historical writing, and a received interpretation of some individual texts, such as the understanding of Genesis 3:15 as a promise of Christ's victory over the Devil. It has inferred from the view that the Bible is the work of one divine author, and thus in some sense a unified whole, that the same theological convictions can be inferred throughout and thus that the "us" and "our" of passages such as Genesis 1:26 and 11:7 hint at God's being as Trinity.

Criticism asked whether these various beliefs or understandings were justified. It concluded that there were good grounds for doubting whether Moses wrote Genesis or Paul wrote Hebrews, for instance, and also for doubting whether Solomon wrote Ecclesiastes, whether Isaiah wrote the whole Book of Isaiah, and (perhaps) whether Paul wrote the Pastoral Epistles. It concluded that Jonah was more like a work of fiction than one of history and that many other narratives in the First Testament could not be judged by our historiographic conventions. It found that traditional Christian interpretations of many individual texts could not be justified on historical grounds, and that the various prophets, narratives, and epistles are capable of suggesting very different historical and theological perspectives. Philosophical and scientific theories put exegetes on the track of different approaches to the interpretation of the Genesis creation stories, and Middle Eastern archaeological discoveries suggested new approaches to the background of those stories. All of this suggested a critical stance over the traditional understanding of the stories, but in due course it offered fruitful new insights on their background, meaning, and significance.

In our interpretation of scripture as the word of God biblical criticism can often seem a threat. It is also a friend. At the end of the nineteenth century its development contributed significantly to the demise of scripture's authority. But by questioning the traditions with which we have hedged scripture around, it enables us to listen to the text itself, and it can support scripture's authority. Indeed, in another sense commitment to the authority of scripture works against a recognition of that authority in practice. That commitment means that I need to make scripture say something acceptable to me so that I can accept what it says. As G. Shaw puts it, I turn it into "an instrument of the believer's obstinacy" in the way described by Tolstoy: "having acknowledged it all as sacred truth, it was necessary to justify everything, to shut one's eyes, to hide, to manipulate, to fall into contradictions, and, alas, often to say what was not true."[17] Biblical criticism is the friend of the authority of scripture, because it insists on facing what scripture actually says, rather than what its apologists make it mean. There is a case for reading scripture in the light of an exegetical, expository, and devotional tradition, in the conviction that the Holy Spirit has been active in guiding the believing communities as they have sought to listen to scripture faithfully over the centuries. But for the sake of the authority of scripture we will also read scripture critically, in a way that is willing to question this exegetical, expository, and devotional tradition rather than assume its infallibility. Indeed, if we find that we invariably understand and agree with scripture, that should make us suspicious. It likely indicates that we have closed our ears at some point.[18]

An uncritical commitment to scripture "tends to confirm the Church(es) and Christians in their *status quo* because the Bible so read yields what they have always thought it meant"; it helps them "to prove that they conform to the biblical directives for what the church should be" rather than to discover where they do not conform to what the Bible says.[19] The point of the inspired word of God, however, was to confront the people of God, not to confirm them in the attitudes they already held. So an approach to scripture such as that of biblical criticism can help to clarify the gap between what we are and what scripture says, and it is thus more likely to enable the inspired word to exercise its own critical function than one that reassures us that we already know what it means and do live by it. In this sense "critical interpretation is the soul of theology: it opens itself to the Word of God . . . but it also remains aware of the inadequacy that is always an inherent property of human interpretation."[20] Critical methods express "the necessary reformatory impulse at the heart of the gospel and

17. *The Cost of Authority* 273, quoting Tolstoy's "An Examination of the Gospels" in *A Confession* (The World's Classics edition, 105).
18. Countryman, *Biblical Authority or Biblical Tyranny* 96.
19. Brown, *The Critical Meaning of the Bible* viii-ix.
20. Jeanrond, *Text and Interpretation* 153.

the Christian tradition": They look for failure of fidelity to the Jesus re-membered by the church and the sentimentalization of love that sidesteps necessary conflict, the fatalism that endorses poverty and suffering, and the existentialist individualism that avoids political commitment.[21]

Admittedly criticism's task is to *test* tradition rather than to ignore it or necessarily to dismiss it. We could hardly be committed to the view that over the centuries God consistently let the believing communities misun-derstand scripture, any more than to the view that they consistently under-stood scripture correctly. We will consider further in chapter 15 how those communities can be the means by which we are delivered from the limita-tions of the century in which we ourselves live and from the misunder-standings that we can ourselves fall into. Nor must we replace tradition with unrestrained individualism in interpretation. The Holy Spirit indwells the church corporately and has done so over the centuries, and the church's interpretation of scripture is more likely to be right than my own inter-pretation (but not *certain* to be so!).

The Presuppositions of Tradition and of Criticism

Many of the conclusions of biblical criticism have seemed at first sight to be incompatible with scripture being the inspired word of God. To question traditional views regarding the origins of scripture appears to cast doubt on its divine inspiration. The whole Book of Isaiah seems to purport to come from Isaiah of Jerusalem; to suggest that a number of writers con-tributed to it (one in the eighth century, one in the seventh, one in the exile, one after the return to Jerusalem, one later still — let alone an army of glossators) casts doubt on its genuineness.

The difficulty here is that the literary conventions of the Middle East of two or three millennia ago were different from ours, and we find ourselves imposing our cultural practices on another culture. It is strange to us, but ancient authors did often attribute their works to earlier figures, perhaps those whom they saw as their particular inspirations, rather than claiming responsibility for their work themselves.[22] Jewish and other Middle Eastern peoples during the first millennium were well acquainted with quasi-prophe-cies that related past events as if they were still future, perhaps thus affirming

21. Tracy, *The Analogical Imagination* 324-25.
22. See Metzger, "Literary Forgeries and Canonical Pseudepigrapha."

the belief that these events were under the control of God.[23] The Book of Enoch, quoted in Jude 14, is one example. The Qumran covenanters took the Torah itself very seriously but also valued the Temple Scroll, which restates much of the Torah, presenting itself as given by God through Moses.[24] Its laws have no historical connection with Moses, but the book's authors perhaps believed that those laws expressed what Moses would say if he were among them and had the kind of authority that his words had. Two of the Gospel writers copied substantial parts of their work from an already existing Gospel. None of these literary practices is accepted in the modern Western world; we cannot infer from this that they could not have been used by God in a world in which they were accepted.

In general, indeed, it may be argued that

> one of the most crucial distinguishing marks of a critical approach to the Bible — or, indeed, to any book — is some attention to the genre of texts. Reading the Bible critically means knowing what kind of literature particular portions of the text are, and therefore what sort of question it makes sense to ask of it. Until we have assigned a text to some genre or other, we do not know how to understand its individual sections, sentences, even words.[25]

For related reasons, when Jesus refers to Moses and David in connection with passages that critical theories conclude were not authored by those men, this does not drive us to the conclusion that he is giving authoritative information on the passages' authorship. It is not that he consciously adopts the popular opinion of his day while knowing better or that he inevitably shares the trivial misapprehensions of his day. Either assumption would presuppose that the question about authorship was a live one for him and his contemporaries. He can only be treated as authoritative, misleading, or mistaken on the matter once we think that the question was a real one. While *we* cannot avoid the question, Jesus presupposes a framework of thinking in which it has not yet been asked. In general the question that he and the Second Testament writers are presupposing when they connect a passage with Moses or Isaiah is whether it comes from authoritative scripture and where in that scripture it can be found. Their reference is conventional and phenomenological, like many of the Bible's references to nature.

23. See Goldingay, *Daniel* 282-83.
24. See Vermes, *The Dead Sea Scrolls in English* [3]128-58.
25. Barton, *Oracles of God* 141.

When Jesus says that the sun rises or that the seed in the ground dies (Matt 5:45; John 12:24) he makes points that a prosaic scientist would dispute, but we recognize that he is simply talking the way people talk about the world as it appears to us. The same is so with references to passages from scripture.

Even in connection with Psalm 110 (Mark 12:35-37) Jesus is not really concerned with the question of authorship but with the person of the Messiah, and he argues over the matter on the basis of what he and his contemporaries can agree on. "We must not invoke our Lord's authority to decide a question that He was not answering."[26] Jesus' exegesis is also phenomenological and conventional. On the basis of the generally accepted understanding of the psalm's origin and meaning Jesus proves from it that the Messiah is not (merely) the son of David, because the author (assumed by the tradition to be David) addresses the recipient of Yahweh's word (assumed to be the Messiah) as lord. The generally accepted approach to the psalm's origin and meaning is now that the speaker is a priest or prophet while the addressee is David or the Davidic king. What is said about this person is larger than life and expresses an ideal that never found realization in the monarchy. It was in a sense always implicitly future hope rather than present fact; from the exile when the monarchy disappeared it became explicitly so. The psalm taken in accordance with this current understanding still proves Jesus' point. What is said of the "lord" spoken of would not be fulfilled in one who was (merely) a son of David. The passage tests but exemplifies a recurrent issue in Christian study of the First Testament. At this point, at least, we can follow the Second Testament's theological approach, but work it via the method of critical interpretation.

As well as being written according to ordinary literary conventions the Bible is written in three ordinary human languages. There is no special "biblical Hebrew" or "New Testament Greek" that God or scriptural authors speak. Those authors used the language of their particular day, with the distinctive vocabulary and style peculiar to them as individuals. They used human voices and their words were written down on ordinary human scrolls. When the exiles listened to Ezekiel, they used the same ears, eyes, and minds that they applied to other exilic prophets. That, too, implies that interpreting the Bible against its historical background and taking its full humanity seriously involves expecting that its authors will use the speech

26. Hebert, *Fundamentalism and the Church of God* 69; cf. Huxtable, *The Bible Says* 74; Orr, *Revelation and Inspiration* 149-54.

forms of their day. It is scripture itself, interpreted in the light of the speech forms of its day as these are known from other sources, that must tell us what these acceptable speech forms are.

The text of scripture has also been transmitted to us by the ordinary processes of copying, and textual criticism of biblical documents proceeds according to principles similar to those used for other ancient documents. We have seen that here, too, one can illustrate the ease with which people's faith commitments can influence them in their interpretation of scripture. In the patristic period Christians whom we would now call the orthodox periodically suggest that those whom we would now call heretics base their arguments on a wrong version of the biblical text or on a wrong interpretation of the text, accusations that begin with 2 Peter 3:16. On some occasions they were quite justified. On other occasions, however, the orthodox themselves were guilty of the same faults. With regard to textual questions, Sanday instances the various readings at John 1:13; 3:6; 7:53–8:11 and Luke 23:44.[27] The question whether such alterations or misinterpretations amount to deliberate falsification may be artificial. Both parties worked in the light of their different convictions; these convictions gave them clues as to what the right textual reading or the right interpretation must be. Faith and criticism exercised a mutual influence on each other. People read and interpreted the text in the light of what they knew it *must* say and mean.

The same process can be observed in the modern world in the varying approaches to writing a critical history of Israel or life of Jesus. It appears more subtly in biblical translations. Versions such as the RSV, for instance, have been accused of reading their own theological preferences into the text when they render the Greek noun *hilastērion* (Rom 3:25) as "expiation" rather than the traditional (!) "propitiation." Conversely the NIV contains a number of innovative renderings designed to harmonize texts with other texts or with extrascriptural information (e.g., Gen 1:2 margin; 2:8, 17; 12:1). This points us to another significance of criticism, especially as practiced by people who do *not* accept the inspiration of scripture or who interpret it in different ways from our own (e.g., for Protestant Christians, Jewish or Roman Catholic interpreters). We will consider further in chapters 14 and 15 how our interpretation of scripture can usefully be tested by criticism offered by people who work on a different basis and may be more likely to expose to us the points at which we are unconsciously distorting evidence.

We have argued that historical criticism is appropriate to Christian faith

27. *Inspiration* 41.

and to the nature of scripture because of their own investment in history. As we experience historical criticism in practice, it indeed manifests its prejudices and presuppositions; E. Linnemann expresses the point particularly trenchantly.[28] A form of rationalism makes historical criticism inclined to question whether knowing about the future and thus speaking of it is possible at all, and inclined to assume that any account of a miracle is questionable. Historically it was such convictions that led to the prevalence of the view that Isaiah 40–55 was written in the exile rather than in the eighth century, even if there are also compelling nonrationalist considerations that lead to that conclusion. Gabriel Hebert has remarked that though there is no real tension between faith and criticism, since both are needed if we are to make a full response to what is both a divine and a human word, critical study can bring to the surface a real tension between two worldviews, one including God, one excluding God. "Behind the issue of Faith and Criticism there lay concealed the deeper issue of Faith and Secularism."[29]

Romanticism is a second significant influence on criticism. It contributed to the shaping of the view that the J material in the Torah (e.g., Genesis 2–3), with what was felt to be its attractive primitiveness, is old and thus more authentic, whereas the P material (e.g., Genesis 1), with what was considered its unattractive cultic concern, is younger and less authentic.[30] Again, this view of the relative age of the material is probably correct, but some of the reasoning that led to it was certainly questionable.

Existentialism is a third influence. Bultmann's criticism is a function of his theology: The act of existential commitment needs no justification from history, and to seek such is to seek justification by works. Better, then, to remove that possibility by removing the possibility of historical certainty about Christ.[31]

More conservative interpretation of scripture can be affected by the same presuppositions. Barr notes a rationalistic flavor in conservative interpretations of the exodus, paralleling rather than standing out from that of more liberal interpretations.[32] Anticritical interpreters have a number of

---

28. See her *Historical Criticism of the Bible*, where she describes herself as engaging a lifetime of scholarly practice, only then coming to know Christ and disowning her scholarship.

29. Hebert, *The Authority of the OT* 117.

30. Cf. R. J. Thompson, *Moses and the Law in a Century of Criticism*, chapter 4.

31. See, e.g., "The Significance of the Historical Jesus for the Theology of Paul," in *Faith and Understanding* 220-46; and further chapter 13 below.

32. See his *Fundamentalism* 235-59.

more distinctive additional presuppositions, even apart from their commitment to seeing scripture as the word of God, such as an inclination to prefer traditional views to novel ones, to date biblical documents early rather than late, and to connect those documents with significant individuals rather than letting them be anonymous. These presuppositions, too, need to be tested, and allowance needs to be made for their influence on the conclusions of conservative scholars.

• 12 •

Hearing the Words of God
in the Words of Human Writers

We have considered the interpretation of scripture in the light of its being words from God and in the light of its being the words of human authors. How far can we bring these two together?

The Risk, Promise, and Ultimate Aim
of Historical Interpretation

The risk and the promise of critical interpretation is that it fixes the Bible in history. The risk is that it may imprison the biblical writers in their time. Pannenberg speaks of the double crisis of the scripture principle.[1] While one aspect of that crisis is the gap between the scriptural narrative and the historical events to which it witnesses, the other is the gap between the ancient text and the modern context in which we need to hear God speak. Similarly, James Barr notes that the contemporary emphasis on hermeneutics makes discussion of the inspiration of scripture and of the relation between divine and human in scripture seem insignificant. Our age has become distinctively aware of the difference between the ancient world and the modern world, and this makes it more urgent to know how to restate what was said in biblical times than to know how what was said in biblical times was said. Answering the latter question does not help with the former, and in that sense it gets us nowhere.[2]

---

1. See, e.g., *Basic Questions in Theology* 1:6.
2. Barr, *The Bible in the Modern World* 21. Cf. his parallel comments on the question of scriptural authority, noted on p. 91 above.

Yet fixing the prophets in their time is the promise as well as the risk of critical interpretation. "The true use of interpretation is to get rid of interpretation, and leave us alone in company with the author."[3] A historical approach contributes to our hearing the prophets today, insofar as the distancing effect of a historical approach can help us to grasp their own meaning.

One of the most significant modern attempts at a historical under-standing of the First Testament is that of Gerhard von Rad.[4] His study has the potential to take one into the specifics of the ministry of a prophet such as Isaiah or Jeremiah or Ezekiel. What happens in the course of such study is not that the prophets are seen as dead figures from the past. On the contrary, they come alive. Similarly, it is tempting to believe that focusing on the pastness of the Second Testament risks irrelevance, but it is in "passing over" into the Second Testament's scandalous and disturbing past-ness that we may discover how it can enrich because it speaks so specifically and so appropriately in relation to its unique context.[5] We meet God precisely by entering into a particular situation whose distance from our-selves we emphasize. "God's word is always something *concrete* and *alive*": Its concreteness and ongoing relevance are not in tension but are interre-lated.[6] Through the ministry of the prophets God relates to people in the specific circumstances of their lives, speaking a concrete word that confronts them where they are and demands a response from them. It is precisely this application of God's word to specific situations that enables it also to speak as God's word to us. Scripture proves that it is not timeless but does possess a "permanent timeliness."[7]

Walter Wink has spoken forcefully of the bankruptcy of the historical-critical method.[8] The method often fails to produce meanings that seem spiritually helpful in the way that a precritical reading of the text can be. There could be several reasons for this. One is that God may not be as concerned with conveying devotionally helpful material through scripture as we are with receiving such; that could be implied by the explicit warnings from the prophets and Jesus about the ease with which religious devotion replaces God's real priorities. The Bible's purpose lies elsewhere, in more

3. Jowett, "On the Interpretation of Scripture" 466.
4. See esp. his *OT Theology.*
5. Nineham, *Explorations in Theology* 1:163-64.
6. Mowinckel, *The OT as Word of God* 120.
7. Tracy, *The Analogical Imagination* 102.
8. *The Bible in Human Transformation* 1.

foundational areas of God's concerns. It is no problem that we may then find more devotional help in *Pilgrim's Progress* or the hymns of Charles Wesley than in the Book of Numbers.

Often investment in critical study may not seem to yield a worthwhile return because of the narrowness with which the historical-critical method is utilized. The aim of any interpretive method should be to help us read the text in accordance with its own concerns. As Barth puts it, it is precisely our taking the humanity and historicality of the Bible seriously that involves us in looking to that which as human words it points.[9] Investigating the background and sense of its words is merely the preparation for actual understanding. Even understanding the speaker's aim in speaking is not the heart of the matter. Understanding someone's statement is not complete until we have considered the object to which that person refers. Objectivity in interpretation involves interest in this object for its own sake. Reading the text in this way may mean de-pietizing it, but it may be that the text is concerned with the things of God in a way that the critical method finds difficult to handle. The solution is not to abandon the method and thereby forgo its strengths but to see that it is used in way that corresponds better to its own goal, that of enabling us to appreciate the text as it is in the light of its own concerns, not in the light of a narrowed-down version of its concerns. A Christian use of historical method will not omit God from literature any more than from history. The tools of biblical criticism need to be not abandoned but brought under new management.[10]

Another way to make the point would be to note that interpretation often involves a move from fusion through distancing to communion.[11] In our study of scripture we commonly begin by assuming that we identify with it, share its basic concerns, and are committed to shaping our lives and thinking by it. In order to maintain that understanding of our own position in relation to scripture, as we have noted in chapter 11, we are likely to have to make scripture mean something that is more acceptable to us. If we are to grow in our grasp of what scripture actually says, in particular at the points where it would make us uncomfortable, we may be helped by moving from fusion to a more neutral and distanced relationship with it that enables it to be different from us, instead of forcing it to be the same. Distancing oneself from scripture in this objectivizing way by means

9. *Church Dogmatics* I/2, 464-72. See further in chapter 16 below.
10. Wink, *The Bible in Human Transformation* 60.
11. So Wink; see *The Bible in Human Transformation* 19.

of a critical approach will not suffice as the end of our relationship with God's word, but it may play a significant role in the development of that relationship by protecting us from identifying with it too easily, projecting our own beliefs and commitments onto it, and missing the challenge in what it is saying.[12]

Where historical criticism again risks bankruptcy is where it forgets that the original object of distancing was to move toward communion. Once criticism performed an iconoclastic function in relation to an ideological orthodoxy; now postcritical faith performs an iconoclastic function in relation to an ideological criticism that methodologically excludes commitment and considerations of ultimate truth, in a "second naïveté."[13]

Interpretation That Goes Deeper Than the Historical

A further aspect of the Prophets points toward another limitation of a narrowly conceived historical-critical approach. The Prophets are among *the* examples of biblical poetry. As prophetic texts they invite a historical approach that takes account of their historical reference and their historical context. Yet as poetic texts they have an irreducibly metaphorical form whose nature is to obscure access to their historical reference and context. This fact contributes significantly to the difficulty in arriving at a historical interpretation of chapters such as those that refer to Hosea's marriage or to the servant of Yahweh. These chapters have a historical reference and context, and a historical approach to them is in principle appropriate, yet such an approach fails to achieve results that are satisfying either in its own terms or in the light of the texts' own nature. The texts are emotional and evocative as well as deliberate and logical and are thus ambiguous and plurisignificant, "suggestive of multiple meanings."[14] Their power and effectiveness has part of its basis here. Their authors may have spoken further than they knew; they may not have perceived all the implications of their words, and the meanings of the words may go beyond the comprehension

12. Cf. R. M. Fowler, "Who is 'the Reader' in Reader Response Criticism?" in *Reader Response Approaches to Biblical and Secular Texts* (ed. Detweiler) 8-10.

13. Ricoeur, *The Symbolism of Evil* 347ff., as quoted by Wink, *The Bible in Human Transformation* 13.

14. Exum, "Of Broken Pots, Fluttering Birds and Visions in the Night" 333; cf. R. J. Weems, "Gomer," in *Interpretation for Liberation* (ed. Cannon and Schüssler Fiorenza) 88-89.

of the authors. But any further meaning interpreters find in their work is to be expected to be a deeper grasping of what the prophets themselves grasped rather than an allegorizing of their words. It will be a fuller understanding, not an unrelated one.

We noted in chapter 9 that in the Second Testament the idea that the Holy Spirit was involved in inspiring biblical texts is designed to draw attention to and to account for their capacity to speak beyond their original context in ways that their human authors could not have guessed. They have a depth dimension, and we may therefore consider them in the light of the category of "classic texts" as Frank Kermode[15] and David Tracy[16] have analyzed it, those texts that continue to be read over generations and centuries, which in their richness invite a multiplicity of readings, which challenge our sense of what is important and possible, and which represent a resource for abiding truth.

We thus approach them with a special openness and expectancy. In his study of the phenomenon of translation, George Steiner includes an analysis of "the hermeneutic motion, the art of elicitation and appropriative transfer of meaning." Its starting point, he suggests, is an act of trust that "there is 'something there' to be understood." Without this, the effort to understand will soon collapse. " 'This means nothing,' asserts the exasperated child in front of his Latin reader or the beginner at Berlitz"; to give in to that tempting conclusion is to forgo the prospect of reaching understanding.[17] This is all the more true with the trusting conviction that we are reading words that God spoke. For the task of interpretation this carries the significant implication that these words are neither unintelligible nor trivial, and it encourages us to persist in the effort to understand even when we are tempted to give up.

These words of God are thus full of potential, yet not predictable. The inspired scriptures speak in unpredictable and unprogrammable ways. Scripture cannot be forced to speak, and in one context will speak as in another it did not. "It does not lie — and this is why prayer must have the last word — in our power but only in God's. . . . We are therefore absolved from trying to force this event to happen. . . . The Word of God is so powerful that it is not bound by what we think we can discover and value as the divine element, the content, the spirit of the Bible. . . . We can and

---

15. *The Classic* 117, 121.
16. *The Analogical Imagination* 154.
17. Steiner, *After Babel* 296-97.

must be summoned by it to thankfulness and hope."[18] We relate to it not merely as people using our reason to decipher a human artifact but as people of prayer seeking to overhear what God has been saying. That consideration makes interpretation a charism.[19] The inspiration of the writing of scripture needs to be complemented by the inspiration of the reading of scripture;[20] one may compare "reader-response" approaches to interpretation, considered already in chapter 3.

From these considerations emerge some of the ways in which the Holy Spirit is involved in interpretation. First, the Spirit is involved in the intellectual work of exegeting an ancient text. Understanding a passage of scripture in order to see what it has to say to me and what it has to say to a congregation often requires hard mental labor of an analytic, reconstructive kind. The Spirit is the one breathed into humanity by creation and the one who works through the mind. But second, insight is not merely a mental matter. 2 Corinthians 3 suggests that "only readers made competent by the Spirit can throw back the veil and perceive the sense of Scripture; those who have not turned to the Lord who is Spirit are necessarily trapped in the script, with minds hardened and veiled."[21] There is a general point here about the way a person's mind has been transformed through turning to Christ. There is also a specific point about seeing the meaning of specific passages. Interwoven with the active analytic work of my mind is a periodic receiving of a spark of insight on the actual subject matter of the text I am wrestling with. Without the mental exegetical effort to grasp the meaning of my "given," the scriptural text, my sermon will be mere blessed thoughts. But without the received sparks of insight by means of which I perceive the text's essential significance, the sermon will be mere antiquarianism. The Holy Spirit is behind both the mental labor and the intuitive insight.

The Holy Spirit is also involved in the exercise of the charism that perceives how the ancient word speaks today; preaching involves being open to God, asking "What does this passage mean for me — what does God want to say to me through it?" (not "What does it say to *them?*"). Preachers are people passing on what they have heard God speak to them through scripture. Not that this task is confined to preachers. The whole church, indwelled by the Holy Spirit, has the capacity and the responsibility to

18. Barth, *Church Dogmatics* I/2, 531-32.
19. So Macquarrie, *God-Talk* 152.
20. Vogels, "Inspiration in a Linguistic Mode" 90.
21. Hays, *Echoes of Scripture in the Letters of Paul* 148; cf. Fowl and Jones, *Reading in Communion* 62.

identify what scripture signifies for us.[22] Finally, the Spirit is perhaps most crucially involved in softening the hard heart of the individual interpreter and the community, enabling them to see things that they would prefer to miss because these things will demand a change in commitments.[23]

Hearing the Word of God in the Words of Isaiah or Ezekiel

The Late Great Planet Earth approach rightly presupposes that God spoke through the Hebrew prophets: Their words are not merely human guesses as to how the future would work out but promises and warnings that came from God. They are included in scripture as promises and warnings whose significance is not confined to the prophets' own day. They are important for the people of God AD as well as BC and have implications for the contemporary Middle East. As the words of God they continue to be effective in implementing God's purpose and to speak beyond the situation in which they were first spoken. If *The Late Great Planet Earth* nevertheless offers a questionable model for our interpretation of inspired words of God such as those of Ezekiel 34–48, then how are we to interpret those words?

These chapters in Ezekiel offer a series of promises and warnings: of a new David to be king over Israel, of the destruction of Edom because of its hatred for Israel, of the restoration of Israel's land and people, of the resuscitation and reunification of the nation itself, of God's judgment being put into effect in a last great battle, and of a new temple in Jerusalem to which Yahweh returns in glory. Behind all this is the concern that the whole world should acknowledge that Yahweh is truly God.

Rather than being taken as a mere preview of events in the last quarter of the twentieth century, these chapters need to be interpreted in the light of the rest of scripture. They belong in the context of the purpose for the world's blessing that God has being pursuing from the beginning. After humanity's turn into the way of disobedience, God promises to a certain man, Abraham, and his family that they will enjoy a special relationship with God, will grow to become a nation, and will come to possess a particular land as their own. God's judgment will come on people who oppose

---

22. Cf. Brown, *The Critical Meaning of the Bible* 34-43 — though the point is not formulated in quite these terms; also Dunn's "fourth level of canonical authority," the ecclesiastical level (see *The Living Word* 152-53).

23. See further pp. 259-60 below.

them, but God's aim for the world in general is that its inhabitants should seek the blessings that Abraham enjoys. These promises begin to be fulfilled in the story told in Genesis to Joshua. In due course two further promises are added. God makes a commitment to Israel's royal line descended from David and to Israel's temple in Jerusalem, which will become God's very home.

All the central features of God's promises through Ezekiel involve a reaffirmation of this plan for blessing. God's glory will be revealed by what God will do for Israel as their age-long destiny is brought to fulfillment. To treat these promises as a coded preview of twentieth-century events in the Middle East takes insufficient account of the significance that attaches to them as part of the outworking of God's purpose for the blessing of Israel and the world.

Ezekiel's words are a reaffirmation of God's ancient words. But they are an affirmation that belongs in a particular context in the story of God's relationship with Israel, and they need to be seen in that context. It is not only the case that Isaiah, Jeremiah, and Ezekiel differ as people. The Judah to which they speak also varies. The introductions to the prophetic books reflect this in drawing attention to the historical periods that the individual prophets address. They imply that we need to understand the addressees as well as the speaker if we are to understand the address. The prophets' messages are not general truths, statements that could have been made to any people in any country in any age. They come from someone to someone in a particular place in a particular time and situation.

Beyond their personality differences it is this particularity that lies behind the great differences among the prophets. Isaiah, for instance, says to the people of Judah: "Do not think that God has abandoned you. God will not let Jerusalem be captured. God is committed to Jerusalem." Jeremiah says to the people of Judah: "Do not think that God is committed to Jerusalem. God is going to let it be captured. God has abandoned you." Jeremiah, again, tells people that God is not interested in the temple at Jerusalem or in the sacrifices that are offered there. Ezekiel speaks similarly, specifically prohibiting appeal to the example of Yahweh's blessing of Abraham as a key to hope of return from exile (33:23-29), whereas Isaiah of Babylon offers precisely this example as a key to such a hope (Isa 51:1-3).[24] Then in later chapters Ezekiel himself relates a vision of a renewed temple in Jerusalem where God will dwell in glory and where sacrifices will

---

24. Cf. J. A. Sanders, *From Sacred Story to Sacred Text* 66-67.

be duly offered; people will once again know the love and the presence of God that Jeremiah has said were to be taken away from them.

Such formal differences among the prophets arise from contrasts in the situations they address, which make different messages appropriate. Isaiah's words were God's message to Judah in the eighth century in the context of its people's fear of the Assyrians. Jeremiah's words were God's message to them at the end of the seventh century when they felt insufficient need to fear anyone. Ezekiel's words were God's message to them in the sixth century before and after their final defeat by the Babylonians. Isaiah of Babylon's words were God's message to them when the end of the exile was imminent. With outward diversity but inner consistency God used prophecy to confront people where they were, encouraging the fearful and admonishing the confident. As a result, the prophets' words apply directly to people in certain circumstances, but less directly to others. We cannot apply every prophetic message as it stands to every age. We have to take account of the circumstances of the prophets' original hearers and of our own circumstances if we are to appreciate the significance of the prophets' statements.

That was where Judah itself was inclined to fail. In Jeremiah's day people remembered Isaiah's message and clung to it, but did so mistakenly because that message did not apply to them. In Ezekiel's day they remembered the message of Jeremiah, realized that he had been right after all, and were demoralized — but wrongly because the arrival of the moment of judgment meant that God could now begin to restore them. Ezekiel's prophecies were given to people in exile. Their relationship with God had been broken and their temple — the place where that relationship was a living experience — had been burned down. As a nation they had been defeated and shamed; their kings had been deposed and humiliated. Their land had been devastated and captured, their God discredited. They were experiencing at every point the opposite of the promise of blessing made long ago to Abraham and developed in the promises concerning monarchy and temple. Through Ezekiel God asserts that those promises are not finished. Ezekiel restates them in more glorious technicolor than they have ever been displayed in before.

To some extent these reaffirmed promises then came true very soon, when the Persians defeated the Babylonians and encouraged the Judeans to return to Palestine to rebuild their temple and their community. Ezra 1–6 alludes to various prophecies that were thus fulfilled, and the partial fulfillment that then came to Ezekiel's promises should not be ignored. But

Ezra and Nehemiah, and other material from the period after the exile such as the prophecies of Haggai and Zechariah, illustrate a gloomier side of the community's experience. Partly because of failures in the people's trust and commitment, such fulfillment as they experienced lacked the technicolor of the reaffirmed promises. The great moment of final judgment and renewal had not yet arrived.

What therefore happens to Ezekiel's promises? The *Late Great Planet Earth* approach assumes that they stand as given, bound to be fulfilled one day in precisely the form that they were given in. The Book of Jeremiah, however, itself makes clear that whether or not warnings or promises are fulfilled depends at least in part on the response they receive when they are given (see Jer 18:7-10). The warnings and promises are part of a living relationship between God and Israel; whether or not they are fulfilled depends on the reaction of those who receive them. If the nature of that response means that they are not fulfilled for their actual recipients, it does not follow that they must be fulfilled someday. In that form, they simply fall. When God's apparently unconditional decision to bring down Nineveh is revoked, as Jonah feared it would be, this did not mean that it nevertheless remained hanging over the city to be fulfilled on some other occasion. In the form in which the decision was made with regard to this particular people, it was simply revoked, like Yahweh's word to Hezekiah in Isaiah 38:1 and to Jehoiakim in Jeremiah 22:19; 36:30 (with which contrast 2 Kgs 24:6), and the one that Amos hears in Amos 7:4. It is significant in this connection to note the important part that intercession played in the prophets' vocation: They were called to pray that their own prophecies would not be fulfilled.

This fact about prophecy suggests a nuancing of our understanding regarding the dynamic power of God's word. The dynamic power of the word is the dynamic power of God; it has no dynamism of its own, and it is not irrevocable in the manner of the Medo-Persian law made fun of in Daniel. In determining whether a promise or warning should have its natural effectiveness God takes account of the response that word meets, and reconsiders it in the light of that response. Yahweh's words do not offer infallible accounts of how the future will turn out. It is the serpent in Genesis 2 who gives Adam and Eve the most accurate account of what will happen to them if they eat of the fruit of the tree.[25]

An unfulfilled warning remains significant as a statement of how history threatens to work out, by the will of God, and thus remains instructive

25. Barr, *Escaping from Fundamentalism* 33-34.

for us as we seek to apply prophecy to history. Ezekiel's promises, too, remain instructive as expressions of the positive purpose of God for Israel and for the world. Once the situation in which they were given has passed, there is no reason to expect them to be fulfilled in their precise form. But as the embodiment in that situation of the age-long purpose of God, they do suggest priorities that God will continue to pursue in history.

To reject the *Late Great Planet Earth* approach to prophecy as misguided is not to affirm the approach that simply affirms the prophets' significance as social reformers. There has been a long-standing debate over whether the prophets' calling was fundamentally to declare that inevitable calamity was about to fall on Israel or whether it was to challenge Israel about its life and to call it to repentance so that calamity might be averted. In seeking to apply the Bible to their society, people naturally presuppose the second understanding, which looks more immediately promising, but the first is actually at least as plausible. The prophets were people who lived in the midst of calamity, in vision or in reality. Their vocation was to prepare people for calamity, to interpret it, and to respond to it.

They did not behave like social reformers. Historically, classical prophecy begins with the appearance of the Assyrians on Israel's northern horizon and with the need for Israel to discover what God is doing with the nation in this context. The first of the prophetic books opens by presupposing that disaster has overtaken the cities of Judah: Isaiah's aim is to try to explain this and to help Judah learn the lesson (see Isaiah 1). Prophets do call for repentance, but too hasty a desire to link them to programs for social reform may in the long term obscure their importance for us. Isaiah goes on to declare to the people of God the fact and the significance of the judgment that hangs over their city, and this is a warning rather than a program for reform. The latter is more the business of Israel's lawmakers, as Deuteronomy in particular shows. The order of the canon is significant, even if books such as Deuteronomy and Leviticus come from later than many of the prophets. The witnessing tradition narrates the events that establish Israel's relationship with God, the authoritative canon lays down the terms of that relationship, and the inspired word declares what is to come on people who ignore God's will.

The prophets' message concerns both Israel and the nations around. A prophet such as Isaiah explicitly addresses himself to the destiny of the nations (see especially Isa 13–27). Jeremiah 18 considers the question whether a nation can evade the judgment of God if it repents; in affirming that this is possible, it regards Judah as at this point in a similar position to that of other nations and as dealt with in a parallel way. In line with this another prophetic book tells that eyebrow-raising story about a prophet sent to a foreign city with the warning that it was about to be overthrown. He did not invite Nineveh to repent, but to his disgust it did so, and his awful fear was realized. God relented (see Jonah 3–4). God does deal with foreign cities on the same basis as Israelite cities. God's message as announced to Israel remains relevant and effective for the people of God; it can be preached to the church as it was once preached to Israel. But God deals with other peoples on the same moral basis as that for dealing with the church, so that the message to Israel can be applied to nations today, though not in such a way as to imply that the household of God is not also the concern of that message — for judgment begins in God's household (1 Pet 4:17).

Critical Interpretation and Interpretation in Faith

We have seen in chapter 9 how Matthew invites us to put alongside each other God's speaking through the prophets and God's speaking through the Son (Heb 1:1) in such a way as to understand the words of God in the First Testament in the light of Christ as well as vice versa. The notion of "God-with-us" is capable of suggesting a presence of a much fuller kind than would be guessed from the words in their context in Isaiah. The darkness into which God brings light is not merely the darkness of this-worldly suffering but that of the absence of God. The growth from the felled tree is, in the person of the Branch-man, more extraordinary even than Isaiah pictured it.

At the same time considerations we have noted suggest we should also study such "prophetic" texts in a way that takes account of their meaning for their authors and first hearers. Even our interpretation of passages such as those that Matthew quotes will not confine itself to noting the significance Matthew finds in them when interpreting them in the light of the particular circumstances of Christ's coming. Isaiah 7, for instance, addresses a context of dire peril for preexilic Judah and relates how its king was challenged to a radical trust in God despite the reality of this threat. Such a trust would issue in doing the right thing before God and before human pressures, despite the temptation either to yield to the pressure from Syria and northern Israel to join their rebellion against Assyria, or alternatively to react by seeking help against Syria and Israel from Assyria itself. The power of Syria and Israel threatens to destroy Judah; but within a year, Isaiah says, it will all be over, and people will know that it is true that "God-is-with-us." That promise is reserved in scripture for the impossible situations that need it (see, e.g., Gen 28:15; Exod 3:12; Jer 1:8; Ps 46:7, 11; Matt 28:20). In these contexts it lifts people back onto their feet, promising them that they do not face the future alone and that God will deal with whatever crisis threatens. So it does in Isaiah 7:14 (see also 8:8, 10); so it does also in that other situation of crisis in Matthew 1:18-25.

Isaiah 9, too, though declared to be fulfilled in Jesus' preaching (see Matt 4:12-17), needs to be understood in its own right. Its context speaks of the darkness, anguish, gloom, and distress of war (8:21-22) — and these are the darkness, anguish, gloom, and distress of the Day of Yahweh's judgment (cf. Amos 5:18-20), which has been embodied in historical events for northern Israel, now the despised "Gentile Galilee." It then portrays darkness dispelled, anguish and distress comforted, the grief of a funeral replaced by the joy of a wedding (Isa 9:1-2). It goes on to speak of a son of David ruling the world in his active justice (9:3-7) — not a vision we yet see fulfilled, but one that must be fulfilled.

The significance of the prophecy concerning a branch to grow from the stump that is all that is left of Jesse's "tree" (11:1) also reaches beyond the link it may have with the name of Jesus' hometown. If a new branch can grow from a tree that has been felled, then no one or nothing is ever finished. If God says that there will be new growth, there will be. For five centuries it must have seemed as if that promise was as dead as the trunk it referred to. Then there *was* new growth, in the person of the Nazarene.

To perceive the fuller implications of prophecies such as these for our understanding of the Christ event and of what God says through such prophecies to us, we need to go back to their own historical meaning. And what is true for passages quoted in the Second Testament will be true for the interpretation of other aspects of the First Testament as the words of God, effective and significant for later generations. The prophets in general present themselves to their hearers as bringing God's words, and the Second Testament accepts that claim. Its utilization of a number of specific passages hardly indicates for us the total range of words of God that it would expect to illuminate the Christ event for us. Rather it initiates us into the task of studying these words as a whole in order that we may understand more fully the one in whom all God's promises find their "Yes" (2 Cor 1:20). These extend right back to God's promise to Abraham of the blessing of family, land, and a secure relationship with God — and beyond to the words of God about blessing and removal of the curse — in the opening chapters of Genesis.

In the story from Genesis to Kings these words from God keep receiving fulfillments of a kind, yet no fulfillment is complete or final, and each experience of fulfillment or loss stimulates renewed hope in God's over-arching promise. This hope is more overt in the prophetic books themselves. What they offer is an updated version of the ancient promises of God to Israel. It is this overarching and ever-reformulated promise that is fulfilled in Christ. So he is to be understood in the light of this ongoing promise to Israel, and we are encouraged to look at those promises in order to under-stand what he came to achieve. At this point, as much interest attaches to aspects of those words of God that were not obviously effective in the Christ event as to aspects that were. For insofar as all God's promises are reaffirmed in Christ, all reveal to us aspects of his significance and calling. Thus if God's words about a new world of active justice have not been effective through Christ's first coming, they must be through his Appearing still to come — must be, because (if one may put it this way) if Jesus is God's Messiah he has no choice but to be the one through whom God's words have their effect.

If God's overarching promise receives a restatement in Ezekiel, that restatement in turn has its effect in the story of Jesus and is retrospectively reinterpreted by it. Ezekiel 34 promises a new David reigning over Israel. Jesus is the fulfillment of that promise, initially in his lifetime, consum-mately at his Appearing. Ezekiel 40–48 promises a new temple more glorious than Zerubbabel's or Herod's. Jesus is that new temple in person, the place of God's dwelling among humanity; the church is then the temple of the Holy Spirit in the world; and the new Jerusalem where God dwells — in a picture colored by Ezekiel — brings God's presence with such reality that it leaves no place for a temple. Ezekiel 38–39 speaks of a coming great final battle. Jesus' ministry, death, and resurrection are the last great battle, to be consummated at the End, which we still await. Ezekiel 37 promises the renewal of Israel and of its relationship with God. Jesus comes to effect that, and Paul reaffirms the promise in Romans 11. The fundamental com-mitment that goes back to Genesis 12 still stands: God will so bless Israel (the Jewish people — the element that belongs to the modern state of Israel is only a small proportion of the people to whom these promises apply) that they will become the means of the world's blessing.

Perhaps an implication of that blessing on the Jewish people is that they will once again enjoy their promised land, as Ezekiel 36 promises. The

Second Testament does see even the promise of the land as fulfilled in Jesus: People enjoy Christ as their inheritance and rest (1 Pet 1:4; Hebrews 3–4). Yet unlike the promises that relate to king and temple, the promise attached to their land goes right back to the beginning with Abraham, no doubt because the notions of land and peoplehood belong closely together. They could hardly be a people without a land. But the possession of the land was always a moral question. Their original possession of it was delayed for four hundred years because God was unwilling to be unfair to the people who were already living there (Gen 15:16). That again draws our attention to the fact that God's promises and warnings attach inextricably to moral questions. Prophecy is not a coded preview of twentieth-century history but an affirmation of God's moral will. It is as such that prophecy has to be applied to the contemporary Middle East, just as to Britain or America. The prophetic word is a promise of God's purpose to renew Israel and to bless the largely Gentile church through Israel, a warning of God's activity in judgment and a challenge to the church, which does not escape the judgment that falls on the world if it becomes indistinguishable from the world. Prophecy is a portrait of the blessing that God intends for Israel and for the church and an invitation to enjoy the abundance of riches that is ours now in Christ and in the Spirit and that will be ours in fullness in the new Jerusalem. Ezekiel 36:24 is inscribed on the wall in the main hall of the President's House in Jerusalem.[26] The prophets' moral challenges also stand written before the nation's government.

Thomas Cranmer once described scripture as the "fountain and well of truth."[27] The phrase recalls Moses' "song of the well" in Numbers 21:17-18, which the Qumran community applied to scripture as a source of the people's sustenance, which interpreters "dig."[28] John Muddiman takes the two images to suggest that "the Bible is like a well, deep and inaccessible, from which truth has to be extracted laboriously by study through the method of biblical criticism," but also "like a fountain, fresh and accessible, with its own power to communicate truth to the receptive mind."[29] Both hard-thinking critical study and simple openness in faith respond to aspects of scripture, and each is incomplete if unaccompanied by the other. Critical

26. According to Fackenheim, *The Jewish Bible after the Holocaust* 49.

27. *Sermons, or Homilies, Appointed to be Read in Churches* (first published 1547; reprinted London: Prayer-Book Society, 1817) 1.

28. See the *Damascus Rule* (CD) 6:4-10, also 3:14-17; cf. Fishbane, *The Garments of Torah* 76.

29. *The Bible: Fountain and Well of Truth* 2; see further 2-7.

method drawing from the well expresses a concern for truth and safeguards us from delusion, while reality itself can rise to the surface of its own accord as from a fountain, fresh and immediate. Roger Lundin contrasts the interpretive stances of Augustine and Descartes, the first finding himself vividly and forcefully addressed by scripture as if it was written to him personally, the second determined to follow measured and objective study that takes nothing for granted. Lundin comments:

> Our deepest sympathies very likely lie more with Augustine and our actual practices resemble his, while our theory demands that we think of the pursuit of truth in the way Descartes seems to do. We live as Augustine and dream we're Descartes.[30]

On the other hand it is the critical approach to interpretation that recaptured the literal meaning of the Song of Songs — even if precritical interpretation then functions to remind us that the Song may also be aware of a link between human and divine love (cf. 8:6-7).[31]

Historical interpretation of scripture and interpretation that is existentially meaningful would ideally occupy concentric circles. In practice, in our age, they occupy overlapping circles.

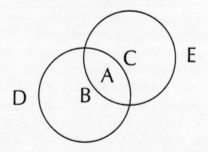

A represents the ideal: Historical and existential interpretation coincide. B and C represent the acceptable if the less than ideal: Historical interpretation that operates within a framework of faith but offers no message that speaks existentially, and religious interpretation that is unrelated to the historical meaning of the passage but works within the parameters of the

30. *The Responsibility of Hermeneutics* 3-4.
31. Murphy, "History of Exegesis as a Hermeneutical Tool."

rule of the faith and serves love and steadfastness. D and E stand outside the limits of the acceptable: Historical interpretation that operates outside the framework of faith and existential interpretation that attributes a significance to the passage that does not correspond to the historical meaning of any part of scripture.

On occasions when a historical approach leaves us only with history we can accept that for the sake of the rigor and honesty of faith. Even when its results seem to offer us nothing directly edifying (perhaps especially when this is so) it thus draws our attention to the fact that God is involved in real history with its specificity, oddness, foreignness, and nastiness — which is good news if we want to believe that God also speaks in our specific historical situation.[32] Conversely, when a nonhistorical approach generates a sense of God addressing us with a word that coheres with the gospel but that we cannot justify through historical exegesis, we can also accept that for the sake of its witness to the true word of God. The eschatological goal for interpretation of inspired scripture is concentricity of the circles in our diagram, interpretation in which history and faith, criticism and devotion are one. That is also an appropriate goal for now. With many parts of scripture in many contexts it is an attainable goal.

In principle an academic or historical approach and a believing or theological approach are in no tension with each other. They can be partners, and either on its own is inadequate as a means to interpreting the text. To put it another way, in interpreting a text we may see ourselves as subject in relation to object, master in relation to servant. We are doing the text the favor of letting it speak once more. But if it is the word of God we are reading, the interpretive movement operates in the reverse direction. God is the subject, we are the object, God the master, we the servant. God is doing us the favor of letting us overhear what our ancestors in the faith once heard. At least, God *may* do so; we cannot assume or imagine that we can force God to speak. That is why prayer must have the last word.

---

32. So Peta Sherlock in a private communication.

PART IV

SCRIPTURE AS EXPERIENCED REVELATION: INTERPRETING APOCALYPSE, TESTIMONY, AND THEOLOGICAL STATEMENT

• 13 •

Interpreting a Revelation

The approaches to interpretation we have considered so far match scriptural narrative, instruction, and prophecy — while also applying more broadly (if in less sharp focus) to all scripture insofar as the whole can be seen as a witnessing tradition, an authoritative canon, or an inspired word. We have finally to consider the apocalypses (Daniel and Revelation), the Psalms, and the wisdom books, and also the Epistles. The Epistles are from our perspective the most complicated genre to handle, but in different ways all these works combine divine revelation, human experience, and human reflection and in this respect may appropriately be considered together. They do not form as simple a model as the first three models we have utilized, but neither are they as disparate as they might at first seem.

The experience in prayer to which the Psalms witness, for instance, often presupposes or looks for an experience of a revelation from God, and also presupposes reflection on experience; psalms, like hymns, are more likely written in the light of reflection on experience, and indeed as a form of reflection on experience, than in the midst of the experience. The wisdom books emphasize experience and are the fruit of reflection on experience, but even this material, which is the nearest thing in scripture to theological reflection in a modern sense, does not regard revelation as something foreign, as Job makes especially clear. The apocalypses bring direct revelation from God in such a way as to make an explicit link with an experience on the part of the seer, and their intrinsic relationship with earlier scripture suggests that they have a "scribal" or reflective as well as a revelatory aspect. The Epistles testify to the human experience of their writers, depend on revelation they have received, and mediate their reflection on experience and revelation. Revelation, experience, and reflection form a triptych, or even a trio of overlapping circles like those in a Venn diagram.[1] Interpretation needs to work with the differing potentials of revelation, experience, and reflection.

Revelation and Myth

The nature of "revelation" is to offer an unveiling of realities that would otherwise remain hidden, and the nature of the Jewish and Christian apocalypses is to unveil aspects of the truth regarding realms that are inaccessible to human investigation. They thus unveil things above and below, things in front and behind (see Mishnah Ḥagigah 2:1):[2] the world of heaven and hell and the world of the future and the past. Their object is not to satisfy mere human curiosity about these realms, just as the object of biblical stories is not merely to entertain. The apocalypses aim to enable people to live in faith and hope, with the right kind of confidence based on a true understanding of Beginning and End, of the realm of heaven and the realm of death.

How are we to interpret the factual significance of their descriptions of the realms above and below and of Beginning and End? Rudolf Bultmann's essay "New Testament and Mythology," published in 1941, set in motion a debate regarding the biblical depictions of Beginning and End and of heaven and hell, declaring that these needed to be demythologized if they were to be interpreted appropriately. More recent discussion in Britain and elsewhere of "The Myth of God Incarnate"[3] continues this debate. The attempt in the United States and elsewhere by theologians such as George Lindbeck to formulate a "post-modern" theology also relates to this debate but seeks to move beyond its parameters.[4]

Bultmann argued the importance of examining critically the differences between what authors actually say and the reality of which they speak. They may not speak of this reality as well as they could, or the words and concepts available to them may be inadequate to that reality.[5] It is our own religious and theological awareness that enables us to discern where this is so. Consciously or unconsciously all interpreters measure what the Bible says by their

1. See further p. 287 in my *Models for Scripture*.

2. See Rowland, *The Open Heaven* 75; see further my *Models for Scripture*, chapter 20.

3. See the book of this name edited by Goulder; also Wiles, " 'Myth' in Theology"; Sykes and Clayton (ed.), *Christ, Faith and History*.

4. See Lindbeck, *The Nature of Doctrine*.

5. See, e.g., Bultmann's "The Problem of a Theological Exegesis of the NT," also his critique of Barth's commentary on 1 Corinthians 15, *The Resurrection of the Dead*, in *Faith and Understanding*, especially 71-72, 80-86.

own religious and theological awareness; Bultmann was unusually self-aware and open about this feature of interpretation. Though the biblical documents may be subject to limitations, Bultmann saw his task not as encouraging Christians to trim the gospel so that it becomes acceptable to a scientific age, but as encouraging them to use their scientific awareness to enable them to see where scripture's message really lay. To believe things merely because on the surface scripture requires them or to believe on the basis of "objective" evidence is to reduce faith to works; demythologizing carries the doctrine of justification by faith to its logical conclusion in the realm of epistemology.[6] To insist on basing belief on such evidence is also dangerous because it may imply an unwillingness to take responsibility for ourselves.[7]

To infer from our experience of the world that the Bible writers' account of it is mythic rather than factual is not to imply that what it says is valueless. It means that we have to get beyond the words that the Bible uses to its real subject matter. Demythologizing is the process of getting behind the words, and existentialist thought helps us identify what their real subject matter is. It does that because existentialist philosophy offers the most penetrating analysis of the human situation and of human needs, of which and to which the gospel is speaking in its mythic manner. Existentialist philosophy can be a means of discovering and living by the message of scripture, and not of discarding it as unacceptable.

Bultmann suggests that whether the Bible talks about past or future, the realm above or the realm below, its true concern is life here and now as we are involved with it. In discussing "the meaning of Christian faith in creation," for instance, he suggests that in any religion "faith in creation is the expression of a specific understanding of human existence." It provides ways of coping with a feeling of anxiety about one's place in the world, of being at a loss as to the meaning of one's situation in the world, of uncertainty as to one's relationship with the rest of the cosmos. Bultmann illustrates this faith mainly from the Psalms, which often speak explicitly of humanity's *present* relationship with creation. Genesis 1–2, in contrast, speaks of creation as a past event, but despite the narrative form of those chapters,

> faith in creation . . . is not a theory about the past. It does not have its meaning by relating what took place at some earlier time and no longer

6. "Bultmann Replies to His Critics," in *Kerygma and Myth* (ed. Bartsch) 1:210-11.

7. Bultmann, *Jesus Christ and Mythology* 16; cf. the comments at the end of chapter 11 above.

concerns man in the present, but rather speaks precisely about man's *present* situation. It tells him how to understand himself *now;* and the reference to the past is only for the purpose of teaching him to understand his situation in the present.[8]

The past must not be objectivized, treated coolly and rationally without personal involvement.[9] To use Bultmann's later terminology, the reference to the past has to be demythologized. The present concern of the Psalms shows where the real concern of Genesis also lies; Bultmann is fond of suggesting that demythologizing has its justification in the moves in this direction within scripture itself. Genesis 1–3 as a whole is of course widely believed to be really concerned with the present realities of human experience rather than with giving an account of human origins, so Bultmann's demythologizing is not in principle as heterodox as it is often portrayed.

Thus far Bultmann has not been talking of distinctively Christian faith in creation. What Christianity reveals is that our human anxiety about our place in the world has its basis in sin, that we find meaning by finding God's grace and forgiveness, and — in keeping with the existentialist understanding of faith — that we are then free of the world and free to be ourselves authentically in it.

Bultmann takes a similar approach to biblical talk about the future. The idea of a future consummation of God's purpose is not meant to give us mere objective information on how as a matter of fact the future will work out. It is meant to call us

> to be open to God's future which is really imminent for every one of us; to be prepared for this future which can come as a thief in the night when we do not expect it; to be prepared, because this future will be a judgment on all men who have bound themselves to this world and are not free, not open to God's future.[10]

In general, then,

> to affirm that Jesus Christ is the pre-existent Son of God, that he was born of the Virgin Mary, that he descended into hell, that on the third day he rose again from the dead, that he now sits at the right hand of the Father

8. See Bultmann, *Existence and Faith* 207-9. Cf. the sermon on "Faith in God the Creator," in *ibid.*, 171-82.

9. See more generally Bultmann's *History and Eschatology.*

10. *Jesus Christ and Mythology* 31-32.

from whence he shall eventually come to judge the quick and the dead —
in short, to affirm any or all of the church's traditional assertions about
Christ is in reality simply to affirm the authentic self-understanding presented in the Christian message.[11]

Paul Tillich approaches the "principalities and powers" of Romans 8
in a parallel way. He suggests that the passage speaks to us of the risen
Christ's lordship over the entities that we realize are our masters. These are
not otherworldly demonic powers but the driving forces of love, power,
knowledge, success and failure, present and future, and death and life. It is
from these all too real overlords that Christ wonderfully frees us.[12] In
general, says Bultmann, talk about supernatural forces intervening in the
course of nature and in what human beings think, will, and do is a mythic
way of speaking of this-worldly and human experiences and responsibilities. Conversely, to declare that Jesus is Lord is not to make a factual
objective metaphysical statement. It is to declare a personal commitment.

Bultmann has a particular concern to avoid appeal to miracle. Like the
being of God, the acts of God are real but cannot be apprehended apart
from their existential reference. They are thus not objectively visible or
attainable like ordinary worldly events. Nor do they involve a disturbance
of the closed weft of history as this presents itself to objective observation.
They do not provide proof to the eyes of the uncommitted.[13] Bultmann's
concern is to deny both that miracles happen and that in any case we could
have access to them as objective facts in the sense of access independent of
our personal involvement with them. The danger of mythic language is that
its objectivizing talk can obscure the point that Christian faith is about a
personal relationship between us and God.[14]

Indeed, Bartsch argues that the very fact that science may allow miracles
illustrates that in themselves miracles can establish nothing. The message
lies in the miracle story, which expresses what an event means for people,
not in the event's mere having-happenedness.[15] "This is not to say that faith
is merely 'making up their minds,' merely a subjective experience. Bultmann
never says that nothing happened between the Risen Christ and his dis-

11. Ogden, *Christ without Myth* 114.

12. See "Principalities and Powers," in *The New Being* 50-59 = *The Boundaries of Our Being* 189-97. See also Bultmann, *Theology of the NT* §§21.3, 26.3.

13. "Bultmann Replies to His Critics," in *Kerygma and Myth* (ed. Bartsch) 1:196-97.

14. Owen, *Revelation and Existence* 16-19; cf. Henderson, *Myth in the NT* 47.

15. *Kerygma and Myth* 2:19.

ciples. All he says is that our only access to what did happen is through their proclamation." The salvation events occurred outside us, but for us; Bultmann wishes to avoid a stress on the former that undermines the latter.[16] His own discussions of the acts of God make it particularly clear that he does not imply that they are merely a "symbolical description of a subjective experience"; this is analogical language.[17] He does not develop the implications of the difference between analogical and mythic language, perhaps partly because the former is also rather objectivist in implication.[18] Even analogically we can only talk of God as known in connection with our own life, not as an object of abstract thought; for Bultmann it is very important that the revelation of God is not a matter of abstract truths but of personal encounter. We are not speaking about God when we treat God as a mere object of thought.[19]

The idea that biblical narrative gives a mythic account of events has been taken up in liberation theology. An event such as the escape of oppressed people from Egypt turns out to be of such deep significance for Israel that it is portrayed in supernaturalist terms, which externalize and objectify the event's transcendent significance. The ongoing hope for the future that these events stirred in Israel leads to that hope being projected back so that the events themselves are portrayed as the planned outworking of a promise on which people could set their hope; Moses' significance as a leader brings about the attribution of a call experience to him; the people's actual escape from the Egyptians acquires miraculous elements such as the parting of the sea and the pillar of cloud; events are portrayed as directly divine rather than as human events that had a transcendent significance.[20]

---

16. Bartsch, *Kerygma and Myth* 2:71-72, 79; cf. D. S. Fergusson's comments on Bultmann's "theological realism" in his "Meaning, Truth, and Realism in Bultmann and Lindbeck" 186-91. Bartsch notes Barth's comment that "the real Easter event . . . is the rise of the Easter faith of the first disciples" (*Church Dogmatics* III/2, 444), apparently misunderstanding this as Barth's own view rather than his summary of Bultmann's. But see Bultmann's own remarks on the past factuality of the events in *Kerygma and Myth* 1:37, also J. Schniewind's quotation from Bultmann in *Kerygma and Myth* 1:77; also Henderson's understanding of the comment by Barth in *Myth in the NT* 41, and Ogden's in *Christ without Myth* 87.

17. *Kerygma and Myth* (ed. Bartsch) 1:196, 197; cf. Bultmann, *Jesus Christ and Mythology* 68-73.

18. Ogden, *Christ without Myth* 150-51.

19. See Bultmann's "What Does It Mean to Speak of God?" in *Faith and Understanding* 53-65.

20. Croatto, *Exodus* 15-16, 25-27.

The Concepts of Myth and Demythologizing

Like revelation, myth and demythologizing are categories with a number of meanings, even for Bultmann himself.[21]

A mythic statement may, for instance, be one that

- sees transcendent significance in the realm of nature as opposed to that of history or seeks to undergird the secure relationship — even oneness — of the realm of nature and the human realm;
- refers to supernatural realms, primal events, or future destiny rather than to matters open to empirical investigation;
- uses forms of expression from human and this-worldly experience to speak of heavenly realities, rather than attempting to speak of them literally (because to do so is impossible);
- is humanly generated rather than divinely given;
- communicates figuratively rather than literally regarding matters that cannot be represented conceptually or expresses the significance of primary symbols in narrative form;
- uses a form of speech that on the surface refers to objective external realities rather than using self-involving, performative language, but whose underlying concern is to express or to evoke certain attitudes or existential commitments;
- utilizes ways of conceiving of supernatural powers of good and evil, or of the Beginning and the End, that derive from the Hebrew or Greek scriptures' relationships with their surrounding cultures;
- expresses itself primitively rather than scientifically, perhaps talking in terms of a three-story universe or picturing Jesus' ascent to heaven with his feet sticking down out of a cloud;
- explains the origins of something in a way that does not correspond to our scientific or historical reasoning;
- constitutes one element from a total perspective on reality and experience and their ultimate significance, expressing in narrative form something of a people's faith, hopes, and ideals, their "intuitions of transcendent reality,"[22] and not wholly capable of being translated into conceptual terms;

21. See further, e.g., J. D. G. Dunn, "Demythologizing," in *NT Interpretation* (ed. Marshall) 285-88; Rogerson, *Myth in OT Interpretation*; Caird, *The Language and Imagery of the Bible* 219-23; also the essays in *Sacred Narrative* (ed. Dundes). In defense of Bultmann, see Ogden, *Christ without Myth* 28-31, 166-70.

22. Rogerson, *Myth in OT Interpretation* 188.

- claims to record the intervention of the supernatural in the course of nature in such a way as to make the sun stand still or axheads float, an idea that Bultmann declared in a famous phrase to be incredible to us who are accustomed "to use electric light and the wireless and to avail ourselves of modern medical and surgical discoveries";[23] or
- expresses a transcendent truth: Bultmann speaks of God's love, demands, wrath, promise, grace, fatherhood, and acts, refers them to the actual "objective" God, and sees that this could also be termed mythic talk, though he prefers to describe it as analogical — the difference being that it is a matter of self-involving terms and terms expressive of a relationship; they are not objectifying and theoretical.[24]

"In both scholarly and popular usage *myth* has acquired a variety of meanings; we throw traditional tales, magico-religious beliefs, theology, false beliefs, superstitions, ritual formulae, literary images and symbols, and social ideals into a common pot and call the mixture mythology."[25] In general myth is not a flattering expression but one to which negative value-status is attached. To describe something as a myth casts doubt on its worth. The term suggests "false" over against "true."

As the nature of myth is understood in different ways, so the meaning of demythologizing varies, and one may say that scripture is thoroughly mythic, or thoroughly demythologized, or occasionally mythic. If myth is understood, for instance, as a way of undergirding the secure relationship of the natural and the human realms, demythologizing involves breaking that pattern of linkage. If myth is understood as a total perspective on reality and experience and their ultimate significance, superficially mythic elements of expression can survive in a nonmythic system with quite different meanings. Thus the biblical use of mythic material is often reckoned to involve demythologization of them or at least theological reinterpretation of them (so, e.g., Genesis 1, Job 41, and Isaiah 14). The three-story universe and other features of Genesis 1 are then not myth but a "residual and sterilised fragment" of what was once myth, and even the more widespread utilization of mythic motifs in the Psalms and the apocalypses may

23. "NT and Mythology" 5.

24. *Jesus Christ and Mythology* 68-69; cf. Henry, *God, Revelation, and Authority* 1:60.

25. J. Fontenrose, *The Ritual Theory of Myth* 53; cf. Rogerson, *Myth in OT Interpretation* 173.

need to be considered in this light.[26] A passage such as Isaiah 14 not only historicizes mythic motifs but also implicitly criticizes the whole mythic way of expression.[27] The Bible does its best to avoid satisfying the human desire for myth. Therefore the Bible's contents had to be remythologized later by the likes of Milton in *Paradise Lost*.[28]

In general the debate over demythologizing strangely ignored the extensive way in which the relationship between faith and myth is handled in the First Testament.[29] It also ignored the way the Second Testament in turn dismisses myths as elaborate and speculative, godless and humanly devised, alien and in conflict with the gospel, contrasting *mythos* and *logos* in a way that stresses that the gospel is the latter, not the former (1 Tim 1:4, 15; 4:7-9; 2 Tim 4:2-4; Titus 1:9, 14; 2 Pet 1:16-19).[30]

A range of further questions about Bultmann's use of the concept of myth might be raised. It is particularly telling that his hesitation regarding miracle on the basis of the scientific worldview and his understanding of worldly causality is itself questioned by philosophers, not only Austin Farrer but Bultmann's own pupil Hans Jonas and the German existentalist Karl Jaspers, to both of whom Bultmann has referred approvingly.[31] It is by no means clear that the gospel that emerges from Bultmann's commitment to modernity is one that meets people where they are; the "mythic" worldview is much more widespread than Bultmann or a sympathetic critic such as Ogden allows.[32]

26. Barr, "The Meaning of 'Mythology' in Relation to the OT" 8; cf. Childs's *Myth and Reality in the OT*.

27. Fisch, *Poetry with a Purpose* 2.

28. Schneidau, *Sacred Discontent*, e.g., 2, 12.

29. Barr, "The Meaning of 'Mythology' in Relation to the OT" 1. See later Rogerson, *Myth in OT Interpretation*.

30. R. Trigg, " 'Tales Artfully Spun,' " in *The Bible as Rhetoric* (ed. Warner) 129.

31. See Farrer, "An English Appreciation," in *Kerygma and Myth* (ed. Bartsch) 1:216; Jonas, "Is Faith Still Possible?" 11-23; Jaspers, "Myth and Religion," in *Kerygma and Myth* 2:134-35. For Bultmann's allusions see "NT and Mythology" 12, 24. See also Jonas 22-23 and Jaspers 144-47 for the place of myth.

32. See Ogden, *Christ without Myth* 127-32. This is not to imply that Bultmann's concern is apologetic, as can seem to be implied by his phrase about what is incredible to people who are accustomed to using electricity and other modern discoveries. His primary concern is the nature of true Christian faith and the appropriate way in which we as Christians should understand the Bible in the light of its own intrinsic concerns, not the establishment of the minimum we should expect of outsiders. See Tracy, *The Analogical Imagination* 138.

The coherence of Bultmann's proposal has also been questioned. Is there some randomness in his stopping short of demythologizing the notion of God and of God acting?[33] Is there some randomness in his retaining reference to Jesus Christ? "One wonders whether there is not a measure of inconsistency between the claim that a truth is, on the one hand, based on human experience generally but, on the other hand, brought home very potently by certain events in history. If it is based on human experience why is it not brought home potently by such experience?"[34] If myth only symbolically represents what is cognitively inaccessible and historically nonfactual, what is the basis for preferring one myth to another?

Further, it is disquieting that Bultmann's affirmation of modernity as the criterion for interpreting scripture was made at the very moment when "the pitiless consequences of this spirit, and of the technological mind to which it has given birth" were reaching their apogee in World War and Holocaust.[35] Bultmann was not historical in the sense that most mattered.

The Complementarity of the Objective and the Self-Involving

With regard to the world of the past, scripture gives great prominence to narrative accounts of events in history, to which human commitment is a response. Bultmann systematically questions both the factuality and the relevance of this narrativity of scripture. As a consequence, Barth suggests, Bultmann risks putting the emphasis on the Christ *event* as opposed to the *Christ* event and gives the impression that talk in terms of God raising Jesus

33. So, e.g., Kee, *The Way of Transcendence* xi-xxii. Cf. Abraham's criticism of M. F. Wiles in *Divine Revelation* 204 and Buri's criticism of S. M. Ogden in *How Can We Still Speak Responsibly of God* 35-38 (cf. Ogden, *The Reality of God and Other Essays* 90-93). See also H. Braun, "The Problem of a NT Theology," in *The Bultmann School of Biblical Interpretation* (ed. Funk) 182-83. In defense of Bultmann as by no means merely Feuerbach in disguise, see Ricoeur, *The Conflict of Interpretations* 394, and for Bultmann's own dissociation of himself from Feuerbach, see *Jesus Christ and Mythology* 70. Moore notes that deconstruction also takes up where Bultmann leaves off (*Literary Criticism and the Gospels* 175-76).

34. Abraham, *Divine Revelation* 83. See the discussion in Ogden, *Christ without Myth.*

35. Füssel, "Materialist Readings of the Bible" 15, following G. Casalis, *Correct Ideas Don't Fall from the Skies* (ET Maryknoll: Orbis, 1984), chapter 4; also Belo, *A Materialist Reading of the Gospel of Mark* 286.

is only a dispensable explanation of the message about Jesus' ongoing subjective significance for believers. We cannot speak of cross and resurrection having their own intrinsic meaning, which is the basis for the message about them and the ground and origin of faith. Whereas the modern instinct is to begin with human experience, scripture begins with God's act, and even its description of our being in Christ is not primarily a statement about subjective human experience.[36]

In Bultmann, the gospel is not so much demythologized as dehistoricized.[37] Indeed, the removal of the gospel's concern with the past and the future and thus of its orientation to humanity's temporal existence is a mythologizing of the gospel rather than an act of demythologizing.[38] Bultmann's convictions about the historical value of scriptural narrative not only mesh with his theology but have their origin there. The narrative itself shows a concern with history that links with its own understanding of the nature of the gospel.

With regard to the worlds above and below, Croatto uses Bultmann's method and infers from the nature of the Latin American experience of oppression and liberation what must have taken place at the exodus. Yahweh's action would have been an immanent providence giving transcendent meaning to events that can be described in human terms. Now such an understanding of the relationship between divine and human action is one that appears in scripture, in the opening chapters of the exodus story (Exodus 1–2). Sometimes Yahweh is described as involved "behind the scenes" in human battles (Exodus 17), so that holy war can be described as a "synergism," "a fusion of divine and human activity."[39] But precisely in the light of this it is noteworthy that Exodus's own interpretation of the exodus itself does not take this form; instead it puts exclusive emphasis on divine activity. It is implausible to claim that Croatto's understanding is one that meshes with the text. This interpretation in the light of the contemporary event rules out the interpretation offered in Exodus.

As the First Testament generally stresses the battle against earthly enemies and only occasionally emphasizes a heavenly battle, so the Second expects people to find it natural to visualize themselves fighting against mere this-worldly enemies and warns them against this (Eph 6:12). Again

---

36. Barth, "Rudolf Bultmann — An Attempt to Understand Him," in *Kerygma and Myth* (ed. Bartsch) 2:92, 95, 101, 110.

37. Cf. Dahl, "Rudolf Bultmann's *Theology of the New Testament*," in Dahl, *The Crucified Messiah and Other Essays* 96.

38. Rahner, "The Hermeneutics of Eschatological Assertions" 331.

39. Miller, *The Divine Warrior* 156.

it seems implausible to suggest that the writer's covert concern is the perspective against which he gives his overt warning. The supernatural forces of evil surely stand for more than those driving forces analyzed by Tillich. The way in which we conceptualize the world above and the world below may need adapting, but there is something ontological to reexpress.[40]

With regard to the world of the future, too, Bultmann suggests that when Paul speaks about the imminent End the deeper meaning of his preaching is that we are all called to be open to God's future, which really is imminent for us all. When scripture depicts the events associated with the End, its intention is to affect life in the present and not to make a statement about the actual historical future.[41] But there was no necessity for the scriptures to emphasize a purpose of God at work on a temporal time line from creation to the End. The First Testament is somewhat distinctive in relating creation, history, and future in this way, and Bultmann notes that it is itself also capable of emphasizing our present relationship with the created world and of writing history without projecting it into eschatology. This suggests that the scriptures' view that history is a time process that will have an End (one that leads into a new Beginning) is not merely a metaphor. In Second Testament times it was quite possible to envisage a worldview that omitted resurrection (Mark 12:18). To operate with a worldview that included resurrection was a matter of choice. As is the case with the being of God and the acts of God, scripture also insists on the world having significance in its own right, which seems a wasteful way of saying that the significance of the world is exclusively that it provides the stage for human life.[42]

The Bible speaks of history both as humanity's responsibility and as determined by cosmic forces. It refers both to a future passage from death to life and to such a transition taking place now. It is concerned with both factual matters and personal commitment. The former provides grounds for the latter, for taking up committed attitudes of faith, hope, and obedience: Scripture assumes that the leap of faith is not a blind one but one that has a basis.[43] Mythic interpretation takes personal commitment alone as scripture's real concern; where scripture seems to make more factual statements, they are regarded as a metaphorical way of expressing or evok-

40. Cf. Goldingay, "Expounding the NT," in *NT Interpretation* (ed. Marshall) 359.

41. *Jesus Christ and Mythology* 31.

42. Cf. E. Lohmeyer, "The Right Interpretation of the Mythological," in *Kerygma and Myth* (ed. Bartsch) 1:128.

43. Owen, *Revelation and Existence* 48-49.

ing this commitment.[44] Demythologizing arises out of a concern to deobjectify scriptural language. Within scripture, the more demythologized language is corrective of the more mythic language.

It is more plausible to see scripture as affirming what Bultmann affirms, that its statements are self-involving, but also affirming what he denies, that behind the self-involving statement is a factual statement. The objective and the self-involving are distinguishable and interdependent, not alternative expressions of the same thing. The two forms of language complement and correct each other. The subjective and the objective elements in revelation are not to be put into a radical disjunction.[45] We should refuse to play theological ping-pong, or at least refuse to play it by Bultmann's rules.[46]

Bultmann contrasts demythologizing with allegorical interpretation of the Second Testament,[47] but the parallel between the two is more striking. He seems to interpret scripture in the light of a principle alien to it and to disregard scripture's right and capacity to provide the categories for interpretation of scripture.[48] As well as seeming more confusing than illuminating, in the interpretation of biblical revelation the category of myth seems to simplify a double concern within scripture: Scripture is concerned for the factual reality of the realms above and below, ahead and behind, even while it assumes that our apprehension of them is always self-involving rather than "objective."

When we say "Jesus is Lord" or "Yahweh is a great God" we are not merely conveying information but declaring our commitment and our worship. (The "deep structure" of these statements is similar to that of declarations such as "We believe in Jesus Christ" or "We praise you, O God.") For such true statements to be truly interpreted, to be authentic on my lips, part of their significance must be to indicate my commitment. But Bultmann went too far when he implied that "Jesus is Lord" indicates mainly or even exclusively that commitment. "For a certain performative utterance to be happy, certain statements have *to be true.*"[49] Revelation is both objective and self-involving.

---

44. Cf. Abraham, *Divine Revelation* 74, with specific reference to the incarnation.

45. Owen, *Revelation and Existence* 138-39.

46. Mitchell, *How to Play Theological Ping-Pong and Other Essays on Faith and Reason* 166-83.

47. "NT and Mythology" 13.

48. H. Thielicke, "The Restatement of NT Mythology," in *Kerygma and Myth* (ed. Bartsch) 1:149.

49. Austin, *How to Do Things with Words* 45 (emphasis original); cf. Thiselton, e.g., "The Use of Philosophical Categories in NT Hermeneutics" 96.

14

Interpreting Accounts
of Human Experience

Because it is a human book, the whole of scripture reflects human experience, though material such as the Psalms and some of Paul's letters is more explicit in its relationship to human experience, and specifically human experience of God. Approaches to interpretation that treat texts as essentially expressions of human experience that have been put into writing are especially appropriate to material in scripture that directly witnesses to the writers' experience, though, like other models, this understanding and approach can be stretched to apply to scripture more generally as issuing from human experience.

How Such Interpretation Starts

How do we go about interpreting this material in which people explicitly focus on relating their own experience?

One major tradition of interpretation over the past two centuries has treated written texts in general as the reflection of the particular historical (concrete, existential) experience of their authors, to which interpreters can gain access through their own analogous historical experience. The fountainhead of this tradition is the work of Friedrich Schleiermacher (1768-1834), in which can be perceived an interest in both a more "grammatical" or objective approach to interpretation and a more "psychological" or subjective approach. The former corresponds to the nature of texts as expressed in language, the latter to their nature as expressions of an individual's creativity. Schleiermacher recognized that texts belong on a spectrum from chronicle and didactic to lyric poetry and letters; objective interpretation has a more prominent place at one end of this spectrum, psychological interpretation at the other.[1] He also brought about a related turning point in the understanding of the aim of hermeneutics. It not merely supports, secures, and clarifies an already accepted understanding; it seeks to make understanding possible, to initiate understanding.[2] Wilhelm Dilthey (1833-1911) shared Schleiermacher's interest in feelings and inner experience and took up the second approach, describing hermeneutics as the "art of understanding expressions of life fixed in writing"[3] and emphasizing the importance of empathy in interpretation.[4]

While building on the work of Schleiermacher and Dilthey, Rudolf Bultmann emphasized that the interpreter's focus lies not on the inner psychology of the writer but on the subject matter of the text, to which writer and interpreter have the same life-relation.[5] The counselor's empathy therefore provides an analogy for the task of interpretation, rather than a definition of it, as that which has as its goal an understanding of the author's mind. Hans-Georg Gadamer similarly took up the more linguistic or objective side to Schleiermacher's approach to interpretation, declaring that "to understand what a person says is . . . to agree about the object, not to get inside another person and relive his experiences."[6] One may grant the fruitfulness of that point without accepting the inference that the original author, audience, and context simply disappear when we are seeking to understand a text. Such an inference

---

1. *Hermeneutics* 103. The relative place of each in Schleiermacher is a matter of dispute: See the "Introductions" by J. Duke and H. Kimmerle to Schleiermacher's *Hermeneutics*. Thiselton's *New Horizons in Hermeneutics* 225 offers a wonderful diagrammatic account of Schleiermacher's understanding of the interpretive process in the context of an appreciative account of Schleiermacher's "brilliance" and "balance" (228).

2. H. Kimmerle, "Hermeneutical Theory or Ontological Hermeneutics," in *History and Hermeneutic* (ed. Funk) 107; cf. Thiselton, "The New Hermeneutic," in *NT Interpretation* (ed. Marshall) 310-11; *idem, New Horizons in Hermeneutics* 204-5.

3. As quoted from *Gesammelte Schriften* (1924) 5:332 by Bultmann, "The Problem of Hermeneutics," in *NT and Mythology* 69; cf. Dilthey, "The Rise of Hermeneutics" 233.

4. "Empathy" is H. P. Rickman's rendering of *hineinversetzen* (to place oneself mentally into something) in Dilthey: see *The Hermeneutics Reader* (ed. Mueller-Vollmer) 159, 164. It is also the rendering of *Einverständnis* (common understanding) in Fuchs, "The Hermeneutical Problem" 270; cf. Thiselton, *The Two Horizons* 343.

5. "The Problem of Hermeneutics," in *NT and Mythology* 69-74.

6. *Truth and Method* 345.

threatens to dissolve Schleiermacher's tension in the opposite direction to that of Bultmann.[7]

An understanding of interpretation as the art of understanding expressions of life fixed in writing provides a suggestive way into material in the prophets (especially Hosea and Jeremiah), Paul (e.g., Romans 7 and Philippians 3), and most systematically the Psalms that directly reflects personal feelings, attitudes, and experience.[8]

The beginning of communication between two people (parent and infant, foreigner and native, counselor and client) depends on two things that they share. One is objects that both can point to: mother, daddy, teddy; tree, house, food; experiences of fear, loss, and anger. The other is a mutual interest in these objects and a mutual involvement with them: If one party is unwilling to look in the direction that the other points, there can be no communication. Communication takes place in the home in a common language based on a world of shared assumptions, attitudes, and experiences: "At home one does not speak so that people may understand, but because people understand."[9] They share a common world shaped by their shared experience and articulated in their common language. Conversely, if a lion could talk, we could not understand him.[10] Communication begins on the basis of a shared interest in something that people have in common.

So it is also with communication in writing. Gadamer takes as the motto for the central section of *Truth and Method* Luther's observation: "The person who does not understand a thing cannot draw out meaning from the words."[11] Experience of something is a precondition of understanding a text that refers to it. "A text can be explained only when one has an inner relationship to the matter with which the text deals," that is, a preunderstanding that one shares with it.[12] In particular, our ability to hear

7. Against Croatto, *Biblical Hermeneutics* 16-17; cf. p. 171 above.

8. Thiselton applies Schleiermacher's romanticist hermeneutics to the broader interpretation of Pauline and comparable texts in *New Horizons in Hermeneutics* 237-71.

9. E. Fuchs, "The NT and the Hermeneutical Problem," in *The New Hermeneutic* (ed. Robinson and Cobb) 124; cf. Thiselton, *The Two Horizons* 344.

10. Wittgenstein, *Philosophical Investigations* 223.

11. See *Truth and Method* 151; cf. Hirsch, *Validity in Interpretation* 248.

12. Bultmann, in a review of Barth's *Romans* reprinted in *The Beginnings of Dialectic Theology* (ed. Robinson) 118. For the term "preunderstanding" see, e.g., Bultmann, "Is Exegesis without Presuppositions Possible?" in *NT and Mythology* 145-53. There is a useful analysis of the various ways of speaking of preunderstanding in Ferguson, *Biblical Hermeneutics* 6-22.

what the Bible is saying begins with the fact that we share things with it (we are also human beings relating in the one Spirit to the same God on the same basis) and that we want to grow in that understanding, relationship, and commitment to God that is expressed in these texts. "The principle of the empty head" — the principle that in interpretation we can and must set aside all preconceptions and approach the text with no assumptions — is a fallacy resting on "naive intuitionism."[13] To put it another way, interpretation involves starting from an appropriate hermeneutical principle. "If you want to understand what a cat is, put a mouse in front of it, and see what happens. The mouse is here the 'hermeneutical principle' that sets the 'catness' of the cat in motion. The mouse is that which causes the cat to show itself for what it is."[14]

It has sometimes been asked whether "modern man" might no longer possess the religious presuppositions that would make understanding of God and therefore of scripture possible. More recently surveys have suggested that even though churchgoing may have declined in some traditionally Christian countries, the vast majority of people still profess to believe in the existence of God, in the possibility of a relationship with God, and in the hope of an afterlife.[15] It is still true that people's hearts are restless until they find their rest in God.[16]

Nevertheless, one problem in understanding scripture may be that we lack the preunderstanding to make sense of what we read. On the way to Gaza (Acts 8:27-39) the Ethiopian's difficulty in understanding Isaiah 53 lay in his not knowing about Jesus. To use Paul's image, a veil may lie over the mind, preventing it from understanding; only through Christ is it removed (2 Cor 3:14-18). Beyond the veil-removal that Paul refers to, a specific enlightenment may be required if one is to understand a particular passage (Ps 119:18, 125). A shared relationship with what we are seeking to understand is a necessary though not a sufficient starting point for interpretation. Interpretation happens because we hazard a guess as to what a person or a text may mean, and then test out our guesses. Schleiermacher defines interpretation as "the historical and divinatory, objective and subjective reconstruction of a given statement."[17] It involves imagination, divi-

---

13. Lonergan, *Method in Theology* 157.
14. P. J. Achtemeier, *An Introduction to the New Hermeneutic* 125, following E. Fuchs, *Hermeneutik* (Bad Cannstadt: Mullerschön, [3]1963) 109ff.
15. See, e.g., Wcela, "Who Do You Say That They Are?" 2-3.
16. Augustine, *Confessions* 1.1.
17. *Hermeneutics* 111; cf. Palmer, *Hermeneutics* 87-90.

nation, inspiration, and intuition.[18] Beginning from an insight — or rather from a striking possibility — suggested by some aspect of the text, we leap into the midst of the hermeneutical circle (better, spiral) and intuitively essay a grasp of whole and parts from this vantage point. We then systematically explore, refine, and test that tentative purported insight more analytically. Ricoeur comments "If there are no rules for making good guesses, there are methods for validating those guesses we do make."[19] The notion of preunderstanding thus suggests our utilization of both an experience we have in common with the text and a preliminary understanding or hypothesis that we then test by the text.

Interpretation has often been understood by analogy with the workings of science and history, as if science and history involved standing in pure receptivity before data that we seek to understand in their own terms, according to their categories, in keeping with their emphases. That is indeed the aim, but in all these disciplines understanding characteristically depends on bringing to the data some hypothesis that helps to make sense of them. One then seeks to discern whether the data fit the hypothesis or whether some different hypothesis is needed. In a parallel way, a preunderstanding or preliminary understanding of a text is our way of opening ourselves to the biblical text. It is "not a prejudice, but a way of raising questions."[20] The divinatory and the grammatical sides of Schleiermacher's thinking about interpretation complement each other.[21]

Schleiermacher's notion of a hermeneutical circle has other facets. "Complete knowledge always involves an apparent circle, that each part can be understood only out of the whole to which it belongs, and vice versa."[22] We understand a word in the light of its place in a sentence, a sentence in the light of the words it uses; a sentence in the light of its place in a work, a work in the light of the sentences it comprises; a work in the light of its author's works and person as a whole, the works and the person in the light of the individual works; an author's writings in the light of the vocabulary and history of the age as a whole, and the age in the light of the author's

18. Hirsch, *Validity in Interpretation* x; cf. Ricoeur, *Interpretation Theory* 75; Kermode, *The Genesis of Secrecy* 7, 16-17.

19. *Interpretation Theory* 76.

20. Bultmann, "Is Exegesis without Presuppositions Possible?" in *Existence and Faith* 293 (Fontana ed., 346); cf. Thiselton, "The New Hermeneutic" 313. See also Heidegger, *Being and Time* 194-95; Hoy, *The Critical Circle.*

21. See Ricoeur, *Interpretation Theory* 76.

22. *Hermeneutics* 113.

writings. "One must already know a man in order to understand what he says, and yet one must first become acquainted with him by what he says."[23] Further, interpretation cannot be forced. "There is no technique or method in the world that will get us in one step from a text that we have never looked at before to an interpretation of it. . . . In the vector that makes up the possibility of exegesis, method may be one component; but experience with the texts involved is another, and probably a more necessary and central one."[24]

How Such Interpretation Develops

Communication begins on the basis of a shared experience and shared interest. It develops by means of an ongoing conversation. At first we only approximately grasp what the other person means; our categories of apprehension are rough and ready. A persistent, careful listening is needed if we are to come nearer to understanding what the person is pointing to. We never totally grasp someone else's perspective, but that is the ultimate goal that we nevertheless strive toward. Understanding at every point involves an ongoing, back-and-forth, spiraling process, one never completed. Two friends or a married couple will recognize (perhaps ruefully) that they will never fully understand each other, yet they may also recognize that they do understand each other a little better each year. Their understanding develops as both are prepared to keep asking questions of each other and listening to each other's answers, to keep revealing themselves to each other and being open about how they see things. Asking the right questions is of key significance in a personal relationship, because they enable other people to express themselves to us.

Something similar is again true of the Bible. A strange conversation is involved, of course, because the outward form of the answers we receive from it are fixed. One aspect of the conversation, then, is that in seeking to discover the significance of these answers, I need to identify the question to which this text is a response. "When documents contain answers to questions, the answers must be brought into relation with the questions that are presupposed, and not with some other questions."[25] So I keep

---

23. Schleiermacher, *Hermeneutics* 56.
24. Barr, *Old and New in Interpretation* 199.
25. Barth, *The Epistle to the Romans* 8.

coming to the Bible with the questions that I can bring on the basis of what I have in common with it, and it keeps responding. As particular aspects of its meaning grasp me, this enables me to formulate some further, fresh questions that may free new facets of its meaning. Admittedly I must also be able to recognize when a text refuses to answer my questions, when pressing the text would be to overinterpret it.[26] Morna Hooker suggests a different image from conversation, that of finding one's way. The Bible offers a series of signposts that tell me the way to A, B, and C. I want to get to X, Y, and Z. To extend her analogy, it is only by following the signposts to A, B, and C that I will find my way to X, Y, and Z; if I try to do the latter too early, the journey will abort.[27]

The questioning process is very different from the one envisaged by Immanuel Kant, in which reason asks questions "not . . . in the character of a pupil who listens to everything that the teacher chooses to say, but of an appointed judge who compels the witnesses to answer questions that he himself has formulated."[28] The image of question and answer may illumine further the discussion of determinacy and the contribution of readers to interpretation, which we looked at in chapter 3. H. R. Jauss implies that "a work does not have an inherent meaning: it does not speak, as it were, it only answers."[29] This makes it sound as if "readers make sense." But if we can formulate the right question, we can access the text's own sense. Indeed, "among the greatest insights given us by Plato's account of Socrates is that, contrary to general opinion, it is more difficult to ask questions than to answer them. . . . Discourse that is intended to reveal something requires that that thing be opened up by the question."[30]

In an ordinary personal relationship I am not merely concerned to understand another person. In learning to look at the world through that person's eyes I hope not only to understand them, but also to understand the world. For I recognize that my own perspective on reality is limited by the fact that it is my perspective; it may be as good as anyone else's, but that does not mean I have nothing to learn. One of the devastating fruits of close friendship or marriage is the discovery that there are other per-

26. Haller, "On the Interpretative Task" 160.

27. "The Bible and the Believer" 86-87.

28. Preface to the second edition of *Critique of Pure Reason* 20; cf. Gunton, *Enlightenment and Alienation* 6.

29. The words are Culler's (*The Pursuit of Signs* 54) summarizing Jauss's work in *Literaturgeschichte als Provokation* (Frankfurt: Suhrkamp, 1970).

30. Gadamer, *Truth and Method* 326.

spectives on the world than my own. It is a positive fruit because it can offer me the opportunity to broaden my horizon.

> As the classic model for conversation in the Western tradition, the Platonic dialogue, makes clear, real conversation occurs only when the individual conversation partners move past self-consciousness and self-aggrandizement into joint reflection upon the subject matter of the conversation. . . . Real conversation occurs only when the participants allow the question, the subject matter, to assume primacy.[31]

So it is, again, with the Bible. Samuel Taylor Coleridge, who was born later than Schleiermacher but died the same year, described the way in which he found in scripture "words for my inmost thoughts, songs for my joy, utterances for my hidden griefs, and pleadings for my shame and my feebleness."[32] "Coleridge's reading leads him into the world of the text, which becomes in turn fit echo of and expression for his own experience of religious transformation."[33] But interpretation goes beyond sharing a subjective experience. I seek to empathize accurately with the psalmists in their situation before God, so that I can look at God and at life through their eyes. Understanding involves learning to stand where someone else stands, seeking to look at the world through their eyes; and our shared involvement with the topic we are discussing is an indispensable aid toward a shared understanding of what they refer to. So our understanding of scripture and of the God it refers to (not merely of its writers' feelings and experiences in relation to that God) is facilitated by our sharing in a relationship with the God to whom and of whom it also speaks. This preunderstanding makes possible an understanding that allows scripture to be "its own interpreter," in keeping with Luther's principle.[34]

There is a negative aspect to the fact that we only understand on the basis of a preunderstanding. The nature of the ongoing conversation reveals that our being the people we are with our experience of God is our privilege but also our limitation. Our involvement with the conversation's subject matter is a potential liability as well as a potential asset. It may encourage us actually to identify our experience or our way of looking at things with

31. Tracy, *The Analogical Imagination* 101; he compares Gadamer, *Truth and Method* 325-41.

32. *Confessions of an Inquiring Spirit*, Letter 1.

33. Dawson, "Against the Divine Ventriloquist" 296.

34. Stated, e.g., in *Assertio omnium articulorum* (*WA* 7:97), quoted by Ebeling, *Word and Faith* 306.

the ones we are seeking to understand. We squeeze other people into our own mold and thus misunderstand them; we subsume what we think we hear within the categories of what we think we know already, and thus we miss distinctive features of what is said.

In a similar way, again, the experiences, needs, and desires that we bring to the biblical text ("what rings a bell with me") are both an asset and a liability. They give us a starting point in asking questions of the text, but they may hinder us from hearing what the text says that does not correspond to what we have experienced or are already interested in. We listen to the text's answers to our questions, but ignore other aspects of the text that do not relate to those questions. As we may put it, only part of the text is "relevant." But if our questions, arising out of our experiences and interests, are to be our way into understanding the text itself, then realizing that the text is actually the answer to a question rather different from the one we have asked must lead, not to our ignoring these other aspects of the text, but to our seeking to formulate a new question that will open the way to hearing some of these other aspects. Our questions and experiences are our point of entry to understanding wider aspects of the text that do not have close points of contact with our previous experience but that may nevertheless be very important — or rather, may *consequently* be very important.

It is easy for our questions finally to determine the answers that the text is permitted to give and for our blinkers to determine what we are able to see — if we ignore the hints, given by those answers, that there are other things visible outside their parameters. We may be drawn to a text for preaching because it relates to a particular theme, and we may consciously decide to take up those aspects of the text on which we wish to preach. But it may be that staying with the text beyond those aspects to other themes with which it associates that one theme will adjust our agenda to God's and enable us to see our theme in better perspective. Scripture is there, in part, to broaden our horizons, and this broadening may require that we cease to be limited by the questions we have brought to the text. The apparent irrelevance of parts of scripture we read devotionally may indicate that our agenda needs adjusting to God's, perhaps by moving away from our dominant individualism to the Bible's characteristic concern with the people of God corporately. Conversely, the clear relevance and apparent straightforwardness of other texts makes it difficult for us to hear them. The easy texts are often the difficult texts.

Generally, we hear "as though we know already, and can partly tell ourselves what we are to hear. Our supposed listening is in fact a strange mixture of hearing and our own speaking, and in accordance with the usual rule, it is most likely that our own speaking will be the really decisive event."[35] "The ordinary, careless way is to be satisfied with a vague impression of the parts so long as one thinks one has caught the general context."[36] The assumption that we understand is most threatening to understanding; suspicion of ourselves of the kind encouraged by the three "masters of suspicion," Marx, Nietzsche, and Freud,[37] is indispensable to growth in understanding, for immediate consciousness is always likely to be false consciousness.

Who we are individually influences what we hear and what we miss. I read scripture as a twentieth-century, male, middle-class, heterosexual, middle-aged, comfortable, intellectual clergyman, as a person with his own joys and pains and loves and temptations. These make it possible for me to see certain things in scripture, but they also limit my horizons, at least whenever I fail to keep in mind that they are likely to do so. We all come from experience to scripture and need to be aware of this fact if we are not to be misled or trapped by it.

I inevitably view the world from the vantage point where I stand, which fixes a horizon for me, determines what I can see, and influences how well I see it. If I can look at it from someone else's vantage point, then, first, I have the opportunity to understand this other person. Then, if I am open to the possibility that this other perspective may also open out onto reality itself, that broader horizon of which both it and my perspective are but part, my horizon is extended. I see reality more fully. The process of interpretation involves a merging of horizons.[38] Indeed, in this process "as the historical horizon is projected, it is simultaneously removed." A dialogue takes place between scripture and contemporary perspectives.

> The dialogue assumes real differences between biblical perspectives and categories and those operative in the consciousness of contemporary thinkers. It does not venture to bypass the hermeneutical problems posed by these differences. It calls attention to them and seeks to work them

---

35. Barth, *Church Dogmatics* I/2, 470; cf. W. W. Johnson, "The Ethics of Preaching" 423.

36. Schleiermacher, *Hermeneutics* 44.

37. So Ricoeur, e.g., *The Conflict of Interpretations* 148 (cf. p. 107 above).

38. See Gadamer, *Truth and Method* 216-18, 269-74, where Gadamer attributes the metaphor to E. Husserl; and Thiselton, *The Two Horizons*.

through critically. The goal of the dialogue is the achievement of a common mind, a "fusion of horizons," between biblical worlds of meaning and those that make up our sense of reality.[39]

To use Fuchs's terms, there then takes place a new language-event and the creation of a new world and a broader common understanding than the one I already have.[40]

Interpretation in the Context of an Interpretive Tradition

An important further insight emerges from Gadamer's *Truth and Method:* Interpretation takes place not only on the basis of the individual's preunderstanding but also on the basis of one's place in a tradition of interpretation. This is already true, for instance, of the reading of Greek myths by the Stoics. Like our individual experience, our interpretive tradition and its understanding provide us with a necessary and unavoidable way into a text. This tradition of interpretation has already shaped our own experience and thinking — indeed, it has made our experience and thinking possible. We do not understand the past except by way of the present, but neither do we understand the present except by way of the past. We are part of a stream of tradition, not readers coming to texts that have never been read before in our community. This stream of tradition helps to form the preunderstanding that makes understanding possible. The temporal gulf between us and the text "is not a yawning abyss, but is filled with the continuity of custom and tradition" and gives us the benefit of historical distance, which may make some aspects of interpretation more difficult but may also give transient preunderstandings time to pass and more significant aspects of the text's meaning time to emerge.[41] "Every reading of a text always takes place within a community, a tradition, or a living current of thought, all of which display presuppositions and exigencies," no matter how committed the reading also is to discovering what is there in the text itself.[42] So "every classic text . . . comes to any reader through the history of its effects (conscious and unconscious, enriching and ambiguous, emancipatory and distorted) upon the present horizon of the reader." But it "can

39. Ogletree, *The Use of the Bible in Christian Ethics* 175.
40. See, e.g., Fuchs, *Studies of the Historical Jesus* 207-28.
41. Gadamer, *Truth and Method* 264.
42. Ricoeur, *The Conflict of Interpretations* 3.

become a classic for the reader only if the reader is willing to allow that present horizon to be vexed, provoked, challenged by the claim to attention of the text itself."[43]

As well as providing us with a way into interpretation, our tradition provides us with a check on our interpretation. If our understanding differs from that to which people open to this text have previously come, this is at least food for thought. The tradition can thus help safeguard us from interpretation that merely reflects our own personalities.[44] For instance, certain sorts of personalities seem instinctively to prefer interpretation that comes to few firm conclusions and enjoy living with uncertainties in interpretation and with as many questions as possible left open, while other types instinctively prefer results that are cut-and-dried and conclusions that are invariably clear. Whereas interpretation can often seem a quest ever to say something new, Jonathan Magonet relates the fear his own teacher felt when he felt drawn to a new reading of a text and his relief if he could discover it had been anticipated somewhere in the tradition.[45]

How a text has been read before is a check but not a final norm for interpretation. In the end the text has to be its own norm; tradition cannot be absolutized. Jürgen Habermas has pressed this point in controversy with Gadamer, stressing that the consensus of the interpretive tradition may well be the product not of reason but of (apparently) accidental pseudocommunication and ideology, of "the repressiveness of a power relationship that deforms the intersubjectivity of understanding as such and systematically distorts colloquial communication." If one fails to question tradition, then one has "allowed hermeneutical insight into the prejudicial structure of understanding to rehabilitate prejudice."[46] Thus while tradition is of value as criticism of and an alternative to modernity, which is not to be treated as if its position was privileged, it is also to be treated as inevitably ideologically suspect — the tradition that limits the priesthood to men is a male one — and thus treated attentively but not uncritically.[47] There is tradition that accumulates insight and brings home the original message afresh for each age, and there is inauthentic tradition, which waters down

43. Tracy, *The Analogical Imagination* 105.
44. Cf. Culler, *The Pursuit of Signs* 52.
45. *A Rabbi's Bible* 7.
46. "On Hermeneutics' Claim to Universality" 314, 315.
47. Bauckham, "Tradition in Relation to Scripture and Reason" 138-39. He compares L. Boff's comments in *Church: Charism and Power* (ET New York: Crossroad/London: SCM, 1985) 43.

the original message.[48] The very study of the text made possible by the tradition that has flowed from it makes possible, and necessary, criticism of this tradition to which we owe so much, and disagreement with it.

We have referred to biblical tradition in particular as the passing on of witness concerning the gospel events and as the development of insight and custom within the gospel community. The subsequent Christian tradition also functions in the way just described to provide the church in particular with its preunderstanding in reading scripture.[49] Scripture is, after all, not a newly discovered Gnostic text, and "the idea of a 'direct access' to the Bible, ignoring two thousand and more years of history of interpretation" is untenable.[50] To insist on it is to refuse a resource that offers vantage points for surveying the biblical landscape and helping us to see its features in perspective. Historically the church's doctrinal tradition issued from this text, even if it was also influenced by other sources on the way and conceptualized in thought-forms that are as strange to us as they would be to the Bible's first hearers (e.g., the ideas of incarnation and of God as Trinity).[51] It is thus not inappropriately utilized as a source of insight on that from which it came.

Tradition is not an absolute; only the text is. In chapter 11 we have therefore noted the role of criticism in enabling us to hear the text itself and to query our traditions about its origin and meaning. But tradition is no more relative than my own present perspective, to put it at its lowest, and thus deserves open if critical attention as a source of possible insight. Luther disputed the novel and idiosyncratic tradition of the medieval church and was always prepared to say "No" to tradition when it did not match the scripture whose ongoing significance it was supposed to mediate. "The tradition grounds the reading and opens up understanding for the individual, while the principle or standard of criticism (in Luther's case, Scripture) provides a check upon that tradition."[52] Scripture must be its own interpreter.[53] Yet Luther also affirmed the value of the church's tradi-

---

48. Lonergan, *Method in Theology* 162.

49. Lonergan, *Method in Theology* 161-62; cf. Montague, "Hermeneutics and the Teaching of Scripture" 9-11.

50. Ritschl, "A Plea for the Maxim: Scripture and Tradition" 121.

51. Cf. Nineham, *Explorations in Theology* 1:137, 139.

52. Lundin in *The Responsibility of Hermeneutics* 28, commenting on Althaus, *The Theology of Martin Luther* 335. Cf. also Pelikan's comments on Luther in *Luther the Expositor* 71-86.

53. See the *Assertio omnium articulorum* of 1520 (*WA* 7:97), noted in n. 34 above.

tion and would have assumed with the Fathers that the "rule for the faith" was a proper guide to interpretation.[54]

Interpreting scripture in the light of how it has been interpreted can offer some safeguard against the limited perspectives of one age and against interpretations that make scripture merely mirror our own (secular or Christian) culture. Understanding a biblical text is not a once-for-all act; different texts can be heard at different times. I can perceive aspects of it today, but miss others, which I may be able to see tomorrow. One generation becomes blind to insights that were once well appreciated (hence the value of using the commentaries of other centuries), but is in a position to perceive things long neglected. The story of biblical scholarship does include some ongoing development of insight and emancipation from error, like that which is usually (though partly mistakenly) assumed to characterize the story of science. More fundamentally, however, it is the story of an attempt to appropriate the biblical message on the part of each generation in its context, and it follows a zigzag line in which insights are sometimes lost, sometimes regained.

When we interpret specific scriptural texts, we do so on the basis of a personal preunderstanding, but we work as members of communities, formed both negatively and positively by our communities and their traditions.[55] This shaping will likely include preunderstandings of the particular text, because as the years pass there will be less and less texts that we approach for the first time. Interpretation is a matter of reconsidering what we and others have made of this text.[56] We want to see things afresh, but if we see fresh things, we are probably the victims of over-fertile imaginations.

Interpretation in the Context of History

Gadamer emphasizes the link with the past that tradition gives us. Is continuity with the past an unvarying reality? Emil Fackenheim begins a discussion of "the Jewish Bible after the Holocaust" by commenting that Gadamer, along with Ricoeur and Heidegger, never "face up to the Holocaust, as an event by which historical continuity might be ruptured."[57] The

---

54. A. T. Hanson and R. P. C. Hanson, *The Bible without Illusions* 24.
55. Tracy, *The Analogical Imagination* 118-19.
56. Barr, *Old and New in Interpretation* 185-86.
57. *The Jewish Bible after the Holocaust* viii.

modern reader has a radically different starting point from that of commentaries written before that event. "In reading their Ta'nach as never before, Jews are, as it were, themselves naked" — naked before the naked text. It is all very well for Exodus 17 to side with Moses and God against the murmurers, but when the bitter test is of the scale that twentieth-century Judaism has seen, Exodus 15–17 as a whole may read differently.[58] At the same time Fackenheim demonstrates that even the Holocaust opens up Judaism to scripture and opens up scripture to Judaism. This is specifically so with Esther, the book that is a threat to Luther because it seems to shut him out but that draws Jews in by virtue of the kind of world it portrays, with the activity and inactivity of Esther, Haman, Mordecai, and God — and challenges Christians, too, for "perhaps [Luther's] discovery that Esther's judaising is incorrigible must become a light for post-Holocaust Christianity."[59] A suspicious hermeneutic, one that is aware of the fact of anti-Jewishness, helps us to recognize anti-Jewish readings of some texts,[60] though it needs to be wary of reading its own concerns into other texts.[61]

We have to seek to understand texts in their historicity; but we have to do so out of our own historicity, the assumptions and horizons that affect how we see and what we see. My personal situation and context shape the way I read just as the authors' situation and context shaped the way they wrote, and I have to reflect as carefully about the former as I do about the latter. It has long been a familiar idea that the scriptures themselves, like any other texts, belong in history and have to be understood in the light of the historical contexts in which they came into being. The crucial insistence of hermeneutical study since Dilthey is that we as interpreters also belong in history and have to go about understanding in the light of the historical contexts in which we live. We have to do this in the sense that we cannot avoid it. The experiences as human beings and as believers that we bring to the text, our perceptions and our questions regarding life and God, and the shared assumptions that make thinking and communication possible in our culture — all these shape what we are open to seeing in the text. A human being is "a historical being," shaped by history and taking shape in history.[62] "Experience is intrinsically temporal (and this means historical in the deepest sense of the word), and therefore understanding

58. *The Jewish Bible after the Holocaust* 27-35.
59. *The Jewish Bible after the Holocaust* 91; see further 60-62, 71-77, 87-99.
60. Milavec, "Mark's Parable of the Wicked Husbandmen."
61. Hvalvik, "A 'Sonderweg' for Israel."
62. Dilthey as quoted by Palmer, *Hermeneutics* 116.

of experience must also be in commensurately temporal (historical) categories of thought."[63] The usefulness of the unfamiliar word "hermeneutics" is that it draws attention to this new awareness, the awareness that we understand the task of understanding in radically historical fashion.

My historicity means that I not only occupy a different context from that of the text; I occupy a *later* context, and all that has happened between the emergence of the text and my own life both links me positively to the text and makes it a demanding task to hear the text as I would have heard it when it was first uttered. "The Waste Land" in 1972 is a different poem from the poem that was printed in October 1922 in *The Criterion:* Familiar and famous, not new and exciting; fixed in a certain period of the past, not contemporary; located in the midst of the total T. S. Eliot corpus, not at the culmination of his corpus as it then stood.[64] Elvis Presley's records of the 1950s can be appreciated now in a way that they could not then, even though (or rather because?) they cannot now strike us with the shock and offensiveness that they then had. The Hebrew Bible cannot be the same for the reader who comes to it as a Christian as it was for the believing Jew of pre-Christian (or post-Christian) times.

Our historicity makes some texts more difficult for us to hear than others, and then it opens us to them once more. In the 1920s Romans suddenly became audible again in Germany, as had happened in the sixteenth century. Over the past 25 years 1 Corinthians 12–14 has become audible again in many parts of the world. Some groups who had been unable to hear books such as Exodus, Amos, and Daniel, with their stress on God's political involvement, have heard them again. Contemporary concern with questions of sexuality and gender has made it possible to read the Song of Songs and Genesis 1–3 more openly or discerningly or truly than the interpretive tradition did. It may be suggested that our time now needs to consider the implications of the Psalms for prayer, and of scripture as a whole for attitudes to other religions.

Of course, the Luther and the Barth for whom Romans came alive misheard the letter in marked ways; their commentaries on Romans make strange reading in a number of respects. The people who have suddenly made sense of 1 Corinthians 12–14 then read into it the meaning that has

---

63. Palmer, expounding Dilthey, *ibid.,* 111; most of the sentence is italicized. See also Nineham's paper on "NT Interpretation in an Historical Age," in *Explorations in Theology* 1:145-65.

64. Gardner, *"The Waste Land"* 1-2.

recently come to be attached to phrases such as "word of wisdom" and "word of knowledge." The prophets are turned into social activists, who thus happily anticipate the role to which we aspire. The Song of Songs becomes merely an affirmation of our own enthusiasm for sex. We understand these books and others in anachronistic ways; we read our concerns, perspectives, and priorities into them.[65] But at least some appropriation of these books is now going on. Questions and experiences belonging to our historical context are our way into the text; our historicality is an asset as we seek to gain acces to scripture in its historicality. But it can be our way of silencing the text as we force it to do our business.

The historicity that enables us to perceive the significance of some aspects of some texts hinders us from perceiving others. A Latin American Roman Catholic sees how prominent the theme of political and national liberation is in scripture, which people in more privileged situations have often taken little note of, but it may miss the equal emphasis on spiritual liberation that also appears even in books such as Exodus. A North Atlantic evangelical notices the stress on personal salvation, but misses the emphasis on the church, and may feel that Ezekiel's stress on individual responsibility was a turning point in Israelite thinking when that value judgment reflects more the individualism of an age that needs to learn from the corporateness of Israelite faith. An Israeli Jew or a Christian supporter of Israel finds it so easy to identify with the story of the conquest of Palestine in Joshua that he or she may miss other features of the story such as God's concern to be fair to the existing inhabitants of Palestine. People who enthuse about charismatic gifts need to hear the warnings of Matthew 7, while people who avoid charismatic gifts need to study 1 Corinthians 14; in practice enthusiasms tend to run the opposite way around. Our historicity shapes our preunderstanding and does so to both positive and negative ends.

65. So C. S. Rodd; see his review of S. Terrien's *Till the Heart Sings* in *ExpT* 97 (1985-86) 258-59; also Clines, *What Does Eve Do to Help?*

15

The Corporateness
of Scriptural Interpretation

In discussing texts as expressions of human experience and interpretation that begins from preunderstanding (both in chapter 14), we have already begun to note that interpretation is not a task undertaken by isolated individuals. Individuals live and work in corporate contexts and interpretation is also, perhaps more naturally and fundamentally, a communal enterprise. We have access to scripture not merely on the basis of individual experience and involvement but also on the basis of corporate experience and involvement. Interpretation belongs in a number of corporate contexts.

The Context of a Confessional Community

"Virtually everything in scripture is written to a faith-community, usually in the style of communal address. Therefore biblical texts must be set in *communal* consciousness to be understood"; they invite us to apply them to communal consciousness rather than to individuals in their existential self-awareness.[1] "Christian communities are central for the ongoing task of enabling people to become wise readers of Scripture."[2] The interpreter studies scripture as a member of the church committed to and involved in a believing, expectant, obedient approach to scripture and is drawn to share

---

1. Buttrick, *Homiletic* 276-77 (his emphasis).
2. Fowl and Jones, *Reading in Communion* 35; as the title implies, this theme is central for Fowl and Jones's book.

its faith, expectancy, and obedience. Scripture itself of course had its origin in the life of such communities of faith and obedience. The stance of these communities contributes to the interpreter's approach to scripture with a preunderstanding that corresponds to its own nature. By sharing in a similar community's intuitive corporate study of scripture, which arises out of and coheres with its attempts to discover scripture's implications for discipleship, the interpreter may hear things that would otherwise be missed. Once again, the community's interpretation is not a norm, but it is a check; if the community in discipleship cannot recognize the individual interpreter's understanding of scripture, that does not demonstrate that this understanding is mistaken, but it does constitute grounds for reconsideration.

In group Bible study it commonly happens that one is amazed at what other people perceive in scripture, insights that were present in the text but that only those people could see because they started from where they were. From Latin America we have received an emphasis on the reading of scripture in grassroots Christian communities ("base Christian communities").[3] Indeed, Gerald West suggests, while the primary dialogue-partners of Western theology and biblical studies are the educated and powerful, the primary dialogue-partners of liberation theologies are the uneducated and oppressed. Admittedly his suggestion that this might even be seen as the defining characteristic of liberation theologies sits uneasily with his awareness that black theology and Latin American liberation theology are open to the charge of being educated middle-class phenomena.[4] It can be argued that liberation hermeneutics simply has both a grassroots strand and an academic strand and that this is a significant strength.[5]

A balanced and insightful response to scripture is unlikely to emerge from individual study, particularly the individual study of scripture in a secular context such as a university religious studies department, against the background of the priorities and criteria of academic study as set by a faculty in relation to students and by an academic guild in relation to faculty. It can seem as if biblical scholars are the privileged interpreters of

3. For the image of "grassroots" see Croatto, *Exodus* 6.

4. See *Biblical Hermeneutics of Liberation* 5; cf. 171-73 (referring to P. Frostin, *Liberation Theology in Tanzania and South Africa* [Lund: Lund UP, 1988] 6); also 58-60; cf. Segundo, "The Shift within Latin American Theology."

5. Cf. Boff and Boff, *Introducing Liberation Theology* 11-21 (with Thiselton's comments in *New Horizons in Hermeneutics* 411-14); they also refer to — and attach great importance to — an intermediate level, the pastoral level.

scripture. They alone can determine what the Bible means. But the Bible was written for believing communities, not critics, and real biblical interpretation happens when scripture does something to such a community. In that context "the role of the critic is primarily to explain how and why and in what way the Bible does what it does."[6] When the church places special emphasis on an academic and critical approach to scripture it easily sets up a new type of priestly control of the Christian community by a guild of experts whose work is authoritarian, not in the sense that it cannot be questioned but in the sense that it is the privileged responsibility of an elite. The development of approaches to interpretation that restore attention to the final form of the text has the potential to restore some power to the grassroots Christian community.[7]

The church's familiarity with and commitment to scripture is an important asset in its interpretation of scripture. It is also a liability. It may give us a way into understanding, but it may also blunt scripture's cutting edge. Unfamiliarity with scripture may enable people to hear it quite freshly, or may make it difficult to hear it at all. Participation in the realities that scripture speaks of helps us to perceive them there and to respond to them. The holy scriptures are texts that command reverence and restrict a free play of response; the appropriate response to them will come from people who are in touch with the Holy One themselves.[8] Awareness that a purely clinical, analytical approach misses the most vital dimensions of these texts led Barth to speak scathingly of standard approaches to exegesis, which reconstructed the outward form of the text's significance but did not penetrate to the truly historical understanding that involves the interpreter in grappling personally with the realities to which the text refers. Exegesis is not the same thing as understanding. Yet that identification with scripture and commitment to it unwittingly hinder our perceiving aspects of the text that do not already have equivalents in our faith. We feel, and are, one with the scriptures, and we may therefore mishear what they are saying. Those who are most committed to the biblical gospel may be hindered from understanding that gospel by the combination of this loyalty and their need to maintain their present position. "Whether or not you subscribe to

6. Keegan, *Interpreting the Bible* 9-10.

7. Brett, *Biblical Criticism in Crisis?* 165-66. Cf. West's further comments in his discussion of different South African approaches to interpreting Genesis 4 in *Biblical Hermeneutics of Liberation* 42-62 and in "Reading 'the Text' and Reading 'Behind-the-Text'" in *The Bible in Three Dimensions* (ed. Clines and others) 299-320.

8. Cf. Detweiler in *Reader Response Approaches to Biblical and Sacred Texts* 214.

the notion of episcopacy ultimately determines . . . how you read the New Testament, rather than vice-versa."[9]

The Context of the Academic Community

We have referred to the limitations of that study that takes the characteristically cerebral and uninvolved stance of the academic community over against the committed stance of the church. But we have also hinted at the positive features of this context. Here the interpreter is able to enjoy the virtues of being distanced from the text, and is then in a position to attempt to bring these two approaches together.

The biblical criticism fostered by the academic community, having begun as an iconoclastic movement concerned to undermine an authoritarian establishment, is itself now an authoritarian orthodoxy receiving its deserved undermining[10] and is now challenged to struggle against the bourgeois state even as once it struggled against the absolutist state.[11] There is need to question the academic community's characteristic post-Enlightenment confidence in reason, "to call attention to the limits of critique's false claim to universality" as well as to the equivalent claim for hermeneutics.[12] The stance of Western critics presupposes "an uncritical acceptance of the implicit faith-commitment that has dominated the culture of the (admittedly large and influential) tribe to which they have belonged since the Enlightenment."[13]

Some suspicion is in any case appropriate in relation to the actual commitments of the academic community with its institutional interests and constraints. That community, too, needs to be committed to truth and right living if it is to have eyes to see what lies in texts. Biblical scholarship now expects of its exponents "a self-consciousness about theoretical perspective, the interests at stake in the reading, and the pragmatic consequences," including the ideological issues and "questions of *institutional control* and *power*" in church, synagogue, seminary, and university that underlie readings.[14] Uni-

9. Jasper, *The NT and the Literary Imagination* 87-88.
10. Wink, *The Bible in Human Transformation* 11-15, 29.
11. See Eagleton, *The Function of Criticism* 124; Mosala (following Eagleton), "Social Scientific Approaches to the Bible" 15.
12. Habermas, "On Hermeneutics' Claim to Universality" 317.
13. Newbigin, *The Open Secret* 177-78.
14. Phillips, *Poststructural Criticism and the Bible* 1-2 (his emphasis). Cf. p. 43 above.

versity-based experts have vested interests in making biblical study difficult and thus worthy of a place in the university in the first place.[15]

The academic community's historical-critical method requires its practitioner to bracket out the believing community.[16] Precisely because of this it has the potential to enable us to handle questions of interpretation and truth more openly than may be the case in the believing community, with its commitment to the tradition. Biblical critical methods encourage the person who identifies with the text to distance himself or herself from the text, to treat the text as an object independent of me; this may be a bad way to start reading the Bible and is certainly a bad way to end doing so, but it may facilitate our perception of where the differences between our own experience and perspective and those witnessed to in the text lie, and it may place a check on our misreading experiences and perspectives into a text that speaks of different ones. It may have liberating potential. Historical-critical study had this potential at the beginning, when it could provide avenues of escape from dogmatic traditions that imposed frameworks of interpretation on scripture. We have noted that in many contexts it has now itself become a bondage from which biblical study needs deliverance. Feminist and black liberation theologians have rediscovered its liberating potential to subvert traditional interpretations imposed by male and white interpreters.[17] For other readers, too, historical-critical study may be able to facilitate the move from a first naïveté to a second naïveté, a post-critical naïveté, a move via a hermeneutic of suspicion to a hermeneutic of recovery.[18] The distancing procedures of biblical criticism can help believing students pay attention to scripture itself.

The highly cerebral exercise of learning the biblical languages also has its place here. The task of translation is, after all, the culmination of the act of interpretation, not a mere preliminary to it. It is an attempt to express the meaning of the words that I have sought to understand. It parallels the counselor's attempt to reexpress in his or her own words what the client first said, to establish to both parties that he or she has heard aright. We can attain an accurate enough understanding of a biblical text from a translation (better, by comparing translations). But there are insights as to the nuances of the text that seem to come only through close attention to

---

15. Brett, *Biblical Criticism in Crisis?* 166.
16. Keegan, *Interpreting the Bible* 20.
17. See, e.g., Schüssler Fiorenza, *In Memory of Her; Bread Not Stone*.
18. Ricoeur's terms; see, e.g., *Freud and Philosophy* 28-36, 496.

its actual words, just as counseling demands thorough, close attention to the very words of the client. Understanding a statement in a foreign language through an interpreter is quite possible, but one is bound to miss something, unless the material is of a very down-to-earth kind. Sharing someone's language is part of being willing and able to listen to them at all.

Interpretation takes place in the context of both the church community and the academic community. "Theologians who continue to seek a way between the horns, and thus to remain within the secular academy without abandoning the community of faith, have often been reduced to seemingly endless methodological foreplay."[19] We must believe and strive for interpretation that enables these to complement each other even insofar as they stand in tension with each other.

The Context in Society

Individual interpreters belong to social groups and bring to their interpretation a "horizon of expectations" shared with their particular culture and period.[20] The text will have presupposed some such communal horizon; that shared by its interpreters in any particular cultural context will likely be rather different. Our social context is thus influential on what we are able to hear and what we miss. Some prayer texts (e.g., Psalm 72) and some other parts of the Bible are difficult to hear in an industrial rather than an agricultural society. We may need to imagine ourselves in a developing country rather than a developed one in order to interpret them.[21]

The Bible, religious experience, and our relationship with God are not matters of unchanging abstraction and individual piety. They involve our humanity as a whole (body and spirit) in a network of relationships in a concrete context, and specifically a socioeconomic context. They need a materialist interpretation — not one that treats people as if they are merely bodies, but one that recognizes that they *are* bodies. Commitment to liberation opens the interpreter's eyes to the prominence of the theme of liberation in scripture itself, and behind that to the prominence of God's

19. Stout, *The Flight from Authority* 147.
20. So Jauss; see, e.g., "Literary History as a Challenge to Literary Theory" 14; cf. Suleiman, *The Reader in the Text* 31-38.
21. On this problem, cf. Rohrbaugh, *The Biblical Interpreter*.

involvement with the whole human person, with body and not merely spirit. Liberation theology takes seriously the involvement of God in history, takes it seriously by taking it politically.[22] Their particular experience of life means that the poor "have riches in plenty to equip them for exegesis."[23] At the same time, scripture arises from specific socioeconomic contexts in which poverty, for instance, takes a particular form (or takes a number of particular forms) and has particular significances because of the distinctive socioeconomic features of the contexts. Our interpretation also takes place in specific socioeconomic contexts in which poverty (for instance) takes other forms and has other significances. We have to think contextually rather than generally and abstractly. Materialist reading is concerned to take account of "bodies and their desires in the symbolic networks of relationships, and . . . of texts and their codes as products of an economic-political-ideological formation."[24]

At this point, as at others, the awareness that interpretation is shaped by considerations we bring to the material does not imply a hopeless relativism over whether we can reach anything that can rightly be called knowledge. People can transcend their cultural history.[25] It does imply that biblical interpretation needs to be as incisive, critical, and systematically suspicious in its understanding of itself and its own present as it is in its approach to the ancient documents of the faith, if it is to grow in its perception of scripture's significance. The religious, secular, and supernatural powers of Jesus' day all demonstrate how the people who know their Bible may not be those who can see and respond to what God is doing in their day. Biblical learning can be not only useless but destructive of the very foundations of the faith.[26] Reflectiveness concerning their commitments may help historical-critical interpreters perceive the bias in their interpretation. Historical-critical method may help consciously committed interpreters distance themselves from the text so as to be sure they are

22. Assmann, *Practical Theology of Liberation* 76; cf. Kee, *The Scope of Political Theology* 16-17.

23. Rowland and Corner, *Liberating Exegesis* 45.

24. F. Belo, "Why a Materialist Reading?" in Küng and Moltmann (ed.), *Conflicting Ways of Interpreting the Bible* 17. Cf. Belo's *A Materialist Reading of the Gospel of Mark;* also Schottroff and Stegemann (ed.), *God of the Lowly;* Gottwald [and Wire] (ed.), *The Bible and Liberation;* Schüssler Fiorenza, "The Ethics of Biblical Interpretation."

25. Cone, *God of the Oppressed* 49.

26. Segundo, *Liberation of Theology* 9 (he goes on to illustrate a four-stage hermeneutical circle in process), 81-82; Bojorge, "Para una interpretación liberadora" 67.

responding to its actual expectations regarding faith and commitment rather than to expectations they are reading into it because it is just those expectations that they hold dear.[27]

Biblical criticism itself has as one of its concerns that we should understand the Bible against its social context, seeking to identify the conventions of speech that lie behind its various texts. In any culture there is a range of attitudes, assumptions, ways of thinking, and ways of behaving that all who live in that culture accept without thinking about them. They are taken for granted to such an extent that we are not even aware that we are taking ours for granted until we enter another culture that does not do so and that has its own habits and assumptions. For us the Bible is such a culture, and one aspect of the complex task of understanding it is to come to discover what are its conventions of thinking and speaking. Form criticism deals with one aspect of this task by seeking to identify the basic genres or forms that appear in a literature and the social context *(Sitz im Leben)* to which they belong.

That such study is to be expected to illumine our understanding of a literature can readily be illustrated from our own culture. The various items that arrive in the mail (a letter from a friend, an advertisement, a bill, a wedding invitation, a greeting card, etc.) all have forms of their own. What kind of paper is used, the format, the language, and the opening and closing phrases all constitute signals that take us a substantial way toward understanding the meaning of each item before we examine what the words actually say. One can imagine, then, how difficult it would be for people in Africa in three thousand years' time to understand this material, given their unfamiliarity with the conventions that we take for granted.

This is our own position in relation to the Bible, which is a wide-ranging collection of works from a different age, culture, and civilization. Form criticism, then, seeks to recover the way things were said and written in that world and to devise the right kind of question-and-answer procedure that will open up the distinctive meanings (and expose the distinctive sets of possible misunderstandings) that belong to each genre.

As it happens, form-critical study of texts expressive of human experience has been a particularly fruitful exercise. The Psalms were among the first subjects of the pioneer form critic Hermann Gunkel, who analyzed basic ways of speaking to God represented in them.[28] His work was taken

27. Miguez Bonino, *Doing Theology in a Revolutionary Situation* 101-2; cf. Miranda, *Being and the Messiah* 73.

28. See, e.g., Gunkel, *The Psalms*.

further by Sigmund Mowinckel, who looked at the Psalms, with greater awareness of their social context, as the vehicles of Israel's corporate worship, expressions of its self-identity, and the means of its mutual fellowship.[29]

Although such study takes us into the shared conventions of prayer texts, form is not all; a person uses form to express something unique. Comparing examples of various genres helps one to perceive the individuality of particular prayers and praises. Psalms 95 and 100 (the *Venite* and the *Jubilate*), for instance, are psalms of praise with close parallels to each other, except that there is nothing in Psalm 100 that corresponds to the closing stanza of Psalm 95, where the movement of communication turns: Whereas in the first part of Psalm 95 human beings address God, in this closing stanza God addresses the enthusiastic worshipers and urges them to be silent for a moment and listen. It is ironic that it is this last, distinctive section of Psalm 95 that is now commonly omitted from worship.

Sometimes the individuality of an author takes up a familiar form in order to make it do something quite different from its normal function. My mail includes advertisements that are personalized in the hope that I may treat them as "proper" letters; British newspapers include "advertisement features" designed to attract the credence given to editorial matter and satire that could be taken by the unimaginative (or by a person from another culture) as a serious leader. We noted in chapter 5 how Amos uses the form of an oracle of judgment on the nations to soften up Israel for an oracle of judgment against itself, the form of an invitation to worship to indict Israel about the true nature of its worship, and the form of a funeral dirge to picture Israel fallen by God's judgment (1:3–2:16; 4:4-5; 5:1-2).

Such creative individual use of forms makes it clear that texts such as psalms that reflect basic forms are not mere formal, institutional texts written to order for an institutionalized cult. They reflect the real experience of nation and individual. Claus Westermann has especially emphasized this;[30] it is significant that he came to his research on the Psalms from the background of the experience of the Confessing Church in the 1930s and from his personal experience of being in a prison camp. Walter Brueggemann has taken this study further in the light of Ricoeur's work on hermeneutics, seeing the Psalms as representing various stages of a personal experience of orientation or equilibrium, disorientation, and reorientation

29. See especially Mowinckel, *The Psalms in Israel's Worship.*
30. See especially *The Praise of God in the Psalms.*

in a new faith.[31] This process reminds one of the new hermeneutic's approach to the parables, considered already in chapter 5, which begins from the hearers' familiar world and disorients them with God's unfamiliar world in order to lead them to "reorientation."[32] It is another variant of the dialectic also present when people's interaction with biblical criticism works well: It takes them from a fusion with scripture that provides an "orientation," by way of a distancing from this heritage that can demystify it and thus enable it to be heard in its own terms, as they move toward the goal of communion, genuine dialogue between interpreter and text.[33]

The Context of the Universal Church

Interpretation is an inherently catholic enterprise. The whole church needs the ways into scripture that the church's different parts can offer us: the Fathers and the Puritans, liberation theology and Western theology, the suburban church and the urban church, women and men, Jews and Christians. The limitations of individual study of scripture are paralleled by the limitations of study of scripture within homogeneous groups. Particular parts or themes in scripture may speak to a particular group with a special directness. They address the questions, needs, and experiences that the group bring to the text and come to form that group's effective canon within the canon. For evangelicalism Romans 3–8 and the theme of justification by faith has traditionally fulfilled this function, followed perhaps by John 3 with its theme of new birth. For charismatics it may be the accounts of Jesus' healing ministry in the synoptic Gospels, or parts of Acts, 1 Corinthians, or Ephesians. For groups who stress social involvement it may be Jesus' proclamation of God's rule.

Interpretation of scripture involves letting parts of scripture that immediately speak to us be our way into grasping scripture as a whole, of which those parts are but part, our point of entry to set us on the road of understanding and appropriating other aspects of scripture. Reading scripture through other eyes is one safeguard against getting stuck with those

31. See especially his *The Message of the Psalms*. He alludes to Ricoeur's *Freud and Philosophy; The Conflict of Interpretations;* "Biblical Hermeneutics"; and *Interpretation Theory.*

32. Thiselton, "The New Hermeneutic" in *NT Interpretation* (ed. Marshall) 321, following E. Fuchs, "Proclamation and Speech-Event," *ThT* 19 (1962-63) 349.

33. Wink, *The Bible in Human Transformation* 19-80.

aspects of the richness of scripture that correspond to our immediate needs. We will be able to find a starting point in scripture for a message that speaks to the experiences, needs, and context in which we live, but these need to be only entry points to grappling with scripture as a whole.

What can happen in practice is that our starting point becomes also our sticking point, and if we read other parts of scripture we do so to reinterpret them in the light of our starting point. One can see this in liberation theology's reading of Romans and in evangelicalism's typologizing of Exodus and its pietistic, christological, or futurist reading of the Prophets, which remove the political implications from each of these parts of scripture. One can see it in the narrowness that affects even our reading of our inner canon. It has inclined evangelicalism to read Romans as if it were purely concerned to minister to "the introspective conscience of the West"[34] and to ignore Paul's history-long and cosmic perspective and his concern with the destiny of Israel in Romans 9–11. It has inclined socially concerned Christians to ignore the fact that Jesus' concern is the destiny of Israel even when he is talking about the poor. It has inclined liberation theology to read Exodus as if it were describing only a humanly inspired act of political liberation and not a God-given experience of release from political service to service of God. It is reflected also in the difficulty each group has in recognizing other groups' use of scripture.

Christian readers of the Hebrew Bible have to make the most of the advantages of their preunderstanding, yet be open to the actual text. Sometimes Jewish readings will enable them to do that. Thus Fackenheim notes that in Jeremiah 31 contemporary Jews may instinctively find the focal point in Rachel's weeping for her children (vv. 15-16) while Christians find it in the promise of a new covenant (vv. 31-34). Even when Christians notice the former they may only read it through Matthean eyes — and even where a Jew considers the latter he may do so through Kantian eyes. So Fackenheim asks whether the day is near when there can be a "fraternal Jewish-Christian reading of the Book belonging to both."[35]

Liberationist interpretation in its several forms illustrates the needful catholicity of interpretation. The work of an interpreter such as José Porfirio Miranda arising out of his experience and involvement in Latin America

---

34. Stendahl, "The Apostle Paul and the Introspective Conscience of the West."

35. *The Jewish Bible after the Holocaust* 71; see further 73-74, 80-86, on Jeremiah 31: Fackenheim notes that Bright has nothing to say on vv. 15-16 but views vv. 31-34 as a high point (see Bright's *Jeremiah* 286-87). See also the evidence and testimony in Magonet, *A Rabbi's Bible*.

points to insights on "obvious" biblical texts such as the eighth-century prophets and on less obvious ones such as Romans 7 that are also of benefit to people outside his context.[36] Western interpreters thus learn from Latin American interpreters. One strength of liberation theology's approach to scripture is that its starting point enables it to make creative theological use of the First Testament in a way Western theology fails to do. Another is its capacity to enable retrieval of themes in Christian theology such as the patristic church's concern for the social demands of the gospel, its awareness of the prophetic dimension of the church's mission, and its sensitivity to the poor.[37]

In seeking the right questions to introduce into its conversation with scripture, liberation theology has utilized materialist perspectives from Marx, just as Bultmann used existentialist perspectives from Heidegger. In principle that is not to be criticized; at least it is self-conscious in method. All interpreters approach scripture with perspectives from their culture; more commonly they are not aware of this and think they are quite un-biased. A framework such as that of Marxism provides a way of raising questions or a setting for understanding answers. It need not be assumed to correspond completely to the biblical perspective, but it opens people to emphases of the biblical message that they might otherwise miss or make too little of. The secular sciences may facilitate both exegesis and contemporary application of the text and may thus enable the text to speak, because they enable us to "relate the 'word' to the facts of present-day human experience."[38]

Liberation theologians thus read scripture out of a situation that enables them to hear aspects of its message that the church has often missed, but this also opens them to the danger of missing what at first sight does not correspond to their concerns or ignoring what does not directly confirm their convictions. Current Christian praxis suggests the questions with which the interpreter comes to scripture; these questions are an inevitable and right starting point for interpretation, but they must be open to refinement on the basis of what we discover in scripture.

Liberation interpreters have been able to see the political significance of Exodus and the Bible's broader implications regarding justice, human beings as workers, the unfinishedness of this world, and its stress on praxis

---

36. See his *Marx and the Bible*.
37. Boff and Boff, *Introducing Liberation Theology* 36.
38. Assmann, *Practical Theology of Liberation* 64.

and on the recognition of truth through involvement. As we have noted, the liberation interpreters' preunderstanding has made it more difficult for them to see the Bible's concern with God as the key actor in the story, with the service of God as that for which the people are liberated, or with the acknowledgment of God by oppressed and oppressor as the aim of the event.[39] Arguably these are vital and distinctive aspects of the biblical testimony. To ignore them is to let a preliminary understanding derived from modern contextual factors freeze into a final understanding, and thus to become the helpless prisoner of a hermeneutical vicious circle (rather than spiral). Even liberation theology needs liberating from its own questions so that it can allow itself to be questioned by scripture.[40]

Liberation theology can thus be criticized as one-sided. But critics who see it in this way likely do so on the basis of a one-sidedness of their own; and were not Augustine's *Confessions*, Luther's polemics, and Barth's *Romans* one-sided? Witvliet argues that the question is whether in its one-sidedness interpretation addresses the particularities of the historical moment of which it forms a part and is aware that this is its task: "What causes real problems is theological thought that does not recognize its own one-sidedness and provisionality."[41] There is an irresolvable tension between the need to see clearly and say sharply what needs specifically to be seen and said in a context and the need to see and say this in the context of the whole counsel of God.

Western interpreters need to hear Latin American interpreters if their openness to scripture is to be extended. Diffidently one may ask whether Latin American interpreters may also gain from looking at the biblical text and at their own interpretation through Western eyes. Western Christians cannot assess the situation in Latin America and the propriety of liberation theology as someone inside that situation can. They interpret scripture not as "prophets" involved in the struggle for change but as "scribes" studying scripture in a more detached way. But "truth can be gained in both ways. While at all times there seems to exist a certain amount of tension between 'scribes' and 'prophets,' the two must check one another and learn from each other." Prophets can stimulate scribes, but then "the insights gained by the 'scribes' can . . . perhaps test and inform the work and struggle of the 'prophets.'"[42] It is thus unwise for liberation theology, for instance, to

39. See further Goldingay, "The Man of War and the Suffering Servant" 89-93.
40. Miguez Bonino, *Doing Theology in a Revolutionary Situation* 87; cf. Bojorge, "Para una interpretación liberadora" 68-70.
41. *The Way of the Black Messiah* 104.
42. Weber, "Freedom Fighter or Prince of Peace" 1.

refuse to talk theology with other Christians on the grounds that only the oppressed can evaluate the actions of the oppressed.[43]

Something similar will be true about the interpretation of scripture in the light of feminist concerns. Men need to open themselves to women's perspectives on scripture because those concerns can help them discover things in texts that they would not otherwise discover and live in the light of those discoveries. In recent years feminist interpretation has emphasized the value of bringing one's own experience, and specifically women's experience, into the interpretation of the biblical text. Like any allowance for involvement of human experience in interpretation, this can sound as if it encourages the introduction of subjective factors into an otherwise objective process. The considerations we have already noted, however, make it clear that subjective factors, and specifically gender factors, are always involved in interpretation. The alternative to subjective experiential interpretation based on feminist values advocated from a position of institutional powerlessness is not objective interpretation but subjective experiential interpretation based on patriarchal values assumed from a position of institutional power.

It is when this fact is acknowledged that we can then see if our subjective interpretation corresponds to the objective nature of the text. "The criteria of public evidence, logical argument, reasonable hypotheses, and intellectual sophistication still adjudicate acceptable and unacceptable positions." The vindication of feminist interpretation in this connection is that by working in the light of women's experience and feminist conviction it has indeed been able "to retrieve texts overlooked or distorted by patriarchal hermeneutics" and "to uncover the counter-cultural impulses within the text."[44] Thus Genesis 1–3 has come to be seen as undermining rather than affirming the idea of a created hierarchy of male over female.[45] A patriarchal preunderstanding affects even the translation of scripture. Translations tend to obscure the fact that in Romans 16 the apostle Junia was a woman and Phoebe was a deacon or minister (they often have "servant"). In 1 Corinthians 11 women are said to have authority (not a "veil") over their own heads. The verb for "submit" is rendered "obey" distinctively when women are the subjects.[46] At the same time, women would be unwise methodologically to

43. Banana, "The Biblical Basis for Liberation Struggles" 422; cf. Cone, *God of the Oppressed* 206.

44. Tolbert, *The Bible and Feminist Hermeneutics* 118, 122. Culler makes the same point with regard to literary interpretation generally (see *On Deconstruction* 55).

45. See Trible, *God and the Rhetoric of Sexuality* 72-143.

46. See, e.g., C. Clark Kroeger, "A Classicist Looks at the Difficult Passages," in

ignore male critique of feminist interpretation because that critique may be able to deliver them from reading their concerns into the text or even missing further liberating features of it.

Western theologians and Latin American theologians, women and men, are all in danger of seeing their own face at the bottom of the hermeneutical well and thus equally need to work in hermeneutical fellowship with each other and with believers in other contexts both past and present to widen their perspectives and test their visions. Criticism from perspectives with which we sharply disagree — for example, left-wing ones for traditional Western theologians and right-wing ones for people influenced by liberation theology — is to be especially welcomed. It has the capacity to remind us of what we might well have forgotten or to insist that we face what we may deliberately avoid. If interpreters react with hysteria or rhetoric to critique from an opposite political perspective, it neither commends their case nor bodes well for their prospects of refining their vision. We all need to listen to the people who for us count as outsiders in order to have our interpretive practice constructively challenged.[47]

The Universal Human Context

The more general implication of our historicity is that the Bible as a whole is separated from us by the deep gulf that divides us from the biblical world (worlds, indeed), a gulf carved out by differences in people's beliefs and assumptions, in how they think, behave, react, feel, and experience life, differences left unmentioned by the text itself because they separate not author and original reader but author and modern reader. This gulf forms part of what Wolfhart Pannenberg called "the double crisis of the Protestant Scripture principle."[48] Whereas Luther, for instance, could assume that biblical narrative both corresponds with what actually happened and remains meaningful today, subsequent study found gaps where Luther assumed identity. What the Bible said was not necessarily what happened, and how the Bible spoke was not how modern Christians could speak, even though they wanted to identify with it.

Perspectives on Feminist Hermeneutics (ed. Gerber Koontz and Swartley) 11-12. Cf. Schüssler Fiorenza, *In Memory of Her.*

47. Fowl and Jones, *Reading in Communion* 110-34.

48. *Basic Questions in Theology* 1:12.

Dennis Nineham often returns to this theme and indeed presses a further aspect of it.[49] He questions not only whether we can identify with the way the Bible speaks, but whether we can even understand it. From literary, anthropological, and theological perspectives one may question his more extreme statements that doubt whether any satisfactory understanding of the Bible is possible, with the theological inference he builds on these statements, namely, that contemporary Christian faith cannot base itself on the Bible. As we have noted, perfect understanding by one person of another is a goal we never reach, just as perfect translation from one language into another is an impossible ideal.[50] Yet these are the goals we nevertheless seek. Partial and growing understanding we believe we do reach.

> Relativism here is only true as the obvious refutation of a naïve and childish, literalist objectivism: it does not tell us that human beings cannot communicate, it merely specifies that all human speech is more or less broken, so that the true communication that all of us from time to time experience is a mystery, a paradox, a waking dream — if we are to speak theologically, an uncovenanted mercy.[51]

From a literary perspective, William Faulkner observes that contact with classic texts presses on us the awareness that "the past is not really dead; it is not even past."[52] While understanding such texts is not a simple matter but one that requires us to feel our way into their world if we are to hear them, Nineham overstates the matter in describing this as an impossible task. If he were right, then we would also be unable to gain any understanding of Aeschylus or Shakespeare, or indeed of our own contemporaries. Biblical writings seem to be among the literature that in practice interpreters find intelligible. The fact that interpreters do seem able to pass over into them suggests that they are not so alien. We have a "spontaneous

49. See *The Use and Abuse of the Bible; Explorations in Theology* 1:92-111; also his and some other contributions to the report of the Doctrine Commission of the Church of England, *Christian Believing*.

50. Steiner, *After Babel* 1-31.

51. Barton, "Reflections on Cultural Relativism" 198; cf. Thiselton, *The Two Horizons* 53-60; Coakley, "Theology and Cultural Relativism"; Downing, "Our Access to Other Cultures"; Preston, "Need Dr Nineham Be So Negative?"

52. Quoted without a reference by Tracy, *The Analogical Imagination* 106. See further Gardner, *The Business of Criticism* 25-51; Trilling, "The Sense of the Past," especially 187.

capacity for understanding others" that "is a factor of our relative freedom from the trammels of our historical situation."[53] We reach a paradox: "While achieving success in unlocking the secrets of the past . . . the modern scholar appeals to a method that, if taken seriously, makes that success impossible."[54]

On the basis of anthropological studies, Rogerson queries whether the gap between biblical and modern outlooks is "vast or unbridgeable."[55] Anthropologists do experience culture shock in seeking to share the life of very different societies, but that in itself reflects the ability to be aware of differences, which then prove capable of being analyzed and understood. One reason for this possibility is that the links between cultures are often stronger than we imagine: Our own societies are in their own way makers of myths, creators of traditions that express hopes and ideals, and mythologizers of history. Sound interpretation may be compared with avoiding committing the unforgiveable sin. People who are concerned that they have done so are those who thereby indicate they have not done so. People who recognize that cross-cultural communication is a demanding task that involves facing the real differences between cultures are then in a position to bridge those differences.

From a theological perspective, Nineham seems to make no allowance for the theological links between us and the scriptural writers deriving from creation and redemption. Interpretation involves building a road across a chasm, but the land on both sides is the same in the sense that we share with the biblical writers a common humanity, a common language (in the broad sense), and a common experience of the same world, as we do with other writings culturally and historically separated from us such as those of Shakespeare or Sophocles or the Gilgamesh epic. That is one factor that makes understanding possible. The air is the same on both sides of the chasm: We are children of the same heavenly Father, brothers and sisters of the same Christ, and partakers of the same Holy Spirit, and this gives us more in common with scripture than with other ancient writings. Furthermore, it is not as if we are the first people to try to cross this chasm, as is the case with some newly discovered ancient text. We are linked by a

---

53. Stern, *On Realism* 174, 183; the first part of the quotation is from E. Auerbach, *Literary Language and Its Public in Late Latin Antiquity* (ET New York: Pantheon/London: Routledge, 1965). Cf. Ford, *Barth and God's Story* 66.

54. Gunton, *Enlightenment and Alienation* 118.

55. *Myth in OT Interpretation* 183. Cf. Preston, "Need Dr Nineham Be So Negative?" 277.

continuity in history with these writings.[56] Each generation has to cross for itself, yet it profits from the way people have been going back and forth for centuries, some by principles of civil engineering that now look shaky, but that seem to have served them.

For reasons such as these, the chasm will often seem easy to cross. We will be almost unaware of it, like a family crossing over a ravine on a modern highway bridge. But the ravine is still there, as we realize when the highway closes for repairs. Furthermore, by its nature the highway makes us miss the delights of the countryside through which we would otherwise travel, unless we leave it and find our own way around. As we have noted, that we feel one and are one with the biblical writers and their original readers is a hindrance as well as a help to understanding them. It can make us think we understand them when we do not and cause us to mishear what they say. Nineham's work is thus valuable because it presses on us the depth of the gulf we have been speaking of. Understanding the Bible is a demanding exercise, like understanding Philo or Origen, Chaucer or Shakespeare. To appreciate these works in their original significance (like fully understanding any other human being) is an ultimately unattainable goal, yet it remains our aim in interpretation, and we recognize that our having to read them in a later context is itself an aid to other aspects of interpretation of them. The works themselves can transcend the gap that separates us from them, and in some ways the passage of time gives us a perspective that makes them easier to interpret.

56. Mark, "Relativism and Community" 162.

• 16 •

Subjectivity and Objectivity in Interpretation

The task of interpretation has a number of aspects. It involves *exegesis,* the attempt to come to an accurate historical understanding of the point that the scriptural text in its own right makes. It involves *synthesis* or *reflection,* where objectivity is again the ideal, but the interpreter is setting the text in the context of scripture as a whole and perhaps some other broad framework of thought such of that of a systematic theology, understanding the obscure and secondary in the light of the clear and primary, and drawing inferences for belief. It involves *appropriation,* a response to the text on the part of a whole person, not at an exclusively cerebral level. It involves *application,* the discovery of the way the God who spoke thus in this text would address concerns of our own day and direct our attitudes and behavior. It involves *communication,* discernment of how the results of interpretation can be shared with other people.

These facets of the interpretive task have commonly been understood as essentially independent of each other and undertaken in linear sequence — usually forming a threefold scheme.[1] In practice they are only notionally distinct: They interweave and contribute to each other. They are coexisting dimensions or levels rather than sequential steps.[2] It is thus particularly hazardous for the tasks to be allocated to different people, as famously happened in *The Interpreter's Bible,* where one section of each page offers

1. E.g., Barth, *Church Dogmatics* I/2, 722-40; Packer, *God Has Spoken* 73-77; also Packer's "Hermeneutics and Biblical Authority" 11-14; Yoder, *From Word to Life* 32.
2. Jeanrond, *Text and Interpretation* 68. Cf. the comments in chapter 1 above.

251

an exegesis of the text and another — on the same page but apparently independently — looks for the text's significance today. Other commentaries are either exegetical or expository; the two are rarely combined. Exegetes, theologians, and preachers alike are thus dangerously constrained in their work because they are encouraged to assume that areas of labor can be divided in this way.[3] It is not so much wrong as impossible. Each interpreter is bound to miss something of importance by looking at the text from one angle in isolation from others.

Exegesis and Appropriation

First, we may note the essential link between historical, exegetical study and the response of appropriation, which involves experiencing the realities of which the text speaks. Scripture is designed to be a means of revelation not merely theologically but experientially, a means of meeting God. During the medieval period this aspect of scripture's importance often became obscured even though — indeed in a sense because — scripture retained central importance as a source of Christian doctrine. The sacraments became the believer's means of a felt relationship with God. The Reformation regained an experiential involvement with scripture, though subsequent doctrinal discussion of scripture can easily give the impression of a return to medieval intellectualism.[4]

The development of biblical criticism encouraged a variant on the same split between mind and spirit. Often biblical critics have sold themselves short, along with everyone who followed them, in two ways. They have become so engrossed in biblical documents, history, and language and with reconstructing what the biblical writers meant in their original context that they have forgotten why they were first interested in the Bible, the attractiveness of biblical faith and of the biblical God. They could say, like Nietzsche, "I have forgotten why I ever began."[5] They are like civil engineers who have

---

3. Cf. Jeanrond, *Text and Interpretation* 6-7; also Lash, "What Might Martyrdom Mean," for a critique of the three-part model. Jeanrond's own "understanding, explanation, assessment" (*Text and Interpretation* xvii) seems rather different. Buttrick reworks the three-part model interestingly in terms of immediacy, reflection, and praxis in *Homiletic* 319-29.

4. See Lindsay, "Professor W. Robertson Smith's Doctrine of Scripture" 243-46, 261; "The Doctrine of Scripture: The Reformers and the Princeton School" 280-81.

5. As quoted by Mannheim, *Ideology and Utopia* 20.

become so thrilled with their bridge that they have forgotten to climb off it to take a look at the country they were making it possible to reach.

On its own, the objective, critical approach to scripture falls short of the hopes both of the readers, who learn by means of this approach nothing from scripture that can relate to their faith, and of the text, because it was written and preserved in order to speak for and to people in their relationship to God. We have noted in chapter 12 Barth's point that it is precisely in following where the text in its humanity points, in treating it historically, that we have to grapple with the divine reality that is its concern.[6] Bultmann speaks similarly of the impossibility of separating historical and theological exegesis as if one could engage in either independently of the other.[7] From the beginning he insisted that we cannot view the text from a distance and perceive what it objectively says without also relating it to our own position and asking about the realities it refers to.[8]

There is a sense in which we do need to quench our subjectivity. We need to silence our personal wishes with regard to the results of our interpretive work, such as any desire to confirm specific doctrinal or behavioral views. But we ought not quench it by attempting to avoid being gripped by and involved in what we study. In this connection "the 'most subjective' interpretation is the 'most objective,' because the only person who is able to hear the claims of the text is the person who is moved by the question of his or her own existence."[9] "Detached neutrality in matters of faith is not neutrality at all, but already a decision against responding" that systematically excludes questions of truth and meaning.[10] The text cannot be understood from a neutral position. The task of interpretation requires that we recognize that our interest is at stake. "Someone who acknowledges the origins of Christianity to be an aspect of *his* past, and not merely of 'the past of mankind' in general, is thereby precluded . . . from regarding the historical study of Christian origins as being 'simply' a matter of 'satisfying antiquarian curiosity.' "[11]

Mere analysis of texts may contribute nothing to understanding, which involves experience of the realities spoken of by the text.[12] Barth sees this

---

6. See *Church Dogmatics* I/2, 464-72.
7. "The Problem of a Theological Exegesis of the NT" 256.
8. "The Problem of a Theological Exegesis of the NT" 238.
9. Bultmann, "The Problem of Hermeneutics," in *NT and Mythology* 86.
10. Wink, *The Bible in Human Transformation* 2.
11. Lash, "What Might Martyrdom Mean" 190, quoting Nineham, *Explorations in Theology* 1:145.
12. Palmer, *Hermeneutics* 231, 248-49.

as a common inadequacy in commentaries, and in the preface to the second edition of his *Romans* defends his insistence on moving beyond text-critical and philological observations to understanding Paul and his subject matter. The Word needs to be exposed in the words.[13] Admittedly Barth's commentary work reveals the dangers in the attempt to think through the Bible's message in the terms of a modern philosophical perspective. The extensive exegetical work in the *Church Dogmatics* is less open to this criticism, despite the common accusation that he ignores historical-critical exegesis; it is important to distinguish theological exegesis, which Barth practices, from charismatic exegesis, which he does not.[14] True objectivity consists in openness to what the text has to say. Concentrating on questions of history or psychology — the reasons for an author's coming to certain views — may be a means of avoiding the text's own concerns and challenges.[15] No doubt historians are entitled to utilize these texts for the purpose of historical study, but that should not obscure the viability and necessity of theological interpretation.[16]

Historical procedures can clarify what is unclear because of our historical distance from the text and thus remove some of the disadvantages of not being the writer's original audience. But they do not in themselves help us to grasp the point the text was making. The old Russian icon had to be " 'discovered' not only physically — in that all the soot and more recent layers of paint have been removed — but also spiritually; we have learned how to look at it."[17] So it has to be with scripture, too. Historical exegesis opens up the possibility of interpretation and helps us check purported interpretations. But our interpretation needs to involve us thinking ourselves into the text's perspective and letting it interact with our own.

Barth and Bultmann thought they disagreed on this,[18] but this understanding was at least partly based on mutual misunderstanding. Both were concerned for matters (such as God) that are real in themselves but can only be real for us through mutual involvement; Barth wanted to stress the

---

13. See *The Epistle to the Romans* 6-9.

14. Berkouwer, *Holy Scripture* 115. Of course Barth, like anyone else, can *accidentally* read alien meanings into the text.

15. So Bultmann; see "The Problem of Hermeneutics" and "Is Exegesis without Presuppositions Possible?" in *NT and Mythology* 69-93, 145-53.

16. Morgan's *Biblical Interpretation* offers a systematic study of the interplay between these two interests.

17. N. S. Trubeckoj in *Readings in Russian Poetics* (ed. Matejka and Pomorska) 119.

18. Cf. Bultmann, "The Problem of Hermeneutics," in *NT and Mythology* 88-90.

"real in themselves," Bultmann the "real for us," and each inferred that the other was denying that to which he gave less emphasis. A similar misunderstanding appears in the more general hermeneutical debate between Emilio Betti and E. D. Hirsch on the one hand and Hans-Georg Gadamer with his links with Martin Heidegger on the other. The former are concerned with establishing what counts as right and wrong interpretation, the latter with how interpretation happens at all; the former can sound as if they are advocating an uninvolved objectivist approach to interpretation when they are not, while Gadamer can sound as if he has abandoned any concern for objective meaning when he has not.[19]

There is an inextricable link between exegesis and appropriation. It implies a reversal of movement in the process of interpretation, noted on page 199 above. I start as the subject, speaking, asking questions, being objective about the Bible, subjecting it to scrutiny, seeking to avoid reading into it the views I already hold, the experience I already have, or the commitments I already accept. In due course it becomes the subject, speaking, addressing, asking questions, challenging my views, my experiences, and my commitments. I am the object on the receiving end of *its* scrutiny. Then "it is not the interpreter who grasps the meaning of the text; the meaning of the text seizes him."[20] This exciting moment unveils whether I really regard the Bible as God's revelation by acting on what I hear.

In the case of prayer texts and other works that directly reflect an author's own experience, that movement naturally has a different dynamic from the one that applies to story, command, and inspired word. There words were spoken to me (or at least I put myself into the position of the people to whom they were addressed). Here a word is spoken for me. Texts such as the Psalms express human feelings and experiences. They are not the words of a "superhuman Ventriloquist" speaking in the name of human beings words never conceived in or uttered from a human heart.[21] Most of scripture speaks to us, but the Psalms speak for us.[22] They articulate expe-

---

19. See, e.g., the quotations and discussion in Palmer, *Hermeneutics* 46-65. Palmer's own sympathy is with Gadamer, but he also notes both that meaning changes and that it does so without being *absolutely* different, because the work's "*essential* truth corresponds to that which originally brought it into being" (184, his emphasis).

20. Palmer, *Hermeneutics* 248.

21. Coleridge, *Confessions of an Inquiring Spirit*, Letter 3; cf. Dawson, "Against the Divine Ventriloquist" 295.

22. Athanasius works this out with regard to different types of psalms in *A Letter to Marcellinus on the Interpretation of the Psalms* 10-33.

riences, attitudes, beliefs, and prayers, and are given to me so that they can go on to articulate my experiences, attitudes, beliefs, and prayers. My "response" to them is to use them in this way, to allow them to call forth from me the praise, the prayer, the act of commitment, the protest, the declaration of trust that the text itself expresses. Like stories, as well as having implied authors these texts have implied readers or ideal readers, and interpretation involves becoming such readers.[23]

Sometimes, admittedly, we find ourselves uncertain as to what kind of reader is anticipated by a text. Some texts are ambiguous, not merely because we lack the right information to enable us to see their meaning, but because ambiguity is built into them. It is there to put further questions to the reader, who learns precisely by having to decide how to read the text.[24] In chapter 3 we considered this "receptionist" approach to interpretation in connection with narrative, but it comes into its own with prayer texts, which speak to me by asking me what (if anything) I would mean by taking this text on my lips. I as the subject questioning the text may be unable to discover whether a psalm that expresses a love for God's law arose out of a "legalistic" attitude — it can be read that way. I may be unable to discover whether a psalm that praises or laments in stereotyped ways arose out of genuine praise or prayer — it need not be read that way. But the text as the subject questioning me penetrates to my inner person (cf. Heb 4:12) to discover whether I have the prayer, praise, or commitment to express by means of this text; not just to discover that, but to evoke that response to God by offering itself as a vehicle for it.[25]

Exegesis and Application

Second, Gadamer has especially emphasized the related intrinsic link between exegesis and application. Ironically, there is a historicist strain to Schleiermacher's hermeneutics. He speaks as if we can completely free ourselves from our own situation and bracket our concern that scripture speak to the present: "In interpretation it is essential that one be able to step out of one's own frame of mind into that of the author."[26] He implies

---

23. Cf. R. S. Cohen in *Interpretation of Narrative* (ed. Valdés and Miller) 5.

24. So Fish, e.g., "Interpreting the *Variorum*."

25. Brueggemann, "Psalms and the Life of Faith" 17-19.

26. *Hermeneutics* 42; cf. the comments of J. Duke and H. Kimmerle in their introductions in the same volume, 11, 30-31.

that one first understands, then applies. The strength of this assumption derives from the fact that concern for the application of the text today, for its relevance, can be a tyranny that inhibits understanding. The approach that hastens to identify its concern with those of the text also easily falls short because it can encourage us to use the text merely to confirm us in the religious beliefs we had before we read it. It was for this reason that in his famous essay "On the Interpretation of Scripture" Jowett especially insisted on a sharp disjunction between exegesis and application.[27]

We easily assume that the experience to which the text witnesses mirrors our own; we look down the well and see ourselves. So here objective, historical approaches can help us to respond in trust and obedience to the scriptural texts themselves, because they help us actually to hear these texts aright. Ricoeur remarks that Freud in his *Moses and Monotheism* "thought he could economize on biblical exegesis" with the result that "he found, at the end of the analysis, only what he knew before undertaking it."[28] "Whether in terms of the current 'contextual' emphasis in the World Council of Churches, or in terms of the charismatic movement, a polarization has emerged between the pre-occupation with present experience and the study of the New Testament. . . . The hermeneutical task is to establish a relationship between two sets of horizons: those of the New Testament itself, and those of the interpreter's present experience and conceptual frame."[29] In a famous article on the nature of biblical theology Krister Stendahl pressed for the maintenance of a sharp distinction between the historical meaning of the scriptural text and its significance for us. He can be chided for hermeneutical naïveté, but his critique of Luther's reading of Romans illustrates the advantage of maintaining this distinction.[30]

Gadamer's point is that application can also be a handmaid to understanding, an aspect of understanding, and an index to whether understanding has actually taken place. "The task of an interpreter is not simply to reproduce what is said by one of the partners in the discussion he is translating, but to express what is said in the way that seems necessary to him considering the real situation of the dialogue, which only he knows, since only he knows both languages being used in the discussion." Thus

---

27. § 5 (pp. 491-508 in the 1862 edition).
28. *Freud and Philosophy* 349.
29. Thiselton, "The Use of Philosophical Categories in NT Hermeneutics" 98.
30. See "Biblical Theology, Contemporary." Cf. Thiselton, *The Two Horizons* 317-18.

application is "an integral element in all understanding." In the process of conversation involved in interpretation "the reconstruction of the question, from which the meaning of a text is to be understood as an answer, passes into our own questioning. For the text must be understood as an answer to a real question. . . . To understand a question means to ask it. To understand an opinion is to understand it as the answer to a question." Indeed "the anticipation of an answer itself presumes that the person asking is part of the tradition and regards himself as addressed by it."[31] The interpretation of a text "always presupposes the horizon of the interpreter, a situation *out* of which and *for* which an interpretation occurs."[32] Even E. D. Hirsch in due course came to acknowledge that application could be seen as part of the text's original meaning insofar as the text looked to have a significance beyond its own day, though he emphasized that this does not indicate that the text's own meaning changes.[33]

Further, Hirsch urges, there needs to be a demonstrable equivalence between the contemporary restatement of the text and the original if it is to count as restatement of *this* text.[34] "If there is no objective meaning, then the text no longer says anything at all; without existential appropriation, what the text does say is no longer living speech. The task of a theory of interpretation is to combine in a single process these two moments of comprehension."[35]

Like concern with appropriation, concern with application corresponds to the text's own aim. Polzin notes that historical-critical study that seeks to interpret Deuteronomy and the deuteronomistic history in the light of their writers' original intention is not, in fact, interpretation of these books in the light of their writers' original intention, because those writers did not concern themselves with such an "objective," historical, uninvolved approach to the texts with which they were themselves working; those works are essentially applicatory, in Gadamer's sense.[36] The significance of this point is qualified by the fact that they these writers do also preserve versions of the texts they were interpreting (e.g., Exodus 21–23 and Deuteronomy itself), which implies some recognition of the ongoing importance of their

31. Gadamer, *Truth and Method* 273, 275, 337, 340.

32. Cady, "Hermeneutics and Tradition" 442 (emphasis original).

33. "Meaning and Significance Reinterpeted" 202.

34. *Validity in Interpretation* 252-53.

35. Ricoeur, *The Conflict of Interpretations* 398; cf. Stanton, "Interpreting the NT Today" 70.

36. *Moses and the Deuteronomist* 11-12.

"texts" in their original meanings. Nevertheless it is true that scripture discourages us from thinking of exegesis and contemporization as independent operations. The urge for contemporization is the motivation to study scripture, the means of insight into its meaning, and the key to the way it is produced in the form it is.

The metaphorical civil engineers referred to earlier in this chapter have also forgotten that their bridge was designed to carry traffic in both directions. It needs two lanes: As interpreters we cross to a different country, but must return to live in our own in the light of the visit there. Our concern to understand the Bible in its day has to be paralleled by a concern to apply it to our day. Indeed "the principal objective of reading the Bible is not to interpret the Bible but to interpret life with the help of the Bible."[37] Our doing that is the evidence that we truly have visited a different country and that we had our eyes open when we did so. Our experience at home enables us to understand our visit to another place, in its similarities and its distinctives, and our visit to another place gives us new eyes with which to look at our home. Exegesis and exposition are distinguishable but interwoven. The image of bridge building is misleading if it implies that we first and once-for-all investigate the far country in an objective, uninvolved way and only then return home.

The process of application does not necessarily look after itself. Clarity of exegesis regarding a miracle story does not establish whether we are to expect miracles today. Sometimes simply to repeat what the scriptural text says is to say something quite different from what it signified in its original context. Condemnation of Jews to their faces by Amos, Jesus, or Paul is one thing; by Gentile preachers before largely Gentile audiences it is another. The equivalent object of condemnation is the church community to which we ourselves belong.[38]

Like the task of exegesis — and like real bridge building, I suspect — the application of scripture to our own age and world and lives means combining hard thinking with inspired intuition. The hard work involves looking for principles that may underlie passages of scripture that do not seem to apply to us as they stand, and comparing those principles with other parts of scripture as a check on our work. It also involves gaining a

---

37. C. Mesters, "Como se faz teologia hoje no Brasil?" *Estudios biblicos* 1 (1985) 10, as quoted in Rowland and Corner, *Liberating Exegesis* 39.

38. Cf. Goldingay, "Expounding the NT," in *NT Interpretation* (ed. Marshall) 353-54, and the comments on p. 125 above.

knowledge of the world in which we live and the situations people today are confronting, to which the Bible needs to be applied. The inspired intuition gives a general principle concrete embodiment in real life.

Hard work seeks to grasp precisely the point a biblical story made; inspired intuition sees how our story can be seen in the light of God's story. Hard work studies the process of reinterpretation within the scriptures, whereby a theme such as creation or God's promise to Abraham comes to have different implications in different periods, or whereby sayings, stories, and events with one meaning in the context of Jesus' actual life come to have further significance in the context of the life of the church, in which the Gospels were written. Inspired intuition sees which of these interpretations especially speaks to us, or what further reinterpretations of themes, sayings, stories, and events is appropriate in our context. Hard work seeks to generate a comprehensive grasp of the variety of messages that appear in the Bible and of the way each of them confronts or encourages people in different situations. Inspired intuition perceives which of these messages has special relevance to us or to the people we have to minister to.

Deuteronomy and the deuteronomistic history also assume that application is not merely a matter of words. The interpretation of scripture takes place in its rendering or embodying in the life of the community and the believer. Faithfulness to scripture is expressed in behavior.[39] Liberation theologians emphasize this aspect of the sense in which biblical interpretation is not the objective, scientific affair that scholarship traditionally assumes it to be. What we see in scripture is very substantially influenced by what we are prepared to see there. Our opening of ourselves to the text is not merely a matter of the mind but of the will. It is not merely possible, preferable, or dangerous to be influenced in the way one reads the Bible by the way one lives. It is inevitable; this is a feature of human understanding in any sphere. Any reading of scripture takes place against the background of some commitment, "reactionary, reformist, or revolutionary"; what is important is to be self-conscious about one's bias rather than pretending to speak from "some sort of ideologically aseptic environment" — and to be self-critical about that bias.[40]

It was commitment to liberation that enabled people to see that liberation is central to scripture. Traditional evangelical reading of Exodus or

39. Lash, "What Might Martyrdom Mean?" 196-98.
40. Miguez Bonino, *Doing Theology in a Revolutionary Situation* 99; cf. Segundo, *Liberation of Theology* 7-8.

the Prophets takes place against the background of a commitment to a more pietistic and politically conservative stance, and to fit in with these commitments adopts hermeneutical devices that enable it not to take these parts of scripture literally. A Latin American evangelical interpreter thus comments that interpretation involves not merely an intuitive, naive move from the text to today but a realization that it is true both that texts are only understood in context and that *we* are only understood in context. The total process involves both historical criticism and hermeneutical re-alization.[41] Bultmann not only anticipates liberation theology's affirmation that "there is no neutral exegesis"; he even anticipates its insight that right interpretation arises only from obedience, quoting John 7:17.[42]

Latin American theologians have been accused of reading into the Bible their own concern with the liberation of their peoples. Their reply would be that their situation enables them to perceive a concern that is present in scripture itself and that Western theologians cannot see because of their hermeneutical bias. People who produce their theology in academic insti-tutions in the West remove the political note from the Bible and treat it as a series of theological and ethical abstractions. Their work is either an exercise in providing ideological support for the political system or part of an academic game; either way it does not impinge on real life and thus misses the point of the Bible. Biblical interpretation is not a matter of mere academic study but a matter of the knowledge of God and of truth: In scripture knowledge implies recognition and acknowledgment, and truth involves faithfulness and constancy.

Understanding is thus furthered rather than hindered by a practical commitment to the ways of the Bible's God, and the attempt to understand the Bible with scientific objectivity may not be fruitful because it does not correspond to the Bible's nature. We may with that kind of study be able to discover certain facts from the Bible, such as facts concerning aspects of Israelite history or of the development of Israelite religion. But we will not reach the kind of understanding for which the Bible looks because it ex-presses, invites, and demands commitment to the One of whom it speaks and for whom it is concerned. For that reason liberation theology doubts whether the academic theology of study and university really counts as theology and questions whether an understanding of scripture that lacks

41. See Padilla, "The Interpreted Word."
42. "The Problem of a Theological Exegesis of the NT" 242, 252. Cf. Rowland and Corner, *Liberating Exegesis* 69-74.

the context of a desire to do what scripture says truly counts as understanding.

Jesus reminds us forcefully of this point by observing in John that people who are committed to doing the will of God will recognize teaching that comes from God (John 7:17). But the people who were most familiar with the scriptures and had committed themselves most unequivocally to following the scriptures had the greatest difficulty in perceiving what they were pointing to. Inability to understand reflects inability to accept what is being said (John 8:43).

In chapter 12 we noted aspects of the Holy Spirit's involvement in the interpretation of inspired scripture, which we have described here in terms of hard work and inspired intuition. It is perhaps most crucial that interpretation involve the Holy Spirit working on the will, which needs the softening that the Spirit has to effect if we are to be open to costly new insights on the meaning of scripture for us. Interpretation is a moral issue. It is through the Spirit's ongoing shaping of individual and community to the likeness of Christ that both may become more and more capable of reading scripture; in particular it makes us more open to the possibility of seeing how to read scripture over against ourselves and not merely to support ourselves.[43]

Appropriation and Communication

A concern with communicating the results of one's study of a text also interweaves with the task of interpretation. It is not merely a stage subsequent to completion of the first task. Teaching also "has an important heuristic rebound and hermeneutical function."[44] It can raise new questions in the mind of the teacher and through the contributions of the taught, who are themselves interpreters, questions that can point toward aspects of the text's meaning that we may have overlooked. Teaching can contribute to understanding.

If appropriation of the experiential material such as the Psalms implies being able actually to say them, preaching on such experiential material has as its aim that people will be able to say them. As human beings we may

---

43. Fowl and Jones, *Reading in Communion*, e.g., 42-43, 84-96, 103-4; they compare Bonhoeffer, "The Interpretation of the NT."

44. Montague, "Hermeneutics and the Teaching of Scripture" 1.

be tempted to the view that in reality either our existence alone truly counts, so that in worship we speak but to empty air and are not addressed, or that God's existence and power alone truly counts, so that in worship we simply submit to God and can hardly utter the rage or hopelessness of our hearts. The preacher is entrusted with the speech of God, which breaks the first form of silence, but also with the speech of the people, which breaks the second form of silence. "The preacher then voices the speech of crushed human voices, persons too long engaged in denial, too long burdened with superfluous guilt, too long pent-up with rage, . . . articulating the protest of self which can then move to praise, risking the candor that becomes the seedbed of communion." This takes place through the use of "the gift of speech that the texts of Israel offer us."[45] It is embodied in the conversations that figures such as Abraham, Moses, Miriam, Deborah, Jeremiah, and Job initiate with God, but particularly in the Psalms, which give expression to the worshiper's pain, protest, and need, to the responsive powerful intervening voice of God, and to Israel's resumed speech of praise and celebration. The preacher's task is to enable the Psalms to be prayed again, to mediate and model a conversation.

A. M. Allchin recalls hearing an Orthodox abbot recite the Psalms.

> But that gives the wrong impression. He spoke them as if they were being spoken for the first time, speaking them from the depths of his heart; and yet at the same time speaking them with the weight of almost three thousand years, a hundred generations of longing after God. It was as if the whole tradition was speaking through him. Scripture comes to fulfilment when it ceases to be scripture and becomes living speech. The Spirit who breathed in the original psalmist breathed in the man who now spoke the psalmist's words. They were words filled with the Spirit.[46]

Our task as preachers is to enable people to make the Psalms their own living speech. We may most plausibly do that by making them our own speech in such a way as to draw others into them. If different types of material in scripture communicate in different ways and point to correspondingly different approaches to communicating them, this also applies to the Psalms. The way scripture itself most systematically goes about teaching people about praise and prayer is by offering models of praise and prayer, by praising God and by praying. As we noted in chapter 1, it does

---

45. Brueggemann, *Finally Comes the Poet* 50; see further 43-77.
46. *The Dynamic of Tradition* 27-28.

not tell people how to do it but shows them how to do it. The style of preaching into which it invites us is an expository approach to the Psalms that preaches them by praying them and letting the congregation overhear what we are saying to God. We praise God and pray in a way that issues from a psalm and thus model what praying the Psalms might be. I have attempted to do this by taking a psalm section by section and talking to God out of my own experience in the light of the psalm, acknowledging to God the ways the psalmist's experience and mine resonate and the ways I need God to bring me into the experience the psalm speaks of.

The Complementarity of the Reflective and the Experiential

The central tragedy of the history of biblical study over the past two centuries is that the objective, distancing, critical approach to scripture and the obedient, trusting, experiential approach have proceeded in substantial independence of each other. The one is appropriate to the scholarly game and the exam treadmill, the other to believers on their knees praying or on their feet preaching. People are brought up on the second approach, struggle with the first approach to get a degree, and then revert with relief to the second when they escape from their tutor's eye. It is the application of the Bible in the contemporary world that counts; there is not enough time for the luxury of the distancing, critical approach. In fact, however, our contemporary application of scripture will be shallow or predetermined by the insights and experiences we bring to scripture or both if we concentrate exclusively on the question of contemporary application.

In discussing how we interpret texts that explicitly evoke human experience, we have brought together two contrasting approaches to interpretation.[47] One begins by assuming that our experience and the experience evoked in the text are parallel, so that the one can be understood in the light of the other; this approach emphasizes the link between the two human experiences. The other approach seeks to distance the interpreter from the text and look at it "objectively" in the light of its context rather than in the light of the interpreter's experience. It is the differences between these two approaches that make them so important to each other.

This contrast links with a contrast between two broad approaches to

47. Martin, "Toward a Post-Critical Paradigm" overlaps with what follows.

interpretation. They are ideal types in the sense that no one operates by either of them all the time, and features of one may become combined with features of the other. That is not a fault, because both approaches are valuable, and they complement each other. The first is more at home with reflective theological material such as characterizes the Epistles, the second more at home with experiential material and with narrative. The first is more traditional, the second is becoming trendy.

The two approaches can be characterized in terms of a series of further comparisons: One is analytic, making discoveries by taking texts apart and analyzing them into parts; the other is holistic, responding to texts as wholes. One is deductive, disciplining itself to starting from texts and moving from there to life; the other is experimental, moving from life to texts. One is concerned with what scripture says to us individually, the other with what scripture says to us communally. One views the study of scripture as naturally undertaken by someone on their own, the other views it as something people naturally do together. One is highly cerebral, left-brain, majoring on hard and careful thinking; the other is more intuitive or right-brain. One tends to focus on otherworldly concerns, the other tends to be more interested in this world. One concentrates more on getting our thinking right, the other more on getting our actions right. One is more objective in its approach, the other more participatory. One is more interested in analyzing texts, the other in being drawn into metaphors. One seeks to distance us from the text so as to lessen the extent to which we may mishear it and to increase our ability really to hear what God was once saying to other people in history; the other emphasizes our appropriation of the text for ourselves as we make our response to the God who speaks in the present to us. One is more interested in correct interpretation, the other more interested in creative interpretation. One tends to look for timeless truths, the other tends to be highly situational. One is inclined to be abstract, the other concrete. One is content with a form of preaching that leaves people to work out the application of scripture for themselves, the other is involved in the explicit application of scripture to people's lives. One tends to be confident about scripture's meaning, the other may be fearful of missing it because of our capacity to avoid the truth.

We need to exercise both of these approaches to interpretation so that we may move nearer to that eschatological goal of a complete grasp of scripture and by scripture, when we will have no more questions and see face to face.

Reflective Expository Preaching

Expository preaching classically denotes any preaching that expounds passages of scripture in a systematic way. It involves a careful analysis of a text's burden, grasping *the* point it makes, construing the text as a whole and in its distinctive singularity,[1] and discovering how its various parts or themes contribute to that whole and relate to that central concern. The preacher then presents the congregation with the results of this analysis in a sermon structured clearly and logically along the lines suggested by the structure of the passage itself, explaining its meaning in clear-cut and unambiguous fashion. Thus described baldly such preaching may sound extremely dull, but it is in fact a way of handling scripture that can open up the text for people very effectively. Its aim is not merely that people should receive some teaching about something but that the intention of the text to do something to people's lives may be realized once again.

Expository preaching is structured, discursive, direct, reflective, and concretely applied, offering explicit teaching and exhortation on belief and behavior. In its nature it is thus hardly appropriate to the narrative material in scripture, but it corresponds well to the form of the Epistles, of the teaching of Jesus, of wisdom thinking, of Torah, and, more surprisingly perhaps, of prophecy. Prophecy has the same characteristics as this other material: Grasping the word of God involves following an argument that God puts before people and responding to it, so classical expository preaching fits the nature of the words of God. Expository material of these various kinds in scripture, then, lends itself to an expository method of preaching.

---

1. Ricoeur, *Interpretation Theory* 77.

How do we discover what to say on the basis of expository texts? And how do they suggest we go about saying it?

Discovering How the Text Addressed Its Hearers

Preaching corresponds to scripture itself in that it is concerned to do something to people on the basis of information it conveys. It seeks to inform in order to inspire. A prophet such as Joel or a letter such as 1 Corinthians leaves the hearer in no doubt as to the fact that it looks for a response, and as to the nature of that response. An expository sermon takes a passage with such an aim, reloads the missile, and fires at the analogous contemporary target. While a story has its effect largely indirectly and subliminally, prophecy and letters aim to hit the hearer right between the eyes.

In seeking to discern how to repeat the effect that the expository text originally achieved, a possible initial question to consider is how the passage confronts its hearers. J. A. Sanders analyzes the way in which at different points scripture speaks to people in a constitutive-supportive way or in a prophetic-challenging way.[2] Even when it is being supportive scripture is characteristically confronting people because they are unsure of God and of themselves and it is offering them a promise of and grounds for security. Scripture's expository teaching is regularly designed to challenge people's current beliefs and attitudes.

Even when being supportive, then, it seeks not to confirm people in their position but to change them, and it is in order to challenge people that it affirms or denies particular attitudes or way of behaving. It aims to reassure the downcast, strengthen the weak, disturb the secure, and expose the sinful. The preacher appropriately begins studying a particular passage by seeking to identify how it is that it brings comfort or discomfort, what central point it makes in order to do so, what sort of people are its implied readers, what reasoning they are urged to follow, and what the text finally aims to do to them. Sometimes exegetical commentaries help the interpreter grasp the significance of passages along these lines, though very many of them mysteriously fail here and may help the interpreter only with trees and not with the wood as a whole; perhaps there is in any case an argument for working first with the Bible on its

2. From *Sacred Story to Sacred Text* 67-68; cf. p. 125 above.

own rather than having one's thinking channeled by commentators too quickly.[3]

Approaching biblical expository material in this way presupposes that although this material (especially the Epistles) contains the nearest thing to a reflective theology in scripture, it is at the same time characteristically situational. It is not mere general truth but specific messages directed to concrete contexts. Systematic treatments of tongues and prophecy, or justification by faith, or Christ's final appearing, feature in 1 Corinthians or Galatians or Thessalonians not as chapters in a dogmatic theology but as messages to particular groups of Christians who had given Paul cause for concern in their attitude to each of these questions.

That scripture's expository teaching is regularly designed to confront people regarding their current attitudes naturally means that it brings contrary messages to audiences in different situations. Words in Ezekiel from the beginning of the exile discourage people from building hopes for the future on God's promises to Abraham, while words in Isaiah relating to the end of the exile encourage people to do just that (Ezek 33:23-29; Isa 51:1-3).[4] In both contexts a prophet is confronting his people, one of them by seeking to rebuild shattered hopes. Paul declares in Romans: "People are justified by faith, not by works; you only have to look at the example of Abraham to see that," while James declares: "People are justified by works, not by faith; you only have to look at the example of Abraham to see that." Paul addresses people inclined to believe that it is what they can achieve that decides whether God accepts them, so he confronts that error; James addresses people who have learned Paul's lesson too well and, confident of God's acceptance, are inclined to believe that they need not bother to try to achieve anything for God, so he confronts that error.

Over many matters, there are not merely two alternative possible errors to be confronted, but a range of possible experiences and needs that the authors address. For instance, Second Testament churches had a variety of experiences with regard to ministerial graces. The church at Corinth was apparently especially excited by "speaking in tongues"; Paul seeks to rechannel their enthusiasm and prefers to emphasize the gift of prophecy.

---

3. Kaiser's *Toward an Exegetical Theology* and Yoder's *From Word to Life* are particularly concerned to help people study scripture in this way for themselves, even if they risk inculcating a hermeneutical naïveté that thinks that there is a linear, one-way relationship between exegesis and application.

4. Again cf. J. A. Sanders, e.g., *From Sacred Story to Sacred Text* 66-67.

The churches in Turkey and elsewhere to which 1 Peter, Revelation, and Ephesians were written had evidently assimilated these graces into their church life, and the writers of these documents could presuppose that they knew how to handle prophecy. Jesus' teaching in Matthew 7:21-23, in contrast, addresses a situation in which people need warning about people prophesying without actually belonging to Christ. The letters to Timothy (also in Ephesus) refer to graces such as prophecy only in connection with Timothy himself as the leader of the church(es) (1 Tim 4:14; 2 Tim 1:6), while the absence of any reference to these graces in Philippians and Colossians makes it possible to question whether they were known there at all. In each case, what the writer says about ministerial graces relates to aspects of the specific situation that the writer addresses.

These are only striking examples of a consistent phenomenon, that scripture's expository teaching is regularly addressed to specific and thus varying contexts. The implication of this phenomenon for preaching is that the preacher has to discern whether certain scriptural contexts correspond more or less to contexts that have to be addressed today. If we preach Paul's message to the kind of congregation that James addressed (or vice versa), we confirm the members of that congregation in their error instead of drawing them out of it. We do the same if we preach Matthew 7's warnings about prophecy's dangers to a congregation like the Corinthians, a congregation inclined to underestimate prophecy. And the reverse is also true. Or perhaps more realistically, we need to recognize that a congregation is likely to include people in different positions with different needs with regard to areas such as these.

Discerning how a passage confronts its readers may naturally lead us to ask how relevant the passage is. If it is a specific message to a particular context, on what grounds can I reapply it to a church today?

There are, of course, issues that tend to need handling in any context, issues that arise regularly in the life of any church in the first century or the twentieth. There are thus passages of perennial relevance. There is often material of this kind in biblical books that make little reference to specific historical contexts, such as Proverbs with its teaching on wealth or the Sermon on the Mount with its teaching on marriage and divorce. Much of the treatment of fundamentals of the gospel in letters such as Romans and Ephesians is similarly of perennial relevance in the Christian church.

Other passages are of specific relevance to particular contexts in scripture, but can easily be imagined to be of specific relevance now. In contrast to the Torah, wisdom, and much of Jesus' teaching, most of the prophetic books and the Epistles are explicitly related (as their introductions and contents show) to the needs of particular periods in Israel's history or of particular early Christian congregations. Thus Isaiah 41 is addressed to the people of God threatened by fear of the future, fear of other peoples, fear of their own weakness and neediness, and fear of having been rejected by Yahweh their God. 1 Corinthians 3 addresses a Christian congregation inclined to attach excessive importance to one Christian leader or another. It is entirely possible to imagine these passages being of specific relevance today.

We need, however, to recognize two problems about the "relevant" themes of scripture. One is that even in those places the differences between ancient and modern contexts need to be honored if we are to do justice to either context. For instance, Ernst Käsemann notes that the idea of the body of Christ is not merely a "beautiful metaphor" nor part of a "timeless metaphysic" that is equally obvious or immediately accessible in all periods, but an image that has a specific background and life setting.[5] It is thus also one that some subsequent generations have been more able to appreciate than others have. We need to understand what Paul meant by it and not just assume we know. Anthony Thiselton makes a similar point about Jesus' image of the reign of God: Even if it is a symbol or metaphor and must be treated as such, it is a symbol that needs understanding on the lips of Jesus and as having reference to his historical reality, his life and deeds.[6]

The other problem is that when we perceive that a particular theme is of great importance today and of greater importance in scripture than Christians have often noticed, it is easy to begin to find this theme everywhere in scripture (a thousand thousand are their texts and all their sermons one). Enthusiasm about the theme of political liberation illustrates this danger. We have to recognize that whatever our favorite theme might be (whatever the central theme of God's dealings with the church in our age might be), there are texts on other themes, texts that are more difficult for us to hear but possibly equally important.

Yet other passages are likely to be of only indirect relevance to any modern context. Ezekiel 8, for instance, warns about idolatrous practices in the temple. 1 Corinthians 9 discusses Paul's attitude to the rights of an apostle. Much of the Torah relates to cultures and to questions that have no direct equivalent in modern North Atlantic countries, though they may

5. *Perspectives on Paul* 103-5.
6. *New Horizons in Hermeneutics* 66-67.

have very direct equivalents elsewhere. 1 Timothy 3 suggests qualifications for church leadership that are very instructive for a young church, but the sharp edge of God's challenge in this matter for an established church may lie elsewhere.

But there will be ways in which such passages can be of indirect contemporary relevance. One is that sometimes a balanced approach to a misapprehension or problem we do not have will also be a balanced approach to one we do have. For instance, the Corinthians were so enthusiastic about heaven that they could not fit the body into their theology or spirituality. Today, we are so enthusiastic about the body that we cannot fit heaven into our theology or spirituality. In 1 Corinthians 15 Paul puts the life of heaven and the life of the body together to help the Corinthians get them into the right relationship, but the way he does so may be just as helpful to us, though our problem is the opposite of theirs.[7]

Another way that a passage can be of indirect relevance is that an "irrelevant" piece of scriptural teaching can nevertheless offer us a paradigm of the application of some principle that we do need to take seriously. In 1 Corinthians 9 Paul talks about the rights of an apostle, which his readers ought to recognize but which he forgoes. The rights of an apostle may be of little relevance to us, but the notion of having rights yet forgoing them might be important to understanding what it means to be a husband or a wife, a parent, a daughter or a son, an employee or an employer. Talk about the rights of an apostle gives a particular example of attitudes to rights in general. Passages cannot be identified once and for all as of specific or indirect relevance; they tend to change places as the circumstances of the church change.

The agenda for scripture's expository material is set by an interaction between the truth about God and the way God deals with people as a whole, on the one hand, and the particular needs of specific contexts, on the other. This suggests that a further question for a preacher to ask about a passage is how it fits into "the whole counsel of God" — how it relates to other scriptures on its particular subject and what the place of this subject is in scripture as a whole. This question draws attention to the fact that preachers have to face two contrary demands, which are placed on them by scripture itself. They are called to be both relevant and balanced. The first obligation is suggested by the situational nature of so much of scripture. This variety of situational material has been collected into a corpus, however, and the

---

7. I owe this insight to a Bible exposition by my former colleague Andrew Lincoln.

implication of having a corpus of writings is that we should take account of the whole range of its perspectives in formulating a view of the whole counsel of God. It is easy to be gripped by only one facet of scripture's teaching on a topic such as healing or spiritual gifts or suffering. Scripture itself offers a wide range of perspectives on such topics, and we have to seek a comprehensive rather than partial grasp of these perspectives in their interrelationships. Again, we can be so overwhelmed by the importance of faith or of evangelism or of divine grace that we fail to see the importance of works or social action or human responsibility (or the reverse in each case).

Expository preaching invites us to a careful historical study of passages in their contexts in order to see how they confronted their original hearers and readers, if we are to see how they might be relevant today. It also invites us into a constructive theological and ethical task that is at least as demanding in different ways, as we seek to turn an understanding of various aspects of scripture's insight on specific themes into a whole that does justice to the individual parts.

Discovering How the Text Applies Today

The preacher's attempt to understand the whole counsel of God from scripture needs to be complemented by the application of this concern to the congregation's life. A lectionary is designed to provide a church with a balanced set of readings that reflects the whole counsel of God as scripture itself expounds it. If the lectionary does so, then the church's preaching program, by following the lectionary, will in turn provide the congregation with a balanced diet that drives home the whole counsel of God to the congregation. At the same time, this preaching program needs to apply the whole counsel of God to the church's specific situation, as scripture itself does, and this will naturally mean ignoring the lectionary at other times in order to focus on issues or to work through particular books of the Bible. In a church worship committee to which I once belonged, we found ourselves discussing two questions: "What does the congregation need to hear at the moment? What subjects should we do a series on?" and "What parts of scripture have we not preached on lately? What themes do the church's year and the lectionary suggest to us at the moment?" The canon of scripture and the calendar and lectionary are the church's aide-mémoire to preaching the whole counsel of God. (Admittedly a hermeneutic of suspicion is also appropriate to lectionaries. Feminist critique, for instance, notes that at Easter they tend to give much more exposure to John 20:19-31 than they do to John 20:11-18. Further, in the Second Testament instructions regarding the submission of slaves to masters accompany instructions regarding the submission of wives to husbands, but the former — which may help to point up the general culture-relativeness of such instructions — are not read together with the latter.)[8]

Scripture itself addresses a wide variety of contexts, and it is quite possible (for instance) to bring scriptural words of comfort to people whom scripture needs to disturb, or to make scriptural demands in situations where scripture would be more inclined to offer encouragement. That is to be a false prophet. We need to be able to set individual scriptural insights in the context of a perspective suggested by the whole and to perceive how the scriptural statements relate to contexts in people's lives and what emphases need to characterize our preaching to people where they presently are. Merely to repeat things that the Bible itself says does not make us biblical preachers. The significance of biblical statements depends on the way they were designed to "cut."[9]

That we are concerned to set each scriptural emphasis in the context of God's truth as a whole does not mean that we abandon scripture's own concern to bring a specific message to particular hearers. We are concerned, therefore, to ask "How does the passage apply to us?" (to me and to the congregation). As scripture's exposition was characteristically direct and applied to particular hearers, so also will exposition based on it be. Some modern expository preaching has been content not to seek to apply the text in specific ways to its hearers but to confine itself to "saying again what St. Paul has already said," in the conviction that applying the text to people is the Holy Spirit's business. Paul himself did not see it that way: He characteristically addressed specific congregations with specific needs and made the concrete application of his message quite explicit.

At one level, the task of perceiving how scripture applies to us may be more or less straightforward. With many texts of perennial or specific relevance little more than restating may seem to be required for their significance to be brought home. Yet they will profit from imaginative working out of their application. The Puritan tradition specialized in this

8. I owe this point to Peta Sherlock.
9. See Thiselton, "The New Hermeneutic" 309, though I think this phrase comes from J. A. Sanders.

approach to preaching. The focus and the very structure of the sermon was determined by the application of scriptural truth to the congregation's needs in the light of the deep and broad pastoral knowledge of people that the preachers brought to their pulpits from their involvement in pastoral ministry. This approach does better justice to this aspect of the texts they preached on. The Puritans sought "to grasp God's truth with the same preciseness of application with which they held that he had revealed it."[10] John Owen suggested that as part of the charism of the preacher this required a knowledge of the particular people we are ministering to, a knowledge of God's general ways of grace on people's minds and hearts, an acquaintance with the nature of temptation, and an understanding of the nature and dynamics of spiritual unhealth and healing.[11] Preaching that does justice to the Epistles, or for that matter to the Prophets, who work in similar ways, will be as concrete, practical, and realistic in its contemporary application as the text was in its original context.

How does the preacher discover the contemporary target that the text now aims at? Our first task is to listen to scripture ourselves. The problem with many understandings of relevance and communication is the assumption that we know the truth, so that our task is simply to make it relevant and communicate it. Instead, we have to discover the truth, and it is as we discover its nature for us that we discover its relevance for others.[12] It is doubtful whether preaching that searches and nurtures generally issues from attempting to discover what the Bible says to *them*, to those other people. It issues, rather, from realizing what the Bible says to *me*. Preaching flows from an interaction between the spirituality of scripture and the spirituality of the preacher. It is a matter of "truth through personality."[13] It depends initially on an expectation that I bring to scripture: Scripture is my resource for preaching because it is my resource for living. Having been nurtured by scripture in the past, I prepare for preaching through a further seeking of that nurturing for myself that may also issue in nurture for the congregation.

The point should not be made too sharply. The congregation needs to be protected from being subjected each week to my latest experience and from being narrowed down to the limitations of what I have experienced

10. Packer, *A Quest for Godliness* 114; see also 116-17, 227-29.
11. *A Discourse of Spiritual Gifts* 510-11.
12. Cf. Barr, *Old and New in Interpretation* 193.
13. Brooks, *Lectures on Preaching* 5.

each week. Our calling as preachers is a "vicarious listening"[14] undertaken on people's behalf. This listening is put in the position of both modern hearer and ancient writer, neither of which is the preacher's own position. It seeks to enter empathetically into the experiences of those to whom the text was originally addressed and also those who are now to be addressed so that the two can come together — first in the preacher's own person, then in his or her sermon. In this sense I forget about my experience and my needs: My listening to scripture is the priestly act that makes possible the prophetic act of preaching itself.[15]

Having granted that, we can reaffirm the significance for preaching of our own relationship with God, our openness to God, our experience of life, and our experience of God. Avoidance of narcissism or self-absorption or self-display must not lead to the opposite errors of depersonalization or of a self-displacement that avoids self-disclosure.[16] While there will be distinctives and limitations to our experience, because each of us is only one person, underlying these limitations is a human being and believer who is one with those to whom that person preaches, in our joy, our sin, our grief, our need, our passion, our doubt, our drive, our hope, our anxiety, our zeal, our shame. It is as a person who rejoices, sins, hurts, strives, doubts, and worries that I come to scripture and hear it reassuring me, confronting me, jolting me out of this preoccupation with my own concerns. It is then as this person who has met God by means of this text that I preach. I may not directly refer to the personal concerns that I brought to the text or that it gave me, but whether I do or not, I preach a living word because I have heard a living word. It is likely that hearing that issues in preaching will take place at least as much through my listening to scripture for its own sake as through my listening simply for the sake of something to preach. Learning to interpret scripture is a means to the preacher's own study of scripture; when the preacher is occupied with this task for its own sake, ideas and possibilities for preaching will flow from it.[17]

"A person will drink from his or her own well."[18] In our lives with God we start from where we are, with our actual experiences, with what God is doing with us, with what we have been led into. We do not pretend that

---

14. W. W. Johnson, "The Ethics of Preaching" 425; cf. p. 9 above.

15. Keck, *The Bible in the Pulpit* 53-54. On the preacher's priestliness see also Barth, *The Word of God and the Word of Man* 127-28.

16. Nichols, *The Restoring Word* 113, 118, 121.

17. Barr, *Old and New in Interpretation* 199.

18. Bernard of Clairvaux, *Consideration* 2.3 [2.6]; cf. Prov 5:15.

we are in any other place — the kind of place we ought to be in, for instance, or where God ought to put us. We acknowledge where we are, not merely because this alone is realistic, but because of the potential that comes from doing so. Whatever is our vale of tears, when it is named as such it can mysteriously become that well from which we may drink.

When Gustavo Gutiérrez adapted Bernard's saying as the title for his book on liberation spirituality, *We Drink from Our Own Wells,* he rendered it into the plural. It is indeed *we* who drink from them: Wells do not belong to individuals. The well that I dig and that I drink from belongs to those to whom I minister. The preacher listens to scripture concerned not merely with the spirituality of individuals but with the church's life as a body before God. Often passages that seem to say little when we approach them out of individualistic concerns suddenly speak when we listen to them on behalf of the church corporately. Indeed, we listen to scripture on behalf of the world outside, which will not hear the sermon. Admittedly there is a danger hear: Preachers have a demonic inclination to berate the absent world in their preaching and thus to encourage their actual congregation to feel very comfortable. But we may be able to address the concerns of the world in a way that enables the sermon's actual hearers to go on to live their lives and fulfill their ministries in that world more fully, and passages that seem mute regarding the preoccupations of the church may suddenly speak when we listen to them with the world's concerns and needs in mind. My vicarious listening to scripture seeks to be sensitive to the personal concerns of the individual, to the corporate life of the church, and to the world that may ignore God and yet belongs to God. Indeed, listening to scripture will itself gain from being undertaken corporately.

If my interaction with scripture is indeed to bring about the digging of a well from which both I and others may drink, then it has to involve a real listening on my part. I find that when I am seeking to listen to scripture for the sake of a congregation to which I have to preach and not merely for myself, that gives an extra edge to my listening. I am not sure this ought to be so. I should surely listen just as keenly when I read scripture simply to hear what God may want to say to me through it, and perhaps that sharper listening to which I have referred reflects a sinful anxiety about having something to say that the congregation will appreciate and be impressed by. Even if my motivations are thus mixed, I am glad that the stimulus of having to preach sharpens listening because a sharpness in my listening is vital for those who have to listen to me. The key to being able to speak is being able to hear (Isa 50:4-5).

There is another sense in which having to preach on a passage may help me to enter into it more effectively. We open the Bible before a congregation on the basis of having opened it on our own beforehand. As we do that we will appropriately utilize the "objective" approach, which is academic study's traditional ideal and which helps prevent our too easily identifying our own concerns with those of the text. But we will be approaching scripture with a view to discovering what this text has to say to a congregation gathered to hear God speak and with a view to communicating that message. If the Bible is itself a collection of sermons, this very aim gives us the preunderstanding[19] or specific concern that can enable us to hear what scripture has to say more fully than purely historical concerns may. It corresponds to scripture's own concern.

We have noted already, however, that a preunderstanding is a notoriously mixed blessing. It is a *preliminary* understanding, which as such puts us on the starting line of understanding but must not be allowed to harden into a final understanding, so that the starting line is allowed to coalesce with the finishing line of understanding and thus becomes misunderstanding. I turn to a particular psalm or epistle because it has some immediate point of contact with my present needs or concerns, and it indeed speaks to those, but I stop, appetite satisfied, at the points I thought it was going to make and thus miss the aspects of its own concerns that I have not yet shared and its capacity to arouse needs or open up questions that I have not yet become aware of. The preacher's listening, in particular, needs to resemble that of the counselor, which is not satisfied with its first rough-and-ready approximation to an understanding, which contains as much of the counselor's imposition of what he or she knew already as it does of the individual uniqueness of the other person, and keeps longing to be refined by the object to which it professes to be paying attention. The preacher also needs to be self-aware regarding the nature of the life-issues with which he or she is currently dealing, because (in the invariable manner of a preunderstanding) these cannot but influence the way we read scripture and preach it. We need to be able to take mature account of how that is happening so as to make the most of its positive features and seek to safeguard against its drawbacks.[20]

The preacher's listening to scripture involves the whole person. It involves

19. So Bultmann, e.g., "Is Exegesis without Presuppositions Possible?" in *NT and Mythology* 145-53.

20. Nichols, *The Restoring Word* 115.

the mind giving itself to the text with the aid of the techniques of criticism and exegesis; the spirit seeking to move beyond the words to the people who wrote and read them, to the One to whom their words referred and to whom they were relating, and to what this One might be saying now; and the will being softened so as to perceive challenges that we might prefer to avoid. These are all processes in which the Holy Spirit is active as the author of thought, insight, and obedience so that each of them will also be the subject of our prayer for God to open our eyes so that we may perceive what scripture has to teach us. That is true of us as believers; it is doubly true of us as preachers, who need to be given and to be exercising the charism of interpretation if we are to be those through whom the Spirit speaks.

In preaching we do not merely report what was once said or relate something we have overheard. Biblical preaching flows from a renewed listening to scripture. In the course of such listening we discover where the text confronts and brings good news to people such as ourselves, and we are thus able to witness in the pulpit to its reassuring and challenging message. Such a listening is thus a matter of our own openness to God, listening for ourselves and putting ourselves into the position of people we have to preach to. It is a central aspect of a preacher's own ministerial grace to be enabled by God to perceive how scripture applies to those we minister to. In my sermon preparation I sometimes ask myself what this would mean for X or Y or Z — particular friends or neighbors or relatives — and I find this can give an edge to my vicarious listening and thus to my speaking. If I am to know the answer to that question, it will involve knowing these people and being alive to the questions that life is raising for them — questions that have to be addressed from scripture — and to the terms and the pictures in which its message can be communicated. Hence the truth in Willi Marxsen's observation that "if I can preach the same sermons today as I preached twenty-five years ago, there is something wrong with my preaching."[21]

However it comes, what is involved is the grace to bring together a text in its own meaning and a congregation in their own situation. The task involves an understanding of both. As interpreters of scripture we have to live in two worlds. We have to be immersed in the world of the scriptures, but we also have to be immersed in our own world, among people of our own time. We then have to be able to bring these two worlds together — to let our world illumine the Bible, and the Bible ours.[22]

21. From a lecture in Nottingham in the early 1970s.
22. Smart, *The Strange Silence of the Bible in the Church* 163.

For a number of reasons the link between the experience of the preacher and that of the congregation is particularly significant in the present age.[23] Traditional expository preaching is linked to traditional rhetoric; that once helped it to be effective but now works against it. This is not an argument for abandoning expository preaching, the significance of which went deeper than merely baptizing that rhetoric and the power of which can survive the rhetoric's death. It does mean that we need to rethink and rework the nature of expository preaching. As was the case with the traditional rhetoric itself, preaching has to reflect contemporary forms; "Preaching in every age follows, to a certain extent, the changes that come to all literature and life."[24] It now has to take account of the way in which television communicates, because of the all-pervasive influence of that medium. As well as being more narrative and more visual, this means being more personal.

The integrity of the preacher's character has always been significant for the effectiveness of the preacher's sermon. That integrity would now be seen in a personal, embodied authenticity that can as such graciously and savingly proclaim an incarnate Christ. As a preacher has and reveals a true self with whom God through scripture has been relating in the concrete fleshly reality of life (not as the preacher merely tells a story about himself or herself) God through scripture speaks to the congregation. Because many men find it hard to discover and speak of a true self in this way, they may find such authentic expository preaching harder to grow into, but the growth is worthwhile for them and for their congregations. Our own experience will be especially significant when we are preaching on experiential texts.

How Expository Texts Communicate, and How We Communicate

How expository texts in scripture actually make their points is also instructive. Two contrasting features are striking: The message tends to be structured and argued, and it tends to be put in pictures. These are not universal

---

23. So Troeger; for what follows see his article "Emerging New Standards in the Evaluation of Effective Preaching."

24. Brooks, *Lectures on Preaching* 19-20; cf. Troeger, "Emerging New Standards" 294.

rules, and one cannot fault a sermon merely on the grounds that it lacks structured argument or lacks picture and symbol. Yet the common presence of those features in the Bible's expository material is suggestive.

An example of the structuring of Jesus' teaching is seen in the Sermon on the Mount in the series of contrasts between what people have heard and what Jesus himself declares and in the warnings about practicing one's piety before other people (Matt 5:21–6:18). The prophets and Paul show the importance of structured argument to the exposition of God's truth: Their preaching is full of words like "because," "therefore," and "but." The structures of their argument provide a structure for the preacher. We have seen that an important aspect of understanding a passage is identifying its central theme and aim and how various parts of it relate to that focal theme and aim. The results of this study also shape the sermon itself, as one aspect of seeking to work with the text's own concerns. Our preaching gains clues for presentation from the ways the passage itself works. Where we can see no surface structure in a passage's argument, it seems appropriate to assume that coherent thinking underlay it in some way, and we may look for some structure in the passage's underlying logic. As with the surface structure of a passage, the test of our understanding of this underlying structure is whether it accounts in a plausible way for all the elements in the passage.

Expository texts tend to express themselves imaginatively as well as cerebrally, and understanding them involves a combination of rigorous thinking and imaginative sensitivity. Communicating their messages also involves this combination. The variety of methods of communication in the first "sermon" in Isaiah (1:2-9) deserves comment. Israel's experience is described by means of symbol (parent and child, vv. 2-3), straightforward theological analysis (sin, turning from God, v. 4), metaphor (a person who has been mugged, vv. 5-6), literal description (invasion, v. 7), simile (like an isolated hut, v. 8), and "scriptural" allusion (Sodom and Gomorrah, v. 9; later passages then refer back to this "text" in developing the notion of "remnant").

Scripture's varied use of pictures is particularly worth noting. Three kinds of pictures can be distinguished. One involves the *comparison* of one thing with another. Thus 2 Timothy 2:1-7 likens the determination and commitment required of a pastor with what is required of a soldier, an athlete, and a farmer. Similarly, preachers will often liken faith as trust to the willingness of a spectator to let Blondin wheel him in his barrow across Niagara, faith and works to a horse and cart needing to be in the right relationship to each other, or the growth of faith by way of challenges to the way muscles grow by physical exercise. A second kind of picture comprises a *concrete example* of the quality or principle being commended or warned against. Jesus, for instance, urges that if someone sues me for my jacket or requires me to carry his bags for a mile, I should also offer my overcoat and offer to go two miles (Matt 5:40-41).

Scripture's most powerful type of picture is the *symbol,* a comparison that appeals to particularly deep and powerful aspects of personal human experiences such as marriage, family life, friendship, community life, and cult. It is these symbols that scripture characteristically uses to convey its vision of the nature of God, the father, the husband, the creator, the king, the shepherd, the judge, the guardian/next-of-kin; to describe humanity's failure, rebellion, disobedience, unfaithfulness, transgression; and to portray the restoration of the relationship between humanity and God: reconciliation, forgiveness, justification, propitiation, redemption.

I think I owe ultimately to Archbishop John Habgood the following re-creation of Paul's taking up of such images as he preaches: Paul stands in the marketplace at Corinth and takes the symbols for his preaching from the scenes around him. There is the slave market, where a man passes from one person's ownership to another's; so the gospel means being redeemed from bondage to freedom or to Christ's service. There are people going to the temple to offer sacrifice as a gesture that seeks to reorder their lives with the gods; so the gospel means Christ gave himself for us as the worshiper gives something valuable to God.[25] There is an embassy arriving from another state that has been at war with Corinth but is now seeking to resume peaceful relations; so the gospel means that Christ effects reconciliation between us and God. There is a man being hauled into court to pay the penalty for his crime; so the gospel means that Christ pays the penalty for us. There are people lining up to be seen by a physician; so the gospel means that Christ saves us from death and from everything that hinders us from enjoying fullness of life.

Paul used such symbols because he was in the best sense a man of his day. When he invited people to envisage what Christ had done for them as an act of redemption or reconciliation or propitiation or justification or healing, these were not technical terms from a theologian's world of discourse but shorthand expressions for experiences of everyday life. Whether you were a slave, a slave owner, or an ordinary free man or woman, the fact

25. See further C. Gunton, "Christ the Sacrifice," in *The Glory of Christ in the NT* (ed. Hurst and Wright) 231-38.

of slavery, slave purchase, and manumission were familiar realities of your day. To use these and other such realities to communicate the gospel and its implications to believers and unbelievers was to speak as a person of your day to other people of your day. They were not trite sermon illustrations but powerful life metaphors and symbols carrying the dynamic reality of what they referred to. Paul was entering the people's world and preaching the gospel from within it, as Jesus did in the parables. Amos, Isaiah, Jesus, and Paul speak as people of their day while they are also people of God; they can therefore bring together God's world and our world in their preaching. It is easy for our preaching to suggest that we are unfamiliar with their world or our world.

Some of these symbols may have lost much of their power because of the familiarity of the language of the Bible. "Its language has been overlayed with tons of obfuscating debris" and "washed clean of resonances by the waters of common repetition and interpretation."[26] Familiar symbols need to be brought back to life. I found some columns by Edith Schaeffer published in *Christianity Today* in the 1970s very effective in this task. She skillfully brought to life such experiences and images as childhood, flood, rock, finding direction, cleansing, and the like by talking about concrete contemporary experiences and events. Sometimes it is possible to talk about one's own experiences of being a spouse, parent, or child, which can enable the significance of biblical use of such images to be grasped and communicated afresh.

The power of Paul's symbols derived from their relationship to everyday life. But they have now become theological technical terms with little relationship to life as we experience it. The release of slaves and the offering of animal sacrifices are not part of many people's lives. It is a consequence of scripture speaking directly to the situation of its day that it does not speak directly to ours. God paid this price in speaking specifically to people living in their concrete situations. What God said directly to them may not be immediately intelligible to people in other contexts. We have seen the importance of taking account of the specific rootage of symbols such as the body of Christ if we are not to fail to see what they signify and then attribute anachronistic meanings to them.

I once thought that the preacher's job was therefore to create new symbols that will bring everyday life and the gospel together in our culture. I now doubt whether this can be done, not merely because I have not yet

---

26. Funk, *Jesus as Precursor* 52; cf. Craddock, *Overhearing the Gospel* 64.

heard it done, but because of aspects of the nature of symbols. I am now satisfied that a lesser task will suffice. The symbols Paul was using were culture-relative in the sense that they were expressed in terms deriving from Paul's social and historical context, but they were at the same time embodiments of symbols of archetypal significance. Our job is not to create new symbols but to let those archetypal symbols find expression anew in our context, looking behind the metaphors for the transcultural experience captured by them so as to give new life to that experience in our day — to bring to life contemporary expressions of release, reconciliation, self-giving, acceptance, and renewal in order to use them as illustrations of what the gospel means, in a parallel way to the way Paul was doing the same thing. Our job is to paint a portrait of the reality that expiation, justification, or propitiation refers to, in such a way that we get in touch with our own and other people's experience of the breaking down and renewal of relationships and can thus also be put in touch with what is going on and could go on between us and God.

Guidelines for the Expositor

There are no rules that guarantee faithful and effective exposition, but guidelines such as the following may aid the preacher in reflecting on his or her preaching.[27] Whatever these guidelines do to the reader, listed thus they frighten me. I cannot claim that I consciously seek to implement them all the time. Their purpose is to provide a checklist that we may use in order to spot what particular items we should take into account at the moment. They cannot be neatly separated or put in strict sequence; like the aspects of the interpretive task — of which, indeed, they are a variant — they tend in practice to interact, and insight on a later point will sometimes further illumine or correct an earlier part of the task.

Become aware of your own world and assumptions, your experience and needs, your vested interests and commitments, which both help and constrain your interaction with scripture (rather than

27. What follows is adapted from my chapter on "Expounding the New Testament" in *NT Interpretation* (ed. Marshall) 361-63, which concluded and emerged from a study of issues raised for exposition from two sample passages, Matt 8:5-13 and 1 Pet 3:18-22. It has been amplified in the light of Montague, "Hermeneutics and the Teaching of Scripture" 13-16; and Yoder, *From Word to Life* 43-47.

assuming that you are an objective person open to what is objectively there in the text).

Base your understanding of the text's significance for us on its own meaning (rather than unconsciously letting it become a mere springboard for your own thoughts: Let your own thoughts stand on their own authority, if necessary!).

Be open to and expectant of finding in the text something fresh, even something that contradicts what you think (rather than letting your theological tradition constrict you to finding only what you already know).

Keep listening to what the text says, hearing it through on the questions *it* raises (rather than cutting it off in midsentence because it has answered the questions *you* were interested in).

Work persistently at a precise understanding of the specific central point of the passage so that you can express in a phrase what holds the passage together, and also work at how the parts relate to the central point and to each other. (Do this instead of being satisfied with an understanding only of individual words and verses or with a general impression that misses the passage's particular purpose or with too narrow a definition that leaves aspects of the passage unembraced.)

Take into account the study of the forms of biblical material and their social context, the text's sources and the way they have been reused, the process of their transmission, development, and redaction by actual authors, using the methods of criticism as creative aids to interpretation, with discernment but openness (rather than reverting to a precritical approach on the assumption that the critical methods can never be of constructive help or can be used only by experts).

Identify the particular circumstances, issues, questions, problems, and mistakes that the passage was addressing and consider how far these were peculiar to its original historical context (rather than assuming that the text lacks such a context).

In the light of this understanding, consider what the passage's specific aim was and what exactly it said to the situation (rather than assuming that its statements and imperatives are necessarily general and universalizable as they stand).

Note the distinctive connotations with which the passage uses theological or other words or concepts such as faith, salvation, and election (rather than reading into such words what they may not mean in this context and thus misunderstanding the point of this particular scriptural statement).

Distinguish symbol, metaphor, and myth from literal statement, for example, by comparing parallel usage elsewhere in the same author's writings or elsewhere in scripture (rather than being literalist).

Allow such images to have an impact on your whole inner person (rather than being exclusively cerebral in your approach to interpretation).

Elucidate what such language is referring to (rather than assuming that the medium is the message or that we know the meaning of familiar images such as the good shepherd or being in Christ).

Establish how concepts reappear in changing ways in scripture — for example, in the First Testament, in early Judaism, between the Testaments, between Jesus and the gospel tradition, between Mark and the other Evangelists, or between Jesus and Paul — so that you can see what they mean in particular contexts and what their significance for us may be (rather than treating this historical study as of purely antiquarian or destructive significance).

Consider how this text has subsequently spoken to the believing communities (rather than assuming that our own contemporary horizon is all we need in order to see how God may speak out of this text).

In these tasks use the resources available, such as a synopsis, a variety of translations, more than one commentary if possible, dictionaries, and wordbooks, treating these tools as witnesses whose testimony can help you make informed decisions as to where the evidence leads (rather than assuming that the clarity of scripture means we can rely on our own uninformed intuition or that its obscurity means we must turn scholarly books into paper popes).

Identify the particularities of your situation today over against those of the passage, including differences in culture, in the church's situation, and the like (rather than failing to locate the exposition's target).

Ask what angles of the biblical message especially apply to your own situation without failing to preach the whole counsel of God or to ask whether it is the passage that is irrelevant, or whether we are (rather than assuming that because all scripture is equally inspired it is all always equally applicable).

Open yourself to the costly demand of the text and commit yourself to repentance and change in the light of it (rather than interpretation being a matter only of theological truth or piety).

Know the congregation: where they are, what connotations words and concepts (such as flesh and soul) have for them, and what hang-ups they have (rather than forgetting that you want to communicate with a specific audience).

Discern how the passage's implicit and explicit attitudes, assumptions, and challenges differ from yours and your congregation's and let these confront you (rather than finding only false comfort in what confirms you in your present position).

Apply without trivializing and reinterpret where necessary without losing the principles expressed in the text (rather than assuming either that this specific word of God directly addresses what is a different age, or that it is so time-conditioned that it can be of no help to us now).

Resymbolize and remythologize so that the significance of the original may be felt anew (rather than confining yourself to biblical symbols just because they are biblical).

Let the dynamic of the passage's own development as you have come to understand it determine the dynamic of your presentation — for example, the sermon's structure (rather than assimilating it to some preconceived sermon pattern).

Avoid flaunting critical data in the pulpit, but where it is relevant be open with your congregation about how you understand the origin of the passage (rather than maintaining a double standard whereby the simple believer is left in blissful ignorance of the facts about the Bible's origin — a practice less defensible now than it was in the days when criticism was carried on without a thought for its implications for the doctrine of scripture or the preaching of scripture).

Seek to lead your congregation into the same position of being addressed by the passage as you have occupied in your presentation (rather than letting it be mere teaching).

Find ways of enabling them to share their insights on the text (rather than behaving as if you alone have the answers).

Let interpretation become active and celebratory worship (rather than only words).

Remember that freshness of approach — not inventiveness but openness and expectancy — is of key importance in the Bible student and preacher, and that the next time you approach this passage you are a different person and may find new light there (rather than assuming that you have now understood it once and for all).

Abbreviations

ATR	*Anglican Theological Review*
BJRL	*Bulletin of the John Rylands Library*
BTB	*Biblical Theology Bulletin*
CBQ	*Catholic Biblical Quarterly*
CI	*Critical Inquiry*
ET	English translation
ExpT	*Expository Times*
HBT	*Horizons in Biblical Theology*
HTR	*Harvard Theological Review*
JBL	*Journal of Biblical Literature*
JRE	*Journal of Religious Ethics*
JSOT	*Journal for the Study of the Old Testament*
JTSA	*Journal of Theology for Southern Africa*
LT	*Literature and Theology*
LW	*Luther's Works* (Philadelphia and St. Louis, 1955-)
ModT	*Modern Theology*
NEB	New English Bible
NIV	New International Version
NLH	*New Literary History*
NT	New Testament
NTS	*New Testament Studies*
OT	Old Testament
OUP	Oxford University Press
RelS	*Religious Studies*
RSR	*Religious Studies Review*
RSV	Revised Standard Version

SAP	Sheffield Academic Press
SJT	*Scottish Journal of Theology*
ThT	*Theology Today*
TynB	*Tyndale Bulletin*
U	University of
UP	University Press
VT (Sup)	*Vetus Testamentum* (Supplement)
WA	*D. Martin Luthers Werke. Kritische Gesamtausgabe* (Weimar, 1883-)

Bibliography

The bibliography includes works referred to in the text above, a few others that I am aware of having utilized but do not happen to have referred to, and articles that I have written from which I have adapted material in this book. In the text, unless otherwise noted, reference is to the latest (British) edition.

ABRAHAM, W. J. *Divine Revelation and the Limits of Historical Criticism.* Oxford/New York: OUP, 1982.

ABRAMS, M. H. "The Deconstructive Angel." *CI* 3 (1976-77) 425-38. = *Modern Criticism and Theory* (ed. Lodge) 265-76.

————. *The Mirror and the Lamp.* New York: OUP, 1953.

ACHTEMEIER, E. "The Impossible Possibility: Evaluating the Feminist Approach to Bible and Theology." *Interpretation* 42 (1988) 45-57.

ACHTEMEIER, P. J. *An Introduction to the New Hermeneutic.* Philadelphia: Westminster, 1969.

ALLCHIN, A. M. *The Dynamic of Tradition.* London: DLT, 1981. = *The Living Presence of the Past.* San Francisco: Harper, 1984.

ALONSO SCHÖKEL, L. "Hermeneutics in the Light of Language and Literature." *CBQ* 25 (1963) 371-86.

————. *The Inspired Word.* ET New York: Herder/London: Burns and Oates, 1967.

ALTER, R. *The Art of Biblical Narrative.* New York: Basic/London: Allen and Unwin, 1981.

————. *The Art of Biblical Poetry.* New York: Basic, 1985/Edinburgh: Clark, 1990.

ALTER, R., and F. KERMODE (ed.). *The Literary Guide to the Bible.* Cambridge, MA: Harvard UP/London: Collins, 1987.

ALTHAUS, PAUL. *The Theology of Martin Luther.* ET Philadelphia: Fortress, 1966.

290

AMIHAI, M., et al. (ed.). *Narrative Research on the Hebrew Bible. Semeia* 46 (1989).

ANDERSON, B. W. "Tradition and Scripture in the Community of Faith." *JBL* 100 (1981) 5-21.

ASSMANN, H. *Practical Theology of Liberation.* ET London: Search, 1975. = *Theology for a Nomad Church.* ET Maryknoll, NY: Orbis, 1976.

AUKERMAN, D. *Darkening Valley.* New York: Seabury, 1981.

AUNE, D. E. *Prophecy in Early Christianity and the Ancient Mediterranean World.* Grand Rapids: Eerdmans, 1983.

AUSTIN, J. L. *How to Do Things with Words.* Oxford: Clarendon/Cambridge, MA: Harvard UP, 1962.

BAILEY, K. E. *Poet and Peasant.* Grand Rapids: Eerdmans, 1976.

———. *Through Peasant Eyes.* Grand Rapids: Eerdmans, 1980.

BAKER, T. G. A. " 'This is the Word of the Lord.' " *Theology* 93 (1990) 266-73.

BAL, M. *Death and Dissymmetry.* Chicago/London: U Chicago, 1988.

———. *Lethal Love.* Bloomington: Indiana UP, 1987.

——— (ed.). *Anti-Covenant.* Sheffield: SAP, 1989.

BALMER, R. H. "The Princetonians and Scripture." *Westminster Theological Journal* 44 (1982) 352-65.

BAMBROUGH, R. *Reason, Truth and God.* London: Methuen/New York: Harper, 1969.

BANANA, C. "The Biblical Basis for Liberation Struggles." *International Review of Missions* 68 (1979) 417-23.

BAR-EFRAT, S. *Narrative Art in the Bible.* ET Sheffield: SAP, 1989.

BARR, J. *Beyond Fundamentalism.* Philadelphia: Westminster, 1984. = *Escaping from Fundamentalism.* London: SCM, 1984.

———. *The Bible in the Modern World.* London: SCM/New York: Harper, 1973.

———. *Fundamentalism.* London: SCM/Philadelphia: Westminster, 1977; rev. ed., 1981.

———. "Jowett and the 'Original Meaning of Scripture.' " *RelS* 18 (1982) 433-37.

———. "Le Judaisme postbiblique et la théologie de l'Ancien Testament." *Revue de théologie et de philosophie* III/18 (1968) 209-17.

———. "The Literal, the Allegorical, and Modern Biblical Scholarship." *JSOT* 44 (1989) 3-17.

———. "The Meaning of 'Mythology' in Relation to the Old Testament." *VT* 9 (1959) 1-10.

———. *Old and New in Interpretation.* London: SCM/New York: Harper, 1966. 2nd ed., London: SCM, 1982.

———. "The Old Testament and the New Crisis of Biblical Authority." *Interpretation* 25 (1971) 24-40.

————. *The Scope and Authority of the Bible*. Philadelphia: Westminster, 1980. = *Explorations in Theology* 7. London: SCM, 1980.

BARR, J., et al. "The Authority of the Bible." *Ecumenical Review* 21 (1969) 135-66.

BARRETT, C. K. *The Pastoral Epistles*. Oxford/New York: OUP, 1963.

BARTH, K. *Church Dogmatics*. ET Edinburgh: Clark/New York: Scribner's, 1936-75.

————. *The Epistle to the Romans*. ET London/New York: OUP, 1933; corrected ed., 1968.

————. *The Resurrection of the Dead*. ET London: Hodder/New York: Revell, 1933.

————. *The Word of God and the Word of Man*. ET London: Hodder/[Boston:] Pilgrim, 1928.

BARTHES, R., et al. *Structural Analysis and Biblical Exegesis*. ET Pittsburgh: Pickwick, 1974.

BARTON, J. *Oracles of God*. London: DLT/Philadelphia: Westminster, 1986.

————. *People of the Book?* London: SPCK, 1988/Louisville: W/JKP, 1989.

————. "The Place of the Bible in Moral Debate." *Theology* 88 (1985) 204-9.

————. "Reading the Bible as Literature." *LT* 1 (1987) 135-53.

————. *Reading the Old Testament*. London: DLT/Philadelphia: Westminster, 1984.

————. "Reflections on Cultural Relativism." *Theology* 82 (1979) 103-9, 191-99.

BARTSCH, H.-W. (ed.). *Kerygma and Myth*. Vol. 1 ET London: SPCK, 1953 2(1964)/New York: Harper, 1961. Vol. 2 ET London: SPCK, 1962. Enlarged one-volume edition, London: SPCK, 1972.

BAUCKHAM, R. *The Bible and Politics*. London: SPCK/Louisville: W/JKP, 1989.

————. *Jude, 2 Peter*. Waco, TX: Word, 1983/Milton Keynes: Word, 1986.

————. "Tradition in Relation to Scripture and Reason." In R. Bauckham and B. Drewery (ed.), *Scripture, Tradition and Reason* (R. P. C. Hanson Festschrift) 117-45. Edinburgh: Clark, 1988.

BEARDSLEY, M. C. See below under Wimsatt.

BECKWITH, R. T. *The Old Testament Canon of the New Testament Church and Its Background in Early Judaism*. London: SPCK, 1985/Grand Rapids: Eerdmans, 1986.

BELO, F. *A Materialist Reading of the Gospel of Mark*. ET Maryknoll, NY: Orbis, 1981.

BERKOUWER, G. C. *Holy Scripture*. ET Grand Rapids: Eerdmans, 1975.

BERLIN, A. *Poetics and Interpretation of Biblical Narrative*. Sheffield: Almond, 1983.

————. See also under Kugel.

BEST, E. "Scripture, Tradition, and the Canon of the New Testament." *BJRL* 61 (1979) 258-89.

BIRCH, B. C., and L. L. Rasmussen. *Bible and Ethics in the Christian Life.* Minneapolis: Augsburg, 1976.

BIRCH, B. C., L. L. RASMUSSEN, et al. Reviews of Childs, *Introduction to the Old Testament as Scripture* (with response by Childs), *HBT* 2 (1980) 113-211.

BLEICHER, J. *Contemporary Hermeneutics.* London/Boston: Routledge, 1980.

BLENKINSOPP, J. *Prophecy and Canon.* Notre Dame, IN: U Notre Dame, 1977.

BOFF, L., and C. BOFF. *Introducing Liberation Theology.* ET London: Burns and Oates/Maryknoll, NY: Orbis, 1987.

BOICE, J. M. (ed.). *The Foundation of Biblical Authority.* Grand Rapids: Zondervan, 1978/Glasgow: Pickering, 1979.

BOJORGE, H. "Para una interpretación liberadora." *Revista Bíblica* (Buenos Aires) 33 (1971) 67-71.

BONHOEFFER, D. "The Interpretation of the New Testament." In *No Rusty Swords* (ET London: Collins/New York: Harper, 1965) 308-25. Rev. ed., "The Presentation of New Testament Texts." In *No Rusty Swords* (ET London: Collins Fontana, 1970) 302-20.

BONINO, J. M. See below under Miguez Bonino.

BOONE, K. C. *The Bible Tells Them So.* Albany, NY: SUNY/London: SCM, 1989.

BOORER, S. "The Importance of a Diachronic Approach." *CBQ* 51 (1989) 195-208.

BOOTH, R. P. *Jesus and the Laws of Purity.* Sheffield: JSOT, 1986.

BOOTH, W. C. *Critical Understanding.* Chicago/London: U Chicago, 1979.

———. *The Rhetoric of Fiction.* Chicago/London: U Chicago, 1961, [2]1983.

———. *A Rhetoric of Irony.* Chicago/London: U Chicago, 1974.

BORNKAMM, G. *Early Christian Experience.* ET London: SCM, 1969/New York: Harper, 1970.

BORNKAMM, G., G. BARTH, and H. J. HELD. *Tradition and Interpretation in Matthew.* ET Philadelphia: Westminster/London: SCM, 1963.

BORNKAMM, H. *Luther and the Old Testament.* ET Philadelphia: Fortress, 1969.

BORSCH, F. H. *God's Parable.* London: SCM, 1975/Philadelphia: Westminster, 1976.

BRAATEN, C. E. *History and Hermeneutics.* Philadelphia: Westminster, 1966/London: Lutterworth, 1968.

BRANSON, M. L., and C. R. PADILLA (ed.). *Conflict and Context.* Grand Rapids: Eerdmans, 1986.

BRETT, M. *Biblical Criticism in Crisis?* Cambridge/New York: CUP, 1991.

BRIGHT, J. *The Authority of the Old Testament.* Nashville: Abingdon/London: SCM, 1967.

———. *A History of Israel.* Philadelphia: Westminster, 1959/London: SCM, 1960; [2]1972; [3]1981.

——. *Jeremiah*. Garden City, NY: Doubleday, 1965.

BROOKS, P. *Lectures on Preaching*. New York: Dutton, 1877/London: Dickenson, 1881; reprinted London: SPCK, 1959.

BROWN, R. E. *The Critical Meaning of the Bible*. Ramsey, NJ: Paulist, 1981.

——. "The Problems of the *'Sensus Plenior.'*" *Ephemerides theologicae lovanienses* 43 (1967) 460-69.

——. "The *Sensus Plenior* in the Last Ten Years." *CBQ* 25 (1963) 262-85.

——. *The* Sensus Plenior *of Sacred Scripture*. Baltimore: St Mary's University, 1955.

BROWN, R. E., et al. (ed.). *The Jerome Biblical Commentary*. London: Chapman/Englewood Cliffs, NJ: Prentice-Hall, 1968; new ed., 1989/1990.

BROX, N. *Die Pastoralbriefe*. Regensburg: Pustet, ⁴1969.

BRUEGGEMANN, W. *Abiding Astonishment: Psalms, Modernity, and the Making of History*. Louisville: W/JKP, 1991.

——. *Finally Comes the Poet*. Minneapolis: Fortress, 1989.

——. "Imagination as a Mode of Fidelity." In J. T. Butler, et al. (ed.), *Understanding the Word* (B. W. Anderson Festschrift) 21-31. Sheffield: JSOT, 1985.

——. *Interpretation and Obedience*. Minneapolis: Fortress, 1991.

——. *The Message of the Psalms*. Minneapolis: Augsburg, 1984.

——. "Psalms and the Life of Faith." *JSOT* 17 (1980) 3-32.

——. "A Shape for Old Testament Theology." *CBQ* 47 (1985) 28-46, 395-415.

——. "Trajectories in Old Testament Literature and the Sociology of Ancient Israel." *JBL* 98 (1979) 161-85. = *The Bible and Liberation* (ed. Gottwald), 2nd ed., 307-33.

BRÜMMER, V. *Theological and Philosophical Inquiry*. Philadelphia: Westminster, 1982.

BULTMANN, R. *Existence and Faith*. ET New York: Meridian, 1960/London: Hodder, 1961/London: Collins Fontana, 1964.

——. *Faith and Understanding*. Vol. 1. ET London: SCM/New York: Harper, 1969.

——. *History and Eschatology*. Edinburgh: Edinburgh UP, 1957. = *The Presence of Eternity*. New York: Harper, 1957.

——. *Jesus Christ and Mythology*. ET New York: Scribner's, 1958/London: SCM, 1960.

——. "New Testament and Mythology." In Bartsch (ed.), *Kerygma and Myth* 1:1-44 (new ET in *New Testament and Mythology* [see below] 1-43).

——. *New Testament and Mythology and Other Basic Writings*. ET Philadelphia: Fortress, 1984.

——. "The Problem of a Theological Exegesis of the New Testament." In *The Beginnings of Dialectic Theology* (ed. J. M. Robinson) 1:236-56.

————. *Theology of the New Testament*. 2 vols. ET New York: Scribner's, 1951 and 1955/London: SCM, 1952 and 1955.

BURI, F. *How Can We Still Speak Responsibly of God?* ET Philadelphia: Fortress, 1968.

BUTTRICK, D. *Homiletic*. Philadelphia: Fortress/London: SCM, 1987.

CADY, L. E. "Hermeneutics and Tradition." *HTR* 79 (1986) 439-63.

CAIRD, G. B. *The Language and Imagery of the Bible*. London: Duckworth/Philadelphia: Westminster, 1980.

CALVIN, J. *The Epistles of Paul the Apostle to the Romans and to the Thessalonians*. ET Edinburgh: Oliver and Boyd/Grand Rapids: Eerdmans, 1961.

CAMPENHAUSEN, H. F. von. *The Formation of the Christian Bible*. ET Philadelphia: Fortress/London: Black, 1972.

CANNON, K. G., and E. SCHÜSSLER FIORENZA (ed.). *Interpretation for Liberation*. Semeia 47 (1989).

CARDENAL, E. *The Gospel in Solentiname*. Vol. 1. ET Maryknoll, NY: Orbis, 1976. = *Love in Practice: The Gospel in Solentiname*. ET London: Search, 1977.

CARROLL, R. P. *Wolf in the Sheepfold: The Bible as a Problem for Christianity*. London: SPCK, 1991. = *The Bible as a Problem for Christianity*. Philadelphia: TPI, 1991.

CARSON, D. A. (ed.). *Biblical Interpretation and the Church*. Exeter: Paternoster, 1984.

CHATMAN, S. *Story and Discourse*. Ithaca, NY: Cornell UP, 1978.

CHILDS, B. S. *Biblical Theology in Crisis*. Philadelphia: Westminster, 1970.

————. *Biblical Theology of the Old and New Testaments*. London: SCM/Minneapolis: Fortress, 1992.

————. *The Book of Exodus*. Philadelphia: Westminster, 1974. = *Exodus*. London: SCM, 1974.

————. "The Canonical Shape of the Prophetic Literature." *Interpretation* 32 (1978) 46-55.

————. *Introduction to the Old Testament as Scripture*. Philadelphia: Fortress/London: SCM, 1979.

————. *Myth and Reality in the Old Testament*. London: SCM/Naperville, IL: Allenson, 1960, [2]1962.

————. *The New Testament as Canon*. London: SCM, 1984/Philadelphia: Fortress, 1985.

————. *Old Testament Theology in a Canonical Context*. London: SCM/Philadelphia: Fortress, 1985.

CLAYTON, J. P. See below under Sykes.

CLEMENTS, R. See below under Schluter.

CLEMENTS, R. E. *Isaiah 1–39*. London: Marshall/Grand Rapids: Eerdmans, 1980.

————. *Old Testament Theology*. London: Marshall/Atlanta: Knox, 1978.

CLÉVENOT, M. *Materialist Approaches to the Bible.* ET Maryknoll, NY: Orbis, 1985.

CLINES, D. J. A. "Notes for an Old Testament Hermeneutic." *Theology, News and Notes* 21 (1975) 8-10.

———. "Story and Poem." *Interpretation* 34 (1980) 115-27.

———. *What Does Eve Do to Help? and Other Readerly Questions to the Old Testament.* Sheffield: SAP, 1990.

CLINES, D. J. A., et al. (ed.). *The Bible in Three Dimensions.* Sheffield: SAP, 1990.

COAKLEY, S. "Theology and Cultural Relativism." *Neue Zeitschrift für systematische Theologie und Religionsphilosophie* 21 (1979) 223-43.

COLERIDGE, S. T. *Confessions of an Inquiring Spirit.* London: Pickering, 1840/Boston: Munroe, 1841; London: Moxon, [3]1853; reprinted Philadelphia: Fortress, 1988.

COLLINGWOOD, R. G. *An Autobiography.* London/New York: OUP, 1939.

CONE, J. H. *A Black Theology of Liberation.* Philadelphia: Lippincott, 1970.

———. *God of the Oppressed.* New York: Seabury, 1975/London: SPCK, 1977.

COOK, E. D. *Are Women People Too?* Bramcote: Grove, 1978.

CORNER, M. See below under Rowland.

COUNTRYMAN, L. W. *Biblical Authority or Biblical Tyranny?* Philadelphia: Fortress, 1981.

———. *Dirt, Greed, and Sex.* Philadelphia: Fortress, 1988/London: SCM, 1989.

CRADDOCK, F. B. *Overhearing the Gospel.* Nashville: Abingdon, 1978.

CRANFIELD, C. E. B. *A Critical and Exegetical Commentary on the Epistle to the Romans.* 2 vols. Edinburgh: Clark/New York: Scribner's, 1975 and 1979.

———. "St Paul and the Law." *SJT* 17 (1964) 43-68. = R. Batey (ed.), *New Testament Issues* 148-72. New York: Harper/London: SCM, 1970.

CRENSHAW, J. L. *Prophetic Conflict: Its Effect upon Israelite Religion.* Berlin: de Gruyter, 1971.

CROATTO, J. S. *Biblical Hermeneutics.* ET Maryknoll, NY: Orbis, 1987.

———. *Exodus.* ET Maryknoll, NY: Orbis, 1981.

CROSMAN, I. See below under Suleiman.

CROSSAN, J. D. *Cliffs of Fall: Paradox and Polyvalence in the Parables of Jesus.* New York: Seabury, 1980.

———. *The Dark Interval: Towards a Theology of Story.* Niles, IL: Argus, 1975; reprinted Sonoma, CA: Polebridge, 1991.

———. *In Parables.* New York: Harper, 1973.

———. "Parable and Example in the Teaching of Jesus." *NTS* 18 (1971-72) 285-307.

——— (ed.). *Polyvalent Narration. Semeia* 9 (1977).

CULLER, J. *On Deconstruction.* Ithaca, NY: Cornell UP, 1982/London: Routledge, 1983.

————. *The Pursuit of Signs*. Ithaca, NY: Cornell UP/London: Routledge, 1981.

————. *Structuralist Poetics*. Ithaca, NY: Cornell UP/London: Routledge, 1975.

CULPEPPER, R. A. *Anatomy of the Fourth Gospel*. Philadelphia: Fortress, 1983.

DAHL, N. A. *The Crucified Messiah and Other Essays*. ET Minneapolis: Augsburg, 1974.

————. "The Origin of the Earliest Prologues to the Pauline Letters." In W. A. Beardslee (ed.), *The Poetics of Faith* (A. N. Wilder Festschrift) 1:233-77. *Semeia* 12 (1978).

————. "The Particularity of the Pauline Epistles as a Problem in the Ancient Church." In W. C. van Unnik (ed.), *Neotestamentica et patristica* (O. Cullmann Festschrift) 261-71. Leiden: Brill, 1962.

DALY, R. J. (ed.). *Christian Biblical Ethics*. Ramsey, NJ: Paulist, 1984.

DANIÉLOU, J. *The Bible and the Liturgy*. ET Notre Dame, IN: U Notre Dame, 1956/London: DLT, 1960.

DAVIS, C. "The Theological Career of Historical Criticism of the Bible." *Cross Currents* 32 (1982) 267-84.

DAWSON, D. "Against the Divine Ventriloquist." *LT* 4 (1990) 293-310.

DERRIDA, J. *Positions*. ET Chicago: U Chicago/London: Athlone, 1981.

DETWEILER, R. (ed.). *Derrida and Biblical Studies*. *Semeia* 23 (1982).

———— (ed.). *Reader Response Approaches to Biblical and Secular Texts*. *Semeia* 31 (1985).

DILTHEY, W. "The Rise of Hermeneutics." ET *NLH* 3 (1971-72) 229-44. = *Selected Writings* (see below) 246-63. = *Hermeneutical Inquiry* (ed. Klemm) 1:93-105.

————. *Selected Writings*, ed. H. P. Rickman. ET Cambridge/New York: CUP, 1976.

————. "The Understanding of Other Persons and Their Life-Expressions." ET in *The Hermeneutics Reader* (ed. Mueller-Vollmer) 152-64.

DOCTRINE COMMISSION OF THE CHURCH OF ENGLAND. *Christian Believing*. London: SPCK, 1976.

DODD, C. H. *The Parables of the Kingdom*. London: Nisbet, 1935/New York: Scribner's, 1936; rev. ed., 1961.

DOWNING, F. G. "Our Access to Other Cultures, Past and Present." *Modern Churchman* 21 (1977-78) 28-42.

DRURY, J. *Tradition and Design in Luke's Gospel*. London: DLT, 1976/Atlanta: Knox, 1977.

DUMAS, A. *Political Theology and the Life of the Church*. ET London: SCM/Philadelphia: Westminster, 1978.

DUNDES, A. (ed.). *Sacred Narrative*. Berkeley/London: U California, 1984.

DUNN, J. D. G. *Jesus, Paul, and the Law*. London: SPCK/Philadelphia: W/JKP, 1990.

————. *The Living Word*. London: SCM, 1987/Philadelphia: Fortress, 1988.

EAGLETON, T. *The Function of Criticism*. London: Verso, 1984.

————. *Literary Theory*. Oxford: Blackwell/Minneapolis: U Minnesota, 1983.

EBELING, G. *Word and Faith*. ET London: SCM/Philadelphia: Fortress, 1963.

EDWARDS, O. C. "Historical-Critical Method's Failure of Nerve and a Prescription for a Tonic." *ATR* 59 (1977) 115-34. = *Ex auditu* 1 (1985) 92-105.

ELIOT, T. S. *On Poetry and Poets*. London: Faber/New York: Farrar, 1957.

————. *Selected Essays*. London: Faber, 1932; [2]1934/New York: Harcourt, 1950.

ESLINGER, L. *Kingship of God in Crisis*. Sheffield: JSOT, 1985.

EXUM, J. C. "Of Broken Pots, Fluttering Birds and Visions in the Night." *CBQ* 43 (1981) 331-52.

————. *Tragedy and Biblical Narrative*. Cambridge/New York: CUP, 1992.

———— (ed.). *Tragedy and Comedy in the Bible*. *Semeia* 32 (1985).

FACKENHEIM, E. L. *The Jewish Bible after the Holocaust*. Manchester: Manchester UP, 1990.

FACKRE, G. *Authority. The Christian Story: Volume 2*. Grand Rapids: Eerdmans, 1987.

FARRAR, F. W. *History of Interpretation*. London: Macmillan/New York: Dutton, 1886.

FERGUSON, D. S. *Biblical Hermeneutics*. Atlanta: Knox, 1986/London: SCM, 1987.

FERGUSSON, D. "Meaning, Truth, and Realism in Bultmann and Lindbeck." *RelS* 26 (1990) 183-98.

FEWELL, D. N. See below under Nolan Fewell.

FIORENZA, E. S. See below under Schüssler Fiorenza.

FISCH, H. *Poetry with a Purpose*. Bloomington: Indiana UP, 1988.

FISH, S. E. "Interpreting the *Variorum*." *CI* 2 (1975-76) 465-85 = Fish, *Is There a Text in This Class?* (see below) 147-73 = *Modern Criticism and Theory* (ed. Lodge) 311-29 = *Reader-Response Criticism* (ed. Tompkins) 164-84.

————. *Is There a Text in This Class? The Authority of Interpretive Communities*. Cambridge, MA/London: Harvard UP, 1980.

————. *Self-Consuming Artifacts*. Berkeley: U California, 1972.

FISHBANE, M. *Biblical Interpretation in Ancient Israel*. Oxford/New York: OUP, 1985.

————. *The Garments of Torah*. Bloomington: Indiana UP, 1989.

FONTENROSE, J. *The Ritual Theory of Myth*. Berkeley/London: U California, 1966.

FORD, D. F. *Barth and God's Story*. Frankfurt: Lang, 1981, [2]1985.

FORSYTH, P. T. *Positive Preaching and the Modern Mind*. London: Hodder, 1907/Grand Rapids: Eerdmans, 1964.

FOWL, S. E., and L. G. JONES. *Reading in Communion*. London: SPCK/Grand Rapids: Eerdmans, 1991.

FRANKLIN, E. *How the Critics Can Help.* London: SCM, 1982.

FREI, H. *The Eclipse of Biblical Narrative.* New Haven/London: Yale UP, 1974.

FUCHS, E. "The Hermeneutical Problem." In J. M. Robinson (ed.), *The Future of Our Religious Past* (R. Bultmann Festschrift) 267-78. ET London: SCM/New York: Harper, 1971.

————. *Studies of the Historical Jesus.* ET London: SCM/Naperville, IL: Allenson, 1964.

FUNK, R. W. *Jesus As Precursor.* Missoula, MT: SBL, 1975.

————. *Language, Hermeneutic, and Word of God.* New York: Harper, 1966.

————. "The Parables." In D. G. Miller and D. Y. Hadidian (ed.), *Jesus and Man's Hope* 2:287-303. Pittsburgh: Pittsburgh Theological Seminary, 1971.

———— (ed.). *The Bultmann School of Biblical Interpretation: New Directions. Journal for Theology and Church* 1 (1965).

———— (ed.). *History and Hermeneutic. Journal for Theology and Church* 4 (1967).

FÜSSEL, K. "Materialist Readings of the Bible." In Schottroff and Stegemann (ed.), *God of the Lowly* 13-25. = *The Bible and Liberation* (ed. Gottwald), 2nd ed., 134-46.

GADAMER, H.-G. *Truth and Method.* ET New York: Seabury/London: Sheed and Ward, 1975; rev. ed., New York: Crossroad, 1989.

GARDNER, H. *The Business of Criticism.* London/New York: OUP, 1959.

————. *"The Waste Land."* Manchester: Manchester UP, 1972.

GERBER KOONTZ, G., and W. SWARTLEY (ed.). *Perspectives on Feminist Hermeneutics.* Elkhart, IN: Institute of Mennonite Studies, 1987.

GLOVER, W. B. *Evangelical Nonconformists and Higher Criticism in the Nineteenth Century.* London: Independent, 1954.

GOLDINGAY, J. *Approaches to Old Testament Interpretation.* Leicester/Downers Grove, IL: IVP, 1981; [2]1990.

————. "Current Issues in Evangelical Interpretation of Scripture." In C. M. Day (ed.), *Anglican Evangelical Assembly Proceedings* 4 (1986) 19-29.

————. *Daniel.* Dallas: Word, 1989/Milton Keynes: Word, 1991.

————. "The Dynamic Cycle of Praise and Prayer in the Psalms." *JSOT* 20 (1981) 85-90.

————. "Expounding the New Testament." In *New Testament Interpretation* (ed. Marshall) 351-65.

————. "The Hermeneutics of Liberation Theology." *HBT* 4/2 (1982) 133-61.

————. "Luther and the Bible." *SJT* 35 (1982) 33-58.

————. "The Man of War and the Suffering Servant." *TynB* 27 (1976) 79-113.

————. "Models for Scripture." *SJT* 44 (1991) 19-37.

————. *Models for Scripture.* Grand Rapids: Eerdmans/Carlisle: Paternoster, 1994.

—. "The Old Testament and Christian Faith." *Themelios* 8/1 (1982) 4-10; 8/2 (1983) 5-12.

—. "The Patriarchs in Scripture and History." In *Essays on the Patriarchal Narratives* (ed. A. R. Millard and D. J. Wiseman) 1-34. Leicester: IVP, 1980/Winona Lake, IN: Eisenbrauns, 1983.

—. "The Stories in Daniel: A Narrative Politics." *JSOT* 37 (1987) 99-116.

—. "Story, Vision, Interpretation: Literary Approaches to Daniel." In *The Book of Daniel* (ed. A. S. van der Woude) 295-313. Leuven: Peeters, 1993.

—. *Theological Diversity and the Authority of the Old Testament.* Grand Rapids: Eerdmans, 1987.

GOTTWALD, N. K. "Social Matrix and Canonical Shape." *ThT* 42 (1985-86) 307-21.

GOTTWALD, N. K. [and A. C. WIRE] (ed.). *The Bible and Liberation.* Berkeley: CRRE, 1976; Maryknoll, NY: Orbis, ^{2}1983.

GOULDER, M. (ed.). *The Myth of God Incarnate.* London: SCM, 1977.

GRAHAM, W. A. *Beyond the Written Word.* Cambridge/New York: CUP, 1987.

GRANT, P. *Reading the New Testament.* Grand Rapids: Eerdmans/London: Macmillan, 1989.

GRANT, R. M. *The Formation of the New Testament.* New York: Harper/London: Hutchinson, 1965.

GRECH, P. "Interprophetic Re-Interpretation and Old Testament Eschatology." *Augustinianum* 9 (1969) 235-65.

GREEN, G. *Imagining God.* San Francisco: Harper, 1989.

—— (ed.). *Scriptural Authority and Narrative Interpretation* (Hans Frei Festschrift). Philadelphia: Fortress, 1987.

GREENSLADE, S. L., et al. (ed.). *The Cambridge History of the Bible.* 3 vols. Cambridge/New York: CUP, 1970, 1969, 1963.

GREENSPAHN, F. E. (ed.). *Scripture in the Jewish and Christian Traditions.* Nashville: Abingdon, 1982.

GREENSTEIN, E. L. "Deconstruction and Biblical Narrative." *Prooftexts* 9 (1989) 43-71.

—. "Theory and Argument in Biblical Criticism." *Hebrew Annual Review* 10 (1986) 77-93.

GREENWOOD, D. C. *Structuralism and the Biblical Text.* Berlin/New York: Mouton, 1985.

GREENWOOD, D. S. "Poststructuralism and Biblical Studies." In R. T. France and D. Wenham (ed.), *Gospel Perspectives* 3:263-88. Sheffield: JSOT, 1983.

GREIDANUS, S. *The Modern Preacher and the Ancient Text.* Grand Rapids: Eerdmans/Leicester: IVP, 1988.

—. *Sola Scriptura: Problems and Principles in Preaching Historical Texts.* Toronto: Wedge, 1970.

GROS LOUIS, K. R. R., et al. (ed.). *Literary Interpretations of Biblical Narratives.* 2 vols. Nashville: Abingdon, 1974 and 1982.

GUDORF, C. E. "Liberation Theology's Use of Scripture." *Interpretation* 41 (1987) 5-18.

GUNDRY, R. H. *The Use of the Old Testament in St. Matthew's Gospel.* Leiden: Brill, 1967.

GUNKEL, H. *The Psalms.* ET Philadelphia: Fortress, 1967.

GUNN, D. M. "New Directions in the Study of Biblical Hebrew Narrative." *JSOT* 39 (1987) 65-75.

————. See also below under Nolan Fewell.

GUNTON, C. E. *Enlightenment and Alienation.* Basingstoke: Marshall/Grand Rapids: Eerdmans, 1985.

GUROIAN, V. "Bible and Ethics." *JRE* 18 (1990) 129-57.

GUSTAFSON, J. "The Place of Scripture in Christian Ethics." *Interpretation* 24 (1970) 430-55. Reprinted in Gustafson, *Theology and Christian Ethics* 121-45. Philadelphia: Pilgrim, 1974.

GUTIÉRREZ, G. *A Theology of Liberation.* ET Maryknoll: Orbis, 1973/London: SCM, 1974.

————. *We Drink from Our Own Wells.* ET Maryknoll, NY: Orbis/London: SCM, 1984.

HABERMAS, J. "On Hermeneutics' Claim to Universality." ET in Mueller-Vollmer (ed.), *The Hermeneutics Reader* 294-319.

————. *On the Logic of the Social Sciences.* ET Cambridge: Polity, 1988.

HALLER, E. "On the Interpretative Task." ET *Interpretation* 21 (1967) 158-66.

HAMPSON, D. "The Challenge of Feminism to Christianity." *Theology* 88 (1985) 341-50.

————. *Theology and Feminism.* Oxford/Cambridge, MA: Blackwell, 1990.

HANSON, A. T. *Jesus Christ in the Old Testament.* London: SPCK, 1965.

————. *Studies in the Pastoral Epistles.* London: SPCK, 1968.

HANSON, A. T., and R. P. C. HANSON. *The Bible without Illusions.* London/Philadelphia: SCM/TPI, 1989.

HARRISON, R. K. *Introduction to the Old Testament.* Grand Rapids: Eerdmans, 1969/London: Tyndale, 1970.

HART, C. *The Use of Miracle Narratives in Mark.* Dissertation, Leeds, 1989.

HART, R. L. *Unfinished Man and the Imagination.* New York: Herder, 1968.

HARVEY, A. E. *Strenuous Commands.* London: SCM/Philadelphia: TPI, 1990.

HAUERWAS, S. "The Moral Authority of Scripture." *Interpretation* 34 (1980) 356-70.

HAWKES, T. *Metaphor.* London: Methuen/New York: Harper, 1972.

HAYS, R. B. *Echoes of Scripture in the Letters of Paul.* New Haven/London: Yale UP, 1989.

————. "Relations Natural and Unnatural." *JRE* 14 (1986) 184-215.

HEBERT, G. *The Authority of the Old Testament.* London: Faber, 1947.

————. *Fundamentalism and the Church of God.* London: SCM, 1957. = *Fundamentalism and the Church.* Philadelphia: Westminster, 1957.

HEIDEGGER, M. *Being and Time.* ET London: SCM/New York: Harper, 1962.

HENDERSON, I. *Myth in the New Testament.* London: SCM/Chicago: Regnery, 1952.

HENGEL, M. *The Charismatic Leader and His Followers.* ET Edinburgh: Clark/New York: Crossroad, 1981.

HENRY, C. F. H. *God, Revelation, and Authority.* 6 vols. Waco, TX: Word, 1976-83.

HERZOG, F. "Liberation Hermeneutic as Ideology Critique?" *Interpretation* 28 (1974) 387-403.

HICKLING, C. See below under Hooker.

HILL, D. *The Gospel of Matthew.* London: Marshall, 1972/Grand Rapids: Eerdmans, 1981.

HIRSCH, E. D. *The Aims of Interpretation.* Chicago/London: U Chicago, 1976.

————. "Meaning and Significance Reinterpreted." *CI* 11 (1984-85) 202-25.

————. "The Politics of Theories of Interpretation." *CI* 9 (1982-83) 235-47.

————. *Validity in Interpretation.* New Haven/London: Yale UP, 1967.

HOOKER, M. "The Bible and the Believer." *Epworth Review* 6/1 (1979) 77-89.

HOOKER, M., and C. HICKLING (ed.). *What About the New Testament?* (C. F. Evans Festschrift). London: SCM, 1975.

HOULDEN, J. L. *Ethics and the New Testament.* Harmondsworth/Baltimore: Penguin, 1973.

HOY, D. *The Critical Circle.* Berkeley/London: U California, 1978.

HUMPHREYS, W. L. *The Tragic Vision and the Hebrew Tradition.* Philadelphia: Fortress, 1985.

HUNTER, A. M. *Interpreting the Parables.* London: SCM/Philadelphia: Westminster, 1960; [2]1964.

HURST, L. D., and N. T. WRIGHT (ed.). *The Glory of Christ in the New Testament* (G. B. Caird Festschrift). Oxford/New York: OUP, 1987.

HUXTABLE, J. *The Bible Says.* London: SCM/Richmond: Knox, 1962.

HVALVIK, R. "A 'Sonderweg' for Israel." *Journal for the Study of the New Testament* 38 (1990) 87-107.

ISER, W. J. *The Act of Reading.* Baltimore/London: Johns Hopkins UP, 1978.

————. *The Implied Reader.* Baltimore/London: Johns Hopkins UP, 1974.

JACOB, E. "Principe canonique et formation de l'Ancien Testament." *Congress Volume: Edinburgh 1974* 101-22. *VT* Sup 28. Leiden: Brill, 1975.

JACOBSON, R. "The Structuralists and the Bible." *Interpretation* 28 (1974) 146-64. = *A Guide to Contemporary Hermeneutics* (ed. McKim) 280-96.

JASPER, D. *The New Testament and the Literary Imagination*. London: Macmillan/Atlantic Highlands, NJ: Humanities, 1987.

JAUSS, H. R. "Literary History as a Challenge to Literary Theory." ET *NLH* 2 (1970) 7-37.

JEANROND, W. G. "Karl Barth's Hermeneutics." In N. Biggar (ed.), *Reckoning with Barth* 80-98, 206-8. Oxford: Mowbray, 1988.

————. *Text and Interpretation*. ET Dublin: Gill and Macmillan, 1988/New York: Crossroad, 1991.

JEREMIAS, J. *The Parables of Jesus*. ET London: SCM, 1954/New York: Scribner's, 1955; ³1972.

————. *Jerusalem in the Time of Jesus*. ET London: SCM/Philadelphia: Fortress, 1969.

JOBLING, D. *The Sense of Biblical Narrative*. 2 vols. Sheffield: JSOT, 1978 (²1986) and 1986.

JOHNSON, E. E. *Expository Hermeneutics*. Grand Rapids: Zondervan, 1990.

JOHNSON, W. W. "The Ethics of Preaching." *Interpretation* 20 (1966) 412-31.

JOHNSTON, R. K. *Evangelicals at an Impasse*. Atlanta: Knox, 1979.

————. "The Role of Women in the Church and Home: An Evangelical Test Case in Hermeneutics." In W. W. Gasque and W. S. LaSor (ed.), *Scripture, Tradition, and Interpretation* (E. F. Harrison Festschrift) 234-59. Grand Rapids: Eerdmans, 1978. = *Evangelicals at an Impasse* (see above) 48-76.

———— (ed.). *The Use of the Bible in Theology*. Atlanta: Knox, 1985.

JONAS, H. "Is Faith Still Possible?" *HTR* 75 (82) 1-23.

JONES, L. G. See above under Fowl.

JOSIPOVICI, G. *The Book of God*. New Haven/London: Yale UP, 1988.

JOUBERT, W. H. *Power and Responsibility in the Book of Daniel*. Diss. University of South Africa, 1979.

JOWETT, B. "On the Interpretation of Scripture." In *Essays and Reviews* (by F. Temple, et al.) 399-527. London: Longman, 1860; 10th ed., 1862.

JUEL, D. *Messianic Exegesis*. Philadelphia: Fortress, 1988.

JUHL, P. D. *Interpretation*. Princeton/Guildford: Princeton UP, 1980.

KAISER, W. C. *Toward an Exegetical Theology*. Grand Rapids: Baker, 1981.

————. *Toward Old Testament Ethics*. Grand Rapids: Zondervan, 1983.

KANT, I. *Critique of Pure Reason*. ET by N. K. Smith, London: Macmillan, 1929, ²1933/New York: Humanities, 1950.

KARRIS, R. J. "Windows and Mirrors." In P. J. Achtemeier (ed.), *Society of Biblical Literature 1979 Seminar Papers* 1:47-58. Missoula: Scholars, 1979.

KÄSEMANN, E. "The Canon of the New Testament and the Unity of the Church." In *Essays on New Testament Themes* 95-107. ET London: SCM/Naperville, IL: Allenson, 1964.

————. *New Testament Questions of Today.* ET London: SCM/Philadelphia: Fortress, 1969.

————. *Perspectives on Paul.* ET London: SCM/Philadelphia: Fortress, 1971.

KECK, L. E. *The Bible in the Pulpit.* Nashville: Abingdon, 1978.

KEE, A. *The Scope of Political Theology.* London: SCM, 1978.

————. *The Way of Transcendence.* Harmondsworth/Baltimore: Penguin, 1971.

KEEGAN, T. J. *Interpreting the Bible.* Mahwah, NJ: Paulist, 1985.

KELBER, W. H. *The Oral and the Written Gospel.* Philadelphia: Fortress, 1983.

KERMODE, F. *The Classic.* London: Faber/New York: Viking, 1975.

————. *The Genesis of Secrecy.* Cambridge, MA/London: Harvard UP, 1979.

————. *The Sense of an Ending.* London: OUP, 1966/New York: OUP, 1967.

————. See also above under Alter.

KINGSBURY, J. D. *Matthew as Story.* Philadelphia: Fortress, 1986.

KIRK, J. A. *Liberation Theology.* London: Marshall/Atlanta: John Knox, 1979.

KLEIN, L. R. *The Triumph of Irony in the Book of Judges.* Sheffield: SAP, 1988.

KLEMM, D. (ed.). *Hermeneutical Inquiry.* 2 vols. Atlanta: Scholars, 1986.

KLOPFENSTEIN, M. A. "1 Könige 13." In E. Busch, et al. (ed.), *Parrhesia* (K. Barth Festschrift) 639-72. Zurich: EVZ, 1966.

KNIGHT, D. A. (ed.). *Tradition and Theology in the Old Testament.* Philadelphia: Fortress/London: SPCK, 1977.

KOONTZ, G. G. See above under Gerber Koontz.

KORT, W. *Story, Text, and Scripture.* University Park/London: Pennsylvania State UP, 1988.

KOYAMA, K. *Waterbuffalo Theology.* London: SCM/Maryknoll, NY: Orbis, 1974.

KRISTEVA, J. *Revolution in Poetic Language.* ET New York/Guildford: Columbia UP, 1984.

KUGEL, J. L. "On the Bible and Literary Criticism" (with response by A. Berlin). *Prooftexts* 1 (1981) 217-36; 2 (1982) 323-32.

KÜNG, H., and J. MOLTMANN (ed.). *Conflicting Ways of Interpreting the Bible.* Concilium 138. Edinburgh: Clark/New York: Seabury, 1980.

LANDY, F. *Paradoxes of Paradise.* Sheffield: Almond, 1983.

LANSER, S. S. "(Feminist) Criticism in the Garden: Inferring Genesis 2-3." In *Speech Act Theory and Biblical Criticism* (ed. H. C. White) 67-84.

LAPOINTE, R. *Les trois dimensions de l'herméneutique.* Paris: Gabalda, 1967.

LASH, N. *Theology on the Way to Emmaeus.* London: SCM, 1986.

————. "What Might Martyrdom Mean?" In W. Horbury and B. McNeil (ed.), *Suffering and Martyrdom in the New Testament* (G. M. Styler Festschrift) 183-98. Cambridge/New York: CUP, 1981. = *Ex auditu* 1 (1985) 14-24. = *Theology on the Way to Emmaeus* (see above) 75-92.

LEACH, E. R. *Genesis as Myth and Other Essays.* London: Cape, 1969.

LEE, D. "Taking Ourselves More Seriously." *Anvil* 6 (1989) 149-59.

LEE, P. "A Land No Longer Desolate?" *Missionalia* 20 (1992) 88-98.

LEECH, K. *True God.* London: Sheldon, 1985. = *Experiencing God.* San Francisco: Harper, 1985.

LEIMAN, S. Z. *The Canonization of Hebrew Scripture.* Hamden, CT: Archon, 1976.

LEMCIO, E. E. "The Gospels and Canonical Criticism." *BTB* 11 (1981) 114-22.

LENTRICCHIA, F. *After the New Criticism.* Chicago: U Chicago/London: Athlone, 1980.

LEWIS, C. S. *Reflections on the Psalms.* London: Bles/New York: Harcourt, 1958; reprinted London: Collins Fontana, 1961.

LICHT, J. *Storytelling in the Bible.* Jerusalem: Magnes, 1978.

LINDARS, B. *New Testament Apologetic.* London: SCM, 1961.

—————. *The Use of Scripture in Theological Debate and in Debate on Moral and Ethical Issues.* London: General Synod of the Church of England, 1982.

LINDBECK, G. A. *The Nature of Doctrine.* Philadelphia: Westminster/London: SPCK, 1984.

LINDSAY, T. M. "The Doctrine of Scripture: The Reformers and the Princeton School." *The Expositor* V/1 (1895) 278-93.

—————. "Professor W. Robertson Smith's Doctrine of Scripture." *The Expositor* IV/10 (1894) 241-64.

LINDSEY, H. *The Late Great Planet Earth.* Grand Rapids: Zondervan, 1970/London: Lakeland, 1971.

LINNEMANN, E. *Historical Criticism of the Bible.* ET Grand Rapids: Baker, 1990.

—————. *Parables of Jesus.* ET New York: Harper/London: SPCK, 1966.

LISCHER, R. "The Limits of Story." *Interpretation* 38 (1984) 26-38.

LODGE, D. (ed.). *20th Century Literary Criticism.* London: Longman, 1972.

————— (ed.). *Modern Criticism and Theory.* London/New York: Longman, 1988.

LONERGAN, B. *Method in Theology.* New York: Herder, 1971/London: DLT, 1972.

LONG, E. L. "The Use of the Bible in Christian Ethics." *Interpretation* 19 (1965) 149-62.

LONG, T. G. *Preaching and the Literary Forms of the Bible.* Philadelphia: Fortress, 1989.

LONGENECKER, R. N. *Biblical Exegesis in the Apostolic Period.* Grand Rapids: Eerdmans, 1975.

—————. "Can We Reproduce the Exegesis of the New Testament?" *TynB* 21 (1970) 3-38.

—————. *New Testament Social Ethics for Today.* Grand Rapids: Eerdmans, 1984.

LÖNNING, I. *"Kanon im Kanon."* Oslo: Universitets Forlaget, 1972.

LOUTH, A. *Discerning the Mystery.* Oxford/New York: OUP, 1983.

LUNDIN, R., A. C. THISELTON, and C. WALHOUT. *The Responsibility of Hermeneutics.* Grand Rapids: Eerdmans/Exeter: Paternoster, 1985.

LUTHER, M. *Lectures on Genesis.* Vol. 1. ET *LW* 1 (1958).

MACDONALD, D. R. *The Legend and the Apostle: The Battle for Paul in Story and Canon.* Philadelphia: Westminster, 1983.

MACKINNON, D. M. *The Problem of Metaphysics.* Cambridge/New York: CUP, 1974.

MACQUARRIE, J. *God-Talk.* London: SCM/New York: Harper, 1967.

MAIER, G. *The End of the Historical-Critical Method.* ET St. Louis: Concordia, 1977.

MAGNESS, J. L. *Sense and Absence.* Atlanta: Scholars, 1986.

MAGONET, J. *A Rabbi's Bible.* London: SCM, 1991.

MALHERBE, A. J. "Exhortation in First Thessalonians." *NovT* 25 (1983) 238-56.

MANNHEIM, K. *Ideology and Utopia.* ET New York: Harcourt/London: Routledge, 1952.

MARK, J. "Relativism and Community." *Theology* 82 (1979) 161-63.

MARSHALL, I. H. (ed.). *New Testament Interpretation.* Exeter: Paternoster/Grand Rapids: Eerdmans, 1977.

MARTIN, J. P. "Toward a Post-Critical Paradigm." *NTS* 33 (1987) 370-85.

MARXSEN, W. *Introduction to the New Testament.* ET Philadelphia: Fortress/Oxford: Blackwell, 1968.

MATEJKA, L., and K. POMORSKA (ed.). *Readings in Russian Poetics.* Cambridge, MA/London: MIT, 1971.

McCONNELL, F. (ed.). *The Bible and the Narrative Tradition.* Oxford/New York: OUP, 1986.

McKIM, D. K. (ed.). *A Guide to Contemporary Hermeneutics.* Grand Rapids: Eerdmans, 1986.

McKNIGHT, E. V. *The Bible and the Reader.* Philadelphia: Fortress, 1985.

———. *Meaning in Texts.* Philadelphia: Fortress, 1978.

———. *Postmodern Use of the Bible.* Nashville: Abingdon, 1988.

——— (ed.). *Reader Perspectives on the New Testament.* Semeia 48 (1989).

MBITI, J. S. *Bible and Theology in African Christianity.* Nairobi: OUP, 1986.

MEADE, D. G. *Pseudonymity and Canon.* Tübingen: Mohr, 1986/Grand Rapids: Eerdmans, 1987.

MENDENHALL, G. E. *The Tenth Generation.* Baltimore: Johns Hopkins UP, 1973.

METZGER, B. M. *The Canon of the New Testament.* Oxford/New York: OUP, 1987.

———. "Literary Forgeries and Canonical Pseudepigrapha." *JBL* 91 (1972) 3-24.

MICHAELS, J. R. See below under Nicole.

MICHIE, D. See below under Rhoads.

MIGUEZ BONINO, J. *Revolutionary Theology Comes of Age.* London: SPCK, 1975. = *Doing Theology in a Revolutionary Situation.* Philadelphia: Fortress, 1975.

MILAVEC, A. A. "Mark's Parable of the Wicked Husbandmen." *Journal of Ecumenical Studies* 26 (1989) 289-312.

MILLER, P. D. *The Divine Warrior in Early Israel.* Cambridge: Harvard UP, 1973.

MILNE, P. J. *Vladimir Propp and the Study of Structure in Hebrew Biblical Narrative.* Sheffield: SAP, 1988.

MIRANDA, J. P. *Being and the Messiah.* ET Maryknoll, NY: Orbis, 1977.

———. *Marx and the Bible.* ET Maryknoll, NY: Orbis, 1974/London: SCM, 1977.

MISCALL, P. D. *I Samuel.* Bloomington: Indiana UP, 1986.

———. *The Workings of Old Testament Narrative.* Philadelphia: Fortress, 1983.

MITCHELL, B. *How to Play Theological Ping-Pong and Other Essays on Faith and Reason.* London: Hodder, 1990/Grand Rapids: Eerdmans, 1991.

MOLTMANN, J. *The Way of Jesus Christ.* ET San Francisco: Harper/London: SCM, 1990.

MONTAGUE, G. T. "Hermeneutics and the Teaching of Scripture." *CBQ* 41 (1979) 1-17.

MOORE, S. D. "Doing Gospel Criticism as/with a 'Reader.'" *BTB* 19 (1989) 85-93.

———. *Literary Criticism and the Gospels.* New Haven/London: Yale UP, 1989.

MORGAN, D. F. *Between Text and Community.* Minneapolis: Fortress, 1990.

MORGAN, R. *The Nature of New Testament Theology.* London: SCM/Naperville, IL: Allenson, 1973.

MORGAN, R., with J. BARTON. *Biblical Interpretation.* Oxford/New York: OUP, 1988.

MOSALA, I. J. *Biblical Hermeneutics and Black Theology in South Africa.* Grand Rapids: Eerdmans, 1989.

———. "Social Scientific Approaches to the Bible." *JTSA* 55 (1986) 15-30. = *Biblical Hermeneutics and Black Theology in South Africa* 43-66.

MOTT, S. C. "The Use of the New Testament for Social Ethics." *Transformation* 1/2 (1984) 21-26; 1/3 (1984) 19-26. = *JRE* 15 (1987) 225-60.

MOWINCKEL, S. *The Old Testament as Word of God.* ET Nashville: Abingdon, 1959/Oxford: Blackwell, 1960.

———. *The Psalms in Israel's Worship.* 2 vols. ET Oxford: Blackwell/Nashville: Abingdon, 1962.

MUDDIMAN, J. *The Bible: Fountain and Well of Truth.* Oxford: Blackwell, 1983.

MUELLER-VOLLMER, K. (ed.). *The Hermeneutics Reader.* New York: Crossroad, 1985/Oxford: Blackwell, 1986.

MUNRO, W. *Authority in Paul and Peter.* Cambridge/New York: CUP, 1983.

———. "Romans 13:1-7: Apartheid's Last Biblical Refuge." *BTB* 20 (1990) 161-68.

MURPHY, R. E. "History of Exegesis as a Hermeneutical Tool." *BTB* 16 (1986) 87-91.

NATIONS, A. "Historical Criticism and the Current Methodological Crisis." *SJT* 36 (1983) 59-71. = *Ex auditu* 1 (1985) 125-32.

NEUHAUS, R. J. (ed.). *Biblical Interpretation in Crisis*. Grand Rapids: Eerdmans, 1989.

NEWBIGIN, L. *The Open Secret*. London: SPCK/Grand Rapids: Eerdmans, 1978.

NEWTON-DE MOLINA, D. (ed.). *On Literary Intention*. Edinburgh: Edinburgh UP, 1976.

NICHOLS, J. R. *The Restoring Word*. San Francisco: Harper, 1987.

NICOLE, R. R., and J. R. MICHAELS (ed.). *Inerrancy and Common Sense*. Grand Rapids: Baker, 1980.

NINEHAM, D. E. *Explorations in Theology* 1. London: SCM, 1977.

———. *The Use and Abuse of the Bible*. London: Macmillan/New York: Barnes, 1976.

NOLAN FEWELL, D. *Circle of Sovereignty: A Story of Stories in Daniel 1–6*. Sheffield: SAP, 1988. 2nd ed., *Circle of Sovereignty: Plotting Politics in the Book of Daniel*. Nashville: Abingdon, 1991.

———. "Feminist Reading of the Hebrew Bible." *JSOT* 39 (1987) 77-87.

NOLAN FEWELL, D., and D. GUNN. "Is Coxon a Scold?" *JSOT* 45 (1989) 39-43.

O'DONOVAN, O. M. T. *On the Thirty Nine Articles*. Exeter: Paternoster, 1986.

———. "The Possibility of a Biblical Ethic." *TSF Bulletin* (UK) 67 (1973) 15-23.

———. "Towards an Interpretation of Biblical Ethics." *TynB* 27 (1976) 54-78.

OGDEN, S. M. *Christ without Myth*. New York: Harper, 1961/London: Collins, 1962.

———. *The Reality of God and Other Essays*. New York: Harper, 1966/London: SCM, 1967.

OGLETREE, T. W. *The Use of the Bible in Christian Ethics*. Philadelphia: Fortress, 1983/Oxford: Blackwell, 1984.

ORR, J. *Revelation and Inspiration*. London: Duckworth, 1909/London: Scribner's, 1910.

OWEN, H. P. *Revelation and Existence*. Cardiff: U Wales, 1957.

OWEN, J. *A Discourse of Spiritual Gifts*. Oxford, 1692. = *The Works of John Owen* 4:420-520. Edinburgh: Clark, 1862.

PACHE, R. *The Inspiration and Authority of Scripture*. ET Chicago: Moody, 1969.

PACKER, J. I. *"Fundamentalism" and the Word of God*. London: IVF/Grand Rapids: Eerdmans, 1958.

———. *God Has Spoken*. London: Hodder, 1965; reprinted Downers Grove, IL: IVP, 1979. = *God Speaks to Man*. Philadelphia: Westminster, 1965.

———. "Hermeneutics and Biblical Authority." *The Churchman* 81 (1967) 7-21. = *Themelios* 1/1 (Autumn 1975) 3-12.

————. *A Quest for Godliness.* Wheaton, IL: Crossway, 1990. = *Among God's Giants.* London: Kingsway, 1991.

PADILLA, C. R. "The Interpreted Word." *Themelios* 7/1 (1981) 18-23. = *A Guide to Contemporary Hermeneutics* (ed. McKim) 297-308.

PALMER, R. E. *Hermeneutics.* Evanston: Northwestern UP, 1969.

PANNENBERG, W. *Basic Questions in Theology.* Vols. 1 and 2. ET London: SCM/Philadelphia: Westminster, 1970 and 1971.

PATTE, D. *What Is Structural Exegesis?* Philadelphia: Fortress, 1970.

PELIKAN, J. *Luther the Expositor.* LW Companion Volume. Concordia: St. Louis, 1959.

PERKINS, P. "New Testament Ethics." *RSR* 10 (1984) 321-27.

PHILLIPS, G. A. (ed.). *Poststructural Criticism and the Bible. Semeia* 51 (1990).

POBEE, J. S., and B. VON WARTENBERG-POTTER (ed.). *New Eyes For Reading.* Quezon City, Philippines: Claretian, 1987.

POLAND, L. M. *Literary Criticism and Biblical Hermeneutics.* Chico, CA: Scholars, 1985.

POLZIN, R. "1 Samuel." *RSR* 15 (1989) 297-306.

————. *Moses and the Deuteronomist.* New York: Seabury, 1980.

————. *Samuel and the Deuteronomist.* San Francisco: Harper, 1989.

PORTER, S. E. "Why Hasn't Reader-Response Criticism Caught On in New Testament Studies?" *LT* 4 (1990) 278-92.

POYTHRESS, V. S. "Analysing a Biblical Text." *SJT* 32 (1979) 113-37, 319-31.

————. "Structuralism and Biblical Studies." *Journal of the Evangelical Theological Society* 21 (1978) 221-37.

PRESTON, R. H. "Need Dr Nineham Be So Negative?" *ExpT* 90 (1978-79) 275-80.

PRICKETT, S. *Words and* The Word. Cambridge/New York: CUP, 1986.

RAD, G. VON. *Old Testament Theology.* 2 vols. ET Edinburgh: Oliver and Boyd/New York: Harper, 1962 and 1965.

————. *Wisdom in Israel.* ET London: SCM/Nashville: Abingdon, 1972.

RAHNER, K. "The Hermeneutics of Eschatological Assertions." In *Theological Investigations* 4:323-46. ET Baltimore: Helicon/London: DLT, 1966.

RASMUSSEN, L. L. See above under Birch.

REED, W. L. "A Poetics of the Bible." *LT* 1 (1987) 154-66.

RHOADS, D., and D. MICHIE. *Mark as Story.* Philadelphia: Fortress, 1982.

RICOEUR, P. "Biblical Hermeneutics." In J. D. Crossan (ed.), *Paul Ricoeur on Biblical Hermeneutics* 29-148. *Semeia* 4 (1975).

————. *The Conflict of Interpretations.* ET Evanston: Northwestern UP, 1974.

————. *Essays on Biblical Interpretation.* ET Philadelphia: Fortress, 1980/London: SPCK, 1981.

————. *Freud and Philosophy.* ET New Haven/London: Yale UP, 1970.

——. "The Hermeneutical Function of Distanciation." *Philosophy Today* 17 (1973) 129-41. = *Hermeneutics and the Human Sciences* (see below) 131-44.

——. *Hermeneutics and the Human Sciences.* ET Cambridge/New York: CUP, 1981.

——. *Interpretation Theory.* Fort Worth: Texas Christian UP, 1976.

——. "The 'Kingdom' in the Parables of Jesus." ET *ATR* 63 (1981) 165-69.

——. "A Response" (to essays by J. D. Crossan and others). *Biblical Research* 24-25 (1979-80) 70-80.

——. *The Symbolism of Evil.* ET New York: Harper, 1967; reprinted Boston: Beacon, 1969.

——. *Time and Narrative.* 3 vols. ET Chicago/London: U Chicago, 1984, 1985, 1988.

RIMMON-KENAN, S. *Narrative Fiction.* London/New York: Methuen, 1983.

RITSCHL, D. "A Plea for the Maxim: Scripture and Tradition." *Interpretation* 25 (1971) 113-28.

ROBINSON, J. M. (ed.). *The Beginnings of Dialectic Theology.* Richmond: John Knox, 1968.

ROBINSON, J. M., and J. B. COBB (ed.). *The New Hermeneutic.* New York/London: Harper, 1964.

ROGERSON, J. W. *Genesis 1–11.* Sheffield: SAP, 1991.

——. *Myth in Old Testament Interpretation.* Berlin/New York: De Gruyter, 1974.

ROGERSON, J. W., et al. *The Study and Use of the Bible.* Basingstoke: Marshall/Grand Rapids: Eerdmans, 1988.

ROHRBAUGH, R. L. *The Biblical Interpreter.* Philadelphia: Fortress, 1978.

ROWLAND, C. *The Open Heaven.* London: SPCK/New York: Crossroad, 1982.

ROWLAND, C., and M. CORNER. *Liberating Exegesis.* London: SPCK/Louisville: W/JKP, 1990.

RYKEN, L. *How to Read the Bible as Literature.* Grand Rapids: Zondervan, 1984.

SAID, E. (ed.). *Literature and Society.* Baltimore/London: Johns Hopkins UP, 1980.

SANDAY, W. *Inspiration.* New York/London: Longmans, 1914.

SANDEEN, E. R. *The Roots of Fundamentalism.* Chicago/London: U Chicago, 1970.

SANDERS, E. P. *Jesus and Judaism.* London: SCM/Philadelphia: Fortress, 1985.

——. *Jewish Law from Jesus to the Mishnah.* London: SCM/Philadelphia: TPI, 1990.

SANDERS, J. A. *Canon and Community.* Philadelphia: Fortress, 1984.

——. "The Ethic of Election in Luke's Great Banquet Parable." In J. L. Crenshaw and J. T. Willis (ed.), *Essays in Old Testament Ethics* (J. P. Hyatt Memorial) 245-71. New York: Ktav, 1974.

——. "First Testament and Second." *BTB* 17 (1987) 47-49.

————. "From Isaiah 61 to Luke 4." In J. Neusner (ed.), *Christianity, Judaism, and Other Greco-Roman Cults* (M. Smith Festschrift) 3:75-106. Leiden: Brill, 1975.

————. *From Sacred Story to Sacred Text.* Philadelphia: Fortress, 1987.

————. *Torah and Canon.* Philadelphia: Fortress, 1972.

SANDERS, J. T. *Ethics in the New Testament.* Philadelphia: Fortress/London: SCM, 1975.

SCHLEIERMACHER, F. D. E. *Hermeneutics: The Handwritten Manuscripts* (ed. H. Kimmerle). ET Missoula, MT: Scholars, 1977.

SCHLUTER, M. *Family Roots and Famility Mobility.* Cambridge, England: Jubilee Centre, 1986.

SCHLUTER, M., and R. CLEMENTS. *Reactivating the Extended Family.* Cambridge, England: Jubilee Centre, 1986.

SCHNEIDAU, H. N. *Sacred Discontent: The Bible and the Western Tradition.* Berkeley/London: U California, 1976.

SCHNEIDERS, S. "Feminist Ideology Criticism and Biblical Hermeneutics." *BTB* 19 (1989) 3-10.

————. "The Footwashing (John 13:1-20): An Experiment in Hermeneutics." *CBQ* 43 (1981) 76-92. = *Ex auditu* 1 (1985) 135-46.

SCHOEPS, H. J. *Paul.* ET Philadelphia: Westminster/London: Lutterworth, 1961.

SCHOTTROFF, W., and W. STEGEMANN (ed.). *God of the Lowly.* ET Maryknoll, NY: Orbis, 1984.

SCHÜSSLER FIORENZA, E. *Bread Not Stone.* Boston: Beacon, 1984/Edinburgh: Clark, 1990.

————. "The Ethics of Biblical Interpretation." *JBL* 107 (1988) 3-17.

————. *In Memory of Her.* New York: Crossroad/London: SCM, 1983.

————. See also above under Cannon.

SCHWARTZ, R. (ed.). *The Book and the Text.* Oxford/Cambridge, MA: Blackwell, 1990.

SEARLE, J. R. *Expression and Meaning.* Cambridge/New York: CUP, 1979.

————. "The Logical Status of Fictional Discourse." *NLH* 6 (1974-75) 319-32.

————. *Speech Acts.* Cambridge/New York: CUP, 1969.

SEGUNDO, J. L. *Liberation of Theology.* Maryknoll, NY: Orbis, 1976/Dublin: Gill and Macmillan, 1977.

————. "The Shift within Latin American Theology." *JTSA* 52 (1985) 17-29.

————. *A Theology for Artisans of a New Humanity.* Vol. 5. ET Maryknoll, NY: Orbis, 1974.

SHAW, G. *The Cost of Authority.* London: SCM/Philadelphia: Fortress, 1983.

SLEE, N. "Parables and Women's Experience." *The Modern Churchman* 26/2 (1984) 20-31.

SLEEPER, C. F. "Ethics as a Context for Biblical Interpretation." *Interpretation* 22 (1968) 443-60.

SMART, J. D. *The Interpretation of Scripture.* Philadelphia: Westminster/London: SCM, 1961.

―――. *The Strange Silence of the Bible in the Church.* Philadelphia: Fortress/London: SCM, 1970.

SMITH, J. Z. "Sacred Persistence: Towards a Redescription of Canon." In W. B. Green (ed.), *Approaches to Ancient Judaism* 2:11-28. Missoula, MT: Scholars, 1978. = Smith, *Re-Imagining Religion* 36-52. Chicago/London: U Chicago, 1982.

SMITH, M. *Palestinian Parties and Politics That Shaped the Old Testament.* New York/London: Columbia UP, 1971. Rev. ed., London: SCM, 1987.

SMITH, R. H. "Were the Early Christians Middle-Class?" *Currents in Theology and Mission* 7 (1980) 260-76. = *The Bible and Liberation* (ed. Gottwald), 2nd ed., 441-57.

SPENCER, R. A. (ed.). *Orientation by Disorientation.* Pittsburgh: Pickwick, 1980.

SPILKA, M. (ed.). *Towards a Poetics of Fiction.* Bloomington/London: Indiana UP, 1977.

SPIVEY, R. A. "Structuralism and Biblical Studies." *Interpretation* 28 (1974) 133-45.

STACEY, D. *Interpreting the Bible.* London: Sheldon, 1976.

STANTON, G. N. *The Gospels and Jesus.* Oxford/New York: OUP, 1989.

―――. "Interpreting the New Testament Today." *Ex auditu* 1 (1985) 63-73.

STEGEMANN, W. See above under Schottroff.

STEINER, G. *After Babel.* London/New York: OUP, 1975.

―――. *On Difficulty and Other Essays.* Oxford/New York: OUP, 1978.

―――. *Real Presences: Is There Anything in What We Say?* London/Boston: Faber, 1989.

STEINMETZ, D. C. "The Superiority of Pre-Critical Exegesis." *ThT* 37 (1980-81) 27-38. = *Ex auditu* 1 (1985) 74-82. = *A Guide to Contemporary Hermeneutics* (ed. McKim) 65-77.

STENDAHL, K. "The Apostle Paul and the Introspective Conscience of the West." *HTR* 56 (1963) 199-215. = *Idem, Paul Among Jews and Gentiles* 78-96. ET Philadelphia: Fortress, 1976.

―――. "Biblical Theology, Contemporary." In *The Interpreter's Dictionary of the Bible* 1:418-32. Nashville: Abingdon, 1962.

STERN, J. P. *On Realism.* London/Boston: Routledge, 1973.

STERNBERG, M. *The Poetics of Biblical Narrative.* Bloomington: Indiana UP, 1985.

STOTT, J. R. W. *Christian Mission in the Modern World.* London: CPAS/ Downers Grove, IL: IVP, 1975.

STOUT, J. *The Flight from Authority.* Notre Dame, IN: U Notre Dame, 1981.

————. "What Is the Meaning of a Text?" *NLH* 14 (1982-83) 1-12.

STROUP, G. W. "Between Echo and Narcissus: The Role of the Bible in Feminist Theology." *Interpretation* 42 (1988) 19-32.

STUHLMACHER, P. *Historical Criticism and Theological Interpretation of Scripture.* ET Philadelphia: Fortress, 1977/London: SPCK, 1979.

SUGIRTHARAJAH, R. S. (ed.). *Voices from the Margin.* Maryknoll, NY: Orbis/London: SPCK, 1991.

SULEIMAN, S. R. *Authoritarian Fiction.* New York/Guildford: Columbia UP, 1983.

SULEIMAN, S. R., and I. CROSMAN (ed.). *The Reader in the Text.* Princeton/Oxford: Princeton UP, 1980.

SWARTLEY, W. M. *Slavery, Sabbath, War, and Women.* Scottdale, PA: Herald, 1983.

————. See also above under Gerber Koontz.

SYKES, S. W., and J. P. CLAYTON (ed.), *Christ, Faith and History.* Cambridge/New York: CUP, 1972.

TALMON, S. "Martin Buber's Ways of Interpreting the Bible." *Journal of Jewish Studies* 27 (1976) 195-209.

TANNEHILL, R. C. "Israel in Luke-Acts: A Tragic Story." *JBL* 104 (1985) 69-85.

TERRIEN, S. *Till the Heart Sings.* Philadelphia: Fortress, 1985.

THEISSEN, G. *Sociology of Early Palestinian Christianity.* ET Philadelphia: Fortress, 1978. = *The First Followers of Jesus.* ET London: SCM, 1978.

THISELTON, A. C. "The New Hermeneutic." In *New Testament Interpretation* (ed. Marshall) 308-33. = *A Guide to Contemporary Hermeneutics* (ed. McKim) 78-107.

————. *New Horizons in Hermeneutics.* London: HarperCollins/Grand Rapids: Zondervan, 1992.

————. *The Two Horizons.* Exeter: Paternoster/Grand Rapids: Eerdmans, 1980.

————. "Understanding God's Word Today." In J. Stott (ed.), *Obeying Christ in a Changing World* 1:90-122. London: Collins, 1977.

————. "The Use of Philosophical Categories in New Testament Hermeneutics." *Churchman* 87 (1973) 87-100.

————. See also above under Lundin.

THOMA, C., and M. WYSCHOGROD (ed.). *Understanding Scripture.* Mahwah, NJ: Paulist, 1987.

THOMPSON, J. B. *Critical Hermeneutics.* Cambridge/New York: CUP, 1981.

THOMPSON, R. J. *Moses and the Law in a Century of Criticism Since Graf.* VT Sup 19. Leiden: Brill, 1970.

TILLEY, T. W. "God and the Silencing of Job." *Modern Theology* 5 (1989) 257-70.

TILLICH, P. *The New Being.* New York: Scribner's, 1955/London: SCM, 1956. Reprinted in *The Boundaries of Our Being.* London: Collins, 1973.

————. *On the Boundary: An Autobiographical Sketch.* New York: Scribner's, 1966/London: Collins, 1967. Reprinted in *The Boundaries of Our Being.* London: Collins, 1973.

TOLBERT, M. A. *Perspectives on the Parables.* Philadelphia: Fortress, 1979.

———— (ed.). *The Bible and Feminist Hermeneutics. Semeia* 28 (1983).

TOMPKINS, J. P. (ed.). *Reader-Response Criticism.* Baltimore/London: Johns Hopkins UP, 1980.

TRACY, D. *The Analogical Imagination.* New York: Crossroad/London: SCM, 1981.

————. *Plurality and Ambiguity.* San Francisco: Harper, 1987/London: SCM, 1988.

TRIBLE, P. *God and the Rhetoric of Sexuality.* Philadelphia: Fortress, 1978/London: SCM, 1991.

————. *Texts of Terror.* Philadelphia: Fortress, 1984/London: SCM, 1991.

TRIGG, R. *Reason and Commitment.* Cambridge/New York: CUP, 1973.

TRILLING, W. "The Sense of the Past." In *Partisan Review* May-June 1942. Reprinted in Trilling, *The Liberal Imagination* 181-97. New York: Viking/London: Secker, 1950.

TROEGER, T. H. "Emerging New Standards in the Evaluation of Effective Preaching." *Worship* 64 (1990) 294-307.

TYNDALE, W. *Works.* Vol. 1. Parker Society Edition. Cambridge: CUP, 1848.

VALDÉS, M. J., and O. J. MILLER (ed.). *Interpretation of Narrative.* Toronto/Buffalo/London: U Toronto, 1978.

VAN BUREN, P. M. *A Theology of the Jewish-Christian Reality.* Vols. 1-3. San Francisco: Harper, 1980, 1983, 1988/Edinburgh: Clark, 1991.

VAUX, DE, R. *Ancient Israel.* ET London: DLT/New York: McGraw-Hill, 1961.

VERHEY, A. *The Great Reversal: Ethics and the New Testament.* Grand Rapids: Eerdmans, 1984.

————. "The Use of Scripture in Ethics." *RSR* 4 (1978) 28-39.

VERMES, G. *The Dead Sea Scrolls in English.* Harmondsworth/Baltimore: Penguin, 1962; 3rd ed., Sheffield: SAP, 1987.

VIA, D. O. *The Parables.* Philadelphia: Fortress, 1967.

VOGELS, W. "Inspiration in a Linguistic Mode." *BTB* 15 (1985) 87-93.

WACHTERHAUSER, B. R. (ed.). *Hermeneutics and Modern Philosophy.* Albany, NY: SUNY, 1986.

WADSWORTH, M. (ed.). *Ways of Reading the Bible.* Brighton: Harvester/Totowa, NJ: Barnes, 1981.

WALHOUT, C. See above under Lundin.

WARNER, M. (ed.). *The Bible as Rhetoric.* London/New York: Routledge, 1990.

WARTENBERG-POTTER, B. von. See above under Pobee.

WCELA, E. A. "Who Do You Say That They Are?" *CBQ* 53 (1991) 1-17.

WEBER, H.-R. "Freedom Fighter or Prince of Peace." *Study Encounter* 8/4 (1972).

WELLECK, R., and A. WARREN. *Theory of Literature.* New York: Harcourt/London: Cape, 1949. 3rd ed., Harmondsworth: Penguin, 1963.

WEST, G. *Biblical Hermeneutics of Liberation.* Pietermaritzburg: Cluster, 1991.

WESTCOTT, B. F. *The Epistle to the Hebrews.* London/New York: Macmillan, 1889, ²1892.

WESTERHOLM, S. *Israel's Law and the Church's Faith.* Grand Rapids: Eerdmans, 1988.

WESTERMANN, C. *The Old Testament and Jesus Christ.* ET Minneapolis: Augsburg, 1970.

———. *The Praise of God in the Psalms.* ET Richmond: Knox, 1965/London: Epworth, 1966. Rev. ed., *Praise and Lament in the Psalms.* ET Atlanta: Knox/Edinburgh: Clark, 1981.

——— (ed.). *Essays on Old Testament Hermeneutics.* ET Richmond: Knox, 1963. = *Essays on Old Testament Interpretation.* ET London: SCM, 1963.

WHITE, H. "Interpretation in History." *NLH* 4 (1972-73) 281-314.

———. *Metahistory.* Baltimore/London: Johns Hopkins UP, 1973.

WHITE, H. C. *Narration and Discourse in the Book of Genesis.* Cambridge/New York: CUP, 1991.

———. (ed.). *Speech Act Theory and Biblical Criticism.* Semeia 41 (1988).

WHITE, R. "MacKinnon and the Parables." In K. Surin (ed.), *Christ, Ethics and Tragedy* (D. MacKinnon Festschrift) 49-70. Cambridge/New York: CUP, 1989.

WHITMAN, J. *Allegory.* Oxford/New York: OUP, 1987.

WHYBRAY, R. N. *Poverty and Wealth in the Book of Proverbs.* Sheffield: SAP, 1990.

———. "Poverty, Wealth, and Point of View in Proverbs." *ExpT* 100 (1988-89) 332-36.

WIJNGAARDS, J. N. M. *Communicating the Word of God.* Great Wakering: Mayhew-McCrimmon, 1978.

WILES, M. " 'Myth' in Theology." *BJRL* 59 (1976) 226-46.

WIMSATT, W. K., and M. C. BEARDSLEY. "The Intentional Fallacy." *Sewanee Review* 54 (1946) 468-88. = *The Verbal Icon* 3-18. [Lexington:] U Kentucky, 1954; reprinted New York: Noonday, 1962. = *Literary Intention* (ed. Newton-de Molina) 1-13. = *20th Century Literary Criticism* (ed. Lodge) 334-58.

WINK, W. *The Bible in Human Transformation.* Philadelphia: Fortress, 1973.

———. *Transforming Bible Study.* Nashville: Abingdon, 1980; ²1990/London: SCM, 1981; London: Mowbray, ²1990.

WIRE, A. C. See above under Gottwald.

WITTENBERG, G. "King Solomon and the Theologians." *JTSA* 63 (1988) 16-29.

WITTGENSTEIN, L. *Philosophical Investigations.* Oxford: Blackwell/New York: Macmillan, 1953.

WITVLIET, T. *The Way of the Black Messiah.* ET London: SCM/New York: Meyer Stone, 1987.

WOLFF, H. W. *The Old Testament: A Guide to Its Writings.* ET Philadelphia: Fortress, 1973/London: SPCK, 1974.

WRIGHT, C. J. H. "Ethics and the Old Testament." In *Third Way* 1/9-11 (1977). = *What Does the Lord Require* (Nottingham: Shaftesbury Project, 1977).

———. *God's People in God's Land.* Exeter: Paternoster/Grand Rapids: Eerdmans, 1990.

———. *Living as the People of God.* Leicester: IVP, 1983. = *An Eye for an Eye.* Downers Grove, IL: IVP, 1983.

WRIGHT, N. T. See above under Hurst.

WRIGHT, T. R. *Theology and Literature.* Oxford/New York: Blackwell, 1988.

WYSCHOGROD, M. See above under Thoma.

YARBRO COLLINS, A. (ed.), *Feminist Perspectives on Biblical Scholarship.* Chico, CA: Scholars, 1985.

YODER, P. *From Word to Life.* Scottdale, PA: Herald, 1982.

YOUNG, F. *The Art of Performance: Towards a Theology of Holy Scripture.* London: DLT, 1990.

ZAHAROPOULOS, D. Z. *Theodore of Mopsuestia on the Bible.* Mahwah, NJ: Paulist, 1989.

Index of Authors

Index of Scriptural and Other Ancient Jewish and Christian Writings